Presenting Persis Khambatta

ALSO BY SHERILYN CONNELLY

The First Star Trek *Movie: Bringing the Franchise to the Big Screen, 1969–1980* (McFarland, 2019)

Ponyville Confidential: The History and Culture of My Little Pony, 1981–2016 (McFarland, 2017)

Presenting Persis Khambatta

From Miss India to *Star Trek—
The Motion Picture* and Beyond

S##### herilyn C##### onnelly

McFarland & Company, Inc., Publishers
Jefferson, North Carolina

ISBN (print) 978-1-4766-8195-5
ISBN (ebook) 978-1-4766-4293-2

LIBRARY OF CONGRESS AND BRITISH LIBRARY
CATALOGUING DATA ARE AVAILABLE

Library of Congress Control Number 2021007027

© 2021 Sherilyn Connelly. All rights reserved

No part of this book may be reproduced or transmitted in any form
or by any means, electronic or mechanical, including photocopying
or recording, or by any information storage and retrieval system,
without permission in writing from the publisher.

Persis Khambatta in *Star Trek—The Motion Picture*, 1979
(Paramount Pictures/Photofest)

Printed in the United States of America

McFarland & Company, Inc., Publishers
Box 611, Jefferson, North Carolina 28640
www.mcfarlandpub.com

For Jeroo and Carol,
who both did their best.

Acknowledgments

Rachel Bernstein, Louise Hilton, and everybody at the Margaret Herrick Library for their invaluable research assistance. Derek Madaris and Abigail Garcia, for rescuing the manuscript from my own carelessness. Robert A. Caro, whose essay collection *Working* came out just when I needed it. Peter-Astrid Kane, for being brave enough to let me speak my mind for so many years at *SF Weekly*. Jaci Rohr, for making me feel welcome at Paramount, and letting me into the vault. Jim and Roxanne, for their hospitality. Genevieve Feldman, for letting me indulge myself at Deep Space Potrero. Michael Kmet and Maurice Molyneaux, for reassuring me that historical truth still matters to somebody somewhere. And Pete Goldie, for joining me on Batuu before he became one with the Force.

Contents

Acknowledgments	vi
Introduction	1
Prologue: The Minneapolis Panic	5

The Early Years

- **1946–1965**   9
  Today Bombay, Tomorrow (Miss) Universe **9**
- **1966–1969**   14
  From *Bheegi Raat* to *Bambai Raat Ki Bahon Mein* **14**

The Seventies

- **1970–1973**   19
  From *Beloved India* to Frozen England **19**; Her First Flight **24**
- **1974–1977**   26
  Khambatta in Kenya **26**; Khambatta in Kohl **29**;
  Siri, the Power-Adjacent Princess **30**; The Eternal
  August, Part I: The Screening of Persis **32**
- **1978**   34
  The Eternal August, Part II: The Shave of Singularity **34**; The
  Eternal August, Part III: Ilia Is Introduced **41**; The Eternal
  August, Part IV: Rush Hour on the Event Horizon **47**
- **1979**   60
  The Eternal August, Part V: The Blinding of Persis **60**;
  The Eternal August, Part VI: Persis Is Presented **62**

The Eighties

- **1980**   67
  Studio 54 on Parallel 42 **67**; The Trouble with Exotic
  Angels **71**; Lovin' that cali lifestyle!! **75**

- **1981** — 79
  Denny, Khambatta, and *Oui* 79; Release the *Nighthawks* 82; The Esquireman Weekend 85; Birds of a Feather Cannot Always Cohabitate Together 89; The (Mega)force of (Tri)illusion 92
- **1982** — 95
  Persis vs. Soup 95; Hunter vs. Khan 97; The Megafudging of Major Zara 103; The Whitewashing of *Octopussy* 109; The Prime Minister of India Meets the Pride of India 112
- **1983** — 115
  Devi, Coelho, and Khambatta 115; I Visited the Lost World and All I Got Was This Lousy Hairline Fracture 118; The Perils of Persis on the Idiot Box 119
- **1984** — 122
  The Saints of Imperfection 122; The Battle of the Bandit Queens 124; First Strikes and Last Resorts 128
- **1985** — 132
  The Pride of India's Perils in the Lost World 132; Waiting for Gandhi 136; Back to Bombay, for Now 140
- **1986–1988** — 142
  MacGyver vs. *Hunter* 142; The Blinking Eye 143; The Flameout of the Phoenix 145; This Is a Lowe 150
- **1989–1990** — 154
  The Triillusion Dissolution 154; Exile on Main Street: Des Moines 155

The Nineties

- **1991–1993** — 159
  Exile on Main Street: Los Angeles 159; The New Old School 160; Persis Reaches Out 162
- **1994–1995** — 164
  Persis Punches Back 164; Her Journey Through the Past 166; Another Dream Deferred 168
- **1996–1997** — 170
  Pride of India Is Begun 170; India's Pride Is Serenaded 173; *Pride of India* Is Published 174
- **1998** — 177
  So Long, It Has Not Been Nice to Know You 177; The Pre-Mortem 179; Persis in the Tower, When the Birds Came 181

Chapter Notes — 185
Bibliography — 205
Index — 219

Introduction

This is a biography of the model and actress Persis Khambatta, best known in the United States for her appearance in the 1979 Robert Wise film *Star Trek—The Motion Picture*. She was so closely associated with the film that its negative reception further hindered a Hollywood career that was already obstructed by Khambatta being a female immigrant of color, at a time when acts of discrimination against women and/or non-whites were forgivable offenses—inasmuch as those as acts were considered offenses, which they were not.

Persis Khambatta was born in Bombay (now Mumbai) in 1946 and died there in 1998 after having spent about half her life abroad. In 1965 she became the third woman to be crowned Miss India, less than twenty years after her country gained independence from England. Though she took great pride in winning the title and representing India, Khambatta had a complicated relationship with her birth country, and no less so with her adoptive home of the United States.

Khambatta was determined to chart her own path in her pursuit of becoming a star, but work was hard to find after the first Star Trek movie. She turned down many of the roles she was offered because they required nudity, a difficulty which was compounded by her being called "exotic." It was a label she had been trying to shake since leaving India in 1971, and she watched as what few Indian characters existed in Hollywood films in the 1980s tended to be cast with white performers. Khambatta died young after a too-brief Hollywood career, but she also achieved a triumph just before her death in the form of her 1997 book *Pride of India: A Tribute to Miss India*, a history of the Miss India contest.

Her story is a reminder of how much things have changed for the better during what should have been her lifetime. In 2016 Priyanka Chopra became the first Indian woman to present at the Oscars since Khambatta in 1980, while Mindy Kaling has found great success as a writer, producer, and star in both television and movies. Chopra, Kaling, and many other present-day South Asian people I mention in this book were able to chart their own paths in a way that Khambatta fought for but was unable to achieve. To be clear, I celebrate their successes, and I only wish Persis Khambatta had lived to see them.

* * *

There are gaps in this history, and while I have tried to find the most likely compromises where the historical records contradict, I take comfort in the fact that people closer to events in question were not always sure. The first entry in Khambatta's book *Pride of India* is for Pramila, who is listed as "Miss India 1947 (Press Award)." The first sentence of this first entry reads: "Amid the euphoria of Independence and the holocaust of Partition, the Miss India title was conferred probably for the first time upon actress Pramila."[1]

The rest of the entry makes no specific references to dates regarding Pramila's award, though it does include a picture of the scroll she received. The scroll's pertinent text follows, and the underlined portions were typed or handwritten onto the blank spaces:

I.F.J.A. AWARD of Scroll of Honours for 1947
  The Judges of the Working Committee of the India Film Journalists' Association, Mysore City (In Co-operation with India's Leading Editors) examine the year's total creations of fine art during their Third Anniversary Session on 31st December, 1948, and Unanimously Declare Pramila winner of the Award: 'Miss India'—1947
  For the year 1947 for the following unduplicated score
  India's Classical film-physique, streamlined and dreamlined with Greek feminine proportions, a Champion of sunshine, outdoor life and professional physical culture—[2]

The scroll goes on to define Pramila as "India's Shapeliest Heroine," and provides plenty for space for the signatures of the committee who declared her as such, with this at the very bottom:

Bombay Seventh April 1949.[3]

Pramila was declared Miss India 1947 by the India Film Journalists' Association during their meeting on December 31, 1948, and the document itself is dated April 7, 1949. As such, it makes sense that Khambatta hedged her bets a half-century later and used the word "probably" for such a seminal event. She had much better access to the relevant primary sources than I do, which makes me feel better about being unable to confirm certain facts such as the launch date of *Pride of India* itself—which was probably October 15, 1997, but I cannot say for sure. Similarly, Ashish Rajadhyaksha wrote in the introduction of the 1995 *Encyclopaedia of Indian Cinema* that he and co-writer Paul Willemen "have endeavoured to produce a book providing the 'most likely' truth on the basis of often deeply conflicting sources." That goes double for *Presenting Persis Khambatta*.[4]

Introduction 3

The one instance in which I outright fudge a fact is the timing of the Las Vegas trip during which Khambatta lost $900 playing blackjack: it happened before April 1981, but I do not know for sure that it was during her otherwise-confirmed Vegas trip in June 1980. But like the banana sticking to the wall in Spalding Gray's *Swimming to Cambodia*, it makes for a better story, so I beg the reader's indulgence.

* * *

The Early Years follows what little I could reconstruct about Khambatta's youth, from the beginning of her modeling career and eventual crowning as Miss India, and her three Hindi films: *Bheegi Raat*, *Pinjre Ke Panchhi*, and *Bambai Raat Ki Bahon Mein*.

The Seventies follows her through this most optimistic of decades, including her participation in the German exploitation film *Kamasutra—Vollendung Der Liebe*, the British films *The Wilby Conspiracy* and *Conduct Unbecoming*, and the American telefilm *The Man with the Power*.

But her role in *Star Trek—The Motion Picture* presents the biggest change from the original conception of this work. I spent considerable time, energy, and money researching the development of the character of Ilia from the earliest treatments for the unmade *Star Trek II* television series, up through the many drafts of the movie's shooting script. It was all fascinating stuff which has never been published in a work of scholarly sparkliness such as this one, and it examined how what could have been one of the most interesting characters in all of Star Trek was reduced to a cipher. The problem was that it shifted the focus from Khambatta to Gene Roddenberry and Star Trek, and there have been more than enough books on those subjects, including my own. This is not a book about Gene Roddenberry or Star Trek, and while Khambatta's participation in the franchise became a singularity from which she never escaped, that was not her choice. She did not want to be defined by having been bald in that one movie, so this book will not do so despite its cover photo. With a few exceptions, this book will focus on her personal experiences working on the first Star Trek movie, and how the character of Ilia was changed in editing.

The Eighties follows Khambatta as a Hollywood career eluded her, as did finding stability in her personal life. This book will also study her roles in the American studio films *Nighthawks* and *Megaforce*; the independent movies *Warrior of the Lost World*, *First Strike*, *Phoenix the Warrior*, and *Deadly Intent*; the Hindi *Shingora* and *Jazira*; and her appearances on the American television shows *Casablanca*, *Hunter*, *MacGyver*, and *The New Mike Hammer*. (Trigger warning: Gene Siskel using the word "erotic.")

The Nineties finds her trying to find a new meaning in her life, which meant returning to India for good and writing *Pride of India: A Tribute to Miss India* before her death in 1998. Though the city of Bombay was renamed Mumbai in 1995, it will be referred to as Bombay in this book.

* * *

As a white person of European descent who has lived in California their entire life, I am aware that I am not the ideal biographer of someone who was born and raised in a country which I have never visited. But Persis Khambatta's story has not been told in print form in the two decades after her death, and I would rather it was by me than not at all. Though she was by all accounts heterosexual, Khambatta was Other enough in both the United States and India that her experiences were much like that of queer people such as myself, and I identify with many of her struggles. She was new and shiny at first, but soon all that was left to most eyes was what made her different. (Been there, done that, though on a far smaller scale.)

Something Khambatta wrote in *Pride of India*'s Author's Note about tracking down the former Miss Indias also resonated with me: "Strangely I felt a close empathy with the ups and downs each girl had gone through in her life and in many ways I could relate to each one of them. It was a feeling of comradeship and female bonding." I get that. I have little in common with Khambatta in the broad strokes, but there are a million little things I relate to, as simple as the fact that she was considered unusually tall, and she eschewed wigs. After writing this book, I love Persis Khambatta like an aunt I never met.[5]

Khambatta described the process of researching *Pride of India* as being like "tracing wayward school friends who have wandered carelessly all over the globe."[6] I can also appreciate that, since researching this book was not even tracing a school friend but the friend of a friend of an acquaintance not only all over the globe but back through time. My hope is that the people who knew her will recognize her in this portrait constructed from shadows and afterimages.

This then is the epic story of Persis Khambatta. Don't be afraid.

Prologue: The Minneapolis Panic

As Persis Khambatta settled into her suite at the Marquette Hotel in Minneapolis on the evening of Sunday, December 2, 1979, she was freaking out a little.[1]

This was the latest stop on a worldwide promotional tour for *Star Trek—The Motion Picture*, which was going to open in over 850 theaters across North America at the end of the week, including at Minneapolis' own Southtown Theater. Khambatta would be in Washington, D.C., for the film's premiere at the MacArthur Theater on Thursday, December 6, and soon thereafter she would travel to the United Kingdom and Australia. In the more immediate future, she was scheduled to speak with writers from two local papers, the *Star* and the *Tribune*. Both would be over meals, though only one would be at an Indian restaurant.[2]

For now, alone in an unfamiliar city on a cold winter's night with nothing to do but relax, she was hit by the latest wave of anxiety attacks about the premiere and her career. She had always known the first Star Trek movie would be a big deal—she was a fan of the television show, after all, and would have been excited about the movie just as an audience member—but the hype and anticipation was far beyond her experience. It was both overwhelming and only the tip of the iceberg: she had been told that fans were camping out in sleeping bags, and some women had shaved their heads. This raised a whole host of other problems, not the least of which was, what if none of the fans recognized her with hair?[3]

The shaving of her head had been such a media event that the first *Los Angeles Times* story had run the day before it happened, with the headline "Shear Terror for Khambatta." Much of the publicity for the film in recent weeks had been about her hair, articles with headlines such as "Bald Is Beautiful for 'Star Trek' Star," "Lt. Ilia Lets Down Her Hair," and "Actress's Cleanshaven Image Lands Role in Star Trek Movie."[4]

Today had been a long day by any measure: she appeared in the Star Trek Shop at the New York Bloomingdale's from 1 p.m. to 3 p.m., autographing photos of Robot Ilia while doing her best to answer questions without giving away too much of the story. She was then hustled to the airport for the three-hour flight to Minneapolis, which gave her more time to ruminate. Her hair had grown back in and she had another movie lined up, but she was having trouble sorting out the advice she had received about sustaining an American showbiz career. When she landed a role in the 1977 television movie *The Man with the Power* she was being managed by Norma Lee, but now her manager was her close friend Bobbie Edrick, who advised Khambatta against doing more small-screen work. Guest spots on television were not the stairway to movie stardom, and even appearing in television specials as herself was not much better.[5]

With nothing else to do, Khambatta turned on the television and flipped through channels. There wasn't much to choose from—American sitcoms, the James Bond movie *The Man with the Golden Gun*, nothing Khambatta's speed—so she settled on a British costume drama. Her mind wandered back to her anxieties, at least until she heard a familiar voice saying that if you enjoyed being able to watch quality programming such as *Masterpiece Theater* on KTCA Channel 2 here in the Twin Cities, please pick up your phone and—[6]

That voice. It couldn't be, could it? Khambatta looked up at the screen. It could be, and it was: Cyrus Bharucha! Though he hailed from Bombay's Parsi community like herself, Bharucha and Khambatta did not meet until London in the early 1970s when he was a producer for the BBC and she was a fashion model. They were good friends back in Blighty, but lost touch when Khambatta left for the United States. Khambatta had not realized Bharucha had done the same, but there he was on the local PBS station standing in front of rows of people on telephones, asking viewers to call the number on the screen and pledge.[7]

Khambatta picked up the phone and called. After apologizing for not making a pledge, she asked the volunteer to please give her name and number to Bharucha. He called right back, and they had a pleasant chat. She had always believed in this kind of serendipity, and seeing an old friend on television (complete with a contact number!) just when she happened to be in town soothed her nerves. It meant things were going to be all right.[8]

She related the story to the *Star*'s Don Morrison the next day at lunch. Morrison was one of the few journalists Khambatta had met who knew that the first Star Trek movie was not Khambatta's first film, or even her first in English: Morrison had been fond of her in *The Wilby Conspiracy*. But she was not there to promote *Wilby*, and after apologizing for circling back around to a topic she was already tired of, Morrison asked what it was like being bald for six months. The article ran on December 5 as "A Friendly Time Warp," making it one of the few headlines to not mention her hair—though Morrison did describe her as exotic, the word she had been trying to shake for the past decade.[9]

As cordial as Morrison had been, things were a little more to Khambatta's taste during her interview with the *Tribune*'s food columnist Will Jones. He was less interested in her exoticness or her onscreen baldness and more in what she had to teach him about Indian food, such as how it was best eaten with your fingers. Sure, Indian restaurants in the United States provided forks and knives, but it never tasted right to Khambatta unless she used her hands, which she did even in classier joints like Gypsies in Los Angeles or Gaylord's in New York. And if you needed a utensil for the curry or lentils, that was what the naan was for.[10]

* * *

When her Minneapolis obligations were complete, Khambatta flew to Washington, D.C., where she was greeted at the Four Seasons hotel by two people who had flown in from farther than Minnesota. One was her live-in boyfriend Pascal Chevillot, who owned the new Benetton boutique on the Sunset Strip, and with whom Khambatta often held court at the hyper-trendy Beverly Hills restaurant Ma Maison. The other, more significant guest was Persis' mother Jeroo, who flew in from Bombay to attend the premiere at the MacArthur Theater. But while Chevillot rode in the limousine with Persis and with her co-star Stephen Collins, who played Khambatta's onscreen lover Will Decker, Jeroo Khambatta opted out because of the photographers waiting on the red carpet. Limousines and spotlights and red carpets were the sort of Western allurements Jeroo feared would have an undue effect on her daughter ever since Persis was crowned Miss India in 1965, but Jeroo still loved Persis enough to be there for this big night, and to consume the media her daughter created.[11]

Though the credits of the film would read "Presenting Persis Khambatta," this was not Khambatta's first movie, nor the first time she had a title card to herself, nor her first movie to play in the United States, nor her first time attending a movie premiere, nor her first time in a literal and/or figurative spotlight. But this was the payoff to all her hard work, and her face was even the focal point of the movie's poster, forming a triangle with William Shatner and Leonard Nimoy. DeForest Kelley was upset that he was bumped from the advertising in favor of Khambatta, though he knew she had no more control over these decisions than he did.[12]

After posing for the professional photographers on the north side of the red carpet outside the MacArthur, Khambatta turned to the fans gathered to the south and spotted a woman dressed as her character of Ilia, complete with a bald cap. Khambatta smiled and pulled at her own hair—her honest-to-goodness, real hair, which most people had never seen. At least this fan didn't shave her head! Paramount asked Khambatta to shave hers again for the premiere, but, no. That time was past, and she was ready to move on to a career in which it was a given that she had hair. Being exotic was already a red flag for producers and casting agents, and she wasn't about to become typecast as a *bald* exotic; nevertheless, Paramount issued a press release in October stating that "eyebrows are being raised even today, more than a year later, when the actress states she'd gladly do it again. Although she does add, 'Maybe.'" Khambatta never stated that she'd gladly do it again, but the studio was selling the picture any way they could.[13]

On a more pragmatic level, Khambatta had been in a car crash this past spring while vacationing in Munich. Her head injury required stitches, and the resulting scar made the thought of going bald even less appealing. That season became all the more frustrating when two film projects fell through: a French picture with Michel Piccoli which was supposed to have begun shooting in April 1979, and a Chopin biopic in which Khambatta would have played George Sand. But that was all right, because a few weeks before the MacArthur Premiere, she signed on to star with Sylvester Stallone in a film called *Attack*. When she auditioned, Stallone asked if she could speak French and German; Khambatta lied and said she had studied the languages in school, and all she needed was 24 hours and a teacher to get brushed up. It worked, and she won the part.[14]

Presently, Khambatta's doppelgänger outside the MacArthur Theater called out, "You look good with hair!" Without missing a beat, Khambatta replied, "You look good bald!" And she was sure that the world would soon forget that she had been bald in that one movie that one time. But not right away, either: in the following day's *Washington Star* coverage of the MacArthur Premiere, Jurate Kazickas wrote that Khambatta's "usually bald head" was now "sprouting black hair."[15]

As Khambatta sat inside the MacArthur with Chevillot later that evening, the lights went low and the opening strains of Jerry Goldsmith's "Ilia's Theme" began. For sure, this was a first for her: starring in a film which not only had an overture, which was rare enough these days, but an overture which was *her* character's musical theme. Khambatta would not know that detail until the soundtrack album was released later that month, and what mattered was that during the opening credits, her name filled the screen in a way it never had before.[16]

She had embarked.

The Early Years

1946–1965

Today Bombay, Tomorrow (Miss) Universe

Persis Khambatta was born in Bombay, India, on October 2, 1946, into the middle-class home of textile manufacturer Feroze Khambatta and his spouse Jeroo Sethna. India achieved independence from the British occupation in 1947, and Feroze achieved a less laudable independence when he divorced Jeroo in 1948; Persis never saw her father again, and Jeroo never remarried, raising Persis and her brother Dinshi alone. Being a child of divorce is hard enough, more so in a culture which stresses the importance of family and tends to victim-blame those who come from broken homes, so while the young Persis Khambatta developed the survival skills of a sense of humor and a tough skin, she still suffered for being different. It helped that she was very bright; she spoke English by the age of four, and also became fluent in Hindi and Gujarati. Khambatta later credited her maternal great-grandfather, Ratanji Framji Sethna, with teaching her charity, compassion, and courage. Though he was not involved in the day-to-day parenting of Persis and Dinshi, Sethna was no slouch in the intellect department, having written a dictionary, an encyclopedia, and a Gujarati translation of Francis Bacon's *Essays*.[1]

Khambatta also found solace in the spiritual master Shirdi Sai Baba, praying to him for guidance and compassion amidst the hunger and poverty of Bombay while also revealing her hopes and dreams of success. Being Parsi, her family were followers of the prophet Zoroaster—also known as Zarathustra, he who spake thusly—but Jeroo took her young daughter to multiple temples where they prayed to all the gods, which Persis found somewhat confusing at the time. Though growing up in Bombay gave her a degree of street smarts which would serve her well in adulthood, she also had what she would later call "the art" from an early age: "Every time I knew that there was a photographer close at hand my expressions would get very animated. I would pose, laugh, give him my profile and offer him all the angles."[2]

One day, the 13-year-old Persis was spotted by photographer Gurmeet Singh as the Khambatta family ate in a Bombay restaurant. Singh asked Jeroo for permission to photograph Persis in his studio, and after being assured that the session would be on the weekend and not interfere with her daughter's schooling, Jeroo agreed. The five dollars Khambatta earned for the shoot wasn't chump change for a tween in 1959 India, and the advertising firm Lintas used the photos for a nationwide Rexona soap campaign. Her image was soon all over the country on cartons, wrappers, newspapers, and billboards in ads which would run as late as 1965. In an effort to look older Khambatta wore more makeup on that first shoot than she would of her own volition later in life, but she loved the camera, the camera loved her back, and their affair would prove long-lived and fruitful.[3]

Khambatta was inspired by photographer David Bailey's doe-eyed muse Jean Shrimpton, and she considered herself more of a facial than fashion model due to her own expressive features. She could give the photographer whatever mood they needed for their products, a range of goods and services she would later sum up as "DCM, Ponds, Hakoba, Bombay Dyeing, pots, pans, shirts, ties, anything." It made modeling feel more like acting than simply looking beautiful in clothes—but she was good at that, too, and Khambatta would one day model for David Bailey as well.[4]

Though she had been professionally beautiful for a few years, Khambatta was first actively honored for it at the age of 17 when she was crowned Film Princess by Hindi film megastar Raj Kapoor in 1963. But Khambatta's entry into competitive beauty came two years later when *Femina* magazine's editor Dr. K.D. Jhangiani encouraged her to enter their Miss India contest. The English-language *Femina* itself was launched in 1959, only a dozen years after the end of the British occupation, and was intended to be read by women around the country "irrespective of her culture, caste, creed or religious background" with the goal of defining what it meant to be Indian. As sub-Editor Vimla Patil would later explain in Khambatta's book *Pride of India*, when *Femina* debuted "there was no such thing as an Indian woman. There was a Bengali woman, a Maharashtrian woman, a Gujarati woman and so on." Early sponsors of both *Femina* and the contest included Pond's and other such cosmetics companies, but the major backers were the native textile mills such as Khatau and Kamala which had struggled under the British occupation, and the Miss India contest promoted both the magazine and the mills. It also helped to have the support of Indira Gandhi, who became Prime Minister in January 1966 and was devoted to the handloom industry which *Femina* championed.[5]

Because orthodox groups felt proper Indian women did not display themselves onstage even when clothed, the contest's first participants were from more progressive communities such as the Anglo-Indians and

The Early Years: 1946–1965

Khambatta's own Parsi sect, while sub-Editor Patil's belief that women should have their own jobs, their own money, and their own position in the household made *Femina* that much more controversial. As a result, the whole Miss India thing was so looked down upon that most "decent" families would not accept a beauty queen in their ranks, and the participants' parents would try to hide their shame by marrying off their daughters as soon as possible. Ratanji Framji Sethna would have preferred that Persis Khambatta became a lawyer, but still supported her right to self-determination and thus her modeling career. It bears repeating that this aging scholar who had the intellectual chops to translate Francis Bacon into Gujarati believed his beautiful great-granddaughter had the brains to be a lawyer—and in 1965, which was not the most progressive era for women in India or elsewhere. Khambatta would take great umbrage in later years at the popular belief that models—and thus beautiful women and just women in general—cannot also be smart.[6]

Jeroo Khambatta also supported her daughter's choice of a life path, and she was certain Persis would become Miss India, for a flower fell into Jeroo's hand from a temple shrine the day of the contest. The Khambatta matriarch's floral prognostication was spot-on: the 18-year-old Persis was crowned both Miss Angel Face (the equivalent of Miss Bombay) and Miss India on the evening of June 20, 1965. The first runner-up for Miss India was Janice Loane from Calcutta, and the second was Annahella Crawford. The whole event was a step up for both Khambatta and the contest, as there had not been a public ceremony when Meher Mistry was the first woman to be named Miss India by *Femina* in 1964.[7]

Though it is clear Mistry won in 1964, it is unclear whether Khambatta was one of her competitors. She makes no reference in *Pride of India* to participating that year, but in 1979 Joan Crosby's *TV Scout* column ran a piece about Khambatta's "hatred (and fear) of black roses" which would seem to stem from the 1964 contest. As the story goes, another contestant handed Khambatta a black rose, after which "I twisted my leg and couldn't compete in the finals." While *en route* to the Miss Universe contest "a year or so later"—Khambatta participated in Miss Universe in 1965, which would have put the initial leg-twisting incident in 1964—a waiter at a restaurant in the Amsterdam airport gave her a black rose as an act of random niceness. "I had a very bad feeling, but I decided that I had to turn it to my advantage. So I said, 'Black rose, black rose, this time you will bring me good luck.'" She further instructed the black rose to manifest that luck in the form of a total stranger giving her a present, and the woman sitting next to her obliged by taking Khambatta by the hand and buying her a toy dog at a gift shop.[8]

For sure, Khambatta's next big destination in 1965 was the Miss

Universe pageant in Miami, which marked her first mention in the pages of the Western showbiz bible *Variety* on July 7, and they almost got her name right: "Pereis Khambatta crowned Miss India and has departed for U.S. and the Miss Universe contest." It wasn't a geodesic from Bombay to Miami, however; the Miss Universe contestants first gathered in Rio de Janeiro for the Carnival, and then stopped off in Washington, D.C., where Khambatta later wrote that she met President Lyndon Johnson and got Robert Kennedy's autograph, as well as Kennedy's monogrammed pen.[9]

Khambatta and the others arrived in Miami for the Miss Universe pageant on Saturday, July 24, 1965. She appears onscreen for about five seconds in a contemporaneous newsreel about the event, in which the narrator proclaims that "the forehead spot Miss India features means that she is a highly fashionable young lady." Her forehead is spot-free in the footage, suggesting that the copywriter was working from Indian stereotypes rather than the film itself. (It may have been the first time, but it would not be the last.) Though Khambatta sported a caste mark in the Rexona ad which made her nationally famous, she did not wear one on a regular basis because she was Parsi, not Hindu.[10]

Even by the standards of an Indian woman in the United States in the mid- to late 20th century, Persis Khambatta's comparative exoticism would always be more of a stumbling block than a steppingstone, a metaphor which took real-life form at the Miss Universe contest. She was not experienced in high heels, since at five feet and seven and a half inches she was already considered tall by Indian standards and had never felt the need to add to her height. But the Miss Universe contest required her to wear a specific kind of stiletto heel, almost as though those rules were designed more for the pleasure of the male viewer than the comfort of the female contestant. (It was never not about legs: since the Miss India contest did not have a swimsuit round, the contestants lifted their saris for the judges, though the gam-inspection was done backstage to maintain propriety.) Khambatta's unfamiliarity with heels was unusual enough to bear mentioning in a wire story about the contest: "Onstage, India's Persis Khambatta of Bombay is practicing to wear high heels. She's never worn them. Pageant officials said she must." (Because they are the worst.)[11]

Miss Bahamas loaned Miss India a pair of heels, but the already too-tall Khambatta's feet were too big, and she was disqualified after developing blisters. Khambatta later wrote that "I blew the chance of a lifetime because the pageant rules wouldn't allow me to wear open sandals or go barefoot," and the way she blames herself for the Miss Universe contest being the worst makes my heart break a little. But she did make it as far as the swimsuit round, and the following year Khambatta loaned Reita Faria her pink bathing costume for the 1966 Miss World competition, since

Faria could not afford her own. (Faria was also of above-average height for a woman, later reflecting with a laugh that "I was mortified that I was so tall.") As though competing with Miss Universe to be the worst, the Miss World officials nixed it once they discovered the suit was a hand-me-down. But Faria's sister was a flight attendant who could afford to buy her a new suit, and that was acceptable, for Faria went on to be the 1966 Miss World.[12]

There's no telling how Khambatta's career and life would have been different had she not "blown the chance of a lifetime" through no fault of her own, though she did receive an offer to screen test for a James Bond film while in Miami. Production on Terence Young's 1965 *Thunderball* had wrapped the month before the 1965 Miss Universe contest, so the next film she could have appeared in would have been Lewis Gilbert's 1967's *You Only Live Twice*. That film was set in Japan and Khambatta was not Japanese, but Sean Connery wears yellowface in the film when Bond goes undercover, so that would have been a minor detail at best. And it is all academic, for Persis had promised Jeroo she would return straight home after the Miss Universe contest, so she declined the screen test.[13]

1966–1969

From Bheegi Raat *to* Bambai Raat Ki Bahon Mein

Had she appeared in a 1960s James Bond film Persis Khambatta likely would have been nothing more than background decoration, such as one of the barely-clad women in *You Only Live Twice*'s bathhouse scene. If it had happened, it would not have been the first time.

Filmed before Persis Khambatta won the Miss India contest, single-name filmmaker Kalidas' melodrama *Bheegi Raat* starring Pradeep Kumar and Shashikala was released in India on August 5, 1965. I will not fully detail the plots for this or Khambatta's other Hindi films, both because of my own monolingualism and because as Ashish Rajadhyaksha and Paul Willemen point out in their 1995 *Encyclopaedia of Indian Cinema*, "most Indian films take many detours and mobilize multiple plot-lines in any given narrative," and there are often "two or three main plot-lines accompanied by a comedy plot and interspersed with song sequences which may or may not advance or impact upon any of the other plots."[1]

Bheegi Raat featured Khambatta's first appearance in a narrative motion picture, and possibly her first credit in the form of "Introducing Poonam." It is also her only Hindi film to be legally streaming with subtitles in the United States at the time of this writing. Khambatta is one of many anonymous women lounging in and around a pool in the first post-credits scene; she wears pink shorts and a black blouse, which may be part of the bathing outfit she would later loan to Reita Faria. Khambatta is being sketched by Pradeep Kumar's character, which leads to Shashikala's character becoming jealous and sketchblocking Khambatta ("Ajay, draw her portrait who will be yours"), which leads to *Bheegi Raat*'s first musical number as the cast Twists by the pool to a song which is by neither Chubby Checker nor Dire Straits. Khambatta herself is only visible in a few medium inserts and is absent from the many wide shots, and she does not appear to have been choreographed as tightly as the rest of the cast. It is notable that while it was the first of her many films to depict a rape—right off the bat in the pre-credits prologue, no less—it is not Khambatta's character who is attacked.

She received far more screen time in Salil Choudhury's 1966 *Pinjre Ke Panchhi*, and a not-terrible fourth billing. Hers is the first on a screenful of names, this time as "Poonam (Miss India 1965)," which is why the "Introducing Poonam" credit in *Bheegi Raat* may have been referring to Khambatta. (Meena Kumari received top billing in *Pinjre Ke Panchhi*, and although she passed away in 1972, in India she was the subject of the daily Google Doodle graphic on what would have been her 85th birthday in 2018.) The escaped-convicts-on-the-run tale *Pinjre Ke Panchhi* gives Khambatta a number of firsts in her role as Amy, the daughter of a train depot manager, including being introduced in a shot which starts at her feet and pans up her body as she enters a room. That the body in question is clothed from head to toe does not keep the protagonist from reacting like a Tex Avery wolf. Shortly thereafter in *Pinjre Ke Panchhi* she sneezes several times, which also qualifies as a first and demonstrates that Khambatta was never afraid to be un-pretty on screen. She spends much of the next ten minutes seated at a table and getting macked on by the protagonist in a series of medium shots with the occasional close-up, and while the specifics are lost on this monolingual viewer, Khambatta gets to act and react and laugh and present something resembling a character. A minor character, to be sure, though Khambatta still gets more to do here than she would a dozen-plus years later in the first Star Trek movie. The other major first in *Pinjre Ke Panchhi* is Khambatta's first featured musical number, as Amy lip-syncs to a piano-driven rave-up and leads a nightclub in the Twist, spotlighting her in a way *Bheegi Raat* did not. This nightclub scene is her last appearance in the film, so it can be concluded that Amy is Khambatta's first speaking character to not get killed.[2]

Being in the right place at the right time was a recurring theme in Khambatta's early career, and once again a chance meeting with a photographer in a restaurant led to her third and most high-profile Hindi film: Khwaja Ahmad Abbas's 1967 *Bambai Raat Ki Bahon Mein*. Since she was acknowledged to be the first Indian model to appear in a film—and under her own name, rather than the Poonam of (possibly) *Bheegi Raat* and (definitely) *Pinjre Ke Panchhi*—this time she earned her own title screen, preceded by "Introducing."[3]

Bambai Raat Ki Bahon Mein is Khambatta's only film to warrant a full entry in the *Encyclopaedia of Indian Cinema*, which says the film is characteristic of the 1960s work of the Communist Party of India's ideologues, being "a demagogic melodrama bewailing the city's effect on 'traditional' values." In an effort to tie it into her performance as both Real Ilia and Robot Ilia in the first Star Trek movie, Paramount's 1979 biography of Khambatta described her as playing a "double role" in the 1967 Abbas film, "as a blonde night club singer and as a simple Indian girl."[4]

In truth, her character of Lily is a woman who sings and dances in a nightclub. After three musical numbers while wearing a blonde wig, one of which involves the Twist, Vimal Ahuja's protagonist Amar barges into Lily's dressing room. After Amar refers to her as his "dream girl," Lily removes her wig, and Amar is reduced to gape-mouthed shock by the big reveal that this young Indian woman has black hair. In addition to being the first but not the last time that a Persis Khambatta character's hair defying expectations would be a crucial element to the plot and/or marketing of a film, there are pictures of Lily on the wall of her dressing room. The odds of *Bambai Raat Ki Bahon Mein* receiving a proper high-definition release are slim to none, but it would be worth it just to get a closer look at these otherwise lost images from Khambatta's 1960s modeling career.[5]

She has a few more musical numbers in *Bambai Raat Ki Bahon Mein*, one of which is in a flashback, and another in which Amar strong-arms Lily into lip-syncing at a party by grabbing her by the arm. But she also has dialog scenes in which she gets to act and emote, and Khambatta seems far more engaged in those moments. This third film appearance also features her first violent onscreen death: as a passenger in a car crash, complete with a *Signal 30*-style shot of Lily's corpse on the road. It is clear that director Abbas considers alcohol to be one of the city's negative effects on traditional values—an unsubtle POV shot through the bottom of a glass hammers it home—but even though Lily declines a drink when offered, just as the teetotaling Khambatta herself would have in real life, she is punished at the end of *Bambai Raat Ki Bahon Mein*. Perhaps simply being a beautiful woman who entertained drunk people was enough.

Khambatta's performance netted her the India Film Journalists' Association award for the Best Newcomer of the Year, but she was growing disillusioned with this career path. She felt the more industrial aspects of the Hindi film industry were suffocating her own creativity, especially because most of the movies were terrible song-and-dance escapist fantasies intended to distract the viewers from their poverty and hunger. Not that that escapism was bad, and Khambatta grew up surrounded by the poverty and hunger from which they were trying to escape, but she knew she was destined for bigger and better things—maybe even movies in which she didn't do the Twist.[6]

Khambatta continued to work as a model, including a February 1968 gig at the Taj Hotel during fashion designer Pierre Cardin's first visit to India. Cardin told Khambatta to try her luck in Europe, which was easier said than done. Her Miss India fame had long since dimmed, and modeling was a disreputable and poor-paying business, but she kept at it. (During the filming of the first Star Trek movie ten years later, Cardin would ask her to work for him exclusively as a bald model, an offer she would decline at Paramount's request.)[7]

In October 1968, Khambatta and her good friend Meher Mistry visited Australia to participate in local parades and to model Indian silk fashions. Khambatta had also just finished working on what the *Sydney Morning Herald* described as a "German semi-documentary" titled *Beloved India*. Though director Kobi Jaeger had received production support from the University of Bombay, and Khambatta's scenes were shot in India, it still counted as her first stab outside the Hindi film industry. In addition to churning out the kind of fluff Khambatta was tired of, it was illegal for Hindi films to show something as basic as kissing, and all evidence suggests her character in the Jaeger film does more than kiss.[8]

Kissing was no less controversial in real life, leading writer James Shepherd to muse in the December 9, 1969, *Life Asia Edition* that the cultural reluctance to exchange spit was "a curious anomaly in a land where the miniskirt has gained at least a foothold." Translation: if a woman wears a short skirt, she must also be willing to put out. (Why else would she dress like that?) Khambatta was among the young Indian citizens who enjoyed breaking the taboo, and Shepherd described her as "a much-photographed model" who said she preferred to kiss Indian men rather than foreigners because Indian men "are more passionate and they don't smell like bubble gum." On the same page was a photo of several people in a shoe store looking at Khambatta, her thick dark hair cascading down past her shoulders, and the caption noted that her miniskirt brought her "even more attention than usual."[9]

However much attention Persis Khambatta was getting, she was all about her friends getting it as well. Like Khambatta and Mistry, fashion model Veena Sajnani toured to promote *Femina* and local textile firms, and one day in 1970 she was surprised to learn she had been removed from a tour. Sajnani's next surprise was learning she was off the tour because Khambatta and Mistry had signed her up for that year's Miss India pageant. Though not competing since they had previously won, Khambatta and Mistry both walked that year's fashion show, and Khambatta spied the judges' notes while on the ramp. Sajnani was skeptical when Khambatta told her the judges were writing down Sajnani's number; how could Khambatta see the tiny writing from a distance? But Sajnani won, and Khambatta and Mistry were thrilled for her, though Sajnani suspected that part of it was because her victory meant her fellow contestant Zeenat Aman lost. There would be a media narrative of a rivalry between Khambatta and Aman in the decades to come, but whatever Khambatta and Mistry's motives for entering her in the contest, Sajnani was happy to become Miss India.[10]

Khambatta was no more of a perfect, selfless human being than you or me, and there are unflattering stories. Shobha Dé's 1994 essay collection *Shooting from the Hip* includes an anecdote about an Ahmedabad fashion show at an unspecified time after Khambatta was crowned Miss India. Dé writes that Khambatta was "the reigning Queen Bee on the modelling circuit" who "had no time for the rest of us greenhorns," instead spending most of her time smoking Salems and going the full Narcissus with a mirror. "She stared as if in a trance changing the angle of her face, dabbing on blushers, pouting her lips in that famous Persis-pout." Khambatta would constantly re-arrange her makeup and hairpieces while continuing to smoke her cigarettes, all while keeping a close watch on herself in the mirror.[11]

But the real sparks flew when the show's organizer came in a few minutes before curtain with news of a change to the running order.[12]

> Instead of Persis opening the show she wanted someone else to do it, God knows why. Khambatta flew into an absolute rage. She stomped her feet, flung her arms around, screamed shrilly and threatened to walk out of the show. "After all, I am PERSIS KHAMBATTA! I am MISS INDIA!!! How can anyone else appear before Me?"[13]

A compromise was reached after this "absolute beaut of a tantrum" during which De was worried Khambatta's lashes would fall off and her pancake make-up would crack, and Dé acknowledges that "if memory serves me well, Persis closed the show with a finale to top all finales." Khambatta high-tailed it out of there afterward to meet a waiting escort, stalking off "without so much as a 'bye' to the rest of us."[14]

Persis Khambatta flaunted it while she had it, and the writer of *Presenting Persis Khambatta* respects her no less for that.

The Seventies

1970-1973

From Beloved India *to* Frozen England

Beloved India was retitled *Kamasutra—Vollendung Der Liebe* for its 1968 German release, and in late 1970 it was released in the United States by American International Pictures with the simplified title of *Kama Sutra* and an X rating from the Motion Picture Association of America. *Star Trek— The Motion Picture* would receive a G in 1979, making Khambatta one of the few actors to appear in live-action films rated both G and X during the brief period when mainstream films could receive those ratings from the MPAA.[1]

Khambatta received second billing after Bruno Dietrich in the *Kama Sutra* promotional materials, which promised that the movie "seen by millions of men and women in Europe and Asia is now free to be shown in the United States ... answers questions even a man and wife don't dare ask each other!" When director Kobi Jaeger went to see his picture in a Philadelphia theater after reading in *Variety* that it received a "sour critical reception," he was shocked to discover that American International Pictures had replaced much of the Indian and European footage with a new 26-minute segment shot in the United States, resulting in what Jaeger called a "butchered, pornographic film." In addition to sending letters "of regret and apology" to the University of Bombay, Jaeger tried to halt the distribution by suing American International Pictures, who claimed they had received the film as-is from the mysterious United Producers Organization and had made no changes themselves. When the 90-minute American International Pictures cut of *Kama Sutra* opened in New York in March 1971, the most enthusiasm the *Times*' Howard Thompson could muster was that it was marginally better than its double-bill partner, *Bora Bora*.[2]

The French skin magazine *Daily Girl* ran a spread on Jaeger's *Kamasutra* around that time which included two stills of Khambatta, while screenshots from a videotape can be found in the ickier parts of the modern Internet. Whatever else is happening in these pictures of the 22-year-old

Khambatta in her role as the young newlywed Nanda, or whatever may be happening to her from outside the frame as she makes facial expressions which infer that Nanda is having sex, Khambatta remains clothed.[3]

The American International Pictures version of *Kama Sutra* does not appear to have made it onto VHS or DVD—not even on Mike Vraney's famed Something Weird Video label, though a 3-minute trailer complete with alleged *Newsweek* quotes was featured on the fifth volume of Something Weird's *Twisted Sex: Trailers from the Sick Sick 60s* in 1993. A German record company released the score for *Kamasutra* by Irmin Schmidt and Inner Space Production (later known as the pioneering German band Can) on CD and LP in 2009, and with "Im Tempel" as the highlight it is the best score to a Persis Khambatta film this side of Jerry Goldsmith's music for the first Star Trek movie. It's also up there with the Electric Flag's score to Roger Corman's 1967 *The Trip* as a great work of late-sixties instrumental psychedelia, and is excellent background music for writing a biography of a former Miss India.

Both pressings of the *Kamasutra* score include promotional photos of Khambatta from the film, and though she bares a scandalous amount of midriff, she is clothed. The liner notes also include excerpts from the original press release, which provide further insight into the film.[4]

> Nanda and Dilip are newly-weds. According to the Kamasutra, any man who marries a young, inexperienced girl should spend ten days under the same roof, get to know her, share a bath with her, make music, eat and play together, coax declarations of love out of her—without attempting sexual union. Only after those ten days should he gently guide her towards intercourse.
> The film opens with these ten days of Nanda and Dilip's tender courtship.[5]

After that the film movies cuts to the European story—which, whatever—before returning to the good stuff.

> Switching back to the Indian storyline, Nanda uses her wits to turn each physical advance into a delightful game. Pursuit and capture are central to the teachings of the Kamasutra. In the end, nightfall rewards the young couple with the ultimate fulfillment of their erotic desires.[6]

It is not surprising that the press release for a film called *Kamasutra* would use the never-not-gross word "erotic," but it is no less disappointing for that. Jaeger's film was available to stream on Amazon Prime in the United States as late as 2018, though not at the time of this writing; the film is listed as 38 minutes on Amazon, and judging from its modern, 30-second trailer this abridged version is just the Indian sequences. (Whether or not Persis Khambatta had any audible lines in any version of the film is unclear; Howard Thompson wrote in the *New York Times* that the AIP cut included "'an English narrator droning away about the wisdom of' the title book" during the Indian sequences, which suggests there was no production sound. As such, *Kamasutra* will be considered an outlier in this book, and beyond the scope of discussions of her Hindi or English-language films.) The Amazon trailer focuses on Nanda, who it again must be stated remains clothed throughout, and there is no evidence that Persis Khambatta was photographed nude for the film. This detail will be important later.[7]

* * *

As Kobi Jaeger and American International Pictures duked it out in the courts in the waning days of 1970, Persis Khambatta was preparing to leave her friends and family. She had gone as far as she felt she could go in India to pursue her dream of being a leading model, and she longed to live in the Western world. Khambatta viewed the Indian woman's role as being an interchangeable moving part limited to tasks such as housework or being a secretary, and she also recognized that like most systems of control it was based on long-standing customs and attitudes: because something had always been done a certain way that was the way it should continue to be done, and those scales were always tipped in the favor of men. So the eternal optimist Khambatta looked to the West, where she was sure things had to be more progressive and less male-dominated, and where being female would not be a detriment to her career.[8]

While she was looking for adventure and challenges in her freedom, she decided she would feel more comfortable with the adventure and challenges of London rather than the other frontrunner, New York. As Khambatta herself later said, and the non-Indian writer of *Presenting Persis Khambatta* stresses that this is a direct quote: "I think Indian people are very close to the British because of the British Raj, and I decided when I wanted to go away from India to model, I chose England because I spoke the language, and there was some affinity with English people."[9]

But moving away was no easy matter. Khambatta managed to get a ticket to England from the Yuvaraj of Dhrangadhra, "Bapa" to his friends, a squash player who had recently returned to India after attending Christ Church at Oxford.[10] Though he arranged for a friend in London to put Khambatta up for a few days, there was nothing Bapa could do about the legal restriction against taking money out of India, so Khambatta landed at Heathrow in January 1971 with only three English pounds on her person.[11] She began cold-calling agents on her first day, three of whom expressed interest. Normally she would have been happy to mail her photos off, but a postal strike had begun on January 20, so she delivered the photos in person despite only owning Bombay-appropriate clothing.[12] Khambatta was sure Londoners were looking at her like she was a crazy person as she walked the snowy streets in thong sandals and a silk sari, but the photos had to be delivered, gawkers be damned.[13] As if that was not sufficiently Dickensian, her food consisted of a bag of potatoes. To help further visualize the bleak landscape, she arrived while Stanley Kubrick was filming the dystopian *A Clockwork Orange* on the streets of London.[14]

Persis Khambatta also arrived at the beginning of the Glam Rock era, and she would leave around the time the scene was dying off. This is a coincidence and there is no evidence that she was involved with or otherwise directly influenced by that scene, but she still lived by manager Tony DeFries' advice to his client David Bowie: to be a star, you had to act like one. Shobha Dé's anecdote suggests Khambatta had already been doing so, and Khambatta would continue to act like the star she knew she herself to be while her career was petering out in the early 1980s. Her star-forming persistence paid off in January 1971: agent Gavin Robinson signed her right away, and by the end of her second week in London, Khambatta earned £200 for appearing in fashion shows for Simpsons of Piccadilly as well as Fortnum & Mason. Converting to dollars and adjusting for inflation, that's approximately $2,100 in mid–2018—not a lot to live on, but a start.[15]

Khambatta did an outdoor shoot for Ronald Spencer in early April, wearing a smart turtleneck sweater against the just-above-freezing temperature. (Full disclosure: this writer's favorite pictures of Persis Khambatta are the ones in which she is dressed for warmth and comfort.) Getting to London had been one battle, but not getting kicked back out was another, so around the time of the Spencer shoot Khambatta enlisted the aid of the UK Immigrants Advisory Service's Praful Patel to help her stay for the next year. It was successful, and she was also famous enough after two months that her efforts to remain in Britain were reported in the *Times*.[16]

Her struggles were far from over, but she had more than a few successes as well. Khambatta modeled for British magazines including but not limited to *21*, *Woman's Own*, and *Harper's*, and in 1972 she did a shoot with Queen Elizabeth's photographer Patrick Lichfield, who called Khambatta one of the ten most beautiful women in the world. Again reflecting the contemporaneous Glam aesthetic, by the time of the Lichfield sessions Khambatta had plucked her eyebrows razor-thin, and kept them that way as late as March 1973.[17]

She was also asked to pose for a brassiere ad shot by photographer Richard Avedon. It would be in good taste as lingerie ads went, and she appreciated it on an aesthetic level, but she could not bring herself to do it. "I didn't think my family in India would understand," she told columnist Earl Wilson. "In India the women keep their faces and everything covered and don't uncover anything." But the work she did accept allowed her to afford climate-appropriate clothes, so she wore pants and a sensible top for the rest of her time in London. She did not like sexy clothes in general and felt too shy to wear a dress or anything low-cut when not on the clock. Having a clock to be on was an adjustment which she welcomed, for she had always been frustrated by how lax Indian culture was about time. As she told an interviewer some years later, she had to be on time when she worked as a model in London "because I was paid by the hour. In India there is nothing like time. People aren't just a half-hour late, they're a half-day late."[18]

Despite her punctuality, Khambatta was frustrated to discover that being a woman was a disadvantage even in London, let alone a career woman, never mind being a career woman who looked and sounded different than everyone else. Khambatta found solace in knowing the bias she faced was not the will of God, whose love she knew to be unconditional, but the will of men who were reveling in their own insecurities. Bapa had bought Khambatta a round-trip ticket so she could return at any time, but she wanted both India and Jeroo to be proud of her, so she refused to let London chew her up and spit her out. That her friends had often called her "Persis-tent" wasn't just wordplay—it was the truth. She also recognized the truth of the saying that behind every great man is a great woman, and that behind a great woman is a man trying hard to stop her, but Khambatta's own spin took the man out of the equation: behind every great woman is the urge to be free.[19]

Persis Khambatta was a feminist. There is no doubt.

To be sure, she willing to use men for practical purposes. Once when there was a mouse in the bathtub of her mews flat, she called a man she was dating who lived several miles away. When he arrived and put the mouse in the dustbin, Khambatta thanked him and said, "Now you can leave." But her desire to be free is why she chose not to marry a London artist whom she had grown close enough to that she was considering taking him to Bombay to get Jeroo's approval. The Londoner himself realized Jeroo's daughter wasn't sure she wanted to get married, as she later told columnist Earl Wilson: "I gave him back his ring and two months later he gave it to my best girl friend. She said, 'You lost him, I'm keeping him.' But I had a letter from him today. He'll never marry her."[20]

Whether or not he did is unknown, but for certain Khambatta felt that he became too possessive of her; she liked to support and encourage struggling artists but would not do so to the detriment of her own ambitions. The danger was real, such as when Khambatta's future co-star Michael Caine married a woman of Indian heritage. Shakira Caine *née* Baksh had been in a few movies, but her new husband forbade her from continuing to work since he did not want to be married to an actress. (Bloody hell, Michael Caine.) Her final film would be John Huston's 1975 *The Man Who Would Be King*, in which she replaced a white British woman who had been hired and then fired when Huston realized she did not look Indian. Michael Caine only allowed Shakira to be in the film out of deference to Huston, which tells you everything you need to know about the pecking order among alpha males, but Caine refused to let her speak to the press. (Bloody hell, Michael Caine.) Writing about this in the *Detroit Free Press* in 1975, Shirley Eder ruminated, "United Artists will spend a whole lot of loot building up their new actress from India, Persis Khambatta, who plays the love interest in 'The Wilby Conspiracy,' to Sidney Poitier and Michael Caine. So why didn't John Huston think of Persis for 'The Man Who Would Be King.' I'm only asking." Not a bad question, but considering what a non-entity the role turned out to be, it was no great loss. (That by the film's internal logic it should have been an Afghan rather than an Indian performer is another matter altogether.)[21]

Khambatta was not waiting for things to happen to her, and she set out to do things she enjoyed. One of her favorite shows on the BBC was *Star Trek*, which she found all the more inspiring since it used exotic women. (Her favorite episode was the awful and misogynistic "Turnabout Intruder," but nobody's perfect.) When Khambatta asked her agent to get her an audition, she was disappointed to learn it was no longer being produced.[22]

Her First Flight

She may not have been able to audition for her favorite show, but Persis Khambatta nevertheless became a fixture on the telly via an Air India commercial which debuted in 1973 and would run in Britain for several years. It was the peak of the jet-age fetishization of flight attendants, which resulted in exploitation films including but by no means limited to Henry Levin's 1963 British comedy *Come Fly with Me*, Al Silliman Jr.'s 1969 softcore 3D film *The Stewardesses*, Norman Panama's 1973 telefilm *Coffee, Tea or Me?* based on the fake 1967 memoir of the same name, and Al Adamson's 1975 nadir *Blazing Stewardesses*. Legitimate airline commercials often used attendants as a selling point, showing them in medium shots featuring their paramilitary uniforms with high collars and/or hats. But Air India's attendants wore saris in both the commercials and in real life, as a 1962 British newsreel noted with horny approval: "All the airlines pick beautiful women to be their stewardesses, but then they dress them up in tunics and sober skirts. Now, feminine frills and gossamer glamor have taken to the air, adding a touch of color to the London tarmac when these shimmering shepherdesses bring their charges to the airport bus."[23]

Khambatta's commercial was an extreme close-up in which she appeared to be wearing nothing but false eyelashes, with a caste mark between her tweezed eyebrows. Though the commercial begins and ends with footage of an Air India plane, the bulk is an unbroken, 33-second close-up of Khambatta welcoming unseen passengers on board. Her hands are together in a *namaste* gesture as she greets the passengers and tries to keep her smile plastered on her face. She presumably also says "namaste" to the passengers, but since the commercial isn't about her as a person, we instead hear a male voiceover[24]:

> As any transatlantic businessman will tell you, flying to the states can become a pretty boring business. The same faces. The same predictable décor. The same airline menus. The same routine service. Which probably explains why flying an Air India 747 to New York isn't half as crazy as it sounds.[25]

Khambatta's face represents the unseen décor and menus that the average transatlantic businessman won't get bored by on Air India, and that she is not referred to as exotic is made up for by the commercial promoting not flights to India, but to New York. It was the best of both worlds for xenophobic white people: get all the exotic sexiness of India without supporting their economy by visiting the country!

Between the commercial and a concurrent print campaign photographed by Jimmy Jarrett, Khambatta became famous as the Air India Girl and/or the Namaste Girl, leading to the *Daily Mail*'s chief feature writer describing her as "the girl who could sell me anything—she conquered England overnight." She might have been able to sell anything to that one ink-stained bloke, but what should have been Khambatta's big break outside India instead became her first exposure to typecasting: she was unable to land other commercial gigs because she was so associated with Air India. Fame was supposed to open more doors, but it was having the opposite effect. Meanwhile, Khambatta had been offered film roles in London as well as during her visits to Australia but declined them all because she refused to take her clothes off.[26]

While riding a London bus one day in late 1973, Khambatta struck up a conversation with a septuagenarian who turned out to be the once-famous bandleader Roy Fox, and who told her the American film producer Martin Baum was in town casting his new film. Fox connected Khambatta with Baum, which landed her a screen test for what would become her first English-language film role: Ralph Nelson's *The Wilby Conspiracy*, starring Sidney Poitier and Shakira Caine's domineering husband.[27]

Baum asked if Khambatta could act, and since to be a star you had to act like one, she replied, "I'm the best actress you'll ever see." Her bluster opened the door, but when she arrived for her screen test, she discovered that she had learned the wrong character's lines. The five minutes Baum gave Khambatta to study the scene were enough, since he told her she got the part before she finished the audition.[28]

1974–1977

Khambatta in Kenya

The casting of Persis Khambatta and *The Wilby Conspiracy*'s other female lead Prunella Gee was announced during a January 24, 1974, photo call at London's Les Ambassadeurs casino. Production began in mid–February in Kenya, where Khambatta declined the first of many offers to pose for *Playboy*, before moving back to Pinewood Studios in London. Khambatta had wanted a different film experience than doing the Twist, and she got it. Her character of Dr. Persis Ray was a dentist, and she got to do her own stunts, including being thrown to her death down a twenty-foot mineshaft. Khambatta was attached to wires and ropes with a half-dozen stuntmen waiting to catch her, and a dummy was used in one shot, so she was as safe as could be expected in a 1970s British film. But her screams of terror were not always acting, such as when Poitier's character Shack Twala picks her up before throwing her.[1]

When the *Wilby* shoot was complete, Khambatta asked Poitier to tell her with absolute candor if she should pursue a movie career. Her own feelings on the subject were mixed; Khambatta had left India without acting in another Hindi picture after *Bambai Raat Ki Bahon Mein* because of her distaste for the country's film industry. It didn't help that Indian magazines such as *Film World* characterized her as having flopped onscreen, while acknowledging the ground she broke with *Bambai Raat Ki Bahon Mein* as well as her more recent and no less unprecedented success as the Air India Girl.[2]

Poitier told Khambatta she was "one of those rare, instinctive actresses"—high praise indeed, for being called a rarity is the best!—but because she lacked technical skills, he suggested Khambatta study with Lee Strasberg, who had trained Marlon Brando and Marilyn Monroe. The problem was that Strasberg was in New York, and Khambatta was not. (Yet.) Poitier also mentored her in less anodyne ways: one day when she was all of sixty seconds late to the set in Kenya, Poitier screamed at her in front of the entire unit. She burst into tears, which you would probably also do if Sidney Poitier screamed at you in public, and Khambatta protested that she was only a minute late. Following the abuser's playbook as expertly as if he had written it himself, Poitier then hugged the sobbing Khambatta and explained how everyone on the unit had to be paid for that extra minute because of her. He then told the woman whom he had just emotionally scarred for no good reason that since being late disrespected the other person, she should always be one minute early. Khambatta endeavored to be on time after that, though she refused to wear a watch since they had the paradoxical effect of making her late.[3]

Her British film career seemed to be on schedule, since by early November 1974 she began work on her second English-language film, Michael Anderson's *Conduct Unbecoming*. The film had a larger cast than *The Wilby Conspiracy*, and Khambatta was so far down the list that her presence was not mentioned in the early announcements.[4]

* * *

By the time both films had been released Persis Khambatta had moved to New York City, where she rented a studio apartment in the East Fifties. Because New York was a small town her upstairs neighbor was Lee Strasberg, who was happy to help her work on her acting chops. "You have a stage presence," Strasberg told Khambatta. "Just work with your fear. Use that energy and dive into theatre." Jeroo Khambatta was still hoping her daughter would return to Bombay to make films or possibly even get married, but by March of 1975 Persis was already hobnobbing with the Gotham glitterati, and being photographed in nightclubs with celebrities like actor Kevin McCarthy. McCarthy was best known for his lead role in Don Siegel's *Invasion of the Body Snatchers*, which hit screens in 1956 when McCarthy was 42 years old and Khambatta was nine, but she also dated men closer to her age—though in the mid-1970s, age-appropriate American men tended to have long hair, which Khambatta didn't care for since it made them look like apes.[5]

Ann Guarino wrote in the August 3, 1975, *New York Daily News* that Khambatta "was born 25 years ago." Khambatta was a few months shy of turning 29 at the time, but that was how the game was played in an industry where women were not allowed to grow old, and this author can only admire Khambatta for keeping her true age a secret up through her death at the age of 51 in August 1998. All the obituaries listed her age as 49 and/or her birth year as 1948; among the great injustices of Persis Khambatta's life was her inability to control her own narrative, but in that respect she was successful.[6]

Buzz started building in March 1975 about Khambatta's "big love scene" with Sidney Poitier in *The Wilby Conspiracy*, which was released in the United States in June. The *San Francisco Examiner*'s Stanley Eichelbaum got both Khambatta's name and her character's profession wrong in his negative review of the film, though his inability to tell the difference between rape and consensual sex was on brand for 1970s men: "The clumsy attempts at humor are only matched by absurd sexual digressions like Poitier's love-making in a hidden closet with a pretty dental assistant (Persis Ray) while the dreaded security police are casing the dentist's office." The *New York Times*' Vincent Canby described Khambatta's character as "a beautiful, perfidious Indian dental assistant, who, according to the film, should never be trusted with anything more lethal than a cotton swab." As things which are "according to the film" go, Dr. Persis Ray is a dentist in her own right, established by a lingering shot on the sign outside her office door. She shares that door with another dentist played by Saeed Jaffrey, but it is clear that she is not his assistant—unless you are a white male film reviewer in the 1970s who cannot wrap your brain around an Indian woman in anything other than a subservient position.[7]

Whether Persis was already the character's first name before Khambatta was cast is unknown, but Dr. Ray was a substantial role for Khambatta's first English-language film. Though she is killed by Shack Twala when she attempts to steal the diamonds which the male protagonists are themselves conspiring to purloin, Dr. Ray has clear motivations and takes decisive actions, which cannot be said for the passive Ilia or most any other English-language role Khambatta would go on to play. But like Ilia, Dr. Ray is portrayed as being irresistible to men, and the aforementioned "big love scene" / "love-making in a hidden closet" is a rape. It is an act which has no bearing on the plot, nor does it deteriorate Poitier's hero status. In his 2004 Poitier biography, Aram Goudsouzian described the *Wilby* rape as "a superfluous romp" injected by the screenwriters because "where once Hollywood sought to purge the screen of black sexuality," that was no longer the case due to "the changes wrought by blaxploitation." This is questionable at best considering that while *Wilby* was domestically distributed by United Artists, it was produced by a British company and thus was not a mainstream Hollywood picture.[8]

The Wilby Conspiracy was followed in October by the American release of *Conduct Unbecoming*, set during the British Raj. Khambatta makes her single scene count as Mrs. Bandanai, a traumatized Indian widow who describes in flashback how after having "lain with" a British officer, she was tortured and raped by a second British officer who forced her to walk on her hands and knees "like a pig" while he stabbed at her from behind with a sword. The flashback is filmed from the unseen attacker's point of view, and the protagonist does not believe Mrs. Bandanai until another man confirms that this sort of "unbecoming conduct" does happen. While many people would go on to criticize her acting abilities, between this scene and Ilia's murder in the first Star Trek movie, Persis Khambatta is always convincing when portraying a woman who has been assaulted.[9]

Khambatta in Kohl

While Persis Khambatta was making the scene in New York, the United Nations held a conference which established a set of goals to advance the rights of women worldwide, declaring 1975 the International Women's Year and the next ten to be the United Nations Decade for Women. It was about as effective as anything the UN ever did, and it was about halfway through the Decade for Women that the United States failed to ratify the Equal Rights Amendment. But the International Women's Year inspired Hari Narain Verma and Amrit Verma to write the reference book *Indian Women Through the Ages*, which was published in mid-1976. As they note in the preface, the book is not a social study but a dictionary of 3,000 "women who matter in the variegated and chequered history" of India. They also disclaim that their alphabetical reference work means to only identify those women, and "there is no effort whatsoever at presenting brief biographical sketches." One of those 3,000 women is Persis Khambatta, whom the Vermas define as "a well known model; has modelled for prominent textile and cosmetics manufacturing concerns in India and abroad." Salome Aaron is the only other model listed in *Indian Women Through the Ages*, and well done to them both.[10]

Khambatta knew she could earn upwards of $500,000 a year in India on the strength of *The Wilby Conspiracy* and *Conduct Unbecoming*, but she considered herself a model first and foremost, so she signed with the Wilhelmina agency in New York. Appropriately enough considering her existing fame in other hemispheres as the Air India Girl, she soon appeared in a Pan Am commercial which both earned her a Screen Actors Guild card and re-upped the acting bug. Her perennial foot in the modeling door also served her well when Europe was swept by a vogue for the dark-eyed look associated with Indian women traditionally known as *kaajal* and Westernized as kohl, and London cosmetics maven Helena Rubinstein further defanged it as the "symphony" look. Rubinstein held a fundraiser featuring the symphony *née* kohl *née* kaajal look in June 1976, an event attended by HRH Princess Anne and featuring Shakira Caine on the runway since her husband was fine with being married to a model so long as she did not also act. (Bloody hell, Michael Caine.) By November, Khambatta was appearing in an ad campaign in London for the Indian cosmetics company Lakme.[11]

The Lakme campaign was welcome work, since Khambatta could not find a Hollywood film role which did not require nudity. While still living in New York she turned down parts in John Frankenheimer's *Black Sunday* and Don Taylor's *The Island of Dr. Moreau* which went to Marthe Keller and Barbara Carrera, respectively. Though it is likely that agreeing to being unclothed was a condition of Keller accepting the part, whether there was full-frontal nudity in the Frankenheimer film depends on whom you ask. In the version of *Black Sunday* available on DVD and streaming services in 2019, Keller appears unclothed from the shoulders up before taking a shower, in a composition similar to Robot Ilia's first close-up in the sonic shower in the G-rated first Star Trek movie. Keller is in the shower about five minutes later when a terrorist bursts in, but is only seen from the neck up; in a promotional photograph used in the newspaper adverts Keller is naked from the navel up and covering her breasts with her hands.[12]

This scene was most likely the dealbreaker for Khambatta, though whether or not it appeared in the theatrical version is unclear. When discussing *Black Sunday*'s R-rating with Rex Reed in the April 3 *New York Daily News*, producer Robert Evans insisted that "there is no nudity or obscene language" in the John Frankenheimer picture, and this is one of those rare times in which Robert Evans' account of history seems worth trusting. And though what was shot on the set of *Island of Dr. Moreau* is unknown, Barbara Carrera's nudity in the PG-rated Don Taylor picture is also a shoulders-up shot which only lasts for two seconds.[13]

The bottom line was that barring a sign from above, non-nude modeling would always be Persis Khambatta's focus.

Siri, the Power-Adjacent Princess

The sign occurred in early 1977 while Khambatta herself was above the Earth: her modeling portfolio was stolen on a flight to New York after visiting Bombay. Khambatta later wrote in *Pride of India* that "strangely enough, it was a friend" who stole the portfolio, and "perhaps because I forgave the person, God gifted me the unexpected chance to be an actress in Hollywood." For sure, it settled that she would move to Los Angeles and break into the film business at the source. As disappointing as it was to only be offered roles which were contingent on her removing her clothes, she was not ready to give up, even if it meant aiming for the small screen.[14]

Khambatta signed with David Moss of Beverly Hills as her theatrical agent, while retaining the New York–based Norma A. Lee as her manager. After a week and a half in Los Angeles, Khambatta won a role in a pilot which began shooting in March called *The Man with the Power*. The job also earned Khambatta her all-important Green Card, so she would not have to keep scrambling to maintain her United States residency.[15]

Khambatta's *Man with the Power* character is a modern-day princess named Siri who is kidnapped in the second act and has to be rescued by the titular telekinetic man. She would not have been on the series if even the pilot sold, and the final product is an eyesore thanks to much of the third act having been filmed in Southern California's bleakest industrial wastelands. But it is also an anomaly in Khambatta's 1970s filmography for two reasons: there is no implication that Siri is raped, and Khambatta gets to have fun. Television movies tended to be 30 minutes of story stretched out to 90 minutes, and *Power* burns five of those minutes as Siri and the Man knock about a boardwalk carnival. It is pure padding as the Man uses his Power to ensure the princess wins at the various games, in particular pinball, but Khambatta radiates joy as Siri gets to indulge in the simplest of pleasures. She would never get to sell such happiness again in an English-language production, though when it was broadcast on British television in early 1980, the UK-based *Star Trek Action Group* newsletter reported that Khambatta "acted well, but did not look very pretty." Priorities![16]

The Man with the Power wasn't much, but Khambatta's manager Norma A. Lee made the most of it. Gerry Levin wrote up Khambatta in an April 11, 1977, *Hollywood Reporter* piece in which Khambatta spoke less about herself and more about the economics of the Indian film industry on both sides of the screen, such as how rich people paid 50 cents to sit in the balcony away from the poor majority down on the floor who paid 10. Khambatta's anxieties about being among the hungry and desperate had not gone away, and she also spoke of her worry that the censorship of Indian films would only get tighter as the outgoing Indira Gandhi was replaced by the new Prime Minister Morarji Desai.[17]

A shorter yet more influential piece ran in Bill Roeder's Newsmakers column in the May 16 *Newsweek*, eight days before the broadcast of *The Man with the Power*. After acknowledging that "TV watchers have seen Persis Khambatta touting Pan Am flights," Roeder wrote that Khambatta has been "publicized as the Sophia Loren of India.'" She was also reported to have been "compared to Sophia Loren and Audrey Hepburn" in a fluff piece which ran in a New York–based entertainment magazine that week, but the Loren comparison would be credited to *Newsweek* going forward. Various versions of the Roeder piece were syndicated to newspapers, truncated for length or on the whims of the given copyeditor, though few retained the most important details: Khambatta's confidence that her acting ability would "help her break the stereotype of 'always playing the princess from some exotic island in the Bay of Bengal,'" and her excitement that even though she was still playing an exotic princess in *The Man with the Power*, it featured "many scenes that allow me to get out of my sari."[18]

But to make sure the men with the power to give her more of those sari-free scenes knew who she was, ads were placed in *Variety* on May 18 and May 23. They featured a photo from the 1972 Patrick Lichfield sessions and contact info for her agent and manager, while the main text read "PERSIS KHAMBATTA Cordially invites you to view her American TV film debut as Guest Star in 'MAN WITH THE POWER,' NBC Movie of the Week, May 24, 8 p.m. EDT."[19] Though she was already more famous than Khambatta would ever be, Aretha Franklin was experiencing career doldrums at the time, and on the same page as Khambatta's ad in the May 18 *Daily Variety* was a slightly smaller advertisement complete with management contact info for Franklin's compilation album *Ten Years of Gold*. Much like shaving a few years off one's age, this was how the game was played at most levels of success or accomplishment.[20]

The Eternal August, Part I: The Screening of Persis

Now that she was back to pursuing an acting career, Persis Khambatta received a call she had long since stopped hoping for: she was asked to audition for a new Star Trek series, appropriately called *Star Trek II*. Knowing the character was from a hairless alien species and determined to prove to producer Gene Roddenberry that she was willing to de-glam for the part, Khambatta wore overalls as well as a bald cap she'd purchased for a dollar from the legendary Columbia Drug Store at Sunset and Gower. As she told the UK magazine *Starburst* in 1979[21]:

> So I walked in to see Gene Roddenberry with it on: "If want you to see me without hair." All the other girls were really dressed up with their best hair-dos and looking beautiful, while I looked ... well, as if I had a swimming-cap on. I sat there, reading and said I'd really appreciate being tested. "I'm not such a fantastic reader," I said, "but I can prove I'm good in a test." They tested two girls—and I got the job.[22]

Khambatta's screen test took place on Paramount's Stage 21 on October 27, 1977. She did her lines from the planned *Star Trek II* premiere episode "In Thy Image" for an acting teacher before the test, later admitting that she "overdid it, in fact. He told me to play it absolutely straight. I was so nervous in the test that my lip was shaking, but I tried to play it as natural as possible. I think I got the part because everybody else was coming on too strong. I was just playing myself."[23]

A color photograph from Khambatta's screen test was later published in J.M. Dillard's 1994 *Star Trek, "Where No One Has Gone Before": A History in Pictures*, and four seconds of silent test footage were released in the bonus features on the 2001 DVD of the Director's Edition of *Star Trek—The Motion Picture*. She wears a gold miniskirt uniform from the first Star Trek series as well as a not-terrible bald cap in the motionless picture from the screen test, and in the film footage she's also wearing the jeweled headband which Robot Ilia would don in the first Star Trek movie. (A similar uniform sold for $8,400 in Christie's 40 Years of Star Trek: The Collection auction in 2006. The description said the uniform was "believed to have been worn by Persis Khambatta in screen tests," but there is no evidence that this belief is true.)[24]

Khambatta was cast as Ilia by October 29, and she signed a six-year contract. That contract was also why she had no problem with *Star Trek II* falling through: "When it was turned into a movie I was really happy. I don't think any of the actors would have come back in a series again. It stops you from working, once you're known as a certain character." Which is true, but like her bald cap from the screen test, the terms of the Test Option Agreement for Pilot and Series she signed were not terrible: $10,000 for four weeks on the pilot, and $2500 per episode for the first year with raises thereafter, including the merchandising clause of "5% reducible to 2½% of net profits after Paramount fees and expenses of 50%." Six years of increasing pay was a step up from subsisting on a bag of potatoes, for sure.[25]

That Khambatta had been cast in a role which required her to be bald soon leaked to the press, and the earliest notice seems to have been in Aaron Gold's Tower Ticker column in the November 15, 1977, *Chicago Tribune*. Gold wrote that since Leonard Nimoy would not be returning for *Star Trek II*, "Capt. (William Shatner) Kirk's aide instead most likely will be played by former Miss India, Persis Khambatta, who will have to shave her beautiful head daily for the role." It is unclear if it had been decided by mid-November whether she would shave her head or wear a bald cap for what was still envisioned as a weekly television show—my previous book *The First Star Trek Movie* goes into detail on the ups and downs of the unmade *Star Trek II* series—but "shave her beautiful head" made for better copy for Gold, and greater fame for Khambatta.[26]

1978

The Eternal August, Part II: The Shave of Singularity

Khambatta's fame had not dimmed in India since she left in 1971, and in two separate articles about fashion and photography in the June 30, 1978, *India Today*, many people took credit. The Spencer Sisters of Bombay claimed to have "groomed" not only Khambatta but also Zeenat Aman and Katy Mirza, though the article points out that "about a dozen others make similar claims in Bombay," while photographer D.L. Oberoi takes credit for "making" both Khambatta and Aman when Oberoi was an art director at Shilpi advertising. That may all be true; after Gurmeet Singh discovered her in that restaurant, it has proven difficult for this biographer to glean who was responsible for what in Khambatta's modeling career. For sure, the single most significant grooming event in her acting career would occur at the hands of Star Trek's once and future make-up guru Fred Phillips on July 26, 1978. It would be associated with her until the release of the first Star Trek movie on December 7, 1979, and never go away, not even decades after her death.[1]

* * *

That the series *Star Trek II* was being upgraded to *Star Trek—The Motion Picture* was announced at a massive press conference on the Paramount lot on Tuesday, March 28, 1978, preceded by a brunch catered by the posh Beverly Hills restaurant Chasen's. Khambatta was present but by no means the focus; reporter Tom Sullivan wrote that Khambatta did "indicate there are Trekkies in her native land, too," though the first Star Trek series would not be broadcast in India until 1984. Charles Champlin wrote in his *Los Angeles Times* coverage that "the only new character will be played by Persis Khambatta, an Indian actress who takes the role of Ilia, an exotic woman from another planet." *Famous Monsters of Filmland*'s Forrest J Ackerman was more effusive about Khambatta's exotic qualities, as well as being the first and last person to compare her to Boris Karloff.[2]

Selected from nearly 100 actresses who were considered for the part, the Hindu star shares the same olive skin of the late Boris Karloff and will portray Ilia (pronounced Eye-lee-ah), an alien female from another planet who joins the crew of the USS Enterprise as a Navigator Lieutenant. For plucky Persis, formerly Miss India, the role in STAR TREK: THE MOTION PICTURE is the culmination of a personal trek toward stardom from India ... to England ... to America. Her exotic qualities should stand her in good stead in her role as a (literally) out-of-this-world woman.[3]

There is no mention in the coverage of the press conference that Ilia would lack hair, though there was awareness in fan circles after Sulu actor George Takei revealed at Liverpool's TerraCon convention in September 1977 that a new female alien character was "a sexy bald woman." The first inklings in the mainstream United States media after the Massive Presser seemed to have been in Hank Grant's *Hollywood Reporter* column known as the Rambling Reporter, which was syndicated to newspapers. As the column ran in the June 18, 1978, *San Francisco Examiner*[4]:

> If you hear **Telly Savalas** growling, "It's about time," it's because **Persis Khambatta** will finally get her head shaved bald this week for her role in Paramount's "Star Trek" movie. Quick, **Eva Gabor**, sell her one of your famous wigs![5]

Khambatta's head would not be shaved for another month because of production delays, but Grant ticked two boxes which would recur in the coverage over the next year and a half: a reference to *Kojak*'s Telly Savalas and/or *The King and I*'s Yul Brynner, and Khambatta as a collector and/or purveyor of wigs to hide her shame. Meanwhile, she sat for photographer Ken Towner in mid–April for what was to be one her last pre-baldness photoshoots, though there would be many during-baldness shoots, and far more post-baldness shoots.[6]

The *Los Angeles Times*'s Fashion78 column reported on July 14 that "Persis Khambatta is facing bald facts" for her upcoming shave, and quoted her: "In India, it's traditional for women to sacrifice their hair for something they want, and I want this success, so I figure if I'm going to be scalped I may as well do it in style." To that end, she said she would wear hats by Zandra Rhodes, Yves Saint Laurent, and Doris Clive. But not wigs; though Paramount supplied her with a baker's dozen to hide her shame, she decided not to wear any during filming, not even when she went out at night. Besides, a wig would have obscured the $10,000 diamond and sapphire earrings Cartier had designed for her to wear while bald. Khambatta had not worn a wig since *Bambai Raat Ki Bahon Mein*, and would not wear one again until her first post–Trek movie, long after her own hair had grown back.[7]

Though Khambatta was fearless about the social aspects of her imminent baldness, she was not going into it without recognizing the physical risks, so she asked for Paramount to take out a Lloyd's of London insurance policy. In a July 19 memo to Vice President of Motion Picture Production Jeffrey Katzenberg, Gene Roddenberry noted with approval that Khambatta "made the request herself on a personal level rather than legalistically through agent or attorney, being that kind of gentle person." (He had a reputation for hiding behind his lawyer Leonard Maizlish, but what was perfectly acceptable for a masculine man's man like Roddenberry would have been unforgivably un-feminine for Khambatta, being a female lady woman and all.) Roddenberry argued in the memo that Khambatta's request should be looked into because there had been similar concerns over Nimoy's eyebrows during the first Star Trek series, it would put Khambatta's mind at ease and thus make her more comfortable in her role, and because publicist John Rothwell assured Roddenberry that if the price was negligible, "we would probably get many times the cost back in publicity about the insurance."[8]

The insurance companies they queried said the price would *not* be negligible, since it would be difficult to prove whether her hair did indeed grow back the way it had been before. Paramount instead paid for a consultation at the hoity-toity Georgette Klinger Skin Care Salon, who recommended that Persis Khambatta come in for six facials and scalp treatments during filming, and to use a cleansing bar rather than shampoo every morning, followed by brilliantine for moisturizing. They further recommended the use of makeup remover and cleansing lotion at the end of a given day, and to use leave-on conditioner for two hours every week.[9]

Roderick Mann of the *Los Angeles Times* reveled in the gender-defying shock of it all in his July 25 piece "Shear Terror for Khambatta," warning that if you were to see Khambatta, you should not ask her to take off her hat no matter the temperature: "She won't! She can't! Because—from Wednesday on—she'll be as bald as a coot." (Similes used to describe her head by other writers included "bald as a doorknob" and "bare as an egg.") The appropriately-named Mann could not have imagined Khambatta would appear in public *sans chapeau* many times in the months to come, writing that "this Bombay-born beauty, whose dark tresses would be the envy of most women," had chosen to go the "Yul Brynner, which-way-is-up, route." Khambatta swerved into the Brynner and Savalas comparisons herself at the end of the article: "I'm not really worried about losing my hair … it's in a good cause. In fact, I'd rather like to have my picture taken with Yul Brynner and Telly Savalas. Maybe somebody can arrange that." She would admit by the film's release in December 1979 that those jokes got old fast, but she did her best to get out ahead of them, including joking that the Hare Krishnas named her their "pinup girl of the year."[10]

Khambatta told Mann that the real bore was going to be "having to be shaved every day for the next three months," an estimate which was too short by half. She had been dating actor Kabir Bedi, and when Mann asked if Bedi would be shocked by Khambatta's tresslessness, she replied that "it won't worry him" because Bedi's "mother was a bald Buddhist nun." Whether memories of his mother would ease Bedi's mind proved irrelevant since he and Khambatta broke up before filming started, confirmed during a trip to Bombay between the shave and the start of principal photography. As Shirjee wrote in the August 28, 1978, edition of the magazine *Sunday*[11]:

> PERSIS KHAMBATTA was in town recently ... presumably to let the Cat out of the bag. What I'd suspected would happen, seems to be happening—Kabir and she are drifting apart. And though she tried to cover it all by saying things like, "I have known all along that Kabir's career comes first with him," fact remains that Persis had hoped that she would be the permanent attachment in Kabir's life. It was silly of her to have imagined such things. What does she think she has that Protima and Parveen don't?[12]

The Protima in question was Protima Gauri, Bedi's former partner and the mother of his children—and in a long-term coincidence, Protima Gauri and Persis Khambatta both died on the same day in 1998. A much shorter-term coincidence was that the next paragraph in Shirjee's column was about how "everybody is so nasty" toward Zeenat Aman, who "does go out of her way to be nice to people but they seem to be instinctively catty towards her," including rumors that she had gone into hiding because "she is so ashamed of all she did for *Saiyam Shivam Sundaram* (and all that it didn't do for her!)." But between the designer hats and high-collared outfits, Khambatta had no intention of hiding for the foreseeable future.[13]

* * *

Khambatta was wearing one of those high-collared outfits when Fred Phillips draped a white barber's cape over her shoulders on Wednesday, July 26, 1978. She was in full makeup, and production hairstylist Barbara Minster set her hair in curls, so much the better for the "before and after" footage. The footage was being directed by Carl Barth, the head of a Continental Films documentary crew which had been hired to shoot every facet of the production. It was intended for use in a television special which never materialized, though Gene Roddenberry later showed the Barth footage of Khambatta's shave during his speaking appearances.[14]

Barth rehearsed the whole procedure with Khambatta, Fred Phillips, and Phillips' daughter Janna, one of the film's credited makeup artists. (During principal photography Khambatta would not let anyone other than Janna Phillips do her makeup; Paula and Mary McKenna of the West Hollywood cosmetics salon Vanity, Inc. would tell *People* magazine in 1980 that they did "Persis Khambatta's bald look for the movie *Star Trek*," but there is no evidence of this.) Christine Chapel performer Majel Barrett and producer Gene Roddenberry were both present for moral support, and they told Khambatta they would understand if she wanted to cry, as they were already getting misty themselves. In addition to her surrogate family in the flesh, Khambatta placed pictures of her mother Jeroo and brother Dinshi on the makeup table. As was her habit, she chain-smoked during the rehearsal and while Barth directed proceedings: "Now, snip a lock of her hair and put it in this box.... Janna, move the box in closer.... Fred, can you cross to the other side? ... Hold the scissors the other way...." Though she was not in the room when it happened (and neither was I), Susan Sackett wrote in her 1980 book *The Making of Star Trek—The Motion Picture* that "Persis looked very small and very vulnerable" during this.[15]

Clutching an unlit cigarette in her left hand like a totem in the Barth footage, Khambatta can be seen holding back tears as Fred Phillips ties the cape while the narrator intones that "for her American film debut, actress Persis Khambatta underwent an unusual transformation." Before breaking out the razor, Phillips cuts off a small lock from the back of her head to show her, and the simple sound of the scissors results in another choked-back sob. He then asks her to remove her large hoop earrings, while the narrator observes that "Freddy arrived at the final decision for the Vulcan ears which became Mr. Spock's trademark, so you might say that one of his specialties is creating unique and unforgettable aliens." This "unusual transformation" into a "unique and unforgettable alien" would be accomplished by shaving a woman's hair. A true wizard, for sure.[16]

Jerry Goldsmith's "Ilia's Theme" plays in the Barth footage as Fred Phillips begins the shearing, and the narrator ponders, "what does it feel like to be instantly bald? Persis' face tells the whole story." She does her best to keep it together as the camera zooms in, trying to maintain a smile through what was by no means an instant process. The footage fades to a wider shot, then zooms back in as Fred Phillips is shaving the back of her head, followed by an extreme close-up from behind Khambatta's left ear as Goldsmith's music swells. Khambatta is full-on crying as both she and the viewer see that the right half of her hair is gone. The film fades to the finished job, and Janna Phillips hands Khambatta a tissue which she dabs at her eyes.[17]

This is followed by a wide shot with Khambatta's earrings already back on, so we do not see her initial reaction to her own baldness—which is fair because she deserves at least that much privacy, though she later said she felt good about the shave, and that her first reaction was "Wow!"[18]

Khambatta brings Roddenberry in for a kiss on the cheek, and he instead kisses her forehead, which would happen a lot in the ensuing months, whether she wanted it to or not. "And to keep her new look in perfect shape," says the narrator, "a special present from Gene Roddenberry." That special present? An electric rotary razor. (See, it's funny because she had just been shaved bald, and—)[19]

Khambatta pulls up the large collar of her blue sleeveless blouse and smiles widely as the narrator concludes: "There's no question about it: for Persis Khambatta, bald definitely is beautiful." That Persis Khambatta's beauty transcended her hair is without question, but there was also no question that Paramount was banking on their film's greatest visual effect being the truly startling image of a bald woman. The story of the shave is told on pp. 6–7 of Sackett's *The Making of Star Trek—The Motion Picture*; the only event considered more important is the first day of shooting on the *Enterprise* Bridge, which is related on pages pp. 1–3, while pp. 4–5 are photos of Khambatta during and after the process. Khambatta's hair was collected in a box, and though she would later make jokes about selling it for a million dollars (possibly to a "rich Arab") if the film were a hit, she never parted with it. Fans began sending her money asking for locks of her hair several months before the film came out, money she always returned without comment.[20]

Much to Fred Phillips' amazement, Persis Khambatta's head was perfectly smooth, so free of bumps that the bust he made of her head felt like a billiard ball. But being bald was not enough; her head had to look like it had never grown hair, and it took Phillips four makeup tests to find a blend which satisfied Roddenberry, director Robert Wise, and cinematographer Richard H. Kline.[21]

Khambatta and Leonard Nimoy were the first to arrive in the morning during production since they required the most work, and it took another 45 minutes to clean Khambatta's head at the end of the day. Her makeup also kept rubbing off on the inside of her costume, leading annoyed costume designer Robert Fletcher to line the collar with a tan felt, which had the unintended consequence of adding an additional splash of color to the film's otherwise aggressively monochromatic palette. The thick makeup caused pimples, and since imperfection was not an option for the film's only sexualized character, Khambatta had to have injections into her scalp on a regular basis.[22]

Knowing her life would involve these early mornings and late nights for the foreseeable future, Khambatta moved into a Hancock Park apartment a few minutes away from Paramount. She also purchased a new flat for Jeroo in Bombay; others tried to dissuade Persis by suggesting that her mother would be fine with the existing family home, but Persis felt Jeroo would be happier in a home of her very own, though in the same building owned by Persis' great-grandfather Sethna.[23]

Persis Khambatta's Paramount proximity would also come in handy when she went out dancing, though she would try to keep it to nights when she did not have to work the next morning. *People* would describe her as "part of the disco glitterati" by the end of 1978, though she was not nostalgic when looking back during a 1981 interview.[24]

Fashion, I'm not with it or without it. Studio 54, I went and now it's closed. It's fantastic being a star. It opens doors for me. I said, "Isn't it sad that this big disco only allows stars inside? Supposing I wasn't a star—just an Indian girl visiting America? Couldn't I come in?" And they said not unless I knew someone. I'm very lucky. I've always known people who can get me in. The press made me into a bigger party girl than I am, you know. I feel sad for the people who live in discos and clubs. They sleep in the mornings and afternoons and go party at night. They have no careers. Even if they go, it's all grogginess. They don't function. They take all those drugs.[25]

In addition to her drug of choice being nicotine rather than alcohol or cocaine, another way Khambatta was not as big a party girl as the press made her out to be was her ongoing refusal to appear nude on film. As the cameras began rolling on the first Star Trek movie, she would face one of her biggest battles on that front.

* * *

Like so many visionary men of his era, the slovenly, out-of-shape Gene Roddenberry pictured a utopian future in which conventionally attractive women had overcome such hang-ups as "wearing clothes" and "not having sex with any man who asks." But Persis Khambatta was troubled that the script required her to be naked in her first appearance as Robot Ilia, and before signing the contract she told Roddenberry that she didn't want to do nudity. He assumed it was because of her ethnicity, so Roddenberry told Khambatta they just wouldn't show the scene in India. The editing of a mega-budget studio film for exhibition in a given country was a decision which was out of Roddenberry's hands to begin with, but Khambatta still had to give the great humanist a basic lesson in human geography and demographics: "Gene, Indians are all over the world. They're not just in India." Susan Sackett later wrote in *The Making of Star Trek—The Motion Picture* that Khambatta's reluctance was due to her "strict religious beliefs and conservative Indian upbringing," and the fact that "in India, people don't even kiss on screen. What would her family think?" In truth, though Khambatta was born into the Parsi sect she did not subscribe to any single religious dogma, and her upbringing had been comparatively progressive by the standards of mid–20th century India, hence her family supporting her decision to pursue a modeling career in the first place, not to mention Sethna wanting her to become a lawyer.[26]

Khambatta further clarified to Roddenberry that her refusal to do nudity was a personal choice, not a cultural or religious one: "It's me. Maybe I will do it one day, but right now I'm not ready for it." Roddenberry was a famous avoider of the unpleasant feelings which come with confrontation—that was what he paid his lawyer for—so he had nothing more to say about it at the time. Khambatta signed the contract, though the issue never left her mind.[27]

The issue of the terrible costumes in the first Star Trek movie is beyond the scope of this book, other than to say that Khambatta was the only performer who managed to make Robert Fletcher's banal uniforms look good. In October 2006, one of the gray uniform shirts she wore in the film was sold for $2,400 in Christie's 40 Years of Star Trek: The Collection auction. Also sold for $2,400 that year was a cream-colored, short-sleeve variation she did not wear on screen, including an orange-colored silk scarf of the sort which Khambatta tended to wear in real life.[28]

But the focus remained above her eyebrows. According to Chekov actor Walter Koenig's on-set diary *Chekov's Enterprise*, while in the makeup room on August 2 he found that he wanted—nay, he *needed* to kiss Khambatta's head. Koenig wrote that she said "of course," because "beautiful women always anticipate aberrant cravings and are, therefore, always gracious in response." (Besides, it was 1978, so did beautiful women expect men to keep their cravings to themselves? That's not women's lib—that's women's lib gone mad!) In addition to putting a "Bald is Beautiful" sticker on Khambatta's dressing room mirror, William Shatner also got into the habit of kissing her forehead. Despite the long shooting schedule with plenty of down time, Koenig would not have an actual conversation with Persis Khambatta for another month and a half. He wasn't alone in not fraternizing with her; Montgomery Scott actor James Doohan told *Cinefantastique*'s Preston Neal Jones that Khambatta and her fellow newcomer Stephen Collins "are very nice people, they really are. Whatever reserve there was was on their part, not ours, trying to find out how they were going to be received." Khambatta later wrote that she came across as aloof due to her inherent shyness, and the fact she was not fully confident at the start.[29]

The Eternal August, Part III: Ilia Is Introduced

Principal photography began on Monday, August 7, 1978. Persis Khambatta came by to watch even though she was not in the scene, as did Leonard Nimoy, DeForest Kelley, and Stephen Collins. Tuesday, August 8 was supposed to be Khambatta's first day, and her head was shaved and made up in the morning and again after lunch, but the picture had already fallen behind schedule.[30]

During a speaking appearance in Washington, D.C., in August 1977, Gene Roddenberry had titillated the crowd by promising that the new character of Ilia in the *Star Trek II* series would be "as startling as anything you've ever seen on TV." As Khambatta sat in Fred Phillips' chair on August 8, 1978, waiting for her hair to be shaved for a day that she did not yet know would be wasted, she noticed Walter Koenig staring at her head. Koenig wrote that he was "startled to see that her hair has already grown back a half an inch." The actress playing that most startling new character pre-emptively offered to let the startled Koenig pet her head, which he found to be soft and fluffy rather than the prickliness of the previous week. Khambatta rolled with the many demands to pet her head in the months to come, often purring like a cat in response. When she bought her first car, she also purchased a personalized license plate which read PURRSIS; not only was PERSIS already taken, like all great minds Khambatta appreciated wordplay, no matter how corny.[31]

Persis Khambatta's first day in front of the cameras for the first Star Trek movie was Wednesday, August 9, 1978. She kept flubbing her lines dues to opening-night jitters, though it didn't help that her first page had been revised the day before. The other problem was that while she knew her character Ilia was Deltan, she still didn't understand who the Deltans were and thus who Ilia was. Roddenberry had written four paragraphs about Ilia for the *Star Trek II Writer's Guide* before she was cast, but Khambatta was not on the production staff and thus was not privy to that document. All she had to work with was what was on the pages she was given on the set of the film.[32]

The writer of *Presenting Persis Khambatta* purchased a copy of the shooting script credited to Gene Roddenberry and Harold Livingston from the Roddenberry Shop in 2017; a copy is also stored at the Margaret Herrick Library, and can be found on the Internet with a minimum of effort. It is dated July 19, 1978, but includes revised script pages up through November 29 to make it resemble the theatrical film. This is the version of the script we will be studying unless otherwise specified, so if you own a copy, please follow along at home.

In both the script and the screen, no character's entrance is as dramatic as Ilia's unobstructed, screen-filling close-up. This is the stage direction in the August 8 revision:

98A ANGLE ON THE ELEVATOR DOORS
as they snap open, and there emerges a breathtakingly beautiful young woman (uniformed as a Navigator Lieutenant) who strides purposefully onto the bridge. A stunning figure, but hairless *[underlined emphasis in script]*, entirely bald but for delicate eyebrows and eyelashes. Her bald head is not at all unattractive, in fact exudes an aura of sensual nudity. Indeed, her whole being exudes sensuality [This is a racial characteristic, not a deliberate presence.].[33]

(In other words, the Deltan girl can't help it if the Earthmen get engrossed.)

Uhura's line in the script before Ilia appears is "she's a Deltan," but in the film Nichelle Nichols drops the objectifying article. I have no proof of this, but I choose to believe it was because Nichols knew how offensive it would have been to introduce Uhura as "she's a Black" rather than simply "she's Black." (Kirk's stated desire to have "a Vulcan" as science officer earlier in the film gets cringier with every passing year.) The stage directions also specify Uhura's "tone and expression" as conveying the D-bomb "in a certain, special manner," and Kirk "reprovingly" states that "there are no finer navigators in Starfleet." If this dialog was filmed it has never surfaced, and while it would have thrown off the pacing of a great introduction, it is no less of a shame that this information about how good Ilia is at her job couldn't have been repurposed elsewhere. But character moments which were not about Kirk, Spock, and McCoy (and to a lesser extent the new character of Will Decker) were undervalued during pre-production and principal photography, and many such moments which were shot were removed by editor Todd Ramsay in post-production.[34]

Ilia is defined on both the page and the screen by how men react to her, and the stage directions note that Sulu eyes her "with unrestrained admiration" throughout her first scene. Sulu's only interaction with and/or acknowledgment of Ilia's existence in the 1979 version is a brief, Kilroy-esque shot of Sulu's eyes over the back of his chair when Ilia first appears, which cuts to a close-up of Chekov breaking into a grin. But Decker's reaction is both more direct and more tender: he and Ilia are happy to see each other, and Decker explains to Kirk (and the viewer) that he had once been stationed on Ilia's home planet.[35]

This tender moment is derailed by the film's most notorious dialog. When Ilia observes that Decker has been demoted from Captain to Commander, thus delivering an important piece of exposition which falls flat due to the weak script and direction, Decker dryly states that Kirk has the "utmost faith" in him. It is a weird thing to say, made weirder by Kirk adding that he has also has faith in Ilia, to which Ilia replies that her oath of celibacy is on record. This line comes out of nowhere and has no payoff whatsoever; the only reasonable interpretation is that Kirk has faith both that Decker will be good at his job, and that Ilia will not fuck every man in sight. (The first rule of rape culture: rape culture perpetuates itself by pretending rape does not exist.)[36]

In a scene cut from the theatrical release, Sulu has to be snapped out of a reverie of staring at Ilia, who reassures the comically bumbling helmsman that she is sworn to celibacy—the word "sworn" is underlined in the script, though Khambatta does not emphasize it in her delivery—and thus is "safe as any human female." (The second rule of rape culture: rape culture perpetuates itself by pretending rape does not exist.) Decker assures Ilia that Kirk "meant no personal insult," and Ilia replies that she would never take advantage of a sexually immature species, adding that Decker of all people should know that to be true. The implication is that Ilia is the predatory figure in this scenario. (The third rule of rape culture: rape culture perpetuates itself by pretending rape does not exist.)[37]

When asked by Preston Neal Jones if "some of Decker's motivation for his final action has been lifted from any of his scenes with the Ilia probe," editor Todd Ramsay insisted that he didn't remove anything which would explain Decker choosing to merge with V'ger because "there never really was a scene which encapsulated the motivation." That the script was starved for character motivations is unquestionable, but Ramsay also said this regarding Decker and Ilia[38]:

> Very little was lost from their relationship *per se*, and what was lost referred to V'ger and not to their relationship, and I think this is important to understand. For instance, nothing was lost before she disappears and returns as the probe. What was lost was what we felt was repetitive, expository information which the audience had already been told once before, which we simply did not feel [bore] being repeated.[39]

The film's climax is a cosmic sex-and-birth metaphor in the form of an interdimensional three-way between a godlike alien (V'ger), a virile young man (Decker), and a robot duplicate of the young man's ex-girlfriend (Robot Ilia), who had been murdered about six hours earlier by the godlike alien. As such, the fact that the young man and his ex-girlfriend had never consummated their relationship would seem to be of the utmost importance, because it provides motivation for that final action: Decker never had sex with Real Ilia, so merging with V'ger is the next best thing. It is an icky and gross motivation for a G-rated blockbuster which was marketed toward families and children, but we are long past notions of taste. The best-case scenario is that Ramsay considered the dialog which established that Decker and Ilia had never had sex to be "repetitive, expository information which the audience had already been told once before," even though the audience had not yet been given that piece of information. Far more likely is the worst-case scenario: Ramsay was under orders to cut as much of the bald chick as he could, no matter how it impacted the film's already muddled story.[40]

The "sexually immature species" scene was restored for the 1983 ABC broadcast which incorporated 12 minutes of deleted footage; the broadcast version was released on VHS and Beta that same year as the Special Longer Version, and will henceforth be referred to as the 1983 version. Though it had been intended for pan-and-scan broadcast and home video, 35 mm widescreen prints of the 1983 version were struck for the 1991 Sit Long and Prosper screenings, and one these 35 mm prints was shown at the Castro Theatre in San Francisco in August 2016. (A digital print of the 1979 version was used for the nationwide 40th Anniversary screenings in 2019.) Though the scene was not restored in the 2001 Director's Edition—henceforth referred to as the 2001 version—it can be found as "Sulu and Ilia #1" deep in the deleted scenes of both the DVD of the 2001 version and the 2009 Blu-ray of the 1979 version. Its companion scene, "Sulu and Ilia #2," was also restored for the 1983 version: Ilia is lost in concerned thought about Decker after he and Kirk leave the Bridge following the Wormhole incident, and Sulu has to say her name twice to bring her back to reality. The last few seconds of Khambatta looking concerned were included in the 2001 version, so hooray for that.

* * *

After Ilia's introduction was filmed, Khambatta asked Gene Roddenberry to do what he should have done in the first place: explain what the Deltans are like as a species. Roddenberry then wrote the longest description he had written of any character in the film, one which gave a better sense of who Ilia was beyond the script's focus on her baldness and her implied sexual prowess.[41]

Well, sort of. Roddenberry wrote that the Deltans' "highly evolved intelligence" allows them to handle "the most complex spherical trigonometric complexities of space navigation as easily as a human learns simple multiplication tables." That's a good start, but Roddenberry characteristically spent far less ink on Ilia's brain than on why her fruit had to be forbidden.[42]

> Unlike the Vulcan race, Deltans value and delight in emotion—they see emotion as one of the myriad delights of being a life form. They are a sensual race—they enjoy the sensation of feeling hunger and fulfilling appetite in every form from satisfying their palates with exquisite foods, to the caress of a warm breeze or the bite of a bitter wind, the touch of an infant's hand, and especially all the shared communications and physical sensations of acts of love. Along its path to individual awareness, all the five (perhaps six) senses of the Deltan become highly acute and sensitive. Their taste buds, the rods and cones of their inner eyes, even their smallest epidermal nerve ending, all are sensitive far beyond the human norm.[43]

Five senses, perhaps six, who knows? Gene Roddenberry was not a detail man. To be fair, he did address Ilia's hopes and dreams and aspirations as a sentient being possessing free will, at least as far as how those hopes and dreams and aspirations intersected with her relationships with men:

> Ilia is different from other Deltans in only one area—as a girl she had considerable contact with humans because of her father's prominence as a Federation historian with special interest in parallels between the civilizations of Earth and Delta.
> Something of a dreamer, Ilia eventually became fascinated with the "primitive" heroic qualities in humans—this led to an interest in 23rd-century space exploration in much the same way that some humans become intrigued with the heroic ocean voyages of the Polynesian people.[44]

This material about Ilia's daddy issues was written after the scene in which it would have been most useful was already filmed, but it is ultimately less important to Roddenberry than Ilia's sexy backstory with Lieutenant Decker:

> Ilia's past connection with Decker is a bit troubling to her. She met Decker while still little more than a girl—her romantic "dreamer" nature saw him loom in her mind as a handsome, primitive young warrior, excitingly different from any Deltan man she knew.[45]

The young Ilia's "romantic 'dreamer' nature saw [Decker] loom in her mind as a handsome, primitive young warrior," Roddenberry wrote, and "her Deltan emotional zest catapulted her into love with this young Starfleet lieutenant"—but Decker's true love was Starfleet, and "his own principal need was for the challenge and adventure he could find only in space as a starship commander."

> When Ilia's interest in him led to preliminary love-play, even this unconsummated sex experience left him so shaken that he saw the trap in time. He fled, realizing he could not risk even a "good-bye"—another hour with Ilia might have brought him to a point of no return.[46]

The adult Decker's "preliminary love-play" with Ilia when she was "little more than a girl" is a power imbalance of the first order, but Ilia's sexuality was nevertheless so powerful, Decker had to leave right away lest he be enslaved.[47]

Roddenberry's belated description of Khambatta's character did not clear up how Ilia being Deltan was relevant, so when Khambatta toured the United States to promote the film in November 1979, he recorded a tape for her to play to journalists explaining her part in the film. The exact contents of the tape are unknown, but whatever he said, it did not help. It is also unknown whether Stephen Collins was given this backstory, and later revelations about Collins' history of sexual abuse of minors are both heartbreaking and beyond the scope of this book.[48]

* * *

It would also go beyond the scope of a Persis Khambatta biography to examine all the bad aesthetic decisions which turned the movie into two hours of drab people in drab costumes doing drab things in drab surroundings. As such, we will not dive into how the use of 8 mm and 16 mm film loops resulted in the low lighting and thus the dim look of the Bridge scenes, or how editor Todd Ramsay's decision to go for "a very Spartan approach" to the sound design makes the film's ambience feel as alienating as sitting in your own home during a power failure, to name two random examples. But the bottom line is that on top of the film's many sensory deprivations, *the new chick is bald*.[49]

To put it in the most heteronormative way possible, the eye candy of Khambatta has all the taste removed because of Ilia's baldness. Robert Fletcher's boring gray uniform doesn't help; had she been able to wear the gold uniform with the headband from the "In Thy Image" screen tests, she might have been remembered as one of the Star Trek franchise's great hotties, up there in fandom fantasies with *Voyager*'s Seven of Nine. Instead, Ilia becomes one more way the film withholds even the slightest sensual pleasures. But since her baldness was a clear-cut example, Persis Khambatta became a shorthand for the film's aesthetic failures, both among the fans and in highest echelons of Paramount.

The Eternal August, Part IV: Rush Hour on the Event Horizon

Shooting began on the Wormhole sequence on Friday, August 18, 1978. Real Ilia gets the most to do in this scene in the 1979 cut because she delivers most of the sacrosanct technological exposition. It does not develop her character *per se*, but at least we get to see that Ilia is good at her job in the most trying of circumstances, Ramsay and his Moviola be damned.[50]

Ilia counting down to the *Enterprise*'s collision with the asteroid was shot on August 22, and during one take she skipped from "four" to "two," leading Walter Koenig to write[51]:

> The set breaks up. The entire company is on the floor. Persis is aghast. She sticks her tongue out, cross-eyed, stares down at it accusingly. Two things about beautiful women: one, even cross-eyed they look beautiful; two, when they make a mistake in their dialogue it's their tongue's fault, not theirs.[52]

Khambatta's was not the only tongue tripping over the unspeakable dialogue, but all was forgiven when she threw a party for thirty members of the cast and crew the following night at an East Indian restaurant called Gypsies, even if the food proved too spicy for some of the more delicate palates.[53]

That Ilia's character began and ended with her body came through in very subtle ways, including in the visual effects of the Wormhole sequence. Effects Production Coordinator Michele Small explained to Preston Neal Jones that Ilia "was conceived to be the most sensual and sensitive of creatures" according to the script's stage directions, but it was never made clear "how absolutely alluring and sensitive she really is."[54]

And I thought, "Well, it's really important to somehow subliminalize that and at least somehow get across the fact that machines like her, too." So during the wormhole sequence, one of the fake lights—which is what we called the lights streaking off panels and consoles—whenever the cut is back to Ilia, is coming up and touching her breasts, very gently, as if they're going, "Nice, nice."[55]

It is probably not a coincidence that the energy tendrils of the probe which murders Ilia also favor Khambatta's breasts, but none of the effects crew copped to this.

* * *

Khambatta attended a party at Chasen's welcoming *The Mike Douglas Show* to Hollywood on the evening of Thursday, September 7, where she was photographed standing next to Lynda Carter and Esther Rolle. Unknown to Khambatta, her best scene had been rewritten earlier that day, and it was this version which was shot the following week: Decker apologizing to Ilia for the way things ended back on Delta. It was both Khambatta's only scene alone with Stephen Collins and Real Ilia's only character moment before she is murdered—and to Khambatta's later chagrin, it would also be the only purely romantic scene in her English-language film career. Ilia freeing herself from Decker's grip and walking away is also the only time the character gets to show any agency in the 1979 cut.[56]

Gene Roddenberry and Harold Livingston were rewriting each other's work on a daily and sometimes hourly basis during principal photography, and as petty and unprofessional as their conduct was, the September 7 rewrite is a vast improvement. In the draft dated August 17, Decker is so busy pouting about being usurped by Kirk that he barely acknowledges his former lover standing in front of him: "This was my ship—my command—and he took it from me." Ilia nods and says she understands his disappointment, but Decker is not convinced, because women cannot understand the importance of ~~penises~~ starships. Indicating the *Enterprise*, he says, "she came so close to being mine." Ilia reminds Decker that she herself also came close to being his, then drops the metaphorical mic and walks away. This version of the scene would have sapped the film of what little emotional resonance it managed, and it is unknown whether Roddenberry or Livingston wrote it, though the scene has Roddenberry's fingerprints all over it.[57]

Persis Khambatta's next significant scene was Ilia relieving Chekov's pain during the first V'ger attack; it was added to the script on September 1, storyboards were drawn on September 7 and 8, the sequence was shot on September 22, and it was cut from the 1979 version but restored for the 1983 and 2001 versions. The stage directions note that while tending to Chekov's wounds, Majel Barrett's Doctor Chapel "gives Ilia a surprised, approving look and a flicker of female friendship passes between the Deltan and Earth woman (setting up a later story point)." That flicker is snuffed out when the Deltan woman is murdered, but it remains the only time in the script two living women speak to each other.[58]

The critical tool known as the Bechdel Test considers whether a given film has at least two female characters who talk to each other about something other than a man, and *Star Trek—The Motion Picture* fails hard, since Ilia's only line to Chapel is "I can ease his pain." No given Star Trek production passes the Test until the 1995 television series *Voyager*—or, to be generous and count by individual scenes, the 1989 *Next Generation* episode "The Dauphin." (The scene in question is of two alien shapeshifters who have taken the form of hot teenage girls for no good reason, but it still passes.) The only other time two women speak to or acknowledge each other in the first Star Trek movie was deleted from the 1979 version: when Chapel enters the Bridge a few moments earlier, Uhura says, "Oh, good, Christine—it's Chekov." Though it fails the Test, it does make Christine Chapel the only character besides Kirk and Decker to be referred to by their first name, which was another ad-lib by the film's unsung hero Nichelle Nichols. (The line was restored in the 1983 and 2001 versions of the film.)[59]

Despite the script noting that the scene sets up a later story point, Todd Ramsay edited both Ilia helping Chekov and the subsequent "flicker of female friendship" between Ilia and Chapel out of the 1979 version. Those removals do hurt the storytelling, and even at age nine the author, watching the film over and over on VHS, could recognize that Chekov standing up from his console after his arm is burned is accomplished via an awkward jump cut. In the 1979 version currently on Blu-ray and streaming services, Ilia can be seen entering the frame briefly at 59:25, Chapel magically appears at Chekov's side at 59:48 with Ilia nowhere to be seen, and a cut back to Kirk at 59:50 shows Ilia's console empty. This writer considers the 2001 version to be little more than a glorified fan edit by the same boys who consider William Shatner shouting "Khaaan!" in the second movie to be Star Trek's high point, but she does appreciate that all the footage of Khambatta with Barrett and/or Koenig was restored.

The filming of the Bridge scene was also when Koenig had his first real conversation with Khambatta, of whom he wrote:

> She possesses a most interesting combination of seemingly contradictory personality traits. By turns, she is the poised elegant international model, a guileless young girl who takes ingenious delight in her own beauty and an actor like the rest of us fraught with self-doubt and insecurity. On the screen the diverse elements come together in a delicate balance of sophistication and vulnerability. The effect is a charisma that has little to do with talent but which, embodied in the right role, can make a performer a star. I am betting that the part of Lieutenant Ilia will do that for Persis.[60]

Koenig's burn on Khambatta's talent notwithstanding, from his lips to the Creator's ears, and Khambatta was striking the iron of stardom while it was hot. Her first high-profile appearance was a fashion show in early September 1978 for Jerry Brown; Jane Fonda and Chevy Chase were among the big attractions, while Khambatta appeared with Isaac Hayes in the finale. (See, it's funny because Khambatta was bald at the moment, and—) Peter Borsari photographed her alongside Hayes as well as Brown, but Khambatta was not yet a big enough name to be listed in the coverage of the event, though she earned her first mention in Marilyn Beck's syndicated column that month: "Indian actress Persis Khambatta reveals she was filled with mixed emotions when she was signed as female star of the big-screen version of 'Star Trek' which is currently shooting at Paramount." The mixed feelings were both from joining an established ensemble and doing so after being shaved bald, but "now, however, after seven weeks of shooting she's here to tell us that 'the people in the company couldn't be nicer,'" and "that she's gotten so used to the bald look she's thinking of maintaining it even after 'Star Trek: The Motion Picture' wraps up."[61]

That same Marilyn Beck column featured a tidbit about how while model Susie Coelho "will be accompanying her man Sonny Bono to Nashville" for the filming of the television pilot *Murder in Music City*, Bono's co-star would be Lee Purcell and not Bono's future wife Coelho as first planned: "Coelho wants us to know it is with her blessings that she bowed out of the project Bono is co-producing because she decided she hasn't had enough experience for such important small-screen exposure." I was not present when the decision was made, but, yeah, sure. Sure it was Coelho's idea and not that of famous control freak Sonny Bono, who existed at a time in which men were allowed to openly curtail the success of their partner, especially after Bono's previous partner was the notoriously un-curtailable Cher. *Suuuuuure*. In any event, Coelho would become a force in Khambatta's life in the years to come.[62]

* * *

Persis Khambatta herself was skilled at sloughing off possessive suitors, and while she would later refer to breaking up with (not-possessive) Kabir Bedi as taking "an oath of celibacy in my life," she had no trouble bouncing back. One of Khambatta's paramours was Los Angeles Museum of Art curator Pratapaditya Pal, who treated her to a candlelight dinner followed by a personal museum tour at midnight. Sometimes her personal life would bleed through to work, as she told *People*'s Sue Reilly[63]:

> I can't remember what humiliation I had suffered at the hands of one of my boyfriends, but one day I was sitting weeping. Director Robert Wise patted my shoulder and said, 'Come on, Persis, this is costing about $10,000 a minute.' He was joking, but I got the point in a hurry.[64]

There is no evidence that Wise said the same thing to Roddenberry and Livingston, whose dueling rewrites were causing more and expensive delays than Khambatta's personal travails. But they were men, so that was different.

However how much the film was costing per minute, it was not enough to get Persis Khambatta to take her clothes off, and on September 25 she revived the issue of Robot Ilia's upcoming debut. Though it wasn't coming up as soon as expected, because nothing on the production was: after a few days of shooting reaction shots to visual effects which were months away from being conceived, rehearsals began on September 8 for the probe sequence which would result in Ilia's murder. Shooting was delayed by the both *de rigueur* technical issues and a party on October 2 for Khambatta's birthday, a celebration shared with Stephen Collins' October 1 birthday. There was a personalized cake for each of them—Collins was turning 31, and Khambatta 32, which was known only to herself—and neither cake specified their age. She knew women in India were considered over the hill after they hit thirty, and she was learning the hard way that the United States was just as bad if not worse.[65]

Ilia's assault and murder were shot on Thursday, October 5. After the probe zaps but does not kill Spock for destroying the computer console in a September 27 script revision, Ilia calls out, "Mr. Spock, don't move…!" Much like how she had gone out of her way to help Chekov earlier, Ilia starts moving toward Spock, which is what draws the probe's attention. Ilia can be seen starting to reach down to Spock after he lands near her console in the film, but Todd Ramsay cuts away in favor of six seconds of the probe, so even this simple act of heroic compassion by Ilia is lost. It remains this writer's theory that Ramsay was under orders to remove as much of the bald chick as possible, and while it is only a theory, it is a theory which fits the facts.[66]

* * *

The publicity machine began gearing up in October 1978 with a *Los Angeles Magazine* article titled "A New Farrah She Isn't." The Farrah in question was Fawcett, who was iconic for a poster featuring her big hair and a prominent nipple. Accompanied by a large photo of Khambatta as Ilia in her Starfleet uniform, the article began by insisting that "not since **Vidal Sassoon** jetted in from London to snip **Mia Farrow**'s hair for Rosemary's Baby has there been such a fuss about a lady losing her tresses." They were not wrong about that, and though Khambatta had just turned 32, it was no small victory that the magazine's writer called her "the 27 year-old black-eyed and once black-haired Khambatta." Persis Khambatta's eyes were brown, not black.[67]

Roderick Mann followed up his coverage of Khambatta's shave and her subsequent unnatural baldness in the October 10 *Los Angeles Times*.

> BALD IS BEAUTIFUL: How fares Persis Khambatta, the Indian actress who shaved her head completely bald for her role in the $15-million movie version of "Star Trek," directed by Robert Wise?
> Just fine, it seems. Whereas some actresses, similarly shorn, might have gone into hiding when not actually working on the set, Persis walks around as if it's perfectly natural for a woman to be bald. Of course she does get kissed on the top of her head by other cast members.[68]

Of course she does! It was 1978, after all. Khambatta described how sensual it felt to shower in the morning, an anecdote she would use a great deal in the year to come, while also expressing confidence that her current baldness would someday cease to be an issue: "I'll never be typecast. Because I'll never look like this again." The second half was true, though Khambatta would stay on Mann's mind for the next few years; writing about an actor who'd shaved his head for a Broadway play which closed after one night in April 1979, Mann mused that "maybe Indian actress Persis Khambatta, who shaved her head for her role in 'Star Trek,' could lend him one of her wigs."[69]

Khambatta was featured prominently in a much longer article by Wayne Warga in the October 15, 1978, *Los Angeles Times*: the header image was of Shatner, Nimoy, Kelley, and Khambatta, and hers and Shatner's photos were twice as large as Nimoy's and Kelley's. Describing herself as a "very lucky lady," she again stated she was not afraid of being typecast "because all I have to do is grow my hair back," while swerving into the Farrah comparison and her tendency to be compared to others: "This is me, right down to the skin. Farrah Fawcett-Majors has too much hair. I'm making up for her. Newsweek once called me the Sophia Loren of India. I am always being compared. Now I am no one but me. And you cannot imagine how marvelous it feels to take a shower, to get that tingling when the water hits you."[70]

Between the publications of the two *Times* pieces with her glowing shower anecdotes came the filming of a make-believe shower about which her feelings were considerably more mixed: Robot Ilia's first appearance on October 11.[71]

* * *

Though Khambatta had long since made it clear to Roddenberry that she did not want to do the scene naked, the stage directions in the October 9 revisions specified that "we SEE, behind the translucent stall door, what is unmistakably the form of a NUDE FEMALE." Kirk "reacts as he sees the NAKED FORM," and even Spock "cannot help repressing an expression of surprise." After again noting that "Kirk's eyes cannot believe what he is seeing," the first description of Robot Ilia is that she is "naked but for a small, multi-colored button imbedded in her throat."[72]

While I have no evidence that Gene Roddenberry was a fan of *Candid Camera* producer Allen Funt in general and Funt's 1970 film *What Do You Say to a Naked Lady?* in particular, I am nonetheless certain of those things. Two more certain things: Roddenberry knew the beam-splitting effect used to create the rippled light on the door of the sonic shower would obscure Khambatta's body on film, and even if it didn't, he knew Paramount would never release this high-profile, mega-budgeted film with unobscured full-frontal nudity. But Roddenberry wanted to see Khambatta naked, and he wasn't the only Gene who wanted it: the *Chicago Tribune*'s Siskel wrote in his "it's just okay" review of the film in December 1979 that Khambatta "is something special" and "as stunning as Bo Derek in *10*," and when she wasn't onscreen "the film teeters toward being a crashing bore." Siskel then parenthetically lamented that "unfortunately, 'Star Trek' is rated G and Khambatta never gets down to basics."[73]

Khambatta was determined to avoid getting down to basics, so she asked Robert Wise to let her wear a body stocking. Roddenberry objected to the stocking because the seams would show, so Khambatta asked the wardrobe department to put the seams and the zipper on the side facing away from the camera. Roddenberry next objected to the lack of nipples, so Khambatta asked the seamstress to add buttons in the appropriate places, and asked Janna Phillips to darken the buttons until they looked realistic. Then came Roddenberry's final, most airtight objection: the whole film would fall apart if this robot replica of the murdered Deltan woman did not show pubic hair. Thankfully, Wise stepped in and put the kibosh on that.[74]

As annoying as it was for Roddenberry to not get to see Khambatta's celebrity skin, nothing can ruin a producer's day like having to jump through hoops to not kill his leading lady. Over a quarter-ton of dry ice was used to provide the moisture of the sonic shower, and filming was delayed by Khambatta stepping out of the carbon dioxide vapor on a regular basis in order to not die. (You may ask why a shower which by definition uses sound waves would create moisture. Yes, you may well ask.) Even more annoying was how the stocking Roddenberry didn't want her to wear provided no protection against the heavier-than-oxygen -109.3° F vapor which gathered at her bare feet, resulting in her developing a case of tonsillitis which required Wise to change the shooting schedule for the rest of the week. As though causing that delay wasn't unprofessional enough of Khambatta, she often caught colds during filming even when she wasn't standing in a cloud of dry ice. Wise and Roddenberry were concerned for her health insofar as a lost day of production cost tens of thousands of dollars, but they would not let her cover her head between takes because of the makeup.[75]

Khambatta's first day standing near-naked in the freezing, poisonous vapor was also her first day wearing the light in the hollow of her throat, which was powered by a battery on her back and connected by wires covered with makeup. The metal doodad heated up as predicted by the first law of thermodynamics when turned on, and Khambatta would cry out, "Switch it off! Switch it off!" It was also discovered at the end of the day in which Khambatta was being simultaneously frozen at the feet and burned at the throat that the light left a red burn mark on her throat, as predicted by the second law of thermodynamics. A plaster impression of Janna Phillips' throat had been used to test the light, but nobody had thought to test it on a human until Khambatta wore it as the cameras rolled. But what could be done? They couldn't *not* use an unreliable incandescent light which seared Persis Khambatta's flesh, so the production grudgingly provided Khambatta with a switch hidden in her sleeve allowing her to turn it on and off herself.[76]

When Khambatta returned to the set on October 18 she was clothed, if only just the short white garment referred to in the script as a "leisure robe," with a high collar intended to emphasize both her bald head and the burning light in her neck. A cream-colored variation of the leisure robe with a lower collar and a cleavage-enhancing neckline was sold for $10,800 at Christie's 40 Years of Star Trek: The Collection auction in 2006. The description says the garment was "worn by Persis Khambatta as the Ilia probe," but it was not, at least not in any known version of the film.[77]

Regarding the leisure robe's all-but-nonexistent hemline, Robert Fletcher admitted to the *Los Angeles Times* that he felt such miniskirted garments were only good for "shock value and occasionally pulling us out of fashion doldrums," and that he "used the look for obvious reasons—to show a very good pair of legs." Fletcher was in a loftier mood when speaking to *Cinefantastique*'s Preston Neal Jones, saying he was trying to create an "ironic juxtaposition of a sexually attractive figure with the soul of a machine." In order to demonstrate that machine soul, Robert Wise did not allow Khambatta to blink as Robot Ilia, even though a big deal is made about how the robot is a perfect replica of the murdered Deltan woman, down to the eye moisture, so by the film's own logic there's no reason for her *not* to blink. This is not to say Roddenberry and Wise made no sacrifices for Khambatta's physical comfort: she was also allowed to wear pants between takes.[78]

But Khambatta was a good soldier, so she did not emphasize the painful scorching of her flesh or the rigors of carbon dioxide poisoning when speaking to the press, but instead the more titillating aspects. In an article in the October 20, 1978, *India West* titled ""Persis Makes a 'Bold' Move—Shaves Her Head," she again described the wonderful feeling of showering when bald as "so different, so sensual, so smooth!"[79]

Robert Kerwin of the *Chicago Tribune* visited the set sometime in October, and when his piece ran the following June, he wrote that Khambatta said she was going to be "so goddamn happy" to grow her hair back. While it is likely that she expressed that general concept, Kerwin's account has Khambatta speaking in a broken English which reflects not the well-educated South Asian woman she was, but instead a white writer who had grown up watching racist caricatures of American Indians in westerns[80]:

> "All other girls come in full dress," she says, "with hair done from beauty shop Afro, curl, wig, everything. Me? Before audition I go buy bald mask, put it on my head, wear overalls. I get hired immediately. I like Hollywood. One thing: I get my head shaved every day for six months now, and when picture wraps, I be so goddamn happy to get real hair back again."[81]

Khambatta did not speak like this. She was fluent in English and knew how to use articles and conjugate verbs, but the *Tribune*'s copy editor was so amused by the notion of her talking like Jay Silverheels as Tonto on *The Lone Ranger* that when the article finally ran on June 3, 1979, one of the pull quotes was "I go buy bald mask. I get hired immediately. I like Hollywood." Them backwards Injuns, they sure talk funny! This may not have been the most egregious display of racism against Khambatta by the United States press, but it is the one which angers this author the most.[82]

* * *

While Persis Khambatta was shooting the film which she had every reason to believe would be her break into Hollywood, the October 22, 1978, edition of the Indian magazine *Sunday* ran an article by Vijaya Irani about the difficulties South Asian actors faced breaking into Hollywood. Zeenat Aman had returned to India after causing "a mighty big flutter" in the Hollywood scene which she had been unable to parlay into a film, while Simi Garewal had expected Conrad Rooks' 1972 *Siddhartha* to be her own entrance to international fame.

Everything seemed to be coming up Garewal when no less esteemed a figure than director Satyajit Ray recommended her to the producers of Michelangelo Antonioni's *The Passenger* as a replacement for the ill Maria Schneider. As Garewal told *Sunday*, "I was keyed up after I had passed my initial tests and interview with the director with flying colours, but Maria's agent, who got wind of my impending entry into the film, worked round the clock to get his client back into the film—she had a contractual edge over me. So there was nothing I could do except turn back home, heartbroken." Back to a home where a different Indian publication had already punished Garewal for appearing in *Siddhartha*, but it is too early to bring Khushwant Singh into our narrative.[83]

Most relevant to our narrative at the moment is Katy Mirza, who was in London at the time of the *Sunday* article. As Irani wrote:

> [Mirza] has this Persis Khambatta complex—the Parsi Miss India who also tried to get into films (to get into Hollywood eventually) and failed—if Persis, who is making it big in Hollywood now, without the help of the Hindi film industry as a stepping stone, so will she! But Katy has not cut off her Indian roots totally—like Persis, she will be hopping homewards during the year in search of a concrete footing in the international world of glamour.[84]

A "Persis Khambatta complex," indeed. When I would tell a Star Trek fan in the late 2010s that I was writing this book, they would often laugh and reply to the effect of "Persis Khambatta? Why her? She didn't do anything else!" But even before she was in Star Trek, snarky columnists named a complex after her, and that's more than enough reason.

* * *

The scene which was supposed to pay off the "flicker of female friendship" was shot on October 30 and 31 as Robot Ilia tries on Real Ilia's jeweled headband. Todd Ramsay again whittled it down in post-production, but even as written the scene had little to do with female friendship—and worse, it tries to let the film off the hook by suggesting that Real Ilia is still alive inside Robot Ilia and thus wasn't *really* murdered. The lion's share of the original scene was restored for the 1983 version, while a truncated version was restored for the 2001 version, and most of the footage can be found as "Ilia's Quarters #1" and "Ilia's Quarters #2" in the extras on the 2001 DVD and the 2009 Blu-ray.[85]

Production shut down on Tuesday, October 31 because Wise had outpaced the usable script, and Khambatta made the most of her impromptu weekday furlough that night when she attended the "Dance with the Stars" Halloween Celebrity Disco with George Takei at the Stardust Ballroom. The United States had been experiencing a craze for all things Egyptian ever since the "Treasures of Tutankhamun" exhibit began touring the country in 1976—a bust of Queen Nefertiti in that exhibit had inspired Gene Roddenberry to create a bald female character in the first place—so Khambatta and Takei dressed in Egyptian garb and makeup. A picture of them with the event's host Jane Fonda made the UPI rounds, and if this author has any regrets, it is that she was unable to present that picture of Persis Khambatta in this book.[86]

* * *

The production was already several weeks behind schedule when filming resumed on November 7, and progress was further stymied by Gene Roddenberry and Harold Livingston continuing to rewrite each other on a daily and sometimes hourly basis. When George Anthony from the Yukon *Whitehorse Star* visited the set on one of those mid–November days, he witnessed an exchange between Kirk and Robot Ilia which was never used in any version of the film. It would have occurred when William Shatner says "V'ger. V'ger!" while breathing down Persis Khambatta's neck both literally and figuratively, and according to Anthony and confirmed by the script, Kirk's unspeakably purple line was "If we are lesser beings we are still, like you, living. And, like you, because we are alive, we wish to survive." Robert Wise then called for a break, which Shatner turned into a conference where he was less concerned with the terrible dialog than with the manner in which he manhandles Khambatta.[87]

> "Bob, the body movement doesn't feel right," said Shatner. "It's just too static. Should I turn when she speaks or should I turn just before? Isn't it more powerful if she turns now"—Ms. Khambatta pivoted slowly on one foot—"as if she's so strong I can't hold her?"
>
> "Yessss," said Wise nodding his head thoughtfully. "Yes, I agree with you. Let's try it."[88]

This day was probably the source of a still photograph which did not accompany the *Whitehorse Star* article, but would be used to promote the film over the years: Khambatta as Robot Ilia is facing the camera but looking to the right of the lens, while William Shatner stands in profile to her left, Shatner's hairy left arm in front of Khambatta as he clutches her right shoulder, while Stephen Collins looms above and behind Khambatta and Leonard Nimoy is almost visible in the background. The photo is murky, confounding, and unpleasant, which can also be said of the corresponding sequence in the film.

As late as the November 5 script revisions, Real Ilia's corpse was found floating inside a cube on the walk to *Voyager 6*, her "eyes closed, hanging within the glowing cube, limp, motionless." McCoy's tricorder finds no life readings, and Robot Ilia says the corpse "is being preserved for further study." Decker is "shaken to the depths of his emotions" by seeing the corpse of his former lover and her robot replacement in the same place, but has "no choice but to follow" Robot Ilia and the others, "glancing back regretfully at Ilia's body, hanging lifeless." This is the last time Real Ilia is seen or mentioned in this draft, and Robot Ilia is just sorta there when Decker merges with V'ger.[89]

The life-size fiberglass replica of Khambatta which Rick Stratton and

Mick Valley built for this scene was later incorporated into Spock's trip into V'ger. Douglas Trumbull told Don Shay in the inaugural issue of *Cinefex* in 1980 that he conducted a photo session of the Ilia mannequin at an unflattering angle with "a combination of blue lights and red lights and rim lights and kickers—all kinds of things—and got some really striking, beautiful photographs." Those photographs were blown up into 16 × 20 color prints, retouched a bit more, then filmed on an animation stand. Seeing Ilia fully clothed once more is a breath of fresh air, and it is the only time Robert Fletcher's fugly Starfleet uniform is a welcome sight in the first Star Trek movie, even in the context of Ilia's murdered body. But as necrophilic as the image already is, it could have been even more violent; aerospace artist Robert McCall designed Spock's trip into V'ger, and Ilia's head is vertically bisected in his original conception of the sequence as printed in the 1982 book *Vision of the Future: The Art of Robert McCall*.[90]

By the time of the November 29 script revisions, the climax plays out much as it does in the film: Real Ilia's corpse is not found, Robot Ilia and Decker give each other sexy looks during the V'ger merge, and in the denouement Kirk wistfully changes Real Ilia's status from "casualty" to "missing." That is a lie, because she was straight-up killed by V'ger. The film takes great pains to establish that Decker consented to his fate, while Real Ilia died with a look of horror while being physically assaulted by an alien probe. Associate producer Jon Povill told Preston Neal Jones at the time: "I'm not sure, but I think it was my idea that Ilia join in the fusing. I know that I was always anti-bringing-her-back." This ignores that it was *Robot* Ilia who joins in the fusing and thus Real Ilia could have been brought back because you can do that in science fiction; the third (and best) Star Trek movie bends over backwards to bring back Spock after he is killed in the second movie. But Povill prevailed, and the Deltan woman remained dead when the credits rolled at the end of the first Star Trek movie.[91]

Ilia was murdered. Never forget.

* * *

Something which many people did not forget so much as never bother to learn was how to pronounce Persis Khambatta's first name. As she told Earl Wilson for his column in the first week of December 1978—in which Wilson described her as having been "a major model who refused nude jobs and bra and pantie ads because in India they wouldn't approve"—she was often called "Precious" and "Princess" by those could not manage "Persis." Most native English speakers could pronounce "persistent," so why dropping the final syllable proved so difficult is anyone's guess. Wilson wrote that Khambatta "wore a cream-colored silk scarf around her bald head when I saw her," and that "boyfriends who take her to dinner don't object when she removes her scarf or hat and emerges looking like Daddy Warbucks in 'Annie,'" though she admitted that "mouths drop open all over the place." Khambatta also dutifully trotted out the already-stale references: "I wonder how I'd look with Telly Savalas or Yul Brynner."[92]

The *New York Daily News*' Phil Roura and Tom Poster went there right away in their December 10 column: "Hey, Yul Brynner, have we got a girl for you!" (At the risk of applying rationality to an irrational thing, how does that even make sense? Did nobody believe Brynner's romance with Deborah Kerr in *The King and I* because Brynner was bald, and Kerr was not?) The piece ran with a photograph of the bald Khambatta standing in a sparse crowd on a New York street, bundled in a large coat and scarf but with nothing on her head. The caption read "Persis has one head turning," and it's true that someone a few feet away is looking in her general direction. It also evokes the picture which ran just shy of nine years earlier in the December 1969 *Life Asia Edition* of the long-haired Khambatta attracting "even more attention than usual" due to her miniskirt.[93]

A December 15 piece by the *Los Angeles Times*' beauty columnist Lydia Lane was among the few in which the accompanying picture was of Khambatta with hair. Lane did not obsess on her subject's current baldness, writing that Khambatta "seemed unself-conscious" and had no regrets: "The beauty inside is what counts. I have more to offer than a head of hair." Lane did note that the interview took place over "a combination salad of raw vegetables, sprouts, fruits, and nuts," and that Khambatta brought her own Thermos, describing the contents as "carrot juice-plus. I have it three times a day when I am working. Its natural vitamins and minerals are a great source of energy." Of the many sober and/or drug-free ways Khambatta was living it up at the Hotel California, proselytizing for carrot juice (plus!) may be the most Californian thing she ever did. She also appeared on *The Merv Griffin Show* in the week leading up to her annual holiday trip to Bombay, though she and fellow guest Irving Wallace only appeared in markets where *Merv* was aired for 90 minutes. The rest of the nation was blessed with Wayne Rogers, Desi Arnaz, Jr., and Robby Benson regardless of local running time.[94]

1979

The Eternal August, Part V:
The Blinding of Persis

Designed by Harold Michelson and built on Paramount's Stage 15, *Voyager 6* was the first Star Trek movie's most dangerous set. The wiring was complicated and overtaxed, and two technicians received an electric shock which might have proved lethal had a third crewmember not tackled them. It was a deathtrap even beyond the risk of electrocution: the fragile floor was 60 feet off the ground, with about 30 people underneath to run the lights, and the wrong place to step on the elevated set was often indistinguishable from the right place until it was too late.[1]

The steps down to *Voyager 6* itself were small, steep, and slippery, and those small steep slippery steps switched from side to side, so walking straight down was not an option. Rugged male leads William Shatner, Leonard Nimoy, De Forest Kelley, and Stephen Collins were playing characters with practical footwear who were allowed to look where they were going, while Khambatta was saddled with the sort of ungainly footwear which had disqualified her from the Miss Universe contest fourteen years earlier. She also had to maintain perfect posture while looking straight ahead at all times even though Robot Ilia was a perfect replica of a murdered Deltan woman who had the physical ability to look down. As such, when Khambatta first saw the set she thought to herself, "I'm going to die." Though stuntwoman Paula Crist appeared elsewhere in the film in a non–Ilia scene, Khambatta did all her own stunts, unlike William Shatner and Leonard Nimoy.[2]

Once again having nobody else to advocate for her self-interest or basic safety, Khambatta asked if she could have a wire or something. It was a reasonable request, but Wise instead decided to get his Eisenstein on and use montage to imply Robot Ilia's descent: she begins walking down for a few seconds, there are about ten seconds of cuts to *Voyager 6* and the *Enterprise*'s landing party, and then *voila!*, she's at the bottom of the steps.

There had been much concern throughout the production that the audience would be confused by things which would have made the film interesting to look at. (*If there's any color in the uniforms, the viewer will be so distracted they won't pay any attention to the dialog! If the walls of the Bridge set can be moved to make room for cameras and lights, the viewer will no longer believe they're on a spaceship!*) But of all the criticisms leveled at the first Star Trek movie, nobody has ever asked *how* Robot Ilia walked down those steps without the audience seeing her doing so. Even so, the film's second greatest stunt is the next ten seconds as Khambatta walks the rest of the way across the level but still fragile set to *Voyager 6*'s much sturdier platform. For the record, it is a greater stunt than William Shatner's double falling ass over teakettle after Robot Ilia pushes Kirk away, though it is nowhere near as satisfying to watch.³

Khambatta has three major close-ups in the film, two of which are tied to entrances. The first is Real Ilia's entrance onto the Bridge, which lasts for about a second before cutting to the reaction of the menfolk. Next is Robot Ilia in the sonic shower for about 11 seconds, during which she has dialog and moves her head. The third is her most impressive and the film's best stunt, running for a whopping fifteen seconds as Kirk and Spock prattle on about *Voyager 6* finding the machine planet. Khambatta has no dialog but being a human in high heels with a burning piece of metal attached to her throat and a large camera a few inches from her face, her body cannot help but wobble. Her eyes do not have the wide, thousand-yard stare as seen in many other shots, and a bit of character leaks through in those fifteen seconds. The lack of an arc for either Real Ilia or Robot Ilia is among the many ways the first Star Trek movie fails as a character piece, but for a non-character who is supposed to be doing nothing, Khambatta's physical suffering during that long close-up reads as Robot Ilia's mental wheels turning.

Speaking of Persis Khambatta in pain, which is synonymous with speaking of Khambatta in the first Star Trek movie, her final day of shooting almost proved to be her final day of seeing: Friday, January 26, 1979. Brian Longbotham told Preston Neal Jones at the time that the melding sequence was lit with two 4,000-watt xenon lights built for drive-in theater projectors, and two 300-watt lights designed for helicopter searchlights, and Longbotham's partner Sam Nicholson noted that everyone involved in the sequence on both sides of the camera got sunburned. *Only* sunburned, if they were lucky: after three and a half months of playing a robot who was a perfect replica of a murdered Deltan woman down to the eye moisture which Deltans blink to replenish and yet being by told by Robert Wise that *robots don't blink* even when they're perfect replicas of murdered Deltans who blink, nobody told Khambatta she should close her eyes when thousands of watts of light was pointed at her. As Brian Longbotham put it,

"Persis was so into the reality of the situation that she kept her eyes open as the turntable spun them slowly around, and looked directly into the lights, which she shouldn't have." Y'think?[4]

Shooting for Khambatta and Collins (who had closed his eyes) wrapped at half past ten, and Khambatta woke up at two in the morning with her eyes burning. When she was able to open her eyes, she could only see black, and justifiably freaked out, she had her neighbor call Paramount, who in turn sent her to UCLA. Khambatta was told it was a kind of snow-blindness, and since her only real exposure to snow had been during her winters in London and New York, she was unsure how this differed from the regular blindness it felt like. The doctors bandaged her eyes and told her not to worry about it. Her vision returned after two days—Army Archerd noted in the January 30 *Daily Variety* that Khambatta was "wearing a patch over her left eye"—though she got splitting headaches for the next week and had to wear dark glasses in the sun for the next few months.[5]

But it was all worth it. From shaving her head to burning her neck, from tonsillitis to blindness, these were all were temporary sacrifices to achieve permanent stardom. The first Star Trek movie's wrap party was held at the Chez Moi disco on February 10, and Susan Sackett wrote in *Starlog* that Khambatta "plans to spend the next several months growing back her shiny black hair! Seems there aren't too many parts for Deltans in Hollywood." Though nobody would ever let her forget she had been bald in that one movie that one time, the true stumbling block to a Hollywood career would not be her make-believe ethnicity on screen but her real-life ethnicity, combined with her stubborn refusal to be naked below the neck.[6]

The Eternal August, Part VI: Persis Is Presented

In an interview with *Fantastic Films* early in March 1979, director Robert Wise described Ilia as "a very interesting new character" played by "a lovely Indian actress named Persis Khambatta," and that "since we reworked the script I think we got a lot more mileage out of her character." This was presumably before Wise knew of, or at least tacitly approved of, Todd Ramsay whittling that mileage down to a few centimeters. Wise also referenced Khambatta as one of the elements of the "abnormal situation" which had been foisted upon him: "I've never come into as ongoing a situation as this. I had sets built without me, a whole troupe of actors, even the Indian lady."[7]

The Indian lady was occupied in the first half of 1979 with nursing both her hair and her vision back, and then her overall health after her auto accident in Munich. But she was no more afraid of public appearances now with short hair than she had been while bald, including appearing on the March 7 episode of *Dinah! & Friends* hosted by Dinah Shore, former partner of Khambatta's future *Megaforce* director Hal Needham.[8]

She was next spotted alongside photographer David Bailey at a private, post–*California Suite* premiere supper at London's Chez Régine nightclub on March 19 by *New York Daily News* gossip columnist Suzy, who noted that Khambatta had "a jewelled skullcap covering her shaved head." Khambatta was still wearing the fancy headgear from the shooting of the film because it looked good, but a picture of her taken the next day by a more prosaic Associated Press photojournalist shows her hair was short and spiky but by no means still shaved. On April 26, the syndicated Dynamite Kids' Page printed in a handful of United States newspapers ran a brief profile by Eve Ronan titled "Star Trek Star Persis Khambatta Sheds Her Locks for Luck!" It featured one of the more flattering photos of Robot Ilia, and Khambatta was quoted as sounding "optimistic about her own future": "'I'm with all these marvelous actors in a project which was already a big success once,' she smiles. 'I can't be typecast because all I have to do is grow my hair back!'"[9]

Khambatta attended the 1979 Cannes Film Festival, later describing herself as having "looked very nice in crew-cut hair." Tom Davies of the London *Observer* encountered her there on May 13, and wrote about it in his May 20 Pendennis column; it included a close-up picture of a melancholy-looking Khambatta with a silk scarf around her head and the caption "Persis Khambatta, an incredibly beautiful actress." While Davies didn't disagree with Khambatta's aesthetic self assessment, he nonetheless compared her to a turtle, and was a tad skeptical about her description of her talent.[10]

> Later I was on the beach getting some sand between my toes when I met an incredibly beautiful actress. Her name was Persis Khambatta, and I fear, the Pendennis Award given to Joan Collins last week, as the most beautiful face of the year, is hereby withdrawn. Persis has vast eyes, as black and mysterious as the French telephone system. There is a long, high neck, wonderful cheekbones and a short thatch of spiky black hair.
>
> It emerged that she's had all her hair shaved off because she's bald for Paramount's forthcoming film 'Star Trek.' She's the navigator who's hitting all those buttons to get Spock and Captain Kirk into the right galaxy. Talking to her put one in mind of a terrapin with a crew cut. I asked her how she rated her acting talent. 'In all modesty I'd rate myself as a very talented and instinctive actress.' Ah.[11]

It's difficult to say how much her terrapin-like qualities may have protected Khambatta during the automobile accident in her subsequent visit to Munich, but by the end of June she was engaged to Alexander Markus Zellermayer, an executive assistant at Germany's largest film studio. Though the engagement would be long over by the time the film was released, Zellermayer came back to the United States with Khambatta, and when Jeroo visited from Bombay, Persis took them both to Paramount to visit Susan Sackett and Gene Roddenberry. Sackett would write of the visit in *Starlog* that Khambatta's hair was "now about as long as the famous Mia Farrow style," and described Jeroo as "her charming, sari-bedecked mother."[12]

The *Hollywood Reporter*'s Rambling Reporter column had small pieces about Paramount asking her to shave her head again for public appearances surrounding the first Star Trek movie, while Roderick Mann wrote in the June 19 *Los Angeles Times* that Khambatta had let her hair "grow back to a healthy bristle, ideal for scouring pans." While she would never shave her head again, her hair had grown out as much she wanted it to by mid–June 1979, later explaining to Don Morrison that "I am keeping it short because it is a more modern look and I'm not doing native-girl films anymore."[13]

Khambatta returned to the *Enterprise* Bridge sets in August when the BBC children's programme *Multi-Coloured Swap Shop* conducted interviews with various cast members. Persis Khambatta and Stephen Collins were interviewed together, and footage like this confirms what the final film barely suggests: they have a terrific chemistry together. The interviewer asked Khambatta if playing an alien posed any problems, and she replied that the "fantastic role" given to her by Gene Roddenberry was "something very similar to my personality." Motioning to the place on her neck where the light had been, she continued, "it was very much spiritual, and what Gene hopes 23rd century people will be." Perhaps conscious of the fact that they were being interviewed for a children's show, she comes across as reluctant to talk about either Ilia's sexual dynamism or her own physical suffering during filming, but Collins prompted Khambatta to talk about the latter, particularly the troubles with the light.[14]

Khambatta was again interviewed on camera on September 29, this time outside the Photoplay Awards along with Robert Wise for the American program *PM Magazine*. Asked by correspondent Dave Sisson about Ilia, Khambatta replied: "Ilia is from planet Delta, and Deltans are bald—that's the character—and they're very sensual people." She was speaking off the cuff, but she also nailed it: Deltans are bald. That's the character.[15]

Wise prompted her, "what is that line of yours again, in the early part of the show about your celibacy?"

"Yes, I have to take an oath of celibacy in the film with Stephen Collins and when I join the crew, because once they...." Khambatta got a case of the giggles at this point. "Once they make love, the Deltans, I don't think anybody else can satisfy them...." Both she and Wise were laughing now as she said, "big responsibility!"

Sisson asked, "How did they convince you to shave your head?"

"I had no problems inside me. I just felt great about it."

"How about your friends? Did they react strangely toward you when you shaved your head?"

"A couple of friends wouldn't take me out to dinner because they didn't know how to handle a bald lady—but on the contrary, I made many new friends, so it was really fantastic."

"Did you feel sexy and attractive with no hair?"

"I think I look more sexy, and I felt more sexy when I was bald then I feel with hair."

Robert Wise added, "we were very lucky, because you don't know what's underneath that hair, y'know? And everybody was kind of standing around as the hair was starting to come off saying, is she going to be all right up there? Is there going to be bumps up there? And fortunately, she has a beautifully shaped head."

Khambatta fought back the giggles and said, "when I first had a shower, I really stayed long in the shower, because it was such a sensual feeling to have water on your head—I mean on your skin—it was the most...." She starts laughing again. "...sensual feeling."[16]

The interview was edited for the broadcast, but even in the final version, Khambatta was getting loopier as she went along. It was far from the first or last interview she gave in any particular medium as the release date approached, always treading the same ground about not having hair in the film, and the final products often imply that she was never not bald.

* * *

After the MacArthur Premiere on December 6, Khambatta returned to Los Angeles. Wanting to see the first Star Trek movie again as soon as possible, she went to the first evening showing at Mann's Chinese Theatre. But her promotional work for the film was far from over, and she and William Shatner traveled to London to promote the film's premiere at the Empire Theatre Leicester Square on Saturday, December 15. From there, she went to Australia for a December 19 press conference with DeForest Kelley. Per usual, the attention was on Khambatta's hair, and Christine Hogan's subsequent article in following day's *Sydney Morning Herald* was headlined "Hair, or Lack of It, the Measure of Her Success."[17]

That same day's *Globe and Mail* in Toronto ran an Associated Press story by Dolores Barclay with the headline "Bald-headed Discovery Just 'Old-Fashioned Girl.'" As was the nature of AP pieces, it ran in many papers with varying headlines and photos, depending on how many column inches were available. The *San Bernardino County Sun* had run it with the rare non-hair headline of "East Indian Actress Maintains She's Just an Old-Fashioned Gal," while the *Ottawa Journal* went with "Persis Baldly

Accepts Stardom." It continued to propagate after Christmas as "Actress Cherishes Old Values of India" in the *Wisconsin State Journal* with photos of Khambatta as herself and as Ilia, and "Actress Goes Bald for Role" in the *Tennessean* with no photos. On January 10 the *Canadian India Times* used the more celebratory "Miss India is Hollywood Star," with no photos, while the *Santa Fe New Mexican* went with "'Star Trek' Actress Old Fashioned Gal" and just an Ilia photo.[18]

But the headline of Christine Hogan's December 20 *Sydney Morning Herald* article ("Hair, or Lack of It, the Measure of Her Success") was not unmotivated, as the article opens with Khambatta saying that "I think I work better with short hair, I look more Western." One of the two photos of Khambatta which ran with the article was captioned "After the film.... Persis Khambatta in Sydney yesterday," and she is pulling at her hair not unlike she'd done in response to her doppelganger at the MacArthur premiere two weeks earlier. What happened before and after the shutter snapped for the Sydney photo is unknown, but Khambatta looks annoyed to once again have to confirm that, yes, her scalp was capable of growing hair. Below it is one of the rare photos of her smiling as Robot Ilia; Khambatta has a far more stern look in most of the photos which ran to promote the film, an image which did not help her long-term viability when "exotic" and "bald" were already strikes against her.[19]

From there Khambatta went on her annual Christmas trip to Bombay, bringing a suitcase full of Ilia merchandise such as shirts, dishwares, and socks. She gave Jeroo the Ilia doll, which Persis found all the more amusing since the mold for the body was the same used for the doll of her media-generated nemesis, Farrah Fawcett. But as Khambatta had learned to do in Hollywood, she laughed to hide her annoyance: "If they're going to the trouble of having the shape of my head, I see no reason why the doll shouldn't have the shape of my shape?"[20]

As annoyances went, the telephoned death threats she had been receiving from several different people were far less laughable. Khambatta had no idea if they were working together or if she had attracted that many random stalkers, but she was relieved the Los Angeles police took it seriously enough to make hourly checks on her safety. She was also relieved that between her promotional obligations for the Robert Wise film and her filming obligations for the upcoming Bruce Malmuth film *Attack*, she would be getting the hell out of Hollywood for a few months.[21]

The Eighties

1980

Studio 54 on Parallel 42

Montreal Gazette columnist Thomas Schnurmacher kicked off the new decade by writing that Persis Khambatta "feels that a bald head with hair slowly growing back won't net her enough publicity, so she has now taken to announcing to any press that will listen that she hopes to marry Prince Charles." Far be it from this writer to suggest Schnurmacher made that up, but if it is true then none of the press that listened to her bothered to print it; I have found no evidence of Khambatta ever mentioning the Prince of Wales in any context, let alone wanting to marry him. Also, she did not have "a bald head with hair slowly growing back" in early January 1980, but a full head of hair which was as long as she wanted it to be.[1]

Persis Khambatta's widest non-syndicated print exposure came in a January 7 *People* profile headlined "Persis Khambatta Suffered the Scrape of Her Locks, but 'Star Trek' Justified the Loss." Sue Reilly described Khambatta as having "a quirky Judy Holliday sense of humor with a background almost as exotic as a Vulcan," and it was the first article about Khambatta to dwell on the negative critical reaction to the first Star Trek movie: "Ridiculing the most expensive movie ever made as 'passive,' 'soporific,' 'sluggish' and a sort of dim-bulb *Spockalypse Now*, the critics would seemingly have dissuaded all but the cult's most ardently oppressive Trekkie fanatics." Khambatta herself refused to feed the trolls, saying "I don't want to spoil my fun by reading negative things" and "I think the movie is wonderful." Always a day late and a dollar short compared to *People*, the concurrent *Us Weekly* ran an article headlined "'Star Trek' Blasts Off for the 80s with Kirk, Spock and a Bald Sexpot," which set a new bar for backhanded compliments by musing that Khambatta "must be the most unique film sex symbol since Miss Piggy." It made Forrest Ackerman comparing Khambatta to Boris Karloff seem downright loving by comparison.[2]

Khambatta hit the chatshow circuit, starting with ABC's coast-to-coast *Good Morning America* on January 9. She next appeared on the also-nationwide *Mike Douglas Show* on January 15, but only in markets in which the show was aired for 90 minutes. Susie Coelho was a guest on the previous day's *Mike Douglas Show* in all markets, while night owls in the Bay Area were lucky enough to hear a pre-recorded interview with Khambatta and William Shatner on the legendary KSAN at midnight on January 14.[3]

Khambatta and her *Attack* co-stars Sylvester Stallone and Billy Dee Williams attended a January 16 luncheon in New York for the Governor's Office for Motion Picture and Television Development. Universal Studios put Khambatta up at the Hotel Mayflower on Central Park, where she was visited by Robert De Niro to commiserate about shaving his head for Martin Scorsese's *Raging Bull*. Principal photography on *Attack* began on January 21 and the working title was soon changed to *Hawks*, but whatever it was called, Khambatta was happy that her fourth English-language film would feature what she described as "a truly spectacular death." Her character is shot in the head by a sniper, so Khambatta was fitted with a squib, complete with a false ear and fake brains to blow out the back.[4]

Khambatta jaunted back to Los Angeles during the first week of filming to attend the Golden Globes at the Beverly Hilton. Not one to miss an awards show with "Golden" in the name—especially when she was participating, unlike at the Globes—she returned to Hollywood again a few weeks later for the Southern California Motion Picture Council's monthly awards luncheon on February 6, where she and DeForest Kelley accepted the Golden Halo for the first Star Trek movie. Khambatta also spoke at a seminar on the making of the Wise film at Sherwood Oaks Experimental College before returning to New York in mid–February.[5]

Just as she had in Los Angeles in 1978, Khambatta availed herself of the New York nightlife in 1980; she and Stallone were present when Studio 54's liquor license expired at midnight on February 29 and the booze was replaced with fruit punch. This suited the teetotaling Khambatta just fine, and a picture of her smiling with a glass of sugar-water went out over the UPI wire.[6]

Khambatta made her second appearance on *Dinah! & Friends* on March 5, and since the death threats had not gone away, she put the gossip columns to good use. From Earl Wilson's column in the first week of March[7]:

> But first I talked to Billy Dee Williams and Persis Khambatta, the girl who went bald in Star Trek. She looked better with hair. She'd gotten a phone threat: "We will come get you tonight." "I was brave," she told me, "I asked them, 'Shall I have tea or coffee for you?' The police told me I should get a gun—or Mace."[8]

She also established in Marilyn Beck's concurrent column that she was leaning toward the former.

"Star Trek" heroine Persis Khambatta is relieved now that she has left Los Angeles for the New York location of "Hawks" because she's leaving behind the barrage of telephone death threats she has received for several weeks. Persis reports the threats were made by a number of different voices and that the Los Angeles Police Department considered them serious enough to have patrolmen make hourly checks on her safety.

She makes a point of adding, that she has become adept at the use of the .38 pistol she's using in Martin Poll's "Hawks" and is seriously thinking of buying her own weapon for protection at home.[9]

Khambatta's next major public appearance in New York was a Kennedy fundraiser at the Magique Disco on Sunday, March 9. The *New York Post* covered it with the headline "A New Look for a Once-Bald Beauty," describing her as having a "dazzling new look—that of a raven-haired, bare-shouldered, exotic beauty." In other words, the look she always had except for the six months she spent making that one movie. The article included a photo captioned "the stunning Persis Khambatta bares a shoulder at a Kennedy fundraiser here yesterday," next to a photo of her as Robot Ilia. She was photographed by the *Post* on March 12 in mid-boogie at the La Boite disco, and her exotic once-baldness was hammered home in the *Post* the next day: "The exotic Persis Khambatta, whose hair has grown out since she portrayed the bald Ilia in *Star Trek—The Motion Picture*, was told she could have a big, juicy part in the much-ballyhooed Academy Awards program if she would just shave off her locks. The former Miss India, who's now working on *Hawks* with Sylvester Stallone, politely turned the offer down...." Later that month she attended another Kennedy event at the Xenon nightclub, where she refused to give a Presidential endorsement beyond saying that she liked Jimmy Carter "because he's a Libra like me." The *New York Daily News*' columnist Suzy noticed that she was not spending her free time sequestered in her hotel room, snarking that Khambatta "remains the most overexposed female in town. She hasn't missed a disco or a club or a night out in weeks. And heaven knows the photographers haven't missed her. She can give Bianca Jagger lessons."[10]

Filming in New York as winter gave way to spring was not conducive to good health even with a full head of hair, and Khambatta had the flu during a shoot on the Roosevelt Island Tramway on March 23 and 24.[11] *Daily Variety* reported a few days later that she and William Shatner would both make their first appearances as presenters on that year's Academy Awards. This made Khambatta the first person of Indian descent to be a presenter—the next would be Priyanka Chopra a mere 36 years later.[12]

When preparing to return to Los Angeles for the 1980 Oscars, Khambatta discovered that her Cartier earrings had been stolen out of her Mayflower room, a theft which Manhattan's 20th Precinct treated as a grand larceny investigation. Though it was fair that the photo which accompanied the April 6 *New York Post* article by Robin Leach was of Khambatta wearing the purloined earrings *sans hair*, it is a safe bet that even if she had acquired the earrings while she had a full head of hair, the headline still would have been "Bald Beauty Loses 10G Gems."[13]

Persis Khambatta was accompanied to the 1980 Academy Awards on April 14 by Vijay Amritraj, a tennis player and fellow Desi. But her co-presenter onstage was William Shatner, and as soon as he and Khambatta reached the podium they began reading the nominees for Documentary Feature and Short Subject. Shatner announced the winner for Feature, and Khambatta for Short Subject, though Khambatta got to hand the Oscar to Feature winner Ira Wohl. Shatner and Khambatta hardly seemed aware of the other's presence, and by some miracle Khambatta's former baldness was never mentioned by host Johnny Carson, who only referred to her as Kirk's "stunning navigator, Persis Khambatta." Rex Reed wrote in his *New York Daily News* review of the broadcast that "Persis Khambatta, the bald robot in Star Trek, turned out to be the prettiest lady on the screen with her real hair," while lamenting that "throughout the night, there was a twinge of nostalgia for the real stars who weren't there." What mattered most was that it was Khambatta's widest global audience, and there she was, with a full head of hair! She was not bald, she would never be again, and finally she could move on.[14]

Moving on almost seemed like an option when Roderick Mann failed to mention her past baldness an April 20 piece about *Hawks*. He even had a perfect intro when he noted that Khambatta "gets her head blown off in her new picture," and yet he resisted the temptation to remind the reader that the head in question once had been bald. Mann then whiffed it in a big and baffling way while relating what should have been a charming anecdote about Khambatta breaking the ice with Sylvester Stallone.[15]

> She got along well with Stallone, despite some early sparring.
> When he arranged to show "Rocky" for some of the unit, she told him she was looking forward to seeing it. "You didn't see it before?" he asked, surprised. No, she said. "But did you see 'F.I.S.T.' and 'Paradise Alley' and 'Rocky II?'" No, she said. "You mean you haven't seen any of my films?" he said. "I can't believe it."
> "Well," countered Persis, who wasn't born Indian for nothing, "I've made four films as well. 'The Wilby Conspiracy,' 'Conduct Unbecoming,' 'The Man with the Power,' and 'Star Trek.' How many of mine did you see?" None, said Stallone. "Well then," Persis said, "we're quits, aren't we?"
> "After that," Persis said, "everything was just fine."[16]

As a white person born in suburban California in the early 1970s I am more well-versed in ethnic stereotypes than I would care to admit, and yet I am well and truly flummoxed by the phrase "who wasn't born Indian for nothing." I do not get it, and I do not want to.

The Trouble with Exotic Angels

Khambatta traveled to Paris the day after the Oscars to shoot her final scene for *Hawks*, and remained in France after filming wrapped. Though she had not yet lined up her next film, rumors had been circulating since February that she and Priscilla Presley were on the short list to replace Shelley Hack on the television series *Charlie's Angels*. Joey Sasso wrote in his syndicated column in early April that "although Persis Khambatta is being bandied about as the most likely choice, I happen to think it's wishful thinking—either on Persis' part or, more likely, her publicist's." Later that month the Tattletales column quoted Khambatta as calling *Charlie's Angels* "a dying show" which "won't last more than another year, and it would be a bad move for me to make," and that for now, "I am waiting for movie offers." She was back in the United States in time for producer Dann Moss to accompany her to the premiere of Chuck Barris' *The Gong Show Movie* on May 13, a gala affair co-hosted by comedian Rip Taylor and *Daily Variety*'s Army Archerd. It is the first known occurrence of Persis Khambatta and Rip Taylor being in the same place at the same time, but not the last.[17]

British gossip columnist Nigel Dempster reported from the 1980 Cannes Film Festival that Khambatta told him she won the *Charlie's Angels* role, adding "considering the series is synonymous with blonde, blue-eyed, all-American heroines, I think it is very adventurous of the producers to have chosen me." It would have been if they had, but they had not, and they expressed that negative in no uncertain terms. In a May 27 *New York Post* article accompanied by photos of Khambatta with and without hair and headlined "Bald Beauty Gets Brushoff," Jack Martin wrote that the show's producers "quickly said the actress' bald boast was nothing but hot air." (See, it's funny because Persis Khambatta had been bald in that one movie, and—) The article quotes many various denials and contradictions, including a spokesman for series producer Leonard Goldberg saying Khambatta "has gone off her rocker if she's announcing herself as hired for the job," while the casting agency was supposedly "just as surprised as the producers of the show." A source at the agency acknowledged that Khambatta had been under consideration at one point, but she was one of many, and "as a matter of fact, we're testing several girls here over the next 10 days—and one of them isn't Persis Khambatta." (Which implies that the other nine girls *are* Khambatta, but the agency no doubt considered it a sick burn.) As this brouhaha brewed, Marilyn Beck reported that after Christopher Walken, Paul Freeman, Tom Berenger, and Jean-François Stévenin had their heads shaved on the set of *The Dogs of War*, director Norman Jewison supplied them with new set-side chairs bearing the names of Yul Brynner, Telly

Savalas, Daddy Warbucks, and Persis Khambatta. (See, it's funny because Persis Khambatta had been bald in that one movie that one time, and—)[18]

The blue-eyed Tanya Roberts won the *Charlie's Angels* role, and in his June 17 *Philadelphia Daily News* piece about the whole affair, Nels Nelson provided a breakdown of who did not get the part and the "obvious" reasons why.[19]

> THE CANDIDATES and obvious Charlie misfits included Jayne Kennedy, of NFL Football halftime renown (black, too tall), Persis Khambatta (Asian, much too exotic), "James Bond" ornament Barbara Bach (too foreign), Suzie Coehlo, Sonny Bono's girlfriend (too Indian), Irene Ferris (too tall, too Russian) and actress Cornelia Sharpe (who ever heard of an angel named Cornelia?).[20]

There is so much racism and fear of the Other to unpack, but, to keep things focused: in addition to Khambatta being merely Asian rather than Indian—no doubt a choice on Nelson's part to differentiate her from Susie Coelho—Khambatta was not only too exotic, she was *much* too exotic.[21]

The May 27 *New York Post* article had not quoted Khambatta, but instead quoted gossip columnist Nigel Dempster claiming to quote her. Khambatta told a different story when speaking for herself in a contentious interview in the March 1981 *Oui*: she said she'd been offered $900,000 for less than six months' work, but turned it down because she didn't want to do television, and because she'd make that much money in movies anyway. Khambatta also told journalist Bert Reisfeld she had declined the televised jigglefest because what she liked about acting was that "you can play out your fantasies, which you couldn't have done in that TV show. Somebody else's fantasies—not my own." Exactly what happened may never be known, but this author chooses to believe Persis Khambatta's presentation.[22]

* * *

A *Charlie's Angels* feature film starring Naomi Scott was released during the writing of this book in 2019, and I was one of the few people to see it in the theater. I went in knowing only that the film was directed by Elizabeth Banks, Kristen Stewart was in it, and its financial failure was being celebrated by many boys on the Internet, which is a subject for another book altogether. I quite enjoyed the film and was struck by how Naomi Scott was the film's protagonist and thus the audience-identification character, but her South Asian descent is never acknowledged, not even in her character's name of Elena Houghlin.

The closest the *Charlie's Angels* press kit came to acknowledging Scott's ethnicity was that she "was recently seen starring as Princess Jasmine in Disney's live-action remake of *Aladdin*" and she "currently resides in London," while the E-bomb is only used in reference to *Charlie's Angels* having been shot "in exotic locales like Istanbul and Germany." Disney's *Aladdin* press kit described Scott as "a singer/actress of South Asian descent who grew up in London," though a May 15 sponsored post by Disney on the Indian edition of *Vogue* titled "5 Things You Didn't Know About Aladdin's Naomi Scott" emphasized her ethnicity, placing it at the first of those five things[23]:

> **She has an Indian connection**
> Scott's father, Christopher Scott is British and her mother, Usha Scott is from Uganda, but of Gujarati descent. Though she's been brought up in London, Scott is proud of her Indian heritage and is often seen celebrating her roots on social media. Back in 2016, she honoured her Indian lineage with a photo on Instagram, sporting traditional Indian jewellery.[24]

Also during the writing of this book, Canadian-born Lilly Singh became the first woman of Indian heritage to host a late-night talk show, and appeared in a commercial during the 2020 Super Bowl. This had been Persis Khambatta's dream all along. It only took until two decades after her death for it come true.[25]

* * *

After leaving most first-run theaters in March 1980, the first Star Trek movie was released on VHS and Beta that October, and on RCA Selecta-Vision VideoDisc in May 1981, the back cover of which described Ilia as "an exotically beautiful, totally bald woman from the planet Delta who becomes Sulu's assistant and Decker's girlfriend." (Sulu's assistant!) But it would not be accessible to most Americans until it was broadcast on ABC in February 1983, which is why the timing was not great back in May 1980 when a children's newspaper supplement called the Mini Page ran a profile of Khambatta with the headline "Meet Ilia of 'Star Trek—The Motion Picture.'"[26]

It was accompanied by the murky, confounding, and unpleasant photo of Robot Ilia with Decker looming behind her—though William Shatner's hairy arm was cropped out, thank goodness—and the caption described Khambatta as "bald but still beautiful." The text was a brief encapsulation of her career thus far[27]:

> A beauty who once held the title of "Miss India" played Ilia (Eye-lee-ah) in the Star Trek movie.
> Persis Khambatta acted the part of a woman from another planet who joins the crew of the U.S.S. *Enterprise* as a navigator.
> She was selected from over 100 actresses for the role.
> She had to shave her head completely for the part. She usually didn't wear a wig when not on the set during the filming. She liked her hairless hairdo.
> Persis began her career modeling at the age of 13. By the time she was 16, she had won her "Miss India" title.

> She left her country to go to London, where it only took her a year to become a very successful model.
> After acting in several movies, she came to the United States and went to New York City as a model. Then she moved to Hollywood, where she got the part in the Star Trek movie.
> She has let her hair grow out and is working on another movie.[28]

When the movie in question was released to theaters the following year, it would go unnoticed by (and be inappropriate for) the Mini Page's readers. Meanwhile, in June 1980 Persis Khambatta left her manager Bobbie Edrick and signed with Jay Bernstein; as the *Herald-Examiner* noted in a brief article headlined "Simply Hair-Raising" about Khambatta getting a new 'do at Adrian Houghton's salon in West Hollywood, "Bernstein had formerly managed another famous head of hair—Farrah Fawcett."[29]

Hitting the newsstands in July, *Starlog* #37 featured a lengthy interview in which Khambatta marveled at the amount of fan mail she had received, though "basically everybody wants a picture of me in a bikini." Regarding the frequent question of whether she would shave her head for another movie, she said, "I don't want to be typecast as a Yul Brynner or Telly Savalas type," and that "it was a once-in-a-lifetime experience. There is one privilege the movie has given me: People don't recognize me with hair." She also observed with a sigh that working on that one movie was "an experience," and that "I have changed as a person" as a result of living in Hollywood. "I have to be more selfish, unfortunately. You have to think of yourself, you have to be tough. But I love acting and I love my profession" She signed off by thanking the readers of *Starlog* for their interest, adding, "I hope they'll see my next movie."[30]

How many *Starlog* readers wrote to the magazine about the interview is unknown, but two letters were published, one of which was from a Georgia man whose respect for Khambatta's autonomy over her body was on par with Gene Roddenberry's:

> As a dedicated baldophile, I greatly enjoyed seeing the hairless Miss Khambatta in Star Trek. I was most disappointed when she grew her hair back. Now, most women's appearance would be greatly improved with the total loss of hair. It is clear that Miss Khambatta looks much better bald than with hair. She could perhaps inspire other women to shave theirs off. Perhaps if enough of her fans pressure her, she will be forced to go bald again. I do not mean threats or violence but gentle fan pressure. There are not many bald women in this world and they are so beautiful.[31]

Thank goodness he did not mean using threats or violence to get a woman to alter her appearance to conform to the demands of strangers! *Starlog*'s editors often wrote short replies to the letters, but they printed this one without comment, beyond giving the baldophiles a little sugar in the form of a picture of Robot Ilia.

Lovin' that cali lifestyle!!

Persis Khambatta did her best to stay in the public eye in the latter half of 1980 as she worked to secure another film role. It was why even though she had no connection to the sports world beyond her friendship with Bapa, Khambatta was one of the presenters at the fourteenth annual Victor Awards in the Las Vegas Hilton on June 14. The show was a nice diversion for Khambatta, who had lost $900 while playing blackjack on this trip. She was spotted at the Victors outside the Hilton's dressing rooms by the *San Francisco Examiner*'s Jane Carroll, who would later write "Persis Khambatta, who appeared bald in the movie *Star Trek*, stands quietly, elegantly in the hallway, her short black hair shining." Projecting elegance while standing quietly is on brand for Khambatta; less so is what Carroll wrote about Khambatta joining the other presenters onstage for a show-closing chorus of "God Bless America" led by Tony Orlando: "'How can I sing "God Bless America"?' mutters Khambatta as she walks into the wings. 'I'm Indian.'" This most American of American cities also gave her one of her subtler moments of culture shock: she wore a long dress to an Engelbert Humperdinck concert at a casino, only to find that "all the people in the audience were dressed like cowboys." Much like Hollywood, Las Vegas was far less glamorous than she had imagined.[32]

She was back in Los Angeles in time to attend a June 16 launch party for the magazine *Biarritz* at the Beverly Wilshire, an event also attended by new *Charlie's Angels* castmember Tanya Roberts and an attendant swarm of paparazzi. Khambatta walked the red carpet a few days later for the premiere of *The Blue Lagoon* at Pacific Theatres' Cinerama Dome to what the *Los Angeles Times*' Lee Grant described as a "rather subdued" response from the crowds. There were no bald-capped Ilia doppelgangers behind the barricades like at the MacArthur Premiere seven months earlier, though "police had to push back the crush of photographers and fans" when *The Blue Lagoon*'s nubile young stars Brooke Shields and Christopher Atkins arrived.[33]

Khambatta was accompanied by John Philip Law on July 26 to the Seventh Annual Saturn Awards, and Khambatta was one of the presenters, though the show would not be broadcast until November. *Daily Variety*'s Army Archerd spotted Khambatta at Morton's with the Ladd Company's Alan Krieger on July 29, and she was among the celebrities on display at the Committee to Cure Cancer through Immunization's 2nd Annual Celebrity Racquetball Tournament in August. Khambatta next modeled alongside Jane Fonda, Loni Anderson, and Pam Dawber in the "Art on the Runway" fashion show at the Ambassador Hotel on September 13, which was a fundraiser for Jane Fonda's Campaign for Economic Democracy Education Fund/Cancer Project.[34]

However many Good Place points Khambatta earned for that charity work may have been canceled out later that month when she participated in the taping of a truly horrible NBC comedy special hosted by Gloria Swanson, Barbara Eden, and *Blue Lagoon* star Brooke Shields. The title was *Men Who Rate a '10,'* a reference to the unfortunate fad popularized by Blake Edwards' execrable 1979 hit film *10* of rating a woman's sexiness on a 1–10 scale. This Dick Clark production was sloppy and thoughtless enough that in a montage of romantic scenes, Sidney Poitier and Diahann Carroll in the gazebo from *Paris Blues* fades into Robert De Niro saying "I think you are the most beautiful woman I have ever seen" to Cybill Shepherd in *Taxi Driver* (presented as romantic because it's a 1980 television special and nothing matters), which fades into Clark Gable taking off his shirt in *It Happened One Night*.

Persis Khambatta's appearance in the October 7 broadcast was blessedly brief, part of a spoken section of "What Do You Think About Men?" from the forgotten Cole Porter musical *Out of this World*. The song is sung in the special by hosts Swanson, Eden, and Shields, who throw the question to a group of five women including Khambatta and her fellow "could never be on *Charlie's Angels* because she's not white" misfit Jayne Kennedy. Khambatta's thought about men is "I don't think I can do without them," which, sure, fine. While the show is presented as a comedy about ogling men—with both a live audience and a laugh track, because women objectifying men the way men objectify women is so silly an idea that no amount of laughter can do it justice—the studio segments nevertheless cater to the male gaze and the atrocious notion of glamor at the dawn of the Reagan Era. Khambatta is not dressed down *per se*, but nothing about her ensemble of a long white dress with a purple scarf is slinky or revealing, and she is the only participant of *Men Who Rate a '10'* who does not embarrass herself.

Her dignity intact, a week after the broadcast Khambatta attended the unveiling of an $8M diamond-and-gold wristwatch at Jewels by Edwar in Beverly Hills, where columnist L.T. Brown described her as being part of a "dazzling trio" along with Loni Anderson and Loretta Swit. Later that month, she presented the American Classic Screen Award to elderly silent actress Carmel Myers at the National Film Society's fifth annual Artistry in Cinema awards. Speaking of the endless awards which Hollywood gave itself—Woody Allen was wrong about a lot of things, but not about that—the Saturn Awards show from July started making the broadcast rounds in November. She attended a fundraiser premiere for Richard Fleischer's *The Jazz Singer* in mid-December with her then-boyfriend *Beverly Hills People* magazine publisher David Gordon, who accompanied her again to a New Year's Eve shindig at the home of Anne and John Aylesworth. Khambatta's hair had grown back in by December 1979, but in December 1980 the *Los*

Angeles Times' Jody Jacobs still wrote that Khambatta "looks terribly chic now that her hair has grown back in."³⁵

Her hair was growing, but the same could not be said for her career. Khambatta's agents and managers kept telling her to trust them to find her the kind of roles she wanted, and she was beginning to realize what "trust me" meant in Hollywood. But a new calendar year was about to start, and she declared that it was going to be the year of her career, and she would get to down business in her own way. As Khambatta explained to syndicated columnist Joan Crosby at the premiere of John G. Avildsen's *The Formula* at the Goldwyn Theatre on December 15, she had declined what would become John Milius' *Conan the Barbarian* because it was "the same sort of exotic role" she had turned down more than once in the past year: "I don't want that kind of part. I want the kind of parts Jill Clayburgh gets to play." *An Unmarried Woman* and *Starting Over* star Clayburgh would no longer get to play those kinds of thoughtful, non-exotic parts by the end of the decade because Hollywood is terrible, but at the beginning of the decade Persis Khambatta started putting together her own projects. She had been hoping since early 1979 to make a television documentary about Zoroastrianism, but she also knew she had to start off with something more commercial, so she optioned a script titled *Just Passing Through* which she described as "the *Alfie* of the 1980s." But it would be several more months before she got the paperwork together to begin pursuing that particular illusion.³⁶

* * *

Also in pursuit of a new illusion was Paramount about the second Star Trek movie.

On December 9, 1980, one year and two days after the release of the first movie, Paramount Television ran a full-page ad in *Daily Variety* announcing the hiring of Harve Bennett.³⁷ After a week on the job, Bennett was called into Paramount president Barry Diller's office, where he was surprised to find not only Diller but executives Michael Eisner and Jeffrey Katzenberg—the latter of whom who was responsible for the first movie's budget spiraling out of control, but who still received a promotion from Vice President of production to Senior Vice President as a reward—as well as head of television Gary Nardino, and Paramount owner Charles Bluhdorn. Bennett spun the following yarn as early as the 1990s, but its first retelling in a Paramount-licensed work seems to have been the August/September 2002 issue of the official fan club magazine *Star Trek Communicator*, four years after Khambatta's death and coinciding with the second DVD release of the second movie.³⁸

As Bennett tells the story in *Communicator*, Bluhdorn asked him what he thought of the first movie. Bennett replied, "I thought it was boring."

Bluhdorn then turned to Eisner and said, "See? By you, bald is sexy!"

To recap: Bluhdorn asked Bennett what he thought of the movie. Bennett said he was bored by it. Bluhdorn used that to criticize Eisner for Persis Khambatta being bald in the film—which is to say not sufficiently sexy, the equivalent of boring.

Bluhdorn asked Bennett, "Can you make a better movie?" Bennett replied that he could, and Bluhdorn further clarified, "Can you make it for less than forty-five fucking million dollars?" Bennett said that he could make four or five movies for that fucking amount, and as a result he got both the gig and a clear message: Persis Khambatta with no fucking hair was what went wrong with the first movie. Eisner and Katzenberg were far more responsible for what went wrong, but Khambatta lacked the white male privilege which allowed them to fail upward.[39]

1981

Denny, Khambatta, and Oui

Persis Khambatta's decision that 1981 was going to be the year of her career did not mean she had not been career-minded every year before, and she had made some difficult decisions in recent months. Not only had she turned down the role in *Conan the Barbarian* which went to the blue-eyed, blonde-haired Sandahl Bergman, Khambatta also declined the lead role in Paul Schrader's *Cat People* because of what the charming website Mr. Skin would later declare to be "Hall of Fame Nudity!" But Khambatta also worried that she'd been preoccupied by her love life over the past year, from former live-in boyfriend Pascal Chevillot to the more recent Robert Sacchi and David Gordon. Being in love took a lot of energy, and she would no longer let it distract her from her career.[1]

Khambatta kept herself out in the world, beginning with a demonstration of Indian cooking on *Hour Magazine* on January 15. Her recipe for the red curry dish Rogan Josh was later printed in the 1985 *Hour Magazine Cookbook*, and according to Gary Collins' ghostwriter, "Indian cooking and heartburn always went hand in hand for me. But thanks to actress and former Miss India Persis Khambatta, this savory entrée for two actually changed my mind!" There was no risk of heartburn for delicate European gastrointestinal systems when Khambatta networked later that month a party thrown by costume designer Ron Talsky, since the refreshments leaned toward vast quantities of guacamole and beer.[2]

The aforementioned contentious *Oui* interview was published in early February, and though writer Jon Denny did not refer to Khambatta as exotic, he did kick off with the other subject she was tired of: "Let's get to the bare facts, Persis. Whatever happened to the Kojak look?" (See, it's funny because Khambatta had been bald in that one movie that one time, and—) After she told the anecdote about Gene Roddenberry insisting she be naked in the G-rated film down to nipples and bush, Denny himself got down to brass tacks: "Persis, you seem to have a real problem doing nude scenes." Y'think?[3]

> I want the public to watch *me*. I want writers writing scripts for *me*. I won't do nude scenes. At least. Not now. I don't want to do them ... if I did nude scenes, they'd say I was in the movie only because I stripped. Do you know what I'm saying? I want to be good. I just refused a movie because there was a lot of nudity. The girl was naked all the time. I couldn't do it.[4]

The timing of the interview suggests the movie was *Cat People*, and Khambatta was not wrong, since the otherwise talented Nastassja Kinski's reputation was forever overshadowed by her willingness to appear nude. For better and worse—better for us because it offers more insight into who Khambatta was a person, worse for her because she was speaking to a scummy interviewer from a porn magazine who was ceaselessly needling her—she opened up about why her relationships had not lasted:

> I also want a man with emotions. Emotions that are working. Men are not supposed to show emotions. I can't find a man who does. I can't find a man who could stay home once and wait for me and say he missed me. Or say he loved me, I want a man who can say those things. Everybody thinks that having a million dollars is the first thing I'd look for. They're wrong.[5]

Denny asked if Khambatta had "encountered any short, balding producers with gold chains and fat cigars? The ones who breathe hard?" (Stay classy, *Oui*!) As was her tendency throughout the interview, Khambatta replied with a more thoughtful answer than the question deserved.[6]

> It's funny, but because of my photographs and movies, men do not know how to deal with a woman like me. They think I'm snobbish and arrogant. In my work, I look unapproachable. I haven't been approached by short, balding producers with casting couches, maybe because of my distant look. My detached look. Lauren Hutton has it. Sophia Loren has it. I've been compared with her. They're not approachable. I'm not some blonde, blue-eyed, fluffy American girl, going, "Yah-yah-yah, wanna party?" I don't have men coming up to me and saying, "Hey, baby, how about coming to bed tonight?" Frankly, they don't think they can conquer me.[7]

Forgetting his mandate to be as creepy and gross as possible, Denny followed up with a question that bordered on thoughtful: "Is it because dark-haired Indian women seem more of a threat to American men? More intimidating?"[8]

> Are you talking about sex? I've been called a sex symbol. My legs have been complimented. But the American system is blonde, blue-eyed. I'm hoping that system could change. I'm hoping a girl like me can be accepted and be number one or two. Every time you see something blonde and blue-eyed, it is a success to the American man. It's the ideal American woman. That's all I've been hearing. "Americans don't accept dark-haired girls, Persis. They can only get off on blondes." I say, how come? Why couldn't I be accepted? People are like machines sometimes. Tell them pink is beautiful, and every time they see pink, it will excite them. People are conditioned. I just hope everybody in the press will talk about the dark-haired beauty from *Star Trek*. Then everyone will say it excites them.[9]

Khambatta briefly wore a blonde wig during the shooting of *Hawks* because Sylvester Stallone could only get off on blondes, and the above paragraph was printed next to a picture of her in that wig. (Stay classy, *Oui*!) Asked if she felt she still had a "legitimate shot at becoming a top sex symbol in America," Khambatta was optimistic, while remaining cognizant of how much it was up to the media.[10]

> Yes. The Eighties can be different. The key thing is: Are they saying it in the press? Americans are like four-year-old children at times. You watch television commercials—I'm not saying I'm any different—you see commercials and they're so stupid. They have Pepsi-Cola and Coca-Cola, and they publicize both at the same time. One says Pepsi's not good—Coke is. They try to put each other down. It's a psychological thing. People look at the woman in the ad and they go out and buy the product. They're spoon-fed. If it's written in the press or shown on TV, they say, "Hey, that's what I like now." Maybe they'll say it about me.[11]

Asked again what she thought of American women, Khambatta dove into gender politics, which was going through one of its dodgier periods: Ronald Reagan had just been inaugurated and the Republican Party had recently withdrawn its support for the Equal Rights Amendment, which was in the process of not being ratified. The term "Women's Liberation" was being replaced with "Feminism," a word which rattled people then and continues to do so; at the time of the interview it tended to be used as a negative to be denied, such as "SJW" and "PC" at the time of this writing in 2019. However, Persis Khambatta was a feminist. There is no doubt.

> I'm an emancipated woman, but not emancipated the way American women think. I work. I support myself. I believe in a career. I believe in marriage. I also believe that men are superior to women. I'm not a slave, but I believe that.[12]

Khambatta's statement about male superiority is troubling, but it is also an outlier: I have never found her expressing a similar sentiment in any other interview, and she contradicted it many times before and after. Denny did not dive deeper into that statement, instead asking, "Have you ever been punched out by a feminist?" There's the word![13]

> I am sensitive. I am emotional. I am all those things that the women who write those feminist books say are wrong. But I am all these things. I hear a lot about American men from women, and I hear a lot about American women from men. From what I hear, the women here are much more domineering. The men are weaker; they're submissive. The women snap their fingers and say, "Let's do this," and the man jumps up and says, "Yes, darling—anything you say, darling." That sort of thing.[14]

Asked if she herself was domineering via the casually anti–Semitic question "are you a closet JAP—Jewish American Princess—deep down?," Khambatta replied[15]:

> I'm changing. The myth I grew up with in India was to give everything to the people, to make them happy. I was in a world of giving. Now I can't please everybody; my time

is limited. If they demand something, I can't always give. People come up to me now and say, "Do you remember me? We met ten years ago at a party." Then they say, "Oh, you won't remember me, because you're a somebody now and you were nobody then." A crack like that … they have such little minds. They feel they're nobodies themselves, and so they put you down. It's a crazy world. Now I'm reading about how to be selfish. I'm OK if you're OK. Be assertive. Pulling my own strings. I want to be happy. I was getting hurt constantly before.[16]

Further pressed to dish on William Shatner, all she would say was:

I learned so much about the movie industry with Star Trek. I learned about acting, about lighting, about editing, about egos. I saw what an ego can do to an actor. I saw what stardom can make an actor into. Of course, they did that series for so long. There's always a clash when that happens.[17]

It is one of many times that a clash is inevitable, and Persis Khambatta did not realize that her own clashes were only just beginning.

Release the Nighthawks

On February 21, Universal sent out a four-page press release about Persis Khambatta to promote the April release of the film which was now called *Nighthawks*. The first page was concerned with Khambatta having shaved her head for a Paramount film in 1978, describing it as "probably the most publicized hair styling for an actress since Ingrid Bergman had her locks clipped short for 'For Whom the Bell Tolls.'" (Which was also a Paramount film!) The document went into some detail about Khambatta's disillusionment with the Hindi film industry, as well as explaining that she had left home because India was "unable to accept the concept of a modern girl" at the time, and ten years later in 1981 "'Women's Lib is just beginning'" there. And as in the publicity for the first Star Trek movie, her Parsi background and Zoroastrian faith were stressed. This was something she did on her own when she was on the chatshows; she wanted to educate Americans about the Parsis, who never got the press (good or bad) of Hindus or Muslims.[18]

Religion was also a handy conversational topic because there was little to say about her role as the terrorist Shakka Kapoor in *Nighthawks*. Like Ilia and Decker before them, many scenes fleshing out Shakka's relationship with Rutger Hauer's main villain Wulfgar were eliminated. As she later told *India West*, this was when Khambatta learned a hard truth about Hollywood: "Unless you have a percentage in the movie, you usually get cut out." Among the footage which survived was a few seconds of her wearing the blonde wig which Stallone favored, and photographs of her in the wig were used in the press kit. That was a lucky break for *Oui*, but it reinforced another hard Hollywood truth for Khambatta: if you are a woman, it helps to be blonde. Another misleading still in the press kit was of a wigless Khambatta sitting on Stallone's lap; it did not represent the film because their characters never interact or even share the frame, but it helped to perpetuate the image of Stallone as a stud who could get the kitties to party, so to speak. To speak less obliquely, Sylvester Stallone had appeared in a 1970 porn film called *The Party at Kitty and Stud's* in which he appeared completely naked on camera, something Khambatta never did. Also, the re-release of *The Party at Kitty and Stud's* under the title *The Italian Stallion* to capitalize on Stallone's post–*Rocky* success did not hurt his career in any way.[19]

Khambatta first appears about eighteen minutes into *Nighthawks* as Shakka exits a train in Paris, takes a cab to the Sainte-Chapelle—footage which was shot in the days following her appearance at the 1980 Oscars—and walks from the cab to the entrance, and finally past the pews to a confessional where Wulfgar is waiting. Their conversation is an exposition dump in subtitled French establishing that Interpol knows Wulfgar's face; Wulfgar and Shakka then go to a plastic surgeon's office to change that familiar face, preceded by another twenty dead seconds of exploitation-film padding of Khambatta and Hauer walking to said office.

We later get a skosh of backstory during a briefing in which a police Inspector played by Nigel Davenport says Shakka "kills without provocation," such as shooting a policeman at point-blank range during an OPEC raid. Setting aside that shooting a policeman during a raid is killing *with* provocation, that still tells us more about Shakka than we ever learned about Ilia. Khambatta next appears around the hour mark when Shakka meets up with Wulfgar in a dank cellar to tell him the cops are hot on his trail. She reappears a few minutes later, and though she is only on screen for ten seconds with one word of dialog ("Yes"), it is one of Persis Khambatta's best moments on film, since she comes across at her most natural. Khambatta is subtly rocking back and forth in a two-shot with Hauer in the foreground, giving him a look which suggests Shakka is losing faith in Wulfgar. Khambatta is wearing a sweater and scarf in the wood-paneled basement room where it was shot during the New York winter of 1980, and she smokes a cigarette. Real talk: smoking is gross, but she makes it look good. This is the only time chain-smoker Khambatta's primary vice made it into an English-language feature film, though she can be seen holding cigarettes in some contemporaneous paparazzi shots.[20]

Khambatta appears in the blonde wig for about five non-consecutive seconds when Shakka shoots Nigel Davenport's character in the head, though she's back to her natural hair in the eleven-minute Roosevelt Island Tramway sequence. It's Khambatta's longest screen time, but she was also battling the flu, so it may have been for the best that her only line is the funny-because-it's-true "it doesn't matter."

Her "truly spectacular death" occurs at about 83 minutes when Shakka is sniped in the head by Billy Dee Williams' character; it could be seen as poetic justice given Shakka's own propensity for headshots, though inferring authorial intent may be giving too much credit. Shakka is drawn out of a crowd and into the path of the bullet by a recording of the Inspector calling her "a spoiled bitch," but because so much of her character was removed in editing it is unclear why that phrase triggers the otherwise stolid Shakka. What matters is that she responds by saying "shit," marking Khambatta's first time swearing in an English-language film. (It's a fine start, but her most glorious profanity was a few years away.) Only the forehead squib is visible in the dark and underexposed shot, but Shakka's brains do get splattered against the side of a bus and remain visible until Wulfgar drives the bus into the East River shortly thereafter.

As excited as Khambatta had been about the scene, she was insulted to learn that the sparse moviegoers were applauding her death, though friends assured her it meant the audience was happy to see the villain get their comeuppance because she had done such a good job in the role. She was not aware of how American grindhouse audiences historically cheered the onscreen deaths of women, and that the promise of such things is what drew many of them to such grimy movies in the first place.[21]

It is considered blasphemy in many cinephile circles to suggest misogyny was at play either behind the camera or in the marketing of exploitation films, and those who consider the suggestion to be counterrevolutionary at the time of this writing tend to refer to an October 1980 *New York Times* article which claimed that 55 percent of the 12 to 17-year-olds who attended low-budget slasher films, such as *Prom Night* or *When a Stranger Calls*, were female. The article itself gave no citation or further background for this statistic, just that it was from an unspecified "research study" which was itself being commented upon by Twentieth Century–Fox's Vice President of Advertising and Publicity. It is nonetheless offered as proof that misogyny was not a factor in the making of marketing of such films—though *Nighthawks* was of a different genre than *Prom Night* or *When a Stranger Calls*, and was marketed to an older crowd. (I was one of the few people at a preview screening of the prequel *Twin Peaks: Fire Walk with Me* in 1992 who had watched the television series. About two-thirds of the vocal, angry audience of mostly men in their teens and late twenties had walked out by halfway through the picture, and as one gentleman made his exit he yelled, "Just kill the bitch already!")[22]

The bottom line is that *Nighthawks* was not a good movie, and the reviews it and Khambatta received were not good. Jack Kroll displayed a

Siskelian perviness when he wrote in *Newsweek* that "Persis Khambatta, who as the bald astronaut in 'Star Trek' made you want to run your fingers through her follicles, plays a vicious lady terrorist with the glazed look of a secretary bombed out on her boss's coke stash." It was a very 1981 sentence by any standard, and Khambatta told *India West* with a grin that the review would have upset her in 1979, but now? "At least he mentioned me." Janet Maslin summed it up best in the *New York Times*: "Persis Khambatta, last seen in the 'Star Trek' debacle, has a full head of hair now, but not much of a role."[23]

The weekend before *Nighthawks* opened, Persis Khambatta tried on another role which did not suit her: an *Esquire* dream girl.

The Esquireman Weekend

Khambatta continued to make the scene wherever there was a scene to be made. She was photographed by Ron Galella at Ma Maison on March 2, and was spotted at the kickoff for the L.A. World Hunger Event at the China Club on March 29. A few days later, a rep from Khambatta's PR firm called the magazine *Esquire*, the motto of which was "Man at his Best." The rep inquired about *Esquire*'s "An Evening With" feature, in which an anonymous writer (henceforth referred to as Esquireman) spent an evening or two with a female celebrity. The perspective was sometimes in the second person; the March 1981 installment began by inviting the reader to "put yourself in our place. You've showered, shaved, and dressed, and in less than thirty minutes you will pick up Michelle Phillips, who at this moment is likely to be putting on her lip gloss for you." Yep, she's putting it on for *you*—man at his best, just like it says on the cover! But more often it was first-person plural, such as "we had made dinner reservations" or "we took a chance: we told Michelle how shrewd we thought she was."[24]

Esquireman wrote that Khambatta's rep told him "Persis was about to appear in a new movie, *Nighthawks*, and that she had some time on her hands. He wondered whether we'd like to meet her, to take her on our customary social trek." Esquireman hadn't thought about her since that one movie had come out a year and a half before, and "having gotten used to predictably fair and well-coiffed starlets," he wasn't sure how to breach the cultural differences between them. Most importantly, because Khambatta was a prize to be won, "what means do you use to win her?" Expecting her to be an aloof, icy princess, he concluded that the key was to "indulge our imagination" and to "play fair but play fancy." Esquireman admitted surprise at Khambatta's engaging, "impish quality" over the phone and she suggested they go to Las Vegas so she could win back her $900. But whatever it meant to Esquireman to "play fair but play fancy," it did not include prioritizing the wants of the woman he was trying to win, so he suggested San Francisco instead of Las Vegas. In a "voice that makes Dietrich's sound squeaky," Khambatta agreed.[25]

Esquireman made reservations at Le Castel in San Francisco's Pacific Heights neighborhood, and Khambatta was disappointed that she would not be able to wear jeans to the fancy-pants restaurant: "'A shame. I'm trying to change my [deleted] image.'" The writer of *Presenting Persis Khambatta* chooses to believe [deleted] was "fucking" since it would be appropriate for how frustrated she had become with her image, but whatever word came out of the same mouth Persis used to kiss Jeroo, Esquireman disapproved of her unladylike lingo: "'Perhaps you might start with your language,' we quipped. 'But that's what I'm trying to change it *to*,' Khambatta replied."[26]

She met Esquireman at the door of her Hancock Park apartment at half past five on Friday, April 3. He wrote that Khambatta's hair had "grown back luxuriantly," which was to be expected after two years, and she was wearing a purple barrette to fasten her hair away from her face "'because it makes me look more American, less exotic.'" Esquireman did not buy her attempt at de-exotification—"less exotic, our foot" was his response, as well as observing that Khambatta wore rings featuring the heads of Shirdi Sai Baba and Zoroaster, a jeweled pendant bearing with the Urdu word for "Allah," and she even smoked Dunhills. The article's subhead further disregarded her stated desire to not be pigeonholed as exotic: "When you take out a former Miss India, the gorgeous navigator in the movie Star Trek, you think exotic." (Does it matter what the former Miss India *wants* you think of her? It does not.) Esquireman wrote that she was "astonishingly beautiful" in person, though her troublesome impishness kept showing through.[27]

> Events turned playful when we finally arrived at the terminal. Persis handed over the tickets to the agent at gate 600B. "These are for me and my father," she told him, gesturing our way. So much for the inscrutable Indian sense of humor, we thought.[28]

He wrote that the plane was packed except for the window seat next to Khambatta, because Khambatta "is not the kind of passenger you like to climb over, settle in next to, and ask, 'Howdy, where ya headin', little lady?'" (Man at his best!) During the flight she transcribed New Zealand poet C.K. Stead's translation of a Japanese haiku about the sadness of dreams into Esquireman's notebook, and said something which summed up the beauty of her life: "'I have always loved sadness. In sadness there is great beauty.'" She also spoke of Jeroo and her brother Dinshi back in India, though she did not see herself living there again: "'I feel like quite an American now.'" Not that American life was without its pitfalls, and as she told the Los Angeles–based Esquireman, "Los Angeles will be my home for a while, even though I have a preference for people from New York. I like their intelligence."²⁹

The teetotaling Khambatta realized as they were being seated at Le Castel in San Francisco that getting through an evening with Esquireman would require breaking a few rules: "They brought us the house aperitif: champagne with a dash of strawberry juice. Persis, who almost never drinks alcohol, took several sips." If he picked up on *why* a woman who had stuck to orange juice while champagne flowed during her nightclubbing excursions now needed to take the edge off with the local booze, Esquireman did not hint at it, any more than he seemed to have recognized her burn about the intelligence of Los Angelenos such as himself. Instead, after Khambatta told her faux-suitor that most American men are either intimidated by her or are "too groping," Esquireman patted himself on the back for being one of the good guys: "As we think of ourself as neither type, we felt encouraged." He soon found they were holding hands, though "she took our hand and held it, or we took her hand and she accepted it—we don't remember which."³⁰

> We do know this: with her eyes fixed on ours, she said in her best husky voice, "Tell me. Do you want to have a passionate, romantic affair with me? With fights and jealousy and making up, the whole thing?" We replied that we didn't appreciate that kind of humor, that she was far too appealing to joke around like this. (Okay, we were a little defensive.)³¹

It's no wonder why Esquireman was a little defensive; Persis Khambatta's impish quality was fine in small doses but joking around was unbecoming of an appealing lady in 1981. The fluffy blonde Michelle Phillips had put on lip gloss for him last time, but now on the return flight to Los Angeles, Khambatta managed to sully the sacred feminine signifier of makeup with more inappropriate humor.

> We nestled into our seats and Persis sighed. She reached into the seat pocket and pulled out, believe it or not, an airsickness bag. This she placed on our shoulder, then rested her head on it. "I don't want to get my makeup on your suit," she whispered, grinning. We leaned over and kissed her. Remember: we are not the groping kind. One way or another she had asked for it.³²

Esquire's motto, right there on the cover under the title, was "Man at his Best." Now, let's revisit that last sentence:

> One way or another she had asked for it.

They were back in Los Angeles by 1 a.m., and Esquireman decided that "we should pick up our own car at the hotel so that we could take Persis home and be alone with her for a few minutes." Whether Khambatta wanted to be alone with this still-strange man in her home is unclear, but as Esquireman wrote about it, she read him some of her poetry and showed him the shrine in the corner of her bedroom. Her living room was decorated with various representations of Khambatta over the years, including paintings, movie posters, and photographs, and on her bedroom wall was a photo of her as Ilia which had been signed by Gene Roddenberry: "To my dream alien. Love, Gene."[33]

Khambatta attended the second annual Group Effort charity auction at the Beverly Wilshire the following evening. She crossed paths with Esquireman briefly after the show, and they met back up for a lobster dinner on Sunday night, talking "the way a comfortable couple does." After dinner they stopped in the parking lot of her apartment afterward to listen to a pre-recorded interview with Khambatta on the radio, and once inside they "huddled closely together" to watch the first night of the miniseries *Masada*. And that, as they say, was that.[34]

* * *

The radio interview was broadcast in the week before *Nighthawks* was released, but otherwise the PR firm's timing was not great. The movie had long since left first-run theaters by the time "An Evening with Persis Khambatta" appeared in *Esquire*'s July 1981 issue, and *Nighthawks* wasn't much easier to find in the second-run houses.

The timing of an interview which ran in the April 8 *Pittsburgh Post-Gazette* with the paper's film critic George Anderson was a little better, despite the publicist giving her the wrong time: Khambatta arrived a half-hour early to meet Anderson at a restaurant in the Sheraton-Universal hotel in Los Angeles. Anderson wrote that "Persis Khambatta was fuming" about the mix-up, and "although the beautiful Indian actress looks fragile, her controlled anger demonstrated the kind of strength needed to compete in the tough worlds of film and fashion."[35]

That strength had always expressed itself in carving her own path, and she mentioned both the script she had optioned and her refusal to be typecast on any continent. She told Anderson said that were she to play a role like *Nighthawks*' Shakka in a Hindi film, "I could be called a vamp, a bad girl," because "heroines are the goodies. In India, all actors are typecast as good or bad. Here, I'm typecast as an exotic woman." Much as with Esquireman and every other white writer to whom she had expressed her frustration, Anderson blamed the victim: "When you sit across a table from her, it's difficult to see how producers could think of her in any other terms. She was wearing a green silk dress with a violet silk jacket, an unexpected color combination that worked for her somehow." In other words, why did she dress like that if she did not want to be thought of as exotic?[36]

One way or another she had asked for it.

Anderson's non-syndicated column only ran in Pittsburgh, where *Nighthawks* opened on six screens. Three other films opened that same day on seven screens each: Alvin Rakoff's *Dirty Tricks*, which you may not have heard of; a re-release of George Lucas' *Star Wars*, which you probably have heard of; and Jeremy Joe Kronsberg's *Going Ape!*, which you probably wish you have not heard of. But *Nighthawks* did play on the same number of screens as Jerry Lewis' *Hardly Working*, which was in its second week.

Receiving more exposure was a piece by Vernon Scott which hit the UPI wire service on April 18. Scott wrote of how "talk stopped and heads swiveled at the posh Polo Lounge of the Beverly Hills hotel the other noon-day when Persis Khambatta whirled in for lunch" in a "gauzy blue, yellow, red, green and purple sari, made into a dress" which "did absolutely nothing to conceal the Khambatta figure."[37]

> An independent and self-assured young woman, Persis looked around at the other diners and returned their interest with a radiant smile.
> 'Nobody recognizes me with hair,' she said.
> Persis is every bit as exotic as her name implies. In appearance, attitudes and personality she is as far from the All-American girl as a female can be.[38]

To review Scott's math: in addition to being "every bit as exotic as her name implies," Khambatta being "an independent and self-assured young woman" made her "as far from the All-American girl as a female can be." (The founding myth of the United States of America is built on independence and self-assuredness—but only for men, not women.) "'I'm well aware of the fact that I look foreign to Americans which is both good and bad for my career,'" Khambatta said. "'I'm trying to look less foreign than in the past.'" Further expanding on the problems with being different, she admitted that "'from the start I wanted a glamour image. Now I'm trying to lose it. Being exotic is enough without wearing flowing silks. I'm getting into jumpsuits.'" Vernon Scott had no more respect for Khambatta's desire to not be pigeonholed as exotic than the Esquireman had, so Scott's UPI piece ran with the headline "Exotic Is the Word for Persis."[39]

Scott wrote that in addition to Khambatta having no plans to become an American citizen, "neither has she thought seriously about getting married." But by the time the article went into circulation in mid–April, Khambatta was giving marriage serious thought.[40]

Birds of a Feather Cannot Always Cohabitate Together

The gritty and masculine *Nighthawks* opened on an April weekend which also witnessed the debut of a venue which was the movie's opposite in all the best ways: Robert Pascal and Lou Paciocco's La Cage Aux Folles supper club on La Cienega in West Hollywood. *Women's Wear Daily* described the turnout for the club—which featured pink stucco walls, stuffed leg sculptures, and a drag show—as "a large gay and celebrity crowd" including not only Persis Khambatta but *The Rocky Horror Picture Show's* Susan Sarandon, and once-and-future Bond Girl Maud Adams. Also present that night was stuntman and actor Cliff Taylor, who was engaged to Persis Khambatta by the end of the month.[41]

Khambatta had long regarded marriage as something unambitious women did, but when she allowed herself to consider it, she imagined they would first stare at each other from across the room, and the man would approach her and say, "I love you. Will you marry me?" Taylor did those very things at La Cage that night, and for Khambatta it felt like the best thing to happen in a long time. In truth, Taylor was everything Khambatta did not want in a man: a blonde, blue-eyed American actor, and not a successful actor at that. But her own star was on the rise, and she intended to boost his as well. Her misgivings about the institution of marriage went on record in the April 18 *Hollywood Reporter*: "Persis Khambatta is credited with this wise observation: 'In Hollywood, all marriages are happy. It's trying to live together afterward that causes all the problems!'"[42]

But their wedding would be in June, so those problems were several weeks away. Khambatta and Taylor attended a fundraising party for the City of Hope Medical Center on May 13, and the Mental Health Association's tribute dinner to Ray Bradbury on May 26. Stage actress Bijou Darden threw Persis a bridal shower in Darden's mansion on Thursday, June 11, and the night before her nuptials, Khambatta was one of the presenters at the 33rd Annual Los Angeles Area Emmy Awards at the Century Plaza Hotel. Unlike the Oscars or the regular, non-regional Emmys, the show was never broadcast.[43]

Persis Khambatta married Cliff Taylor at La Cage Aux Folles on Sunday, June 14, 1981. The reception featured a cake four tiers high, with heart-shaped mylar balloons, and the entertainment was a stage show including Bobby Etienne as Diana Ross, Busty O'Shea as Dolly Parton doing a timely "9 to 5" routine including with a typewriter and telephone, and Jimmy Segovia as Liza Minelli. This may be my favorite paragraph in this entire book for many reasons, not the least of which being that it demonstrates how ahead of her time Persis Khambatta was. She told Liz Smith that the wedding would be at La Cage because that was where Khambatta met Taylor and "she's very sentimental," but as we have seen, there was a tendency by white Americans to write off Khambatta's refusal to appear nude less as a personal choice and more of an adherence to Indian conservatism—but if nudity and kissing were controversial in India, then the open homosexuality represented by La Cage was unspeakable. It was barely speakable in the United States in 1981, and Khambatta's wedding at this very gay venue took place two weeks shy of the twelfth anniversary of the Stonewall Riots. Cross-dressing was done for lowbrow comedic purposes in Hindi films, such as Rajenda Nath's sissy character Pritam wearing a one-piece bathing suit in Khambatta's lone scene in *Bheegi Raat*, but that was quite different from and far less threatening than what La Cage represented, which was all about laughing *with* the crossing of gender lines, not *at* it. (The baldness of Ilia also represented a crossing of gender lines, a transgression for which Khambatta was never forgiven.)[44]

Wedding guests included Jeroo Khambatta—her mother! Persis Khambatta's mother was at La Cage!—as well as Nichelle Nichols and Robert Wise, Khambatta's wedding dress designer Elke Lesso, Francesca Hilton and producer Irwin Yablans, John Saxon, and Persis' former partner Pascal Chevillot. Khambatta and Taylor's first big public appearance as newlyweds would be the following Wednesday at a party at Mary Pickford's old estate honoring sports entrepreneur Jerry Buss, a soiree which was also attended by O.J. Simpson and Nicole Brown. Whether Khambatta met them is unknown, but one can only hope not.[45]

Continuing to have difficulty finding work, Khambatta re-signed with David Moss of the Moss Agency in July. The issue of *Esquire* with Esquireman's account of macking on Cliff Taylor's new spouse soon hit the stands, albeit an account from before Khambatta and Taylor met. That same month Khambatta and the *Los Angeles Times*' beauty columnist Lydia Lane visited paraplegic patients at a veterans' hospital in Long Beach, and along the way Khambatta talked to Lane about how she still followed her grandmother's beauty habits of using honey and yogurt for facials, and how meditation helped her deal with the stresses of North American life. Khambatta's friend Olivia Hussey had introduced her to Swami Muktananda's Siddha Yoga meditation in particular.[46]

The piece ran on July 10 with the elegiac title "Persis Khambatta Had Plan for Life." It did not mention Taylor, and a late-summer honeymoon to Bombay so Taylor could meet Dinshi and the rest of Khambatta's family was canceled when Khambatta and Taylor broke up. She later told Marilyn Beck there was "no bitterness," and that she was trying to be philosophical about the whole misadventure: "It's good to find out very fast if a marriage isn't going to work out. And one grows from both the good and the bad experiences."[47]

Khambatta was more honest and less philosophical about the collapse of her marriage to Taylor when speaking to the *Telegraph* five years later, putting it in the context of her great disillusionment about the world beyond India. (Persis Khambatta was a feminist. There is no doubt.)[48]

I found, to my utter dismay, that even western societies order their laws, psychological and theological systems, marriage and family structures, and their whole economic pyramid on the continuance of woman as cheap, easily controllable domestic and commercial serfs, breeders and child-tenders. I even had a stab at marriage with a foreigner and it only lasted a few months. I am an ideal liberated woman. That marriage made me a half a woman, legally. I just couldn't live like that! At every step along the line, I've felt the weight of this male-oriented system. Even abroad, I became aware of the system's universality, its arbitrariness.[49]

Speaking of arbitrariness, when Liz Smith reported on the end of Khambatta's marriage in her August 19 column, Smith added parenthetically about Khambatta: "Remember, she shaved her head for 'Star Trek.'" Smith never failed to mention Khambatta having shaved her head, and she was by no means alone; the *New York Post*'s Sideliners column quoted Khambatta that "we made a mistake. If we're meant to get back together, we will," and Sideliners reminded the reader that Khambatta "became famous by shaving her head for *Star Trek, the Motion Picture*."[50]

The (Mega)force of (Tri)illusion

Persis Khambatta realized if she was ever going to be famous for something other than having shaved her head for that one movie that one time, she would have to get serious about creating her own illusions. As a result, divorce filings were not the only paperwork she busied herself with in the autumn of 1981. With the help of attorney Gregory Gelfan, Khambatta registered a California Domestic Corporation named Triillusion Co. on October 12 to develop "Entertainment Services" in the form of her own film projects. Her corporation (C 1057069, to be precise) was also authorized to issue 2,500 shares of one class of stock.[51]

The name Triillusion was inspired by a numerologist telling Khambatta that her fortunes would improve if her birth and name numbers were synchronized. She had tossed around adding a second "i" to her name, making it "Persiis," but settled for the double-I of Triillusion. (She also purchased an apartment that year in the same building in Bombay's upscale Nepean Sea Road neighborhood in which Jeroo lived, a building owned by her great-grandfather Ratanji Framji Sethna.) But producing her own films would take a long time, and things were dire enough in the short term that Khambatta auditioned to appear as Tom Selleck's wife on *Magnum, P.I.*, a part she lost to Marta DuBois.[52]

No matter, because the week after registering Triillusion, Khambatta traveled to Nevada for her first movie role since *Nighthawks* had wrapped a year and a half ago: *Smokey and the Bandit* director Hal Needham's would-be magnum opus, *Megaforce*. Produced by Albert S. Ruddy as the Golden Harvest Group's follow-up to their Needham megahit *The Cannonball Run*, it was one of two offers Khambatta received out of the blue, and she chose the Needham picture without reading the other script because *Megaforce* looked fun. Which is not the same as *funny*, and while it may be just as well that Khambatta's character of Major Zara Benbhutto was not responsible for any of *Megaforce*'s attempts at humor, Khambatta told Marilyn Beck she hoped to do a comedy soon. Beck did not mention that Khambatta had been bald in that one movie that one time, though she did undercut Khambatta's attempt to brand herself as something other than exotic.[53]

> She's enjoying the experience of playing a Megaforce military woman, but hopes to get a chance to play comedy soon. "I am thought of as an 'exotic' type," says the beautiful Indian actress, "and I've played a tough terrorist and a robot. People think of me as aloof, but I'm not really that way, and I'd love to hear people say, 'Hey, she can be funny.'"[54]

A beautiful Indian actress who doesn't want to be pigeonholed as exotic and/or aloof? Not on Marilyn Beck's watch! (Or George Anderson's watch, or Vernon Scott's, or Esquireman's, or....)

The National Association of Theatre Owners began a three-day convention in Las Vegas on November 10, and the next day more than a thousand delegates were caravanned to a dry lakebed where they were greeted by Khambatta and her *Megaforce* co-stars Barry Bostwick and Henry Silva. After a barbecue luncheon, the NATO delegates watched the filming of a battle. Location work in Nevada wrapped on November 21, and Khambatta returned to Los Angeles in time to be photographed by *Women's Wear Daily* the following day at a "Very Black Tie" party for the $150-per-ounce perfume Giorgio. The $10,000 Yuki dress Khambatta wore was forever on the verge of tearing due to people stepping on her tail, which may rival "the beauty of sadness" as a metaphor for her life and career. Not that she would have worn it a second time; Khambatta tried to wear something different every day as a rule, and retired anything she was photographed in, including but not limited to the $30,000 dress from the 1980 Academy Awards. She admitted that most of the money she made went into clothes: "I have trunks of clothes in New York and London. In India, I have six closets packed with gowns in addition to eight suitcases crammed with clothes. I guess you'd call me a clothes freak." Several years after leaving Glam-era London, she was still living by the credo that to be a star, you had to act like one.[55]

Khambatta spoke to Associated Press writer Bob Thomas during a break in the filming of *Megaforce* for a piece which was syndicated in the final weeks of December 1981. It had been two and a half years since

Khambatta grew her hair back, but the topic of conversation was "her seven months of baldness and what 'Star Trek' has done for her." Khambatta tried to put a positive spin on the grueling experience by saying that it "opened the door for me professionally, gave me immediate recognition. Even if producers don't remember my name, they recognize me as 'the girl who shaved her head for Star Trek.' I'm glad I did it."[56]

Much like the December 1979 AP article by Dolores Barclay, this December 1981 AP article by Bob Thomas ran in many different papers with varying headlines and photos, depending on the available column inches. The Bridgewater *Courier-News* ran it on as "Bald Beauty from 'Star Trek' Still Has Mega-Career" with a photo of Robot Ilia; the *Santa Cruz Sentinel* as "Young Actress' Hairy Experience" with no photo; the *Indianapolis Star* that same day as "Baldness, 'Star Trek' Spur Persis' Career" with both regular and Robot Ilia photos; the Wilmington *Morning News* as "Baldness Made Actress Famous" with no photos; and the *Longview News-Journal* as "'Star Trek' Baldy's Career Moving Along Nicely" with no photo. Roderick Mann demonstrated his continuing fascination with Persis Khambatta's temporary baldness in a piece about William Shatner and the second Star Trek movie, which was filmed at the same time as *Megaforce*: "And although this one hasn't got a bald-headed beauty like the first film (Persis Khambatta), Shatner thinks it's got a better script and is coming in at a better price."[57]

But when she was one of "50 major celebrities" asked about their New Year's resolutions by the *Tampa Tribune*'s Anthony Bowen, the otherwise media-savvy Khambatta's frustration bled through.[58]

> I broke my resolution last year. I swore I'd put me and my career first from then on. Then I went and got married ... so, you know what happened to those plans. My New Year's Resolution for 1982 is to love people that deserve loving. You see, I think we tend to love a lot of people who don't deserve our love and attention. You love the wrong people, some of the time, and you waste your time and energy on them. Some just take what they can from you and reciprocate not at all. Be careful who you choose to love.[59]

Megaforce wrapped on Christmas Eve, and according to the *Hollywood Reporter* Khambatta's final day of filming involved a death scene. That footage has never surfaced, and had it been used it would have given the Needham film a much darker tone and put Khambatta at four out of five for dying in her English-language films thus far. In any event, as work schedules so often will the shooting schedule threw off Khambatta's usual plans to spend the holiday with her mother. Not only did she miss Christmas with Jeroo but also Dinshi's wedding, which all the more painful because she considered leaving India before getting to know Dinshi to be one the biggest sacrifices she had made for her career—a career which she feared was beginning to stall out.[60]

1982

Persis vs. Soup

It may have looked to an outside observer like that career was going just fine: a January 8, 1982, *India West* article called 1981 "a milestone year for the Indian community in the United States," citing "Kabir Bedi, Persis Khambatta, Ahmed Lateef and Waris Hussain" as having "made progress in Hollywood." In a February 17 *New York Daily News* profile which bucked tradition by not mentioning her hair in the headline "She's Looking for Reel Love," Khambatta said she was tired of playing terrorists and other tough-minded women. "I want audiences to see me in a different light. Right now I'm regarded as an exotic type who is strong, capable, intelligent and who doesn't need anyone or anything else." She described her character in the recently-wrapped *Megaforce* as "a strong-willed woman, a military person who recruits a first class group of men to rid her beleaguered nation of mercenary invaders," the only problem being that she didn't have a love scene with any of her male co-stars. In the concurrent Marilyn Beck column, *Megaforce* producer Al Ruddy was debunking rumors that "his Barry Bostwick-Persis Khambatta 'Megaforce' feature" had been completed for a modest $3M: "It's a massive movie, awesome, overwhelming in size. And, with the very exotic sequences we decided to add, it's a $20 million production." It was one of the rare times the word "exotic" was used adjacent to Persis Khambatta without being used to describe her.[1]

Getting pawed by Esquireman had failed to drum up much publicity for Universal's seedy, R-rated *Nighthawks*, but Twentieth Century–Fox had a more direct approach for the PG-rated boys' adventure film *Megaforce*: they tried to get Khambatta to pose nude for a sixteen-page *Penthouse* spread, but she refused. The somewhat more respectable *Playboy* had been trying to coax her into a shoot since *The Wilby Conspiracy*, so in an effort to split the difference between promoting *Megaforce* and taking her clothes off, Khambatta told *Playboy*'s west coast photography editor Marilyn Grabowski she would consent if she could wear clothes and choose her own photographer. Hugh Hefner was fine with using Khambatta's photographer, but balked at her wearing clothes. Though the *Playboy* shoot never happened, she would later be shamed for both having done it and for *not* having done it.[2]

* * *

The single constant which all observers agreed upon no matter their frame of reference was that Persis Khambatta had been bald in that one movie that one time. Since she wouldn't play ball by doing a nude photoshoot, Twentieth Century–Fox instead sent out a press release titled "The Hair-Raising Adventures of Persis Khambatta," which starts eating its own tail in the opening paragraph.[3]

> One of the most lasting impressions made by an actress in recent motion picture history was that made by Persis Khambatta when she shaved her heard for her unique role in "Star Trek." Even to this day she finds herself being constantly questioned about it.[4]

The reader is assured that the "full head of hair" she sports in *Megaforce* is "the same silky, dark hair that made the exotic East Indian beauty one of the world's top photographic models before she embarked on her movie career." Persis Khambatta never wore a wig while she was making that one movie that one time, but that did not stop the Roderick Manns of the world from assuming that she must have worn a wig, and may still be doing so at any given moment to hide the shame of her surely perpetual baldness.[5]

> "Even today," she says with a grin, "I'm constantly being asked if this is my real hair or am I wearing a wig. Oddly enough, the question comes as often from co-workers as it does from strangers who just come up to me on the street."[6]

Not that she resented the questions, mind you. She was nothing if not a good soldier.

> "I appreciate them, in fact. First of all, it's flattering that people are able to recognize me <u>with</u> hair. After all, I'm a relative newcomer to films. And secondly, those who ask are sincerely interesting in my well being. Some thought I'd never be able to grow it back and that bothered them."[7]

Persis Khambatta had pulled at her hair in public more than once since 1979 to demonstrate that, yes, she was capable of growing the stuff, though it was not until this press release that she acknowledged that other people had done so without her consent. Pulling a stranger's hair is assault, but the story was related in a press release for a boys' adventure film in 1982, so Khambatta being assaulted was downgraded to "one thing that does prove distracting."[8]

> "It's those who are too shy to ask but not too shy to come up behind me and tug at my hair. As you can imagine, that can be awfully upsetting at times, especially when you

don't expect it. I've had my hair pulled by people standing behind me in elevators in the department store and once while I was standing in the ticket line at a theatre."

The worst instance she recalls occurred while dining at a popular Hollywood restaurant. "I was just about to put a spoonful of soup in my mouth when a grandmotherly-type lady gave my hair an extremely hard pull from the rear. Needless to say, the soup ended up in my lap instead of my mouth. It was hot and I jumped up with a scream. The lady who'd pulled my hair was petrified. She didn't realize what had happened.

"She fainted right there on the spot and then I was the one who was petrified. I thought this elderly lady had had a heart attack and died. Fortunately, she regained consciousness almost immediately and the whole matter turned out with the only damage being a large soup stain on my dress."[9]

To say nothing of the psychological damage caused by living in fear of strangers feeling entitled to pull at her hair, and knowing it can happen anywhere (such as a popular Hollywood restaurant) and be done by anyone (such as a "grandmotherly-type lady"). But the release does acknowledge that "Khambatta can't understand all this strange attention as to whether or not she's wearing a wig," and that the most puzzling aspect is how many people seem to believe her hair "fails to grow the same way as theirs."[10]

"It's been a long, long time since I shaved my hair for that role. In fact, I've had it cut several times in the interim. What these people don't seem to realize is that if I hadn't had it cut, it would be down to my waist by this time."[11]

The press release ties it back into the film it's meant to promote by ruminating that the shoot would have been simpler for Khambatta "if her head was still shaved and she was wearing a wig" since much of *Megaforce* takes place in the desert, complete with "swirling sand, blasting gunpowder and harsh sun." The only time she had worn a wig in recent memory was for the few blink-and-you'll-miss-it seconds in *Nighthawks*, but she nonetheless agreed that, yes, wearing a wig would solve some problems—while creating a host of others.[12]

"It would be a lot easier to just change wigs than to continually wash my hair," she admits. "But then, if I did that, how would I explain to all those people why my hair hadn't grown back since 'Star Trek' was filmed?"[13]

Persis Khambatta had been a celebrity long enough to know that she was damned either way, but she was also confident that being in *Megaforce* would finally do for her career what that one movie had not.

Hunter vs. Khan

Nighthawks premiered with little fanfare on domestic cable television in March 1982. The supplement *On TV* described Khambatta's character

Shakka as "an international terrorist who wears a blonde wig," but fear not, for her "real hair finally makes an appearance in *Megaforce*." The small photo accompanying the article was of Khambatta with the aforementioned real hair in *Megaforce*.[14]

Khambatta herself was on a publicity tour that month, including a Bertrand Laforet photoshoot in Paris in which Khambatta wore the Megaforce uniform from the scene in the film in which her character is told why she's not fit to wear the Megaforce uniform. (We'll get to that.) She was back in the United States in time to accompany actor Kip Whitman to the premiere of Robert Dornhelm's documentary *She Dances Alone* on April 20. There also exists a Peter Borsari photograph of Khambatta with *WKRP in Cincinnati* actor Gary Sandy; according to the handwriting on the back the picture was taken at a Cable T.V. Party on January 27, though it does not include the year, location, or any hint as to what a Cable T.V. Party even is.[15]

Buzz was building in 1982 for the second Star Trek movie, and Saavik performer Kirstie Alley told *Starlog* that "they made it very clear to us that no one was to talk about the script. I figured that if I talked about it, I'd be left in space somewhere … either that or be forced to shave my head for the role!" (See, it's funny because Khambatta had been bald in that one movie that one time, and—) The film was released to great fanfare and immediate sanctification on June 4, and Janet Maslin's *New York Times* review did something unusual: she singled out Khambatta for praise. Unable to decide whether Ricardo Montalban looked like "either the world's oldest rock star or its hippest Indian chief" in the second movie, she concluded that "either way, he looks terrific, every bit as happily flamboyant as the first film's characters—notwithstanding the beautiful, bald Persis Khambatta—were drab."[16]

Khambatta continued to get herself out there in the weeks between the release of the second Star Trek movie and the only Megaforce movie. (A second Megaforce movie titled *Deeds Not Words* was slated to start filming in September but was scrapped when the original flopped hard.) She was escorted by Pan Am's vice president Jeff Kriendler to the St. Barts wedding of the airline's president's daughter, appeared on *The Merv Griffin* show opposite Debbie Boone and Ricky Jay, and then on *The Tonight Show* along with Bill Cosby. (Though Khambatta would appear on any chat-show which would have her, her favorite was *The Tonight Show* because she felt most at ease with Johnny Carson.) From there she went to New York, where she told Earl Wilson she wished reporters would stop asking if she was still bald: "That was almost three years ago." Perhaps most excitingly, she was negotiating for a leading role in a film slated to begin filming in New York in July: *The Snake*, to be produced and directed by Alfredo Leone from a script by *Shaft* screenwriter Ernest Tidyman, and starring Cathy Lee

Crosby and Fred Williamson. The picture fell through, though Khambatta would go on to act opposite Williamson in two future movies.[17]

But first she had to survive the crash and burn of her current movie. The high-profile *Megaforce* was getting all the bad reviews of the low-profile *Nighthawks*, and they were delivered with the ire of the bad reviews of the mega-profile *Star Trek—The Motion Picture*, made worse by the fact that Khambatta was just as prominent in *Megaforce*'s advertising. *Megaforce* also had the misfortune to open in a summer which boasted not only the second Star Trek movie but Steven Spielberg's *E.T.*, John Carpenter's *The Thing*, Steven Lisberger's *Tron*, Tobe Hooper's *Poltergeist*, and Ridley Scott's *Blade Runner*. Not all of these films were hits; *Blade Runner*, *Tron*, and *The Thing* were box office and critical disappointments which later found their audiences on home video. But *Tron*, *The Thing*, *Poltergeist*, *Blade Runner*, and the second Star Trek movie all have spawned sequels, prequels, and/or remakes, as well as restorations and multiple special editions in various video formats, and are all integral parts of what many men of a certain age call the best summer movie season ever. To be clear, other films from that summer such as John Huston's *Annie*, Clint Eastwood's *Firefox*, and Sylvester Stallone's *Rocky III* are not remembered as fondly as the others. *Rocky III* was the highest-grossing entry in that franchise to date, yet it is now overshadowed by 1985's more flamboyant *Rocky IV*. But only *Megaforce* is looked back on as the worst movie of the summer of 1982, and there has never been a sequel, remake, or non-rudimentary video release.

Megaforce was not screened for the Southern California press before its June 25 premiere. But the most wide-reaching critical voices in 1982 were based out of Chicago, and on June 24 Roger Ebert and Gene Siskel discussed what Ebert called "a real loser" and "one of the most confusing, pointless, and muddled thrillers I've seen in a long time" on their PBS show *Sneak Previews*. Within the first thirty seconds, Ebert described how the film's hero Ace Hunter "gets involved in a really dumb love affair with Persis Khambatta, a female warrior with romance on her mind." This was accompanied by a clip of Zara and Hunter's first meeting, in which she upbraids him for making them drive into the middle of the desert for no apparent reason. Major Benbhutto does not come across as romance-minded in the clip other than briefly smiling when she tells Hunter to call her Zara, but Ebert has other fish to fry.[18]

> In this life and death mission, we get dialog like women used to use in the movies 30 years ago: "You're going to leave me to bake in the desert." She's supposed to be a warrior, but that's how she talks. You may remember her—that's Persis Khambatta from the first Star Trek movie. I don't think very many people are going to remember her from this movie.[19]

Despite being a screenwriter himself, Ebert does not specify that Khambatta is just reading the dialog she was given, let alone that Zara has a point about Hunter leaving them in the desert. Khambatta is not mentioned again in the *Sneak Previews* segment, but Gene Siskel does make the first of many homophobic jokes about the costume design: "This is Barry Bostwick, who's been terrific in *The Rocky Horror Picture Show*, also in *Movie Movie*, he's a terrific song and dance man. But Ace Hunter? No. And the costume designer who puts him in a gold lamé jumpsuit is, I think, a little bit off—this guy should be hunting for bargains in the supermarket or something." A satirical book about modern masculinity titled *Real Men Don't Eat Quiche* was published the month before *Megaforce*'s release, but judging from Siskel's comment, Real Men in 1982 did pay full retail price when grocery shopping. Insecure male critics would never stop making queer jokes about *Megaforce*: a writer for an Illinois paper described Bostwick's character in May 2019 as "the kind of nominal 'hero' you're supposed to root for as he trots around with his blow-dried coif gently bouncing" and the rest of Megaforce as "just your usual gang of equally blowdried action guys all clad in a wide ranging array of upsetting jumpsuits." We get it, broheim. You are very straight.[20]

The reviews, all negative, rolled out over the next few weeks after the film's release on June 25, 1982. John Dodd wrote in the *Edmonton Journal* that Khambatta was "no longer bald (or very interesting)," while Ernest Leogrande's review headlined "Mega Bomb" in that same day's *New York Daily News* observed that "Persis Khambatta of the first 'Star Trek' movie has hair here. She plays a military officer but she doesn't get to fight, only stand back and admire Bostwick. After all, war is a man's job."[21]

Janet Maslin wrote in her *New York Times* review that Bostwick's "swashbuckling manner" is "lost on Persis Khambatta, his ostensibly romantic co-star. Here and in 'Star Trek: The Motion Picture,' Miss Khambatta has had to wear some of the most ill-fitting outfits ever designed for the screen. Unlike Mr. Bostwick, who at least tries to remain animated, Miss Khambatta has a wooden presence here. She even has trouble with a line like 'I wanted it to be different,' which is about the best line the screenplay allows her."[22]

After having been disappointed that Khambatta never got "down to basics" in the G-rated *Star Trek—The Motion Picture*, Gene Siskel again lamented the lack of Khambatta's exotic skin in his *Chicago Tribune* review of the PG-rated *Megaforce*: "Persis Khambatta, the exotic-looking star of the first 'Star Trek' movie, plays Ace Hunter's love interest, but they don't have a single erotic scene. They only flip each other a thumb's-up sign and promise to meet after the battle is over in a London hotel. 'Megaforce' could have used that London hotel scene." Though Roger Ebert was no less pervy than his onscreen sparring partner Siskel, Ebert was less disappointed in his *Chicago Sun-Times* print review by the lack of an (ugh) "erotic scene" than by the way Khambatta's character was written and directed: "I almost forgot the subplot, which involves a shudderingly stupid romance between Bostwick and Persis Khambatta (the bald woman in 'Star Trek,' this time with hair). She trains to go into battle with the men, but then Bostwick says he just can't take her along, and the not-so-subtle Needham cuts to a backlit silhouette shot of Ms. Khambatta and a piece of sculpture as she portentously pronounces the not-so-original words, 'Is it … because I am a woman?'" However portentously Khambatta may have pronounced the words she was contractually obligated to speak, the fact remains that, yes, it was 100 percent because Zara was a woman.[23]

Daryl Miller wrote in the *Arizona Daily Star* that "Persis Khambatta, who played the bald beauty in 'Star Trek, The Motion Picture,' appears as Zara, daughter of Sardoun's president. Her talent, like Bostwick's, is hidden by her limited role. Khambatta is basically required to look beautiful and little else." The *Hartford Courant*'s Malcolm L. Johnson described her as "last seen bald and bad in 'Star Trek: The Motion Picture,'" though "bad" in what sense is unclear. (Or perhaps the writer of *Presenting Persis Khambatta* just wants to believe it's unclear.) Paulette Henderson in the *Waterloo Courier* gave Khambatta one of her few positive notices for any English-language film, while still acknowledging that she'd been bald in that other movie: "One other bright spot is the performance of Persis Khambatta, who played the bald Lt. Ilia in 'Star Trek—The Motion Picture.' She did a good job of presenting a character of more than one dimension, which is more than her co-stars were able to do."[24]

Though Gene Siskel was officially the first critic to joke about the costume design in *Megaforce* by virtue of his platform on public television, Terry Lawson in the *Dayton Journal-Herald* was probably still proud of himself for his own cleverness: "At first, when I saw the commander and his pals on their garish black and gold motorcycles, I thought it was going to be an all-gay battling brigade, and I saw some promise in that premise. It was wishful thinking. The leader, played by Barry Bostwick, falls for the first woman he sees, who turns out to be *Star Trek*'s Persis Khambatta. I originally failed to recognize her with hair." (It is not the job of film critics to memorize a given performer's filmography, especially back in the analog days, but I did not find any *Megaforce* reviews which acknowledged Khambatta had been in *Nighthawks*.) Harry F. Thermal wrote in the July 4 Wilmington, Delaware, *News Journal* that *Megaforce*'s "silliest dialogue and role are given to Persis Khambatta, whose baldness made her the most memorable character in the first 'Star Trek' film. The former Miss India has her hair this time, but in this film she plays a passive woman who sits on the sidelines while the men go off to do the fighting." Which means that Thermal was not paying attention to any of her scenes in the first act of the film, in which her character is not passive but instead makes an active attempt to join the men in the fighting.[25]

In his review for *Cinefantastique* long after *Megaforce* had left theaters, Mike Mayo got the queer jokes out of the way—"Bostwick and Beck have a great time running around their desert headquarters in tight, quasi-homosexual pastel spandex outfits"—before describing Khambatta as "dreadful in a sop-feminist role as an unbelievable woman general who pouts when Barry-poo won't take her along on the mission. He'd like to, you understand, but the boys wouldn't approve." It is unclear which aspect of her character is unbelievable, unless Mayo considered the very concept of a female military office to beggar belief. His description of Khambatta's role as "sop-feminist" implies that it was some kind of act of tokenism on Needham's part, and also suggests that Mayo did not pay attention to Zara's arc even though he sums it up pretty well, minus the pouting—shades of the *Wilby Conspiracy* reviews which referred to Dr. Persis Ray as a dental assistant, even though it is both shown and told that her character is a dentist.[26]

The *Queen City Mail*'s critic sank to a different low: "Persis Khambatta is dull as yet another liberated woman who has placed armed combat ahead of getting the extra iron she needs on her list of priorities." What can be duller than a woman who isn't just chasing men all the time? Ugh, film critics are the worst. (I was a film critic for eight years, so I can say that.)[27]

A week and a half after *Megaforce* was released, the *New York Times* called it one of the "obvious losers" of the summer of 1982, along with director Sidney Poitier's *Hanky Panky* and Patricia Birch's *Grease 2*.[28] Paid film critics were not alone in slamming *Megaforce*; in November *Starlog* printed a letter from a young man urging readers not to see it for many reasons, the most "shocking" being Persis Khambatta, "who throws the role of women back into the Dark Ages." Not understanding that Khambatta was a professional who was contractually obligated to read the lines which were written by somebody else for her make-believe character, the young man listed off Khambatta's crimes: "Out in the desert, she puts on lipstick; gleefully smiles and waves idiotically as The Boys takeoff on The Mission; and after proving herself worthy of becoming a Megaforce member and being denied entry, she spouts that timeless phrase, 'It's because I'm a woman, isn't it?' with all sincerity." Again, the character of Zara is 100 percent right that she is not allowed to go on the mission because she is a woman—but still, the nerve of Khambatta, playing the part as written! One has to wonder if this young male arbiter of gender equity would have still blamed Khambatta for "throwing the role of women back into the Dark Ages" had she "spouted" the timeless phrase *without* sincerity? He does not blame Barry Bostwick or any of the rest of the cast for the actions of their characters, and it is also worth noting that the last letter about Khambatta printed in *Starlog* had been from the "dedicated baldophile" who hoped that "if enough of her fans pressure her, she will be forced to go bald again." The hostility that Persis Khambatta engendered in *Starlog*'s readers is nothing if not palpable; perhaps in addition to quiche, real men don't like foreign women who were bald in that one movie that one time.²⁹

The Megafudging of Major Zara

Where to start with *Megaforce* itself? The parallels between the Robert Wise and Hal Needham films are numerous, and not just because a big deal was made in the marketing for both about how the props were functional—though rather than the light-switch technology discussed in my previous book *The First Star Trek Movie*, it was real motorcycles with rocket launchers in *Megaforce*.³⁰ More pertinent is that they were Khambatta's first and last Hollywood studio pictures, and the hell of it is that *Megaforce*'s Major Zara could have been Khambatta's best English-language role, but she was once again at the mercy of both an undercooked script and a director with other issues on his mind. By his own admission Needham was never concerned with character or cinematic style, and was already famous in 1982 for saying "if someone handed me *Fiddler on the Roof*, I wouldn't know what the fuck to do with it." But *Megaforce* is nonetheless an outlier in Persis Khambatta's English-language filmography by that point, for only Zara's pride is assaulted, not her body. (Khambatta's next film would reset that counter in a big way.)³¹

Khambatta told the *New York Post* in July that she appreciated how Zara was "an independent, determined woman. Just like me." The tension between who the real-life Persis Khambatta was, who the make-believe Zara was, and who the filmmakers and studio wanted both the real-life and make-believe women to be plays out on both sides of the screen. Twentieth Century–Fox had already hit the "hey, remember when she was bald in a different studio's picture?" angle hard in the "Hair-Raising Adventures" press release, so the first Star Trek movie doesn't come up until the last page of the three-page bio of Khambatta in *Megaforce*'s Production Information package. It describes "the idealistic Ilia" as a role "that left a lasting impression with audiences all over the world," and then uses the same phrasing as the *Nighthawks* press kit, give or take a preposition: "probably the most publicized hair styling for an actress since Ingrid Bergman had her locks clipped short in 'For Whom the Bell Tolls.'" (This was probably not due to Fox actively copying from Universal, but because Khambatta's management provided the same boilerplate to both, and they had no reason to suspect that forty years later some weirdo would go through it all with a fine-toothed comb.) The *Megaforce* bio focuses on the Persis Khambatta who was forever straddling two worlds: East and West in real life, male and female gender expectations on the screen. A sexy woman ... but she talks funny, she was bald that one time![32]

After Zara is described as the "tough but beautiful" daughter of the President and "also a staunch, hard-driving officer in her father's army," Khambatta is directly quoted[33]:

> "It gives me the best of all worlds," the actress believes. "It allows me to be feminine while at the time same it shows I'm as capable, if not more so, than the men. And the icing on the cake is that I'm the only woman in the movie!"[34]

The copywriter's choice of verb is telling: not that the actress *says* the role gives her "the best of all worlds" or that the actress *states* it, but rather that the actress *believes* it, phrasing which cast doubts as to the truth of what she's saying. It may not be true, but she believes it even if nobody else does.[35]

Though not quoted directly, Khambatta is also said to have noted "that the Parsi religion was the first to open schools to women in India, which remains by caste, historical development and the Hindu religion a male dominated society." Heady stuff for the press materials of an adventure film marketed to young American boys, and it ends with Khambatta describing her home as being wherever she is at the given moment: "I'm Eastern and I'm Western. I've built a bridge between the two and I feel it's a rare privilege to be a part of both."[36]

Khambatta affirms her duality elsewhere in the document.

> "I enjoy playing strong women," affirms the actress. "I feel that is a part of my own personality which I convey very well on screen. But I think it is an inner strength not an outward hardness or something that is unfeminine."[37]

In her pursuit to not be unfeminine, she is reported to have said that "she is not a feminist but has always believed in the equality of men and women," and that she "'knew about women's liberation before I even knew what the word was.'" When asked why women walk behind men in India, her response was "because they are the ones pushing the men to the top." This was a more politically judicious response than what she would later write in *Pride of India*: "It is said that behind every great man is a great woman and behind a great woman is a man trying hard to stop her! My own version is that behind every great woman is the urge to be free."[38]

Being outspoken about women's rights and equality was not a way to boost a career in 1982, and refusing to get down to basics in the (ugh) "erotic scenes" men like Gene Siskel wanted to see did not help. It was being bald all over again: she was sexy on paper, but being naked in the wrong place meant she was not masturbation material, which was a fatal flaw in an industry in which the ability to give strange men erections was crucial. It helped that she eschewed the emerging word "feminist," but she also used the already slightly-outdated "women's liberation" in both the *Nighthawks* and *Megaforce* press kits, and it is significant that the publicity departments of both studios chose to retain the references. (It is outside the research scope of this book to determine whether non-exotic performers such as Farrah Fawcett made similar political comments in the publicity materials for films like *The Cannonball Run*, but it feels safe to speculate that they did not.)

Producer Albert Ruddy described Persis Khambatta in *Megaforce*'s Production Information package as "a very determined, very talented actress who was able to bring those traits to her character, Zara. Zara is an extremely capable soldier, a major in her own army, and a very contemporary woman." Director Hal Needham sort of agreed.[39]

> She's the only woman in the movie, so she really is, in a way, representative of all women facing the dangers and challenges of war time. She meets the challenge, actually more than meets it because she wants to fight alongside the men. Persis has all the qualities of this kind of courageous person. She is the embodiment of that kind of inner strength that is characteristic of today's woman.[40]

No one man would ever represent all men in a Needham film—George Furth's Professor Eggstrum and Barry Bostwick's Ace Hunter could not be more different in *Megaforce*—but women are not as complicated as men in his world. Say what you will about Hal Needham as a director, but his ability to give lip service to the equality of women while refusing to permit it on or off the screen is a wonder to behold.

Not only does Persis Khambatta get her first onscreen kiss in a Hollywood film, her character initiates it. The recurring joke on the set was how chaste the film was: here Khambatta was with these handsome men, but all anyone cared about was the vehicles and the weapons. She had been looking forward to "one of those long, luxurious screen kisses," but it was not to be in *Megaforce*. She would get a long kiss for sure in *Warrior of the Lost World*, but whether it was luxurious is another matter.[41]

Zara is also Khambatta's only character in her three American studio films to have an arc. Ilia is killed halfway through the first Star Trek movie and most of Shakka's scenes were cut from *Nighthawks*, but Zara in *Megaforce* is ambitious, and she has the wherewithal to pursue her goals. She is an oft-decorated officer in her home country, and she wears her military uniform for much of the film, but Ace Hunter is not impressed by Zara's medals. When Hunter points out that Zara lacks "the Good Conduct Medal," the words "Author's Message" might as well flash on screen in all seriousness like they did jokingly in Clive Donner's *What's New, Pussycat*?[42]

Being more concerned with technology and optical effects than with its characters, *Megaforce* is top-heavy with exposition and world-building which never pays off, including vast interior sets created with the Introvision front-projection process. These things are also true of the first Star Trek movie (except for the use of Introvision), but that was to show a pre-established world in a scope never possible before. The first act of *Megaforce* spends a great deal of time establishing the title army as a shadowy, crypto-fascist organization which surveils all those deemed worthy of surveillance by Megaforce's even more shadowy parent organization, the Supreme Command United Free Forces.

Megaforce never addresses the ethical ramifications of this invasion of privacy coming from an organization which the opening text informs us is dedicated to "battling the forces of tyranny and evil in every corner of the globe." Instead, the only ramifications the movie cares about are what would happen if the Megaforce branch of the He-Man Woman-Hater's Club were to admit Zara into their ranks.

Even though it is rebuffed, Zara has the most agency of any of Khambatta's characters: she wants to go on the mission; she states that she is going on the mission; and she demonstrates that she has the skills and experience to go on the mission. (Khambatta's last character to have a clear, defined goal and thus a recognizable motivation was Dr. Ray from *The Wilby Conspiracy*.) Hunter tells Zara that "you have more than proved yourself," but that she cannot join the "60 guys" who comprise Megaforce because any outsider "would create enough uncertainty to jeopardize the entire mission." The scene in which Hunter (gently) puts Zara in her place is the only interesting composition in Needham's oeuvre which does not involve stunts: a slow dolly in as Bostwick and Khambatta are silhouetted against a bright purple screen. Khambatta is in the middle with Bostwick on screen right and a souped-up motorcycle on screen left, and at a certain point there are no fewer than seven phallic symbols on the screen: five are protruding from the motorcycle, three of which are pointing at Khambatta, and Bostwick points at her with both hands, though his left hand begins at crotch-level, which in silhouette makes it look like—well, like a phallus. The meat-and-potatoes Hal Needham was no Ridley Scott (or even *Fiddler on the Roof*'s Norman Jewison) when it came to *mise-en-scène*, but this framing was not an accident, and the message is clear: capability is defined by gender, gender is defined by genitals, and Zara cannot join because she does not have a penis. The action scenes never give a sense of Megaforce being such a finely-tuned 60-man dance crew team of mercenaries that the addition of a 61st would imbalance them so much it would create a wormhole, and the subplot takes up seven minutes of the film's 100 minutes—which is more than it sounds like, particularly considering how much of *Megaforce* is ineptly-filmed action and stuntwork.

Beyond introducing her as "Major Zara Benbhutto (PERSIS KHAMBATTA), field officer and the beautiful daughter of Sardoun's President," Twentieth Century–Fox's official synopsis ignores the subplot entirely.

> Following this indoctrination, Zara and Byrne-White are shown to their quarters to clean up for dinner. A little while later, Hunter comes to Zara's rooms to escort her into the dining area. Before they leave, we see a personal relationship developing between them which is definitely NOT military in nature.
>
> On the way to the dining area, they stop off and enter the war room. Zara is awe-struck; as she scans the room, she's seeing something akin to the Eighth Wonder of the World. Floor-to-ceiling fiber optic maps of every country in the world being flashed on screens; wall-to-wall computers; ultra-sophisticated microwave transmitters and receivers; and a multitude of consoles performing unbelievable functions.
>
> Byrne-White, Dallas and Eggstrum, who were already in the war room, join Zara and Hunter as they move on to the dining area. Once there, the two visitors meet the rest of the 60-man unit, all resplendent in their dress military uniforms.[43]

There is no further reference to Zara in the synopsis, not even to her relationship with Hunter "which is definitely NOT military in nature." In Harold Livingston's October 20, 1977, Rough First Draft of "In Thy Image" before Khambatta was cast, Ilia's "stunning figure" was described as "hardly military." Nothing is less military than femininity![44]

Megaforce is "based on a story" by Robert S. Kachler, and the screenplay is credited to "James Whittaker and Albert S. Ruddy & Hal Needham & Andre Morgan." This is an astounding number of cooks for a thin gruel, and who contributed what is unknown, but it is my theory that the "Zara wants to go on the mission but can't because of reasons that totally *aren't* because she's an icky girl, honest" subplot was added by Needham himself.

* * *

This is what happened. In 1970 Hal Needham formed an organization called Stunts Unlimited, and they started admitting women in September 1976, one of whom was Kitty O'Neil. It was soon announced that O'Neil and Needham were going to attempt to break the women's land speed record and the overall record respectively in William Fredrick's "supersonic rocket car" known as the SMI Motivator at El Mirage Dry Lake in Nevada. (Fredrick would later build many of the vehicles in *Megaforce*.) Because of logistical complications the attempts couldn't be made until early December, at which time Needham was unavailable because he was working on his directorial debut *Smokey and the Bandit*.[45]

Kitty O'Neil drove the SMI Motivator across the Alvord Desert at 321 mph on Saturday, December 4, breaking Lee Breedlove's 1965 record of 307 mph. O'Neil reached 524 mph the following day; when asked what it was like to drive that fast, O'Neil replied, "It's just beautiful. It's just spooky." But she also said 524 mph "wasn't scary enough," and she and Fredrick were confident she could break the world record of 622.407 mph. O'Neil hit 591 mph in a test run on Monday, December 6, and her attempt to break the record was scheduled for the very next day.[46]

She was preparing to witness the beautiful spookiness of 750 mph on Tuesday when Hal Needham derailed her by threatening a lawsuit. Needham said he knew O'Neil could pull it off because she was "a very talented little lady," but that O'Neil and Fredrick "got impressed with themselves, started dreaming and forgot to read the contract." The contract limited O'Neil to an average speed of 400 mph, which was enough to break Breedlove's girly record while leaving the far manlier world record intact for Needham. "Yeah, I guess you could put it that I was a spoiler, but your word is your bond," said the man who was editing a fictional film about the joys of breaking the law and doing your own thing by driving very fast, but who was not about to let someone else violate the terms of a legal contract in real life by doing their own thing and driving very fast.[47]

Needham's memoir *Stuntman!* does not acknowledge the existence of Kitty O'Neil, *Megaforce*, or Persis Khambatta, and the SMI Motivator incident was five years and eight movies before the 1981 filming of *Megaforce*, so it being an inspiration for Zara's subplot is speculation. Also of interest is that a stuntwoman named Heidi Von Beltz had been in a car crash during the *Cannonball Run* shoot in June 1980 which had left her paraplegic; she filed a $35M lawsuit against *Cannonball*'s production team in June 1981. The lawsuit included but was not limited to Hal Needham, who was working on the *Megaforce* script at the time and did not exist in a vacuum.[48]

* * *

It is difficult to discern the boundary between insult and injury in Khambatta's career, but both were in ample supply in Robin Sloan's syndicated column on July 15, 1982, by which time *Megaforce* had left most first-run theaters.

> Q. Can you tell me whatever happened to that bald girl who was in the "Star Trek" movie? I don't remember seeing her in any film since then.
>
> A. You most likely have seen actress Persis Khambatta since then, but you probably just haven't recognized her. With her black tresses the one-time Miss India contestant in the Miss Universe Pageant looks far different from the smooth-domed intergalactic character she portrayed aboard the Enterprise. After her next role, in "Nighthawks" opposite Sylvester Stallone, people told her that they loved her performance but didn't know until the end credits it was she. Chances are better she'll be recognized in the new action adventure picture "MegaForce"—she's the only woman in the film.[49]

While that column was propagating on July 17, Persis Khambatta finally got the opportunity to win back her blackjack money: she traveled to Vancouver to be one of the celebrities participating in a $125-per-ticket "offshore legal gambling cruise" on the *MV Britannia*. She was described by the *Vancouver Sun*'s Denny Boyd as "lithe Persis Khambatta, who shaved her head for Star Trek," and the most notable of the cruise's other celebrities was the comedian Rip Taylor. Boyd described Taylor as "the one who cries," which is as reductive a view of Taylor as Khambatta being the one "who shaved her head for Star Trek"—and while this author could go on at length about the confetti-tossing madman, she will save it for *Presenting Rip Taylor*.[50]

The Whitewashing of Octopussy

"I'm going to be honest. I'm sick to death of talking about hair." Thus spake Persis Khambatta in a profile by Diana Maychick which ran in the July 10 *New York Post*.[51]

> I never dreamed it would cause so much fuss. It's as if people don't realize the stuff grows. In fact, I've had my hair cut a couple times since the movie. But the one good thing now to come out of all the attention to my head is that I still have my privacy. Not too many people recognize me with a full head. It's funny, but [producer] Marty Poll saw *Star Trek* and wanted me for *Nighthawks*. I was grateful—he let me have hair in that film. Everybody forgets that *Megaforce* is not my first movie with hair.[52]

People not realizing the stuff grows could account for why Walter Koenig had written that he was startled to see that Khambatta's hair had grown in half an inch overnight in August 1978. But whatever the status of her hair four years later, she was optimistic that her skin could be an asset: "With my coloring I can play lots of ethnic groups: Italian, Spanish, French, South American, you name it. I have to be versatile. How many roles are there specifically for an Indian woman?"[53]

Not many, and there was no guarantee that a role for an Indian woman would be played by an Indian woman. One such role for which Khambatta had been considered earlier that year was the title character in the James Bond picture, *Octopussy*. (According to uncredited writer John Strong III, *Octopussy* was set in India because Strong's treatment for the 1981 *For Your Eyes Only* "had an Indian background and though the film wasn't shot in India, the idea caught on." India: it's a meme!) The Bond pictures were known for using non-white women such as Mie Hama and Akiko Wakabayashi in 1967's *You Only Live Twice*, or Gloria Hendry in 1973's *Live and Let Die*. That was only three roles in two out of the dozen films produced thus far, and one of those parts was played by a Black American—who could never be on *Charlie's Angels*, by some reckonings—but it still brings us to Maud Adams.[54]

Persis Khambatta and the Sweden-born Adams had crossed paths more than once: they were both presenters at the Saturn Awards in July 1980, and Adams attended the opening night of La Cage in April 1981. Adams started out as a model, and while she had some high-profile roles such as Guy Hamilton's 1974 James Bond picture *The Man with the Golden Gun* and Norman Jewison's *Rollerball* in 1975, she found it difficult to get the kinds of parts she wanted. Her most recent theatrical picture was Bob Brooks' controversial 1981 *Tattoo*, in which Adams played a model who was kidnapped and non-consensually inked by an artist played by Bruce Dern. The full nudity was risky enough, and things got far worse for Adams when Dern claimed their sex scenes had been real. It was why Adams was more than happy to accept a role in a television series called *Chicago Story*, which she hoped would repair the specific damage done to her reputation by Dern and *Tattoo*, and help her move beyond the general typecasting as "the beautiful woman in an action-adventure movie." *Chicago Story* premiered in the spring of 1982 and was canceled in June. At the time of this writing, the stud who claimed to have had real sex with Maud Adams onscreen remains a sought-after character actor, having appeared in nine feature films and two television shows in 2019 alone, and the slut who denied having had real sex with Bruce Dern onscreen did not find much work after 1990.[55]

While Adams was shooting *Chicago Story* in early 1982, casting director Jane Jenkins received a most exciting call: Albert "Cubby" Broccoli requesting Jenkins' services for the new James Bond picture. Debbie McWilliams was doing the majority of the casting in London, but Cubby and company wanted to expand their search for the new Bond Girl beyond Blighty. Secrecy was always the order of the day, so all Jenkins knew was that they were looking for an "exotic East Indian dark-skinned beauty." Jenkins reflected in her 2009 memoir *A Star Is Found* that in 1982 "Hollywood was a lot whiter and more European than it is now, and I just couldn't find a dark-skinned actress who fit the bill." Among those she "looked at" were "actual ethnic Indians" such as Persis Khambatta and Susie Coelho, and white Canadian performer Barbara Parkins made it as far as an audition because she could "pass for Indian." Then Cubby saw an ABC broadcast of *The Man with the Golden Gun* in May and decided to cast Adams.[56]

A press release from August 1982 featured a quote from Cubby which demonstrated that Hollywood puffery and chicanery was by no means limited to Southern California: "We have followed Maud's amazing development as an actress over the past years; and I have long thought of the possibility of using her again if the part was right. As the screenplay was being written, it became obvious that Maud would be perfect in this important role." Jenkins wrote in her 2009 book that she was opposed to the decision, but "luckily, I kept my mouth shut, made some calls, and managed to get Adams on board—the only woman in the history of the series who ever appeared in two Bond movies." Lois Maxwell had appeared as Miss Moneypenny in all twelve movies thus far, but she didn't count since Bond never had sex with her, and Jenkins' relief that "luckily, I kept my mouth shut" would require another book to unpack. As for Adams as Octopussy, Jenkins wrote that "they dyed her hair, the writers threw in some lines about her having been raised by an Indian family, and as far as the producers were concerned, problem solved." The idea that a child's hair changes to match the color of her adoptive family is dopey beyond belief, but if those lines were ever filmed they were edited out. Nor did hairdresser Jeanette Freeman receive the memo, since not only is Maud Adams' mane the same chestnut-brown it had been in *Chicago Story*, the color is identical to her costar Roger Moore's mop. The film *Octopussy* never reveals the title character's real name or family history, but we see a picture of her very white father, whom she describes as "a leading authority on octopi" in a way that someone whose father was a leading authority on cephalopods would never phrase it. She also explains that "Octopussy" was her father's pet name for her, which is grody even by the standards of James Bond films.[57]

The bottom line is that instead of hiring an Indian performer to play what was conceived of as an Indian character, the producers hired a white performer and scrubbed all non-whiteness other than her living in India and occasionally wearing a sari. Oh, and Octopussy is the leader of a cult of mostly white women who wear saris and other Indian garb when not in bright orange spandex, while her main henchman is named Kamal Khan and favors Nehru jackets but is played by French actor Louis Jordan making no attempt made to hide his Gallic accent because it was a James Bond film and nothing mattered. Make no mistake: *Octopussy* would *not* have been improved by putting Adams in brownface, or even just darkening her hair and including a line about her having been raised by an Indian family as Jenkins misremembered. But in this case, the fear of the exotic Other resulted in a terrible and dated film which would have been more terribly dated had the producers not erred on the side of white supremacy.

Jenkins later ruminated in *A Star Is Found* that the "big picture" is that "actors, agents, and managers" are focused on "getting the actor a job," and that they assume the performer being "good-looking or talented enough" is going to tip the scales. "Sometimes, of course, it does—but usually only at the Star level. Yes, they rewrote a few lines in *Octopussy* to cast Maud Adams, and I suppose after telling that story, I'll never again have any credibility when I insist on ethnic-appropriate casting." Y'think? After pouring one out for her credibility, Jenkins then added: "But that film was very much the exception." Okay, then! *Octopussy* is not a glaring example of systemic racism: it is an "exception." One which proves the rule, but an exception all the same.[58]

Some Kind of Hero: The Remarkable Story of the James Bond Films co-author Ajay Chowdhury told the *Telegraph* in 2016 that the role of Octopussy "was going to go to the Indian beauty, Persis Khambatta, 'but for various reasons that did not happen.'" Chowdhury did not reveal what those various reasons were in the interview, and the book *Some Kind of Hero* itself relates Jenkins' *A Star Is Found* anecdote—no shade on Chowdhury for that, since *Presenting Persis Khambatta* does the same—while also revealing that *Octopussy* director John Glen had looked into Grace Jones and Cybill Shepherd.[59]

So it could have been worse, but that makes it no less of a shame that nobody tried to do better.

The Prime Minister of India Meets the Pride of India

It is unknown whether Persis Khambatta was aware that she was under consideration for *Octopussy* in 1982, but on the day *Daily Variety* announced the casting of Maud Adams, Khambatta had an encounter which had a more profound and positive impact on her life than starring in a terrible James Bond film would have.

Two years after having been re-elected Prime Minister, Indira Gandhi was on a tour of the United States. Late in the afternoon of Tuesday, August 3, she spoke to about seventy members of the Los Angeles Indian community in the Century Plaza Hotel's Pacific Palisades Room. Among those present were Khambatta and her ex-boyfriend and now regular-friend Kabir Bedi (who would fly to London a week and a half later to start work as one of the few Indian actors with a speaking role in *Octopussy*) as well as musician Ravi Shankar, conductor Zubin Mehta, and Vijay Amritraj's brother Ashok. Vijay missed Gandhi's speech, due to being one of the other Indian actors with a speaking role in *Octopussy*, though in 1986 he would go on to be the first male Indian actor with a speaking role in a Star Trek film—and as a non-exotic human starship captain, no less.[60]

Gandhi encouraged the audience to continue their good work in the United States while keeping India in their thoughts, and "help build bridges of friendship between the peoples of the two countries." She noted with relief that "the image of India with a begging bowl is no more," and that the country was now seen as "a mass of people working together to surmount the several problems"—one of the biggest of which was the poverty which could be traced back to the British occupation. The exhausted Prime Minister apologized for not being able to spend more time with her fellow Indians, but on her way out she saw one whom couldn't fail to speak to. And so it was that Indira Gandhi offered her hand to Persis Khambatta; when one of Gandhi's entourage scrambled to introduce Khambatta, the Prime Minister said, "Who doesn't know Persis? She is the pride of India. She has done India proud." Ecstatic about this unexpected encounter, Khambatta told *India West* that Gandhi's handshake "meant more to me than shaking the hand of any film star in this world!" She would later write in *Pride of India*[61]:

> The magnitude of her comment moved me deeply and has stayed with me ever since. I was blessed to blossom in India's garden of beauty and venture through the paradise of this world. I've always wanted to do something for our Indian women, celebrate them in some extraordinary way. And I had considered three ideas to honour them: a charity show, a movie and a book.[62]

Two of those ideas would eventually happen. In the meantime, Khambatta continued to participate in Indian-themed events in the United States, including the second annual India Independence Day celebration at the Los Angeles Civic Center Mall on Saturday, August 14. She also appeared as a model at a Fendi fur fashion show on Wednesday, September 8; one of her fellow catwalkers was Maud Adams, back in the States during a break in the filming of *Octopussy*.[63]

Though Khambatta had no other films lined up, the Fashion82 column of the *Los Angeles Times* reported on October 8 that "the actress who shaved her head to appear in 'Star Trek: The Motion Picture' three years ago, is now into another form of futuristic fashion" in the form of inflatable plastic boots.[64]

> Khambatta puts them on as part of a body-contouring program at Clinic Les Champs, says owner Mila Moarsi. "The boots are attached to an air pump that helps energize sluggish blood and reduce puffiness and cellulite," Moarsi says. But when it comes to booting herself into shape, Khambatta is as erratic as anybody, it seems. Says Moarsi, "Persis comes every day before she makes a movie. But once she gets down to size, she doesn't come back for six months."[65]

Celebrities who have to live up to impossible beauty standards: they're just like us!

She was reunited with Rip Taylor in Canada later that month as a guest on *The Alan Thicke Show*—in this writer's headcanon, Khambatta and Taylor became lifelong besties—and she appeared in another Beverly Hills fur fashion show in November. On the three-year anniversary of the release of the film that was supposed to make her a star, she attended the UNICEF-benefit Los Angeles premiere of Richard Attenborough's *Gandhi*, where *India West* observed that among the 1400 attendees, "there were nearly 100 people from the Indian community including such celebrities as Persis Khambatta and the Amritraj brothers."[66]

Khambatta was not in *Gandhi*, though by the end of October it had leaked to the trades that she would appear on producer David Wolper's television series *Casablanca*, which was a prequel to the 1942 Michael Curtiz film. The *Hollywood Reporter* noted that in addition to being Khambatta's "first venture into episodic TV," her role would be "a romantic Moroccan, a huge departure from the militaristic characters she has played in features." By the end of 1982 she had finished her one-episode obligation, which would prove to be the last of the five episodes produced.[67]

1983

Devi, Coelho, and Khambatta

Persis Khambatta kicked off the new year by appearing on the cover of the January 1983 *Popular Photography*. There was no content about her in the magazine itself, but it was clear that she still loved the camera, and the camera still loved her back. She also appeared on *The Merv Griffin Show* that month alongside Virginia Ferry, Hala Maksoud, and Joanna Lumley for what a newspaper ad called a panel of "'International Women'—With Outspoken Representatives of France, India, England and Lebanon.'" An interstitial blurb for *Merv* on that same page also promised "A Gorilla Who 'Talks'!" I was unable to track down a copy of the episode, but I suspect the producers gave the, ahem, "gorilla who 'talks'!" equal if not more airtime than the "outspoken" women.[1]

Margo Skinner noted in the January 13 edition of the Bay Area–based *Asian Week* that "Persis Khambatta, the beauty from India ('Star Trek I') has guest starred on an episode of the forthcoming series, 'Casablanca.'" Khambatta attended a reception at the private residence of India's director general of tourism that month and was reunited with her friend Loretta Swit at a Julie Andrews-hosted Operation California fundraiser for a Saigon orphanage on February 11.[2]

Khambatta was in a mood to celebrate that day, having received a game-changing call from producer Robert Evans. He had thought of Khambatta when he read an Associated Press story about 27-year-old "bandit queen" Phoolan Devi, who was about to formally surrender to the authorities in India's Chambal Valley. Though Evans was deep in the pre-production quagmires of what would become the 1984 Francis Ford Coppola film *The Cotton Club*, he knew Triillusion had been looking for a project, and as far as the Kid was concerned Devi's story was tailor-made for Khambatta. Khambatta agreed, and she went to India for two months in 1983 to do research and arrange the below-the-line money.[3]

Khambatta was not the only South Asian woman trying to make a go of it in white-supremacist Hollywood to be inspired by Phoolan Devi's story. Born in England and raised in Paris, Susie Coelho had never been to India, did not speak Hindi or Gujarati, and downplayed her heritage to the extent that she refused to see Attenborough's *Gandhi*. "I dreamed of being blond, blue-eyed, big-boobed and with hips and calves like American girls," Coelho told the UPI's Vernon Scott. "I didn't want to be different. It was only a couple of years ago, after marrying Sonny, that I could deal with the fact that I'm exotic." (Recall that when Khambatta told Scott she was trying to move beyond her exotic image, Scott headlined the piece "Exotic is the Word for Persis."[4])

Coelho told syndicated columnist Dick Kleiner that "I dreamed about [Devi] for weeks" after reading the AP article, "until finally Sonny was exasperated with me and said, 'Look, if you like the story so much, go to India and get it.'" Kleiner described Coelho in that column as "the color of mocha mousse" and as having grown up "out of place" as "an exotic, dark-eyed, dark-haired child," and wrote that while she "turned her exotic looks into an asset and became a successful model," Coelho still believed "she would have been more successful if she had been fairer, and feels strongly that dark people are always being discriminated against here." Kleiner did not note that Coelho's strong feelings about discrimination against dark people in the United States had the benefit of being true.[5]

With Sonny Bono's exasperated blessing, Coelho traveled to India for the first time in April 1983, bringing journalist Rakesh Mathur as both guide and translator. Phoolan Devi was imprisoned in the town of Gwalior, and Coelho did further research during the six days she had to wait there before meeting Devi. As Coelho later told Vernon Scott, "I learned Phoolan was married off by her parents to a 40-year-old man when she was only 11. When the marriage ended she was kidnapped by dacoits and raped. She eventually became the mistress of the gang leader. When the leader was killed, Phoolan became the bandit queen and swore revenge for her lover's death by wiping out his dacoit killers." Coelho told Scott that she soon won Devi's confidence and friendship and learned that her story was even more dramatic than what had been printed thus far. Most importantly, Coelho said she won Devi's permission both to write her life story and to star in the film version. (Phoolan Devi makes no mention of being visited by Coelho in *I, Phoolan Devi: The Autobiography of India's Bandit Queen*, which claims to be based on recordings of Devi telling her life story in the summer of 1994 and transcribed into book form by writers Marie-Thérèse Cuny and Paul Rambali.) Khambatta spent much of 1983 setting up her own film version, though her research trips to India did not include visiting Devi. She could have pulled the necessary strings, but as she later put it, "as an actress, I think it would have had a negative effect."[6]

Another potential negative effect came in the form of the ABC broadcast of the 1983 cut of *Star Trek—The Motion Picture* on Sunday, February 20, the first time it was available to a wide audience after leaving first-run theaters in March 1980. (The 1979 cut had been available on VHS since October 1980, but I as explain in some detail in my previous book *The First Star Trek Movie*, VCRs and video rentals were still a luxury item.) Linda Gross was kinder than most in her *Los Angeles Times* preview blurb; while acknowledging that much of the film "is sluggish and lacks stirring action," she wrote that Khambatta and Stephen Collins are "both attractive players" who "carry the film's parable of looking toward some higher evolution." Gross did describe Khambatta as "of the shaved head," but unlike the many other writers who had mentioned her past baldness, it was in the context of the film for which Khambatta had shaved her head.[7]

The Persis Khambatta of the full head of hair was among the "more than 120 Southern California Indians" whom *India West* described as having "jammed the dining room of the China Palace restaurant in Anaheim" on April 2 for a Nargis Dutt Memorial Foundation fundraiser. It may have been a welcome distraction, for the Academy had just announced that three of Khambatta's former colleagues would be involved with that year's Awards: both William Shatner and the producer of the as-yet-unaired *Casablanca* series David Wolper would present at the 1983 Oscar telecast on April 11, while Robert Wise would moderate the Foreign Language Film Nominees Symposium at the Beverly Hilton on April 9. The press release noted that in previous years, "Shatner presented the Documentary Film Awards along with Persis Khambatta" and "Wolper presented the Documentary Features and Documentary Short Subjects Awards with Mia Farrow." Wolper returned to the 1985 Oscars to receive the Jean Hersholt Humanitarian Award for reasons that seemed to be related to Wolper producing the 1984 Olympics, while Shatner returned as a presenter in 1987 by virtue of having been the star of one of the most profitable films of 1986. Khambatta and Mia Farrow were not asked to return in 1983 or any future year, and their humanitarian work went unacknowledged by the Academy. It should also come as no surprise that Khambatta was not included in the 1999 Oscar telecast's In Memoriam montage after her 1998 death.[8]

Khambatta participated in a three-hour telethon for Jeff Bridges' charity organization End Hunger on Friday, April 9, 1983. The following Monday, Richard Attenborough's *Gandhi* swept the Oscars, including John Mollo and Bhanu Athaiya winning Best Costume Design, the latter becoming the first Indian to win an Oscar two years after Khambatta became the first to present at the ceremony. The day after the 1983 Oscar telecast, the "Pix, People, Pickups" column in *Daily Variety* announced that "Frank Hildebrand has joined Continental Motion Pictures and will oversee 'Warrior of The Lost World,' which will star Robert Ginty, Persis Khambatta and Donald Pleasence."[9]

Donald Pleasence's bald head was a part of his screen persona by the early 1980s; also famous for being bald at least once was Khambatta, who got an unpleasant shout-out in a book published that May titled *George Michael's Complete Hair Care for Men*.

> Unless you can make being bald pay off handsomely in the grand manner of Yul Brynner or Telly Savalas, if you're a man you would rather have a full head of hair than not. As for women, there isn't one in the whole world (with the exception of Persis Khambatta, who starred in the first *Star Trek* movie) who would choose to be bald.[10]

See, it's funny because ... oh, never mind.

I Visited the Lost World and All I Got Was This Lousy Hairline Fracture

Though Persis Khambatta did not regret turning down parts which had required nudity like *Cat People* or *Conan the Barbarian*, she knew she needed more (clothed) exposure to land the romantic and comedy roles she craved, which meant being in front of the motion picture camera as much as possible, which meant making pictures like David Worth's *Warrior of the Lost World*. As she explained it to *India West* in June 1983[11]:

> In a sense I used to be very, very snobbish about my career. I wouldn't do films unless I really like the role. The most important thing for me is to be working and to have the experience of working, instead of waiting for the right role. I've done eight films in eight years. Every year I did a film and that was all my need was. Now I'm saying one movie a year is not really helping me out to be known.[12]

Warrior was an old-school exploitation film in many ways, including being pre-sold at the Cannes Film Market in May on the strength of the poster, which already been printed in *Variety* in April before principal photography began. By that reckoning the first Star Trek movie was no less of an exploitation film, just on a much grander scale. (How it was exploited is detailed in my previous book *The First Star Trek Movie*.) *Warrior* was also old-school in that Khambatta had signed producer Frank Hildebrand's contract with the understanding that the film's budget was $3M, but when she arrived on the set in Rome in the latter days of April 1983, Khambatta discovered the budget was only $1M. Having learned from the Robert Wise and Hal Needham films that megabudgets were no indicator of a motion picture's quality or success, she looked at *Warrior* as a learning experience, and a new way to think of being an actress.[13]

It was fast and cheap work which Jill Clayburgh would not have accepted, to be sure; the shooting schedule was only five weeks, and

Khambatta had to do her own stunts. The hidden blessing of that fast cheapness was that she could make a creative contribution in a way which had not been possible in the slow and expensive Hollywood movies. Like *Megaforce*'s Zara, her *Warrior* character of Nastasia was defined by being the daughter of an important man who needed the help of the male hero. When Khambatta realized that Robert Ginty's title Warrior did not like Nastasia but they still had to come together at the end, she invented a bonding moment in which the Warrior saved Nastasia from a fall. There were no dummies for cutaway shots nor wires to hold her like her mineshaft plummet in *The Wilby Conspiracy* nine years earlier, and certainly not that production's half-dozen stuntmen waiting to catch her. *Warrior of the Lost World*'s budget did not even provide for a mattress to cover the wire bars, broken glass, and stones on the ground, and Khambatta received a hairline fracture from the stunt. Then again, *Warrior*'s budget was 1/44th that of the first Star Trek movie, and the latter's multitude of filmmakers could not be bothered to protect Khambatta's flesh from being scorched or her eyes from being blinded.[14]

Khambatta went into the *Warrior* stunt knowing that the worst could happen, and as she told *India West* after filming wrapped, "if I was going to be dropped, that was my karma anyway." On the subject of her karma vis-à-vis injuries sustained on film sets and the crew making no attempt to prevent those injuries, the current issue of *Starlog* featured an article with Sam Nicholson, who had co-created the lighting effects for the finale of the first Star Trek movie. Nicholson described the sequence as using "about 50,000 watts [emphasis in original article] of incandescent luminescence on two people from a distance of only six feet," and he brushed off the damage done to Khambatta's eyes: "I suppose the best thing about the experience was that we all got great suntans."[15]

But the stunts which injured Khambatta in that one movie—the dry ice which gave her tonsillitis and almost poisoned her, the small light which seared her flesh, the large lights which seared her eyes—made it into all three official versions, while the stunt which fractured her shoulder is not in *Warrior of the Lost World*, which is all the stranger considering *Warrior* does not play like a film in which an action sequence would have been left on the cutting-room floor. Perhaps film editors were just that allergic to anything which may have developed a Persis Khambatta character, even with a full head of hair.

The Perils of Persis on the Idiot Box

While shooting *Warrior of the Lost World* in Italy, Persis Khambatta hung out with her old friend Robert De Niro and new friend Liza Minnelli when they were both vacationing in Rome, so the trip was by no means a waste. When Khambatta returned to the United States in June she bought a West Hollywood penthouse, and she was also briefly engaged to a stock investor from India, a relationship which like so many before and after went nowhere.[16]

There is evidence that Khambatta underwent surgery circa 1983. Depending on which of her obituaries you believe, it was either a cardiac valve operation, open-heart surgery, or a coronary bypass. In 1986 an interviewer would refer to it as "your earlier open-heart surgery," and Khambatta did not correct them on either the nature of the operation or its very existence.[17]

Megaforce made its pay-cable premiere in July, and while it was nowhere to be found when the nominations for the 10th annual Saturn Awards were announced, Khambatta was a presenter at the ceremony on July 30. Her next public appearance was alongside Kabir Bedi at the third annual India Independence Day celebration at the Los Angeles Civic Center Mall on August 13. The temperature was a record-breaking 98 degrees, but Khambatta soon traded the dry California heat for Florida's more familiar tropical humidity when she was one of the celebrity judges of the Miss Teen USA pageant at the Lakeland Civic Arena. Khambatta appeared on the second and third of its three non-consecutive nights, the last of which was broadcast live on CBS on August 30.[18]

She was featured the following Saturday in a broadcast which was more of a stillbirth: "Divorce, Casablanca Style," the fifth and final episode of 1983 Oscar presenter David Wolper's *Casablanca*. The first three episodes had been broadcast in April before the show's May cancelation, and the exposure Khambatta hoped it would provide was mitigated by it being a late-summer burn-off of the latest notorious flop she was now associated with—inasmuch as she could be associated with something which hardly anybody was aware existed.[19]

Casablanca was a product of the post–*Raiders of the Lost Ark* vogue for old-timey colonial adventures, including television series such as *Tales of the Gold Monkey* (starring Stephen Collins) and *Bring 'Em Back Alive*, and feature films too numerous to mention. Persis Khambatta is introduced in "Divorce, Casablanca Style" wearing a hijab for the first and last time in her screen career, and she is being assaulted for neither the first nor the last time: her character Amira is hit twice by her husband, who says "I divorce you" both times. Rick prevents the husband from making it official with a third strike, though Amira does not react much better when Rick puts his hands on her shoulders from behind. Outside the Café Américain, Amira explains to Rick that she cannot stay at her husband's home and no man will ever marry her because she is not a virgin, so she has to go home to her own family. Rick suggests she get a job, and while Amira first scoffs at the idea, she soon comes around and asks for a starter loan. And get started she does, though by the end of the episode the *status quo* is restored as Amira abandons her business and is last seen back in the hijab with her abusive husband and I don't want to talk about *Casablanca* anymore.

* * *

The 1980 *Men Who Rate a '10'* may have been the nadir of Khambatta's television specials, but there was more terribleness to come in 1983 and beyond. She could be glimpsed with Sandahl Bergman, Loretta Swit, and Khambatta's fellow "obvious Charlie misfit" Jayne Kennedy in footage of a fashion show at the Century Plaza Hotel in an overstuffed yet vague NBC special titled *The Best of Everything* on September 18. What was it about? What does it matter?[20]

Though Khambatta was keeping her percolating Phoolan Devi project under wraps, *Daily Variety* formalized Susie Coelho's on November 11: "Susie Bono has acquired rights to the bio of Phoolan Devi, 26-year-old 'bandit queen' of central India, who surrendered to Indian authorities earlier this year. Bono is negotiating for book and film rights to 'The Bandit Queen.'" Margo Skinner did not mention Coelho in her roundup of busy Indian artists in *Asian Week* that December, though she did mention that Khambatta had been one of the Miss Teen USA judges and a presenter at the Saturn Awards, and also predicted that Khambatta would be seen in the movie *Warrior of the Lost World* "at Christmas time." In fairness, Skinner did not specify Christmas of which year.[21]

1984

The Saints of Imperfection

Whether she liked it or not (and she did not), Persis Khambatta continued to be associated with female baldness. She had been name-checked in an August 1983 *El Paso Times* article about Danny and Lavina Vaswani, a local couple who had moved from India to the United States in 1971, the same year Khambatta moved to England. (Lavina had been one of the finalists in the 1969 Miss India pageant, so it is possible she and Khambatta had crossed paths.) The Vaswanis opened a restaurant and four retail stores after settling in Texas in 1977, but there was a dark turn: a 1982 brain scan revealed that the severe headaches Lavina had been experiencing since 1973 were due to a tumor. The subsequent surgery required her to shave her head, and looking back on it, Lavina's husband Danny joked to the reporter, "she was only trying to imitate Persis Khambatta." In the long run, Khambatta would lose her fight against being identified with having been bald in that one movie that one time, but this was one of the first times that her voluntary and quite temporary baldness was invoked in a positive way regarding a woman who had lost her hair for less pleasant reasons.[1]

A February 1984 Fort Myers *News-Press* article about a Florida woman with the disease *alopecia universalis* began by ruminating that "Ilia, exotic creature from the planet Delta and a crewmember of the Starship Enterprise, was beautifully bald. With the movie 'Star Trek,' baldness took on a glamour and sexiness it had never known. But that was Hollywood." The rest of the article was about how the Florida woman had come to terms with her hairlessness, concluding that "as she takes off her wig for the photographer, another advantage becomes apparent—she has a nicely shaped little head, and smooth as baby's skin. Perhaps not quite like Persis Khambatta of 'Star Trek' fame ... but nothing to be ashamed of." The article began by only referencing the character of Ilia, but ended by referring to Khambatta herself, again without clarifying that she had been hairless by choice, and only temporarily.[2]

The Florida and Texas articles would have gone unseen by Khambatta unless she had a clipping service, but the opening paragraph in an April 1984 *People* article about an up-and-coming Swedish model was more likely to be a ping on her radar.

> Her name is Jenny O. And in a fashion world accustomed to the luxurious tresses of Christie Brinkley and Cheryl Tiegs, she is an arresting sight indeed. Sure, Telly Savalas and Yul Brynner have been telling us for years that bald is beautiful, but they are, after all, men. And, yes, an Indian actress named Persis Khambatta adopted a hairless pate for the first Star Trek movie, but that was only temporary. The thing about Jenny O is that she is completely and irrevocably bald, and has been since she was 4, as a result of hormone deficiencies.[3]

Consider *People*'s phrasing: the use of "and, yes" suggests the writer knew the reader was already thinking about Khambatta, because you can't *not* mention Khambatta when talking about bald women in 1984, though it was one of the few to acknowledge that her hairlessness had been temporary.

Jenny O had already been written up in the March 18 *New York Times*, and she appeared on the cover of that month's issue of the Italian fashion magazine *Donna*. While the *Times* article did not mention Khambatta, Ms. O—who wore a wig when not on the clock "because I don't want to cause a sensation in daily life"—acknowledged the fleeting nature of her own fame: "Right now, modeling for me is an ego boost, but I know that I will be a craze for six months and it will be over. That's what usually happens in the fashion world. I'll just enjoy myself until something new comes along." She was described as "hard to miss" due to being "tall, long-limbed, and totally bald" in a May 31 *Philadelphia Inquirer* article about the vogue for androgyny in the fashion world. The problematic way the *Inquirer* headline "The Gender Blenders: Appearances Sometimes are Deceiving as Androgyny Comes into Style" equates androgyny with deception is simultaneously beyond the scope of this book and also illustrates the theme of this book, for the cisgender Persis Khambatta was punished for violating the gender binary by shaving her head (like women are not supposed to) yet refusing to take her clothes off (like women are supposed to). A few months later *Vogue* printed a picture of Jenny O with the caption, "Though she privately wears one of six wigs, Swedish-born model Jenny O is known worldwide for her startling bald head."[4]

(Think of a woman without hair. Boo! You're startled. It's startling.)

Jenny O's prediction about her own shelf life was on the money. She had signed with the modeling agency Click, and a December 1985 *Washington Post* article about Click said the agency was "too weird to last" due to its tendency to sign people like Ms. O or the long-haired male model Attila: "In its willingness to take on the new and untried, the criticism goes,

Click signs up models clients don't want to hire. Jenny O and Attila don't work much anymore." I could not find any references to Ms. O after 1985, and the non-paywalled, Google-indexed Internet does not seem aware she existed; the only Jenny O on Wikipedia at the time of this writing is a singer who was born in 1989. Our Ms. O sat for photographer Alex Kayser's book *Heads*, a study of bald heads which was first published in 1987 and reprinted as recently as 1997 in which her picture is captioned as "Jenny O., New York City: antique dealer and fashion model," but that appears to be it. If Persis Khambatta was aware of Jenny O's existence, she may have hoped that this young Swedish woman would inherent her mantle as the icon of female baldness. It was not to be.[5]

The Battle of the Bandit Queens

While Jenny O was challenging the fashion world with her baldness, Persis Khambatta was challenging the film world with her boldness: the time had come to announce her Phoolan Devi project. *India Today*'s Eye-catchers column reported on the Ides of March in 1984 that Khambatta, who "manages to squeeze her lithe frame into the limelight wherever she may be," had "announced her intention to co-produce a film, for which she claimed she had roped in an American producer and the Hollywood star Omar Sharif." She also hoped it would be directed by Rahul Rawail, helmer of the Hindi hit *Betaab*. (To put it in perspective with her Hollywood career, this announcement came two weeks after Khambatta appeared on *All-Star Family Feud* alongside Rita Moreno and Adrian Zmed.) The *India Today* piece neither said what the film was about nor whether Khambatta would be in it, but the following day's *Hollywood Reporter* had many juicy details, particularly that she would star as Phoolan Devi in a film titled *The Bandit Queen* to be coproduced by Khambatta's Triillusion Co. and Ray Hafeez's Zeray Entertainment. Logan Clarke and Harry Butler had written the script, and Khambatta expected the roughly–$5M production to start filming in India, Pakistan, and/or Morocco in September 1984, provided the financing was firmed up by mid–April.[6]

Khambatta made no bones about why she was interested in *The Bandit Queen*, telling the *Hollywood Reporter*'s Alan L. Gansberg that she was putting it together "because of the difficulties in getting women's roles." It also helped that this "adventure-romance action movie" was "a strong woman's role" and "absolutely tailor-made for me." For as much as she danced around the F-bomb in those days, particularly as the definition of feminism was evolving in a male-dominated business which was decades away from the #MeToo movement of the late 2010s, Khambatta flat-out said she was creating a role that was a strong woman. Even if one chooses to parse the phrase "a strong woman's role" as a strong role *for* a woman rather than a role which is that *of* a strong woman, the fact remains that she was attempting to chart her own course and make her own decisions. Khambatta described the role of Devi as "challenging. It's about a woman's growth, her strength and determination, and how she rose from adversity." And though it would be based on an Indian woman, she described Devi's travails as "a woman's story" rather than an Indian story, and she was open about gearing her take toward American commercial tastes by focusing on the "romantic adventure angle."[7]

Persis Khambatta was unconcerned that others were also working on films about Phoolan Devi, or that those others may have had legal rights which she did not possess: "Phoolan Devi has been written about so much in the newspapers that she's in public domain. It's a matter of who gets there first." For Susie Coelho the project was both a career move and a way of connecting with her long-shunned Indian heritage, but having been crowned Miss India when she was 18 meant Khambatta had nothing left to prove regarding her own heritage, making it a career move first and foremost.[8]

Producer Ray Hafeez was getting bids for *The Bandit Queen* from major studios by late April 1984, while Khambatta was waiting to hear back on two "hot" (read: not Indian) stars and looking for someone new to direct the picture. For as much as she'd wanted *Betaab*'s Rahul Rawail as director and a primarily Indian cast, Khambatta conceded that her American backers had a point: "We have to sell 'The Bandit Queen' to American audiences, and so we need those stars who have box office appeal."[9]

Exploitation producer Sidney H. Levine was also thinking in terms of box office appeal, so in March he hired Sam Locke to write a biopic titled *The Deadly Flower*. That was three English-language Devi films in the works as of Q2 1984 by producers based in the United States, and none of them would get made. Khambatta was also supposed to start filming a non–Devi picture directed by Pierre D'Moro called *Three in Love* in May, but it fell through. However, two Devi pictures were made in India by director Ashok Roy, the first being a Bengali-language film prosaically titled *Phoolan Devi*. Roy then reshot it in Hindi to appeal to the wider market, and there his troubles began.[10]

Though both pictures were shot and edited in 1983, Roy later told *India Today* that due to the disorganized nature of the Central Board of Film Certification, the Hindi version went through 18 Censor Board screenings over the course of 13 months until he realized they just wanted him to change the title *Kahani Phoolan Ki* to *Kahani Phoolvati Ki*. He did so, and the picture finally received its certificate in July 1984. Public interest in Devi had cooled by the time Roy's Hindi picture hit screens in 1985, and Roy estimated that he lost Rs 6 lakh in grosses as a result—which was peanuts compared to the Rs 50 lakh in damages which *India Today* reported that Phoolan Devi herself demanded in a defamation lawsuit against the filmmakers in September 1985. The article claimed that among Devi's objections to the film was that Chambal Valley outlaws such as herself "don't dance around trees when they're in love."[11]

Though she has a few musical numbers, Phoolan Devi's celluloid avatar does not dance around a tree in *Kahani Phoolvati Ki*. The phrase is a metaphor referring to the frothier aspects of Hindi cinema, the sort of escapist elements which were so distasteful to Khambatta in particular, who had found herself doing the Twist in all three of her Hindi films. Whether or not Devi did indeed make the "dancing around trees" comment is another matter. According to *I, Phoolan Devi*, Ashok Roy visited her in prison: "He said he had made a film called *Kahani Phoolan Ki* and that he had been waiting to see if I was killed or put in prison to finish his film." She does not specify the year but it would have been at least 1984, long after Coelho's visits, though she says regarding Roy's visit that while she had been to a cinema once years earlier in Nepal, "I still didn't know what a film was." (I make no claims to being either a Phoolan Devi expert or a Hindi film expert, and this book was researched and written before the publication of Susie Coelho's book *The Bandit Queen, The Warrior Queen, and Me* or the domestic release of Hossein Martin Fazeli and Gillian Greenfeld's documentary *Phoolan*.)[12]

It is unknown whether Devi was aware of Khambatta's attempt to make a film about her, but while still in prison in July 1986 she was angry about Coelho's failure to do so, telling writer Richard S. Ehrlich that Coelho "told lies" and "nothing ever happened." According to Ehrlich, Devi said Coelho promised "they would make a film and pay her 60,000 rupees ($5,000). But all she did was send me some clothing and paid me 3,500 rupees ($290). I feel used because of this."[13]

* * *

Every element of two Indian women duking it out over who would produce and star in a movie about a third Indian woman was a hilarious novelty in the white/male-supremacist Hollywood of the mid–1980s. *Men make movies, not women, and certainly not exotic women with funny accents!* As a result, Coelho and Khambatta's rivalry led to the last bout of sustained attention the latter would receive in the United States press before her death. The May 16, 1984, *Los Angeles Times* headlined it as "Actresses Vie to Screen Bandit Queen's Saga," but that same day's *New York Post* went with "Sari Time in H'wood for 2 Actresses," which is almost subtle by the *Post*'s standards. A June 11, 1984, *People* story was titled "Two Actresses Vie to Escape Hollywood's Caste System—by Playing India's Bandit Queen," and later that week Marilyn Beck described Khambatta and Coelho's vying as a "much-publicized battle."¹⁴

It was not going unnoticed in India, where K.P. Sunil wrote in the July 24 *Illustrated Weekly of India* that "glamour-puss Persis Khambatta, who carved a niche for herself as an actress in Hollywood, is reportedly contemplating a film on the dacoit queen Phoolan Devi, *a la Kahani Phoolan ki*," but that Khambatta "remains tightlipped on this." Sunil also noted that "despite a sensational debut" in the first *Star Trek* movie "Khambatta hasn't gone very far at all" in Hollywood, only receiving "unimpressive, bit-roles in films like Nighthawks."¹⁵

The United States publicity peak was the *People* article, which featured both a photo of Coelho and Devi in Devi's Gwalior cell and a photo of Khambatta in her Devi cosplay, dressed in black and holding a horse's reins. The latter's caption read, "Former Trekkie Khambatta also is saddling up as Devi. 'Anyone who thought about the role thought of me,' she claims." The article quoted Khambatta as finding it "curious" that Coelho had "resented any reference to her Indian heritage" prior to the Devi story, while Coelho faulted Khambatta for "making no effort to meet her incarcerated subject." Khambatta, whom *People* described as "a beauty of strong will," was upfront about why she wanted to make the movie: "'There are not many good roles for women in Hollywood,'" she says. "'So you see Goldie Hawn and Barbra Streisand producing. And that's what I'm doing.'"¹⁶

> Persis, who fashioned her script out of press clips, says she has deliberately not made the pilgrimage to Gwalior. "As an actress," she says, "I didn't want to be influenced by her. I have this romantic vision of her and I don't want to alter it." She adds that Devi is said to be short and unattractive, hardly what she has in mind for herself in the film. Bono vows her movie will be true to the facts, "or I won't make it."
>
> Meanwhile Bono is consulting lawyers to protect her rights. She has also sent news of Khambatta's preparations to the prisoner in Gwalior. This was definitely a less than generous act: It's been rumored that Devi discouraged another would-be filmmaker by threatening to have him shot. Khambatta is not impressed. "I've always done what I wanted to do," she says. "This is no exception."¹⁷

(Much like how Khambatta fashioned her *Bandit Queen* script, the book *Presenting Persis Khambatta* is largely fashioned out of press clips! Great minds and all.) The still-jailed Phoolan Devi was reported to be "generally oblivious to the contention between actresses continents away," and while Coelho described herself and Devi as "two souls" with "a spiritual connection," Khambatta was pragmatic: "I hope this movie does as much good as Star Trek did for me. Only this time with hair."¹⁸

* * *

The 50th annual international feature film, television film and documentary market in Milan, known as MIFED, was held in the late 1984. The centerpiece event focusing on feature films occurred from October 28 through November 3; as it had in past decades and would continue to for years to come it was called (ugh) Indian Summer, a name which this writer is so miffed about that she cannot type it without parenthetically grunting in disgust.[19]

Being their wont for all such film markets, *Variety* published a mega-issue packed with full-page ads from distributors peddling their available, upcoming, and often never-to-exist films. They were not all being sold at (ugh) Indian Summer, but this was how awareness was raised. No iteration of *The Bandit Queen* and/or *The Deadly Flower* is hinted at in the 472-page behemoth, but Susie Coelho and Khambatta were listed in two other films. Included in the 27-page section bought by Cannon Films is a full-page ad for Sam Firstenberg's iconic *Breakin' 2: Electric Boogaloo*, known then by the more embryonic title *Breakin' 2 is Electric Boogaloo*, the credits for which included "Also Starring Susie Bono." Deeper into the issue were three pages purchased by RGH International Film Enterprises Inc., and among them was an ad for Allan Kuskowski's non-iconic *First Strike*, which after listing the main cast included "and Persis Khambatta as Sylvia Kruger." Coelho and Khambatta were both big enough stars to be separated out from the main casts, though only Khambatta's character's name is mentioned. (It is not a competition.)[20]

The last gasp for *The Deadly Flower* came in a *Daily Variety* casting call that December. Due to begin filming in Northern California in March 1985, the leading roles were listed as "Phoolan, 22-28, East Indian, beautiful, lead, star name; femme, 20-25, East Indian, attractive, featured; femme, 25-30, American, blond, stringer for American magazine, supporting; femme, 25-30, American, Red Cross social worker, supporting." These were followed by "male, 30-35, photographer, American, supporting; male, attaché in embassy, sensitive, featured; males, 18-25, East Indian, bits." Heaven only knows how *The Deadly Flower* would have turned out, but this casting data provides more information than is known to this writer about either Coelho or Khambatta's *Bandit Queen* projects, and it is not unremarkable that *Flower* was planned to be a female-led film.[21]

First Strikes and Last Resorts

Persis Khambatta kept busy with non–Devi things in 1984, though not as many as in past years, nor as breathlessly reported. Not only would her final appearance in Marilyn Beck's column be that year, she had not been mentioned in Army Archerd's *Daily Variety* column as a personality rather than as metadata since November 1982. Writing under the pseudonym of Bunny Mars, *Los Angeles Times* columnist Richard Rouilard spotted Khambatta at the closing night of the American Film Market in March 1984, describing her as "perfectly dressed in an outrageously splendid blue-and-silver sequined sari." Later that spring Rouilard spotted Khambatta at a Versace fashion show without commenting on the splendid outrageousness of her clothing.[22]

Khambatta's newest gig in India was far off Rouilard's radar: she was the new main model for the textile firm Garden Vareli, which to some eyes was still plenty outrageous. Khambatta wore Western-influenced but nonetheless Indian dresses, and the slogan was "You Fascinate Me." The campaign won the top honors in the Indian advertising industry awards in Bombay in the spring of 1985, and again in 1986 in 1987, with Khambatta as the primary model. Vareli designer Hemant Trivedi was thrilled to finally get to work with Khambatta: he had been a student in Australia when Khambatta's shaved head was in all the papers in 1979, and though they had never met, Trivedi fibbed to his friends at the time and said he knew her.[23]

Khambatta participated in the festivities for Houston's 1984 India Week beginning on April 29, which included a tour of NASA's Johnson Space Center led by Geotest Engineering founder V.N. Vijayvergiya on the afternoon of Sunday, May 6. Khambatta and Kabir Bedi were among the twelve judges that evening for the regional edition of the Miss India USA pageant, which had been founded by the India Festival Committee in 1980. Khambatta had the honor of crowning Monica Kishnani as the 1984 winner, after which Khambatta told the audience that the finalists' mothers should receive a special thanks for encouraging their daughters. (Word!) Unfortunately, it was discovered the following day that first runner-up Padma Iyer was the actual winner and Kishnani had come in third due to a clerical error. While there is no primary source confirming this, given the proximity to NASA it is a safe bet someone made a joke comparing pageant tabulation to rocket science—and in this writer's headcanon, Khambatta made that joke.[24]

* * *

For the first time since the back-to-back filming of *The Wilby Conspiracy* and *Conduct Unbecoming* nine years earlier, Khambatta began work on a new movie before her previous movie had been released. This was less due to the pace of her career and more because *Warrior of the Lost World* was sitting on a shelf somewhere when she shot Allan Kuskowski's *First Strike*. The Kuskowski picture was also the first of her United States career to receive minimal ink in the trades; its only mention in *Variety* before the (ugh) Indian Summer ad was a piece in the August 3, 1984, *Daily Variety* Film Castings, and even that was just for performers Richard Karlan and Paul Comi. (Because all things on the mycelial network are connected, directly below the *First Strike* listing was: "Susie Bono, John Christy Ewing, Alicia Bond, 'Electric Boogaloo is Breakin' II,' Cannon.") *First Strike*'s second *Variety* shout-out was in a chart accompanying a May 1985 article about what the showbiz bible described with a hint of wounded pride as "secret" feature films: "Many of these pictures are low-budget maiden efforts for the production companies involved (often filmed in 16m for a hoped-for 35m blowup later), made without publicists or knowledge of reporting the shooting to the trade."25

First Strike was indeed the low-budget maiden effort for its filmmakers, but it lacked the budget to be made on film, so in the tradition of indie producers since time immemorial Allan Kuskowski worked with what was available; being the President of the broadcast rental company Trans Northern Television, his own facilities were what was available. This meant shooting on videotape, but the loss of quality would be negligible since the movie was intended to be released straight to video. In addition to being paying work, *First Strike* reunited Persis Khambatta with a fellow Indian by the name of Noel de Sousa. He had played Princess Siri's right-hand man in *The Man with the Power*, and in more recent years de Sousa worked as a makeup artist. He was hired to do Khambatta's makeup for *First Strike*, which would not be the last time they worked together.26

On Saturday, September 8, Khambatta participated in the "Stars of Today" panels at Hollywood International's Celebration II, described as "a weekend-long tribute to the entertainment industry" which also included "a celebrity cocktail party, a beauty pageant and other panel discussions." This writer's research failed to uncover any evidence of the first Celebration or a Celebration III, and your guess is as good as hers as to what "Hollywood International" was or what any of it means. Tickets for the Celebration II were available through TicketMaster, and the event's *LA Weekly* advert promised that "The stars are coming out … and you're invited!" Adam West and Cesar Romero from the 1966 *Batman* series were among those stars, so it was probably all as crass and depressing as it sounds.27

* * *

Proof that *Warrior of the Lost World* had not just been a bone-breaking fever dream for Khambatta could be found in *Fangoria* #40, which went on sale on October 30. It featured a two-page, refreshingly snark-free recap in which Alex Gordon described *Warrior* as "an upcoming epic from Helen Sarlui's Continental Motion Pictures, Inc., a company whose films usually get terrible tradepaper reviews (Variety, etc.) but must be profitable in other parts of the world because they keep making them." He also noted that the picture starred "Robert Ginty, Persis Khambatta, Donald Pleasence and Fred Williamson, and with those names I suppose it has a chance in the North American market place."[28]

Visto International released *Warrior of the Lost World* into a smattering of theaters in Texas and Louisiana on November 21. This film had not yet been rated, but since many newspapers refused to run ads for unrated films, Visto declared *Warrior* was PG. The PG-13 rating had only been put into effect the previous July, and the two PG films which had resulted in the introduction of the new rating—Joe Dante's fun, violent *Gremlins* and Steven Spielberg's grim, violent *Indiana Jones and the Temple of Doom*—were still playing in theaters, sometimes in the same multiplexes as *Warrior*. The mysterious cabal at the MPAA gave *Warrior* an R during the first week of December, though it was often still listed in the papers as PG or PG-13 and would just as often be pluralized as *Warriors* as it made its way through the South, because it's not like it mattered.[29]

* * *

Indira Gandhi was assassinated on October 31, 1984. It was a tragic event for both India and Khambatta, whose brief meeting with Gandhi had been a needed shot in the arm. But she had to keep working no matter the damage to her pride, hence such dubious events as Hollywood International's Celebration II. It is also why she traveled to India later that year to tape a segment for a syndicated pilot from the producers of *Lifestyles of the Rich and Famous* with the working title *Exciting People in Exotic Places*. The further association with the E-bomb notwithstanding, the pilot paid, it allowed her to make it to Bombay in time for her annual holiday trip, it was exposure, and it bears repeating that it paid.[30]

1985

The Pride of India's Perils in the Lost World

To be clear, *Exciting People in Exotic Places* paid only in money, not career dividends. Renamed *Exciting People, Exotic Places* when it aired in mid–January 1985, it got bad reviews across the board and was not picked up as a series. Its ultimate utility was to provide filler material for the 1986 *Lifestyles of the Rich and Famous* book, which included a picture of Pam Dawber and Persis Khambatta riding an elephant in Nepal. This horrible book also described how Khambatta and Dawber "took a *shikara*, or water taxi, to tour the mirrored splendors of Lake Dal" in the "unhurried waterborn society of lotus-eaters" of Kashmir. Also fun is the reflection on how "when the British ruled India, they built houseboats on the water to circumvent the Maharaja's ban against owning their own land—and the decorative houseboats are still the preferred accommodation for residents and visitors alike." The British Raj was a terrible thing for the people of India, but if you were a privileged white person in the mid–1980s, the occupation's spoils were the cat's pajamas.[1]

The same producers asked Khambatta to represent India in another forgotten failed-pilot-turned-special, a "global extravaganza saluting the #1 winners of the wonderful world of entertainment" titled *On Top All Over the World*. While it did no good for anyone at any elevation anywhere when it was finally shat upon the airwaves in April 1985, it was probably seen by more people that year than Khambatta's other seven-syllable project which ended with the word "world."[2]

Though Visto had been distributing *Warrior of the Lost World* throughout the Southeastern United States for three months, the February 5 *Daily Variety* noted that next up for Visto was "an acquisition from Continental Motion Pictures, the R-rated fantasy 'Warrior Of The Lost World,' due to bow in late February or early March in the Southeast." The film was instead exhausting its theatrical run in those regions by then, and it was released nationwide on VHS and Beta by Thorn EMI/HBO the week of May 17, 1985.[3]

Fangoria's Alex Gordon was not wrong about pictures like *Warrior* tending to get terrible reviews in the trades, though *Variety*'s mid–June review of the videocassette release described it as "a well-directed action fantasy which might have been a winner with a better script," which is fair. The review also theorized that director Worth aimed "at a look resembling George Lucas' debut pic 'THX 1138,'" a respectable guess considering that Worth cited Norman Jewison's *Rollerball* and Stanley Kubrick's *A Clockwork Orange* as inspirations in a 1983 interview. Best of all, neither *Variety* nor *Fangoria* mentioned that Persis Khambatta had been bald in that one movie that one time.[4]

When Visto handed *Warrior of the Lost World* off to Aquarius for Northern theatrical distribution in September, the latter company faced a new challenge: not only had the film already been released on cassette, the video box used the same poster art which had been published in *Variety* in 1983, art which was subsequently used in the newspaper ads for the Southern reach. This meant Aquarius had to start from scratch, but they also had a confluence of showbiz fluctuations in their favor. One was that the 1980 film *The Exterminator* starring Robert Ginty was released on cassette in 1983 just as video store shelves were expanding to make room for such schlock. The initial Thorn EMI/HBO release of *Warrior of the Lost World* traded on this association, listing him as ROBERT "THE EXTERMINATOR" GINTY on the cover which I remember well from the video store where I worked as a teenager, along with PERSIS "STAR TREK" KHAMBATTA and DONALD "HALLOWEEN" PLEASENCE.[5]

Ginty also starred in *The Exterminator 2*, which hit theaters a month before the October 1984 release of the James Cameron film *The Terminator*; the latter starred a thickly-accented immigrant who would go on to be one of 1980s Hollywood's biggest stars, and launched a franchise which is still going at the time of this writing. (I was one of the few people who saw the 2019 *Terminator: Dark Fate* in a theater, so the franchise is not going strong *per se*, but it is going.) Adding the nonsense suffix "-ator" to a verb was already a thing when *Warrior of the Lost World* was released in the North a year after *The Terminator*, and it would reach its nadir in 2003 when the aforementioned thickly-accented immigrant was elected governor of California thanks in part to many people thinking the phrase "the Governator" was hilarious.

Aquarius put the nonsense suffix to work in their northern print campaign in 1985 by implying that *Warrior of the Lost World* was now called *The Assassinator*, though the *New York Daily News'* Phantom of the Movies columnist was not fooled:

> **Let the Viewer Beware Dept.: Warrior of the Lost World's** print ads proclaim: "First There Was 'The Exterminator.' Then 'The Terminator.' And Now… 'The Assassinator.'"

> As far as cheap Italo "Road Warrior" ripoffs go, "Warrior" isn't the worst (the recent "Fall of New York" currently owns that dubious distinction), but this postnuke pulp pic, which opened at Aquarius Showcase Theatres last weekend, has been kicking around since 1983 and is already available on video (from Thorn EMI/HBO). Think twice before shelling out for a first-run ticket to see this secondhand, third-rate junk flick. Remember: The bucks you save may be your own.[6]

Note the recurring theme in the reviews: *Warrior of the Lost World* was not a great movie or even all that good, but it was not the worst movie ever. Aquarius' advert used five images from the film, two of which were unflattering shots of Khambatta. One was of her making a wide-eyed, pained expression while being tortured, and the other was her looking sad and frightened with a gun pointing at her head. These kinds of images remained a fundamental tenet of marketing during the tail end of the grindhouse era, particularly in the North. It was fine to play up the fantasy and/or racing elements in the supposedly backward South, but hurting women was the best way to put sophisticated Yankee asses into theater seats.

Though I had been intrigued by the VHS cover's promise of PERSIS "STAR TREK" KHAMBATTA every time I passed it on my store's shelf, I did not watch *Warrior of the Lost World* until it was featured on *Mystery Science Theater 3000* in 1993. Some of Khambatta's best moments were lost when the ninety-minute *Warrior* was edited for both time and content to fit the *MST3K* format, and while the theatrical cut has been released on DVD, it is a bit of a shame that the *MST3K* version is the most readily available. *Warrior* is not very good, but the fact that it delivers on its promise to be a high-speed action movie on wheels keeps it out of the pantheon of the worst movies ever made. Much like *Megaforce* it is hindered by a male protagonist of dubious heroism and regrettable facial hair, but *Warrior* has more kinetic energy than *Megaforce* attempted to create, and in terms of bang for its production buck *Warrior* makes *Megaforce* look like … well, like *Star Trek—The Motion Picture*.

For all its low-rent crudity, the sexual politics of *Warrior* are still more mature than both *Megaforce* and the first Star Trek movie, and *Warrior*'s first act can almost function as a rejoinder to the terrible gender politics of *Megaforce*. Whereas *Megaforce* introduced Major Zara in her brown military uniform but couldn't wait to put her in a slinky red dress because she is a lady who is "representative of all women facing the dangers and challenges of war time," *Warrior* introduces Nastasia wearing her military uniform, and though she has a few story-motivated costume changes, she does not wear anything glammy until the denouement. Even better, Nastasia's first action in her first scene is to take the Warrior's own pistol, press it against his denim-clad crotch and say: "Listen, you dumb motherfucker." After verbally dressing down the Warrior for his self-consciously macho loner ways, Nastasia presses the gun harder into his crotch and says, "either you help me rescue my father, or, I'll blow your balls off."

Major Zara hired Megaforce and then was rebuked when she asked to join them on their mission, while Nastasia makes it clear that she is only retaining the Warrior to help Nastasia on *her* mission. This is a step up for Khambatta characters by any standard—but if you still need proof that there is no justice in this world, it's that the line most associated with Khambatta is Ilia's "My oath of celibacy is on record," not Nastasia's "I'll blow your balls off." (Though taken out of context, it would probably be misinterpreted as a promise of sex rather than violence.) The Warrior's reply of "what's in it for me?" makes no sense considering Nastasia just made it clear that what's in it for the Warrior is Nastasia *not* shooting his balls off, but Nastasia's response is to shoot the gun directly into the air, to which the Warrior replies, "okay." (Our hero, folks!) Khambatta is grinning from ear to ear throughout, and she appears to be having fun for the first time since the arcade filler in *The Man with the Power*. She was putting together *The Bandit Queen* at the time, so this may have been a dry run for how she would have played Phoolan Devi, but either way it remains one of Khambatta's best English-language scenes.

So unlike Major Zara (who was 100 percent correct that she was sidelined because she was a woman), Nastasia not only joins the adventure but leads the Warrior on their mission into the evil Omega stronghold. She is very much the hero as they wander through a cave, batting away a spider and teasing the Warrior for his arachnophobia. Things take a steep dive when the Warrior rescues Nastasia from a mutant attack, and she behaves like a scared ninny from then on—though Nastasia still has to keep him from drinking the mind-control beverage served at a *Brave New World*–style nightclub, because the Warrior is an idiot.

Most of the picture is shot outdoors, and David Worth squeezes every lira of production value he can out of Italy's industrial wastelands. Banners and flags hanging on real buildings hundreds of feet from the camera's wide-angle lens help to create a sense of scale and scope which is far more convincing than *Megaforce*'s use of the expensive Introvision system, and once-and-future cinematographer Worth has a much stronger visual sense than former stuntman Needham. *Megaforce* is never a high bar to clear, but low-budget films by hungry directors tend to be more interesting than big-budget films by bored or complacent directors (cf. the first two Star Trek movies).

Khambatta racks up her highest unconfirmed body count as Nastasia shoots a lot of anonymous baddies with a machine gun, but she is nevertheless captured at the end of the second act, providing one of the stills used in the Aquarius print ad. (When we watched the abridged film on *Mystery*

Science Theater 3000, my mother was appalled by the Warrior escaping in a helicopter while Nastasia is surrounded on the ground: "He's the hero! The hero isn't supposed to leave the woman behind!" She was not wrong.) Khambatta's next scene finds her playing opposite Donald Pleasence's villain Prossor; Pleasence grabs Khambatta by the hair, and after she hocks a loogie onto his face, Pleasence appears for all the world to hit her. It is probably a no-contact stage hit, but it reads on screen as the real thing. Khambatta's next two scenes are of her writhing in pain on a brainwashing table, the source of the other picture of her in the Aquarius print ad.

The Warrior and Nastasia's father sorta kinda rescue her in the end: the brainwashed Nastasia is being held by Prossor, to the extent that Pleasence pets Khambatta's head, which would be the greatest indignity of almost anybody else's career. Prossor orders Nastasia to shoot the Warrior, but Nastasia only wings him because he's the title character. When Prossor next orders Nastasia to shoot her father, she instead unloads the clip into Prossor, his blood splattering against the wall not unlike Shakka's in *Nighthawks*. If *Bheegi Raat*, *Pinjre Ke Panchhi*, and *Bambai Raat Ki Bahon Mein* made the Twist her signature move in Hindi films, it is a net gain that between *Nighthawks*, *Warrior of the Lost World* and the still-unreleased *First Strike*, Khambatta's signature move in English-language films was shooting men at point-blank range. The scene also implies that Nastasia would have saved herself without any intervention from the Warrior, while Khambatta's performance hints at what Robot Ilia might have been like had the character been allowed any development whatsoever. Low-budget films also tend to double as documentaries of their own making, and while *Warrior* has a credited makeup artist and two, count 'em, two credited hairstylists, there is a good chance that this is what Khambatta looked like on a daily basis—and even in the grimiest of circumstances, she was a smokeshow.

Were that *Warrior of the Lost World* ended there, but, no: the infamous denouement is a close-up of Nastasia kissing the Warrior for the longest sixty-two seconds of your life, and in a wide shot for another seven seconds. Eroticism-enthusiast Gene Siskel bemoaned that Khambatta and Barry Bostwick only gave each other a thumb's up at the end of *Megaforce*, but it could have been much, much worse.

Waiting for Gandhi

Like most of the rest of the media, the *Los Angeles Times*' Roderick Mann had lost interest in Persis Khambatta by 1985. As such, there is no indication in Mann's January 29 profile of Calcutta-born actor Victor

Banerjee that he picked up on how Banerjee hit many of the same points as Khambatta had in the mid-1970s, such as being able to play nationalities other than Indian ("I can play lots of nationalities—Greeks, South Americans, Arabs, all sorts"), the lucrative direness of his home country's industry ("Bombay cinema makes mostly terrible films, but that's where the money is"), or how Banerjee couldn't take much money out of India due to foreign-exchange regulations.[7]

Banerjee went on a promotional tour in early February for David Lean's *A Passage to India*, in which he played a doctor accused of raping a white woman. The picture was nominated for 11 Academy Awards, none of which were for Banerjee or anyone else of Indian descent. He was also not among the "celebrities from the Indo-American community" such as Khambatta and Ashok Amritraj who were spotted by *India West* at the February 11 opening of restaurateur Sant Singh Chatwal's Bombay Palace in Beverly Hills. In a March 1 *India West* article which called him "the latest Indian recruit to Hollywood, after Kabir Bedi and Persis Khambatta," Banerjee described how David Lean wanted Banerjee, an Indian man from India, to mimic the accent Peter Sellers had used in his brownface role of Hrundi V. Bakshi in Blake Edwards' 1968 film *The Party*. Lean also darkened Banerjee's skin with makeup because he considered Banerjee's natural tone to be too light for an Indian man from India, though Banerjee tried his best to spin that racist indignity as an example of how he was "not limited to playing Indians." The white Alec Guinness' face was also darkened in *Passage* much as it had been in Lean's *Lawrence of Arabia*, the latter of which continues to be held up as one of the greatest films ever by white people who consider criticisms of the brownface in David Lean and/or Blake Edwards films to be political correctness gone mad. Banerjee noted that some Asian members of the English Equity actors' union were angry that Lean hired Banerjee, an Indian from India, to play an Indian from India in *A Passage to India* rather than hiring an Indian from England to play an Indian from India. He also acknowledged that this greatest fear was "having to go back to India with nothing to show," a fear with which Khambatta could relate.[8]

In a March 17 *New York Times* profile with the no-pressure headline "Victor Banerjee—India Personified," Nan Robertson called Banerjee "the first Indian actor since Sabu, the 'elephant boy,' to win world fame in a Hollywood movie. It is not at all likely that he will fade away and end, as Sabu did, a pauper in his native land." Dying a pauper was all the more unlikely since the article pointed out that he was born into "immense privilege and luxury," and that Banerjee—who, like Khambatta, chain-smoked Dunhills—still lived in "his mother's turn-of-the-century Calcutta palace." All the same, *India Abroad*'s Arthur Pais would look back in 1989 and reflect that "Victor Banerjee could not capitalize on the critical notices he received" for the David Lean film, while "Persis Khambatta returned briefly to India to act in video films, while in Hollywood she gets a few guest roles in television shows."[9]

* * *

Persis Khambatta would not be in India *or* Hollywood by the end of 1989, but in mid–1985 she was in thick of how India was represented in the United States. After a soft launch in May, June was the kickoff of the Festival of India 1985–1986, an eighteen-month event described as "a unique cooperative effort between the governments of India and the United States designed to bring a greater understanding of the complex life and culture of India to the American people." It had been in the works with the Reagan Administration since Indira Gandhi's 1982 visit, and according to the Indo-U.S. Subcommission on Education and Culture's American executive director Ted Tanen, fundraising proved easier than expected in the United States thanks to the public's awareness of India being raised by Indira Gandhi's assassination, as well as by films such as *Gandhi* and *A Passage to India*. Unmentioned by Tanen was that Steven Spielberg's 1984 blockbuster *Indiana Jones and the Temple of Doom* had been seen by twice as many members of that public than the Attenborough or Lean pictures: as of December 1985 *Temple of Doom* had earned $109,000,000 from its theatrical run according to *Variety*, while *Gandhi* made $24,747,883 and *Passage* a meager $13,343,683. In the plus column, the India-set *Temple of Doom* cast Indian performers for the major Indian characters, and the brownface was mostly relegated to the stunt performers—but those major Indian characters were portrayed as savages who commit human sacrifice and feast on chilled monkey brains, so it only resembled progress if you squinted and used your imagination.[10]

The Festival of India's opening was timed to coincide with a visit from current Prime Minister Rajiv Gandhi, who was Indira's son and the "honorary patron" of the Festival along with First Lady Nancy Reagan. But the centerpiece of the Washington, D.C., kickoff was the National Gallery of Art's Sculpture of India exhibit, and the Gallery also held a six-week festival of the films of director James Ivory, producer Ismail Merchant, and writer Ruth Prawer Jhabvala, collectively known as Merchant-Ivory. (This was before their arguable breakout picture *A Room with a View* in 1986, let alone their most famous-to-Americans films *Howard's End* and *The Remains of the Day* in the early 1990s.) Khambatta had never been in a Merchant-Ivory picture and never would be, but she participated in the event at the request of Vice President George Bush.[11]

Khambatta's biggest exposure in the Festival came when she was one of the speakers who introduced Rajiv Gandhi at the Shoreham Hotel in New York on June 14. *Daily Variety* noted that same day that Khambatta and Linda Blair had signed with Contemporary Korman Artists for theatrical representation; this came two weeks after the *Hollywood Reporter* reported that she had "pacted with Talent International for theatrical representation and with Michael Levine Public Relations Co. for public relations." (The PR firm Edward Lozzi & Associates claims Khambatta was referred to them in 1985, but there is no primary-source evidence of this.) While at the Shoreham, Khambatta told *India West* that her home was Hollywood because "my home is where my feet are, but 'India is really special. I love India and I'm an Indian.'" She also mentioned that she and Victor Banerjee were slated to star together in a film called *The Unterman*. That picture fell through, but it was never as exciting a prospect as the other project she mentioned, and in doing so she confirmed a rumor which had been floating around since mid-May: she had auditioned to play Indira Gandhi in a television movie.[12]

A four-hour miniseries, to precise, which as of April was titled *Indira Gandhi: A Tryst with Destiny* and was being produced by the London-based Silver Chalice Productions. That company's CEO Judith De Paul told *India Today* the project had been in the works since before the assassination, and that it had both Indira Gandhi's approval beforehand and Rajiv's approval now. De Paul said the lead would have to "carry the film so we need someone who is a strong actress and can also look something like Mrs. Gandhi," with the two most likely contenders at the time being the India-born Madhur Jaffrey, and the Bronx-born Anne Bancroft. Shooting was expected to begin that autumn.[13]

Shooting did not begin that autumn, though on October 29 *Daily Variety* ran a profile of Silver Chalice's Judith De Paul which said the $6M project was now titled *Indira Gandhi—If I Die Tomorrow* and was due to start shooting in India that January. The rest of the profile read like a press release which bent over backwards to make sure De Paul did not sound like one of those buzzkill feminists ("'I'm not involved in wondering whether or not most women have problems.... It's not my problem'") or to even acknowledge that institutionalized sexism exists ("[De Paul] does not attempt to conceal her femininity. She just denies that it has been a relevant factor in her ascent to corporate command—because she simply has refused to permit it to become a factor").[14]

The January 1986 start date came and went, and in July 1986 *Variety* reported that "Showtime and Viacom are in" for De Paul's Gandhi project, "currently being scripted for a late fall roll." It did not begin rolling in the late fall, and a few days after the 1986 winter solstice *Variety* reported that in addition to producing the television movie *Nazi Hunter: The Beate*

Klarsfeld Story and acquiring the rights to Michael Pearson's book *The Sealed Train*, De Paul's Silver Chalice "has been developing a miniseries on the late Indian leader Indira Gandhi." But *Klarsfeld* would prove to be Silver Chalice's last production, and by June 1990 the four-hour Indira Gandhi miniseries was in the hands of Procter & Gamble Productions—best known for soap operas such as *Guiding Light* and *As the World Turns*—and was slated "to be produced in cooperation with the former world leader's family," though "no network is connected as of yet." None would be.[15]

Speaking of nonexistent things, at the time of this writing the Internet Movie Database and thus many other sources list Persis Khambatta as making an uncredited appearance in Stephen Frears' *My Beautiful Laundrette*, which premiered at the Edinburgh Film Festival on August 17, 1985. This is apocryphal, for if Khambatta is in the film, this writer has not been able to spot her.[16]

Back to Bombay, for Now

After completing her Merchant-Ivory obligations, Khambatta returned to Los Angeles to be one of the Hollywood Foreign Press Association's "celebrity presenters" along with Bud Cort and Maria Conchita Alonso at the Beverly Hilton on July 17, where they gave out grants to various industry-related organizations. Khambatta and Kabir Bedi also appeared at the fifth annual India Independence Day celebration, where *India West* observed that they "were seen many times surrounded by a large group of autograph seekers," which sounds horrible.[17]

Khambatta and Bedi were reunited in much more pleasant circumstances on September 14 at the Embassy Auditorium for the Los Angeles launch of the Festival of India, where they read English translations of the *Bhagavad Gita* along with Martin Sheen. It may not have been up there with Phil Collins playing both sides of the Atlantic within twelve hours during Live Aid earlier that year, but Khambatta was still bicoastal for the Festival of India, and did quite a bit of globetrotting in late 1985.[18]

This included trotting back to India at the request of producer Nari Hira to star in *Shingora*, Khambatta's first Hindi-language production since *Bambai Raat Ki Bahon Mein*, and her second shot-on-video feature after the still-unreleased *First Strike*. Directed by Anil Tejani, *Shingora* was one of the first of a wave of racy, adult-oriented releases by Hira's company Hiba Films. They were intended for distribution in the thousands of video libraries in Bombay and Madras, as well as closed-circuit cable in apartment buildings, hotels, and airplanes, with a planned release of a new movie every 20 days.[19]

Though bits of the dialog are in English, as with Khambatta's earlier Hindi films this writer's monolingualism makes it difficult to examine *Shingora*. However, her character Roma Shinga appears to be a high-powered real estate developer who by day wears the pastels and nightmarish shoulder pads favored by female executives worldwide in the mid–1980s, but by night goes dancing in the black-on-black goth attire favored by this writer during her own clubbing excursions. It is while out dancing that Roma spots Marc Zuber's character, which leads to Persis Khambatta's first fully consensual post-*Kamasutra* sex scene, though Gene Siskel would have been disappointed by the lack of nudity. Things get soapy from there, and Khambatta throws herself into *Shingora*'s broad emotional palette with her trademark lack of self-consciousness, including a lengthy crying scene. For a woman who had been feted for her beauty since she was 13, she was never afraid of being un-pretty onscreen, and while she does not lead any of the musical numbers—which were an unbreakable tradition even for this new wave of Hindi pictures shot on headache-inducing video—Khambatta dances the Twist for the first time since *Bambai Raat Ki Bahon Mein*. Whether anyone on the *Shingora* set was aware of Khambatta's history with that dance is unknown, but Roma has to be coaxed into dancing, and Khambatta's reluctance onscreen plays as genuine.

Khambatta was not *Shingora*'s only former Miss India, or even the only one who traveled from the United States: the video picture also starred Neeta Puri, who won the Miss India USA pageant in New York in 1983. Puri receives the "Introducing" credit in *Shingora* which Khambatta had received twice in the 1960s, while Khambatta shares a title screen with Marc Zuber.[20]

But the potential indignity of the movie's distribution model or of sharing the small screen with a younger model was neither here nor there. "I was really missing home," Khambatta told *India Today*'s Eyecatchers column (which zinged her by referring to her as an "aspiring Hindi actress"). "Some things you wish for subconsciously, and my dream came true." Another dream she was hoping would come true was Jeroo arranging a marriage: "I know I am going to get a wonderful man—I have always got what I wanted. And people are going to say she won." Her hope for an arranged marriage had first been mentioned in the *New York Daily News*, which had reported in August that Khambatta "has returned to her roots for marital bliss and asked her mother to arrange a marriage to a suitable man of the Parsee religion." *India Today*, meanwhile, referred to it as a man hunt. Whether arranged or hunted, however, it was not to be for a few years.[21]

1986–1988

MacGyver vs. Hunter

Persis Khambatta returned to the United States in early 1986 after shooting *Shingora* to make guest appearances on the very American television shows *MacGyver* and *Hunter*, though the most American thing she did was being one of about five dozen "national honorary chairpersons and guest artists" for the celebration of post–*Rambo* national guilt known as the "Official National Welcome Home Celebration for Our Vietnam Veterans," held at the Forum in Inglewood on February 24. There Khambatta was reunited with (or at least was present in the same multi-purpose indoor arena as) her former co-stars Leonard Nimoy and Billy Dee Williams. Khambatta's connection to the war and its veterans was tenuous at best considering she was not born in the Western Hemisphere and did not take up residence in the United States until a few months before the Fall of Saigon—but a gig is a gig, and it was a gig.[1]

Speaking of gigs, the *MacGyver* episode "To Be a Man" was broadcast a few days after the Forum event. Wearing a long native-girl wig, Khambatta plays a widow named Zia who lives with her son next to the Vasquez Rocks in Afghanistan. Zia nurses MacGyver back to heath after his plane crashes, then helps him escape to the Pakistan border. Though MacGyver saves the day using *science!* because that was the show's premise, Zia herself is no slouch in the resourcefulness department, including saving MacGyver's life by cauterizing a wound using a red-hot poker. It is Khambatta's best television guest appearance, and Zia is arguably as much the episode's protagonist as MacGyver himself. It also helps that as Khambatta's dishwater-blonde male leads go, she has far more onscreen chemistry with *MacGyver* star Richard Dean Anderson than she had with Barry Bostwick, Robert Ginty, or *Casablanca*'s sentient block of balsa wood with the ironic name of David Soul.

It is easy to see why *MacGyver* entered pop culture lore judging from "To Be a Man," since the episode is a fun, rousing adventure in which humanity is valued above ethnic or political differences. The title refers to the lesson that MacGyver imparts to Zia's son: violence should always be a last resort, and if you show mercy to your enemies it will come back around. Like karma, if you will.

By comparison, *Hunter* is only entertaining if you are a straight white man who thought things were better back before people who are not straight white men were treated as equals, and Khambatta's episode "62 Hrs. of Terror" makes it clear why Alan Spencer's 1986 parody series *Sledge Hammer!* is more fondly remembered now than *Hunter*. Wearing her own shortish hair in "62 Hrs. of Terror," Khambatta is Dhari Siad, the vice-consul of the "Baraqi" consulate in Los Angeles who comes under suspicion by ostensible hero Rick Hunter after a Baraqi student group claims responsibility for a car bombing. The overall episode is terrible—especially a cross-dressing joke which was no doubt hilarious to the same people who found *Megaforce*'s uniforms too queer—though it does feature Khambatta's first consensual, post–*Kamasutra* English-language sex scene, just a few months after the Hindi *Shingora*. She begins kissing fellow guest star Rod Arrants before the commercial break, and at the beginning of the next act Khambatta is kissing his gross hairy chest in bed after the deed has been done. The best thing that can be said about the episode is that Khambatta survives to the end.

The Blinking Eye

The roles of Zia and Dhari were a long way from Indira Gandhi, but Khambatta came close to playing what the February 20 *Los Angeles Daily News* described as "a classical Indian dancer who becomes a spy investigating the assassination" of the former Prime Minister in B.R. Chopra's film *Awam*. Khambatta told the paper the part was "too good to turn down," and since she was getting domestic television work and was up for a pilot for a network sitcom, she was unconcerned that *Awam* would probably never play in the United States.[2]

> For years I was advised not [to] do television. I was told that I was a film star. But work is work. There's so many things happening on TV there's so many great people doing it. I think it's great exposure. I haven't stopped working since last September. I was offered five guest shots for TV shows in one month. I really think it's all in your mind. Once you decide that you want to do more, it just comes to you.[3]

The sitcom pilot never happened, and while *Awam* ended up not being about Indira Gandhi, in a July 1986 Q&A with the *Telegraph* she denied having lost the part for health reasons.

Q: What happened? They say you couldn't go through the strenuous dances because of your earlier open-heart surgery and that's why you were dropped.

A: That's a lie. I'm absolutely healthy and normal. I was told it was a significant role. But after a few days of shooting, I found it was a "sidey" character. So I walked out. It wasn't what I was looking for.⁴

Khambatta had begun to speak more freely in the half-decade since the *Oui* interview, and it was while talking to the *Telegraph* that she referred to herself as "an ideal liberated woman" who couldn't live with the way that her marriage to "foreigner" Cliff Taylor made her legally "half a woman." Later that month, the *Illustrated Weekly of India* quoted her from the *Telegraph*: "My success lies in being able to combine my good head, good heart and good body to make my mark in this male-oriented society." Persis Khambatta was a feminist. There is no doubt.⁵

She would not appear on American television again in 1986 following *Hunter* and *MacGyver*, but Khambatta temporarily achieved one of her persistent-in-spite-of-herself goals when she became engaged to a wealthy Gujarati detective in Toronto by the name of Naren Parekh. She described him to *India Today* as "a very sexy man" with "eyes like Michael Caine's"—but with more progressive attitudes about his wife's autonomy, one would hope—and Khambatta was confident because "I love him. It'll work out."

Though the *Hollywood Reporter*'s Rambling Reporter reported on August 29 that Khambatta was getting married on September 6, and the *India Today* piece ran on September 30, it is unclear whether she did marry Parekh. In 1998 after Khambatta's death B.R. Srikanth and Shameem Akhtar wrote in the magazine *Outlook India* of her "broken second marriage to Sandy Naren," which may be a reference to Naren Parekh, but that is far from certain.⁶

* * *

In October 1986, Persis Khambatta was one of four dozen guests along with Kabir Bedi and Noel de Sousa at a screening of Jagmohan Mundhra's 1984 film *Kamla*, which starred Deepti Naval and Khambatta's *Shingora* co-star Marc Zuber. Though *Kamla*'s hoped-for domestic release for did not happen, Mundhra went on to become a prolific director of straight-to-video English-language exploitation movies, some of which were written by *India West* correspondent Michael Potts. The VHS-era classics Mundhra and/or Potts created such as *Night Eyes* and *Last Call* did their part to fill the shelves of the video store I worked in as a teenager as much as *Shingora* did in India. No shade is being thrown on Mundhra's movies, but Khambatta had loftier ambitions.⁷

Triillusion rose from *The Bandit Queen*'s ashes in December when a long-simmering project was announced by Potts in *India West*: Khambatta and Noel de Sousa had joined with commercial director Ahmed Lateef to produce a $2M feature film to be shot in India titled *Eye of Katmandu*. (By this time Reseda-based accountant Waldo Brain had become Secretary of Triillusion, and actor Sukhbir Kang was the Chief Financial Officer, though Khambatta remained the Chief Executive Officer and sole Director.) Noel de Sousa initially hired *The Black Hole*'s Gerry Day to adapt Margaret Lawrence's novel *Seven Thunders* into *Eye of Katmandu*, but this screenplay by a female screenwriter based on a female author's book with two female lead characters was rejected by director Lateef for having "too feminine a slant" (Khambatta described Lateef as "very artistic, very sensitive, and very honest." That last one checks out.) A sufficiently not-girly draft was written, and Khambatta was set to play the non-white of the two leads while she was still seeking out half the film's budget from Indian investors living in the United States. It was acknowledged that $2M was a fairly large budget for a film to be shot in India, but they hoped to get big names, including Khambatta's *Conduct Unbecoming* co-star Michael York. Noel de Sousa, Lateef's Silver Eye Productions and Khambatta's Triillusion were also working to secure funding for two other potential projects, *China Love* and *The Locket*, both of which had half of their budgets raised as of December 1986.[8]

Lateef and de Sousa had been close friends since the early 1950s, and when Lateef passed away in 2015, de Sousa wrote a remembrance for the Hollywood Foreign Press Association. He did not mention *Eye of Katmandu*, *China Love*, nor *The Locket*, for none of them were made.[9]

The Flameout of the Phoenix

ABC had pre-bought seven broadcasts of the first Star Trek movie in January 1979, and they burned off one of them on Monday, March 9, 1987. By now it had been overshadowed in every positive sense by the three films which followed, and the buzz building around the upcoming premiere of the television series *Star Trek: The Next Generation* made the first movie look even creakier. ABC also no longer had any exclusivity, given that the Special Longer Version had been a consistent bestseller on VHS since June 1983 in spite of the film's bad-to-horrendous reputation, and it had also been part of Paramount Television's non-network Portfolio X broadcast package.[10]

While the network was determined to get the most of out their ill-considered investment, it was clear from the press materials that they put as little effort into it as possible. In both 1979 and 1987 the bald head of Khambatta was the only visual which translated to newsprint, and they again used the murky, confounding, and unpleasant photo of William

Shatner and his hairy left arm clutching Khambatta's right shoulder as Stephen Collins looms over her, though most papers again cropped it to just Khambatta. Much like the RCA VideoDisc description of Ilia as "an exotically beautiful, totally bald woman from the planet Delta who becomes Sulu's assistant and Decker's girlfriend," the 1987 press material seemed to have been written by someone who hadn't watched the film since 1979. The version which ran in the *New York Daily News* read "Kirk is concerned when a navigator—co-star Persis Khambatta—aboard the Enterprise is overcome by a mystical force." There would be variations as different editors across the country tinkered with it, such as Kirk and/or Decker "registering deep concern," as "Navigator Ilia seems overcome by a mystical force," but they all bring to mind the best line from the best Star Wars film of the 2010s: "Impressive. Every word in that sentence is wrong."[11]

* * *

As she had been during the initial broadcast in 1983, Khambatta was again out of the country during the 1987 broadcast. Nari Hira's Hiba Films straight-to-video releases were doing well, and when his new project *Jazira* required a woman who could look tough and fight, Hira called Khambatta. The role was of a daughter out to avenge the death of her family, and Khambatta told *India West* the character "is more like a female version of a Mithun Chakraborty/Clint Eastwood type, where I'm dressed up like a man. It's not the kind of picture where you have three hours of beautiful fashions. There's a lot of karate fighting, which was fantastic for me because I had to fight in my own scenes." It was still not the kind of part Jill Clayburgh would play, but it was the niche which Persis Khambatta had been able to carve out for herself, and she threw herself into the action as much as she had in *Nighthawks* and *Warrior of the Lost World*. (Or would have in *Megaforce* if Hal Needham had not been ... well, if he had not been Hal Needham.) *Jazira* also reunited Khambatta with her *Shingora* co-star Neeta Puri, who had appeared in Hira's *Kalank Ka Tika* and *Sone Ka Pinjra* in the meantime. Echoing Khambatta's own "I'm the best actress you'll ever see" bravado from her early days, Puri told the magazine *Sunday* regarding her ambition to graduate from video screens to movie screens that "my aim is to make it as an actress solely on the basis of my talent and perfection."[12]

The career momentum generated by previous associates who knew Khambatta could play violent women continued when she returned to the United States on March 15: she received a call that day from her former manager Jay Bernstein, who offered her a guest spot on his CBS series *The New Mike Hammer*. The tricky part was that shooting began on March 16, but Persis Khambatta was never one to let jet lag get in the way of work.[13]

The *Mike Hammer* role was of a kidnapper named Shandra who purloins a blind girl's dog, and Khambatta laughed off Shandra's cruelty: "I love children and I am so unlike my character. But that's what happens when you're an actor. You play better what you really are not in person." The blind girl was the daughter of an arms dealer named Decker, whom Shandra speaks to on the phone and refers to by name. (For such a brief English-language career, Khambatta played opposite male characters with the surnames of Hunter and Decker twice each. Oh, Hollywood.) Khambatta received an "and Persis Khambatta as Shandra" card in the credits during the first act, and she does not kill anyone onscreen—though she does get shot by Mike Hammer, which beats getting shot by Rick Hunter.[14]

Around the time the *Mike Hammer* episode aired in late April, Khambatta attended the premiere of Armand Mastroianni's horror film *Distortions* at the Academy Theater in Beverly Hills. The schlocky picture would go on to play in the Cannes market and be reviewed by *Variety*, which was more dignity than was afforded to the submarine picture Khambatta had made way back when. *First Strike* found its way onto United States video store shelves in July 1987 via Video City Productions, a distributor whose business model was repackaging older exploitation films. Considering their recent releases *Nazi Love Camp 27* and *The Last Orgy of the Third Reich* were both late-1970s Italian films, the 1984-lensed *First Strike* was both one of Video City's newest films, and one of their least tasteless.[15]

Variety's review of the "doomsday submarine thriller" noted that "the use of tape is particularly unflattering to Khambatta, who also suffers from several awkward line readings." Perhaps, but she's as graceful as Meryl Streep compared to most of the other performances in what may be Khambatta's most ineptly produced English-language film. Which is not to say it is her worst, nor is it unwatchable, but it is very clumsy on a technical level. *First Strike* is also a quintessential Dad Movie: if you grew up in a certain socioeconomic class in the United States in the 1980s, it was the kind of movie your Dad gravitated toward, particularly if he lacked the privacy to watch *Nazi Love Camp 27* or *The Last Orgy of the Third Reich*.[16]

A *First Strike* scene in which Khambatta's character of double agent Sylvia Kruger makes her way between submarines was most likely shot in a tank or swimming pool, and while it is unknown if Khambatta knew how to swim, she sure looks like she's trying not to drown. The picture also gives Khambatta her highest confirmed English-language kill count, as Kruger shoots five people at point-blank range just like Shakka and Nastasia, and stabs a sixth. Kruger escapes using her own wits, and is last seen floating in the water, looking at the burning remains of the ship which was supposed to rescue her. She probably dies, but *First Strike* does not resolve its narrative so much as it gets bored and changes the channel.

* * *

Video City Productions' business model was to revive films which had long since been shot and often but not always previously distributed, but David Winters' newly-formed Action International Pictures had a more proactive approach: making new films which were "infused with as much action as possible." (Action International Pictures is not to be confused with *Kamasutra*'s domestic distributor American International Pictures, though the similarity is not a coincidence, either.) After beginning pre-production in May 1987, principal photography on *Phoenix the Warrior* began that July in locations within a few hours' drive from Riverside, California. It was to be the last time Khambatta received star credit, and though not associated with Triillusion it was the first film for which she received a producer credit in the form of the historically meaningless "associate producer." This was part of how Winters lured in names which would be familiar to video store patrons; Dan Haggerty, Erik Estrada, and David Carradine each received associate producer credit for the 1989 Action International Pictures releases *Elves*, *Alien Seed*, and *Future Force*, respectively.[17]

Phoenix the Warrior is a post–*Road Warrior* action movie in the same broad vein as *Warrior of the Lost World*, but *Phoenix*'s core cast led by Kathleen Kinmont consisted of what Khambatta had once described as "blonde, blue-eyed, fluffy American girls," who throw themselves into the nudity which Khambatta herself never stopped refusing. The picture screened in the market at the Cannes Film Festival in mid–May 1988, and *Variety*'s review nailed it[18]:

> "Phoenix the Warrior" is a truly awful offering about a post-apocalyptic future populated solely by slim, long-legged women boasting leather-clad thighs and skimpy animal skins.
> An extended male fantasy more than any serious attempt at general fantasy, pic is destined to be the unavoidable inclusion at the tail end of a cheap homevideo package.[19]

All true. *Phoenix the Warrior* is by far the worst and laziest English-language film of Persis Khambatta's career, making *Megaforce* and *Warrior of the Lost World* look respectable by comparison, and even salvaging *First Strike*. Khambatta gives *Phoenix the Warrior* her all as the black-clad villain Cobalt; to put it in Star Wars terms, Khambatta's Cobalt is the Darth Vader to the Emperor Palpatine that is Sheila Howard's the Reverend Mother. If anything good can be said about *Phoenix*, it is that the Reverend Mother's Palpatine-esque makeup is better than might be expected for such a cheapjack production.

Variety's forecast that *Phoenix the Warrior*'s destiny was to be included in "the tail end of a cheap homevideo package" proved accurate when Sony Video Software released it on VHS in October 1988 for a standalone price of

$79.95, or as part of a three-tape, $159 "Money-Maker prepack" along with the 1988 film *The Rejuvenator* and the 1981 *The Appointment*. Sony's marketing manager predicted that "based on the average retail purchase price, the retailer breaks even on only 15 rentals per title," and *Phoenix*'s cover and poster art by the famous fantasy artist Boris Vallejo did help the film break even at my video store. It was the kind of tape which tended to be returned unfinished and unkindly unrewound: the average young male viewer who was drawn in by the promise of bare breasts would find that promise fulfilled in the first twenty minutes when the fluffy American women bathe under a waterfall, during which time the viewer would reach his own personal climax, then eject the tape and put it back in the box as-is.[20]

This also means that most of the film's viewers never saw Khambatta's second-to-last onscreen death. After Phoenix's band of rebels infiltrate the boiler room which passes for the film's Death Star, Phoenix engages in a deadly game of cat-and-mouse with Cobalt. (Given that Khambatta had mostly been in action films, it is somewhat surprising that she had never been in a deadly game of cat-and-mouse before this. Her deleted scenes from *Nighthawks* have never been released, so it is possible that *Phoenix the Warrior* was just her first deadly game of cat-and-mouse to make it to the final cut.) After some close-up fighting which requires both Khambatta and Kinmont to throw stage punches, Khambatta dies a very late-1980s villain death when Phoenix blows her up with a grenade. Or something like that—the editing is not very clear, but it still qualifies as one of the last examples of the Exploding Bad Guy trend familiar from films like *Rambo: First Blood Part II*, *Invasion USA* and *Wanted: Dead or Alive*, and which made a pleasant return in Cathy Yan's 2020 *Birds of Prey and the Fantabulous Emancipation of One Harley Quinn*.

* * *

Khambatta started shooting director Nigel Dick's *Deadly Intent* in November 1987, a few months after *Phoenix the Warrior* wrapped. It would prove to be Khambatta's final feature film in any language, and while she had been the only famous name in *Phoenix*, producer Chuck Fries rounded up a stable of B-movie stalwarts for *Deadly Intent*. The biggest male name was Lance Henriksen, who became famous in James Cameron's 1986 *Aliens* but never stopped working in smaller pictures. *Deadly Intent*'s biggest female name was Maud Adams, and one can imagine a parallel timeline in which Khambatta was cast in *Octopussy* instead of Adams, and yet they still both wound up working for Chuck Fries a few years later.[21]

Deadly Intent is unremarkable and comparatively inoffensive as straight-to-video schlock goes. Though only a promotional reel of it was ready for the American Film Market in late February, the completed film was screened in the Cannes Film Market in May 1988, and Khambatta's role was so minor she was not mentioned in the subsequent *Variety* review. As Francesca Slate, the partner of Fred Williamson's Curt Slate in both marriage and jewel-thievery, Khambatta first appears after about half an hour, saying nothing and wearing a sweater which is unspeakable even by the standards of the late 1980s. Khambatta and Williamson appear again about 20 minutes later, and this time Khambatta gets the majority of the dialog in a scene opposite Maud Adams.[22]

Francesca and Curt invade the home of the film's female lead Laura played by Lisa Eilbacher just shy of the hour mark; this leads to Khambatta's first and last foot chase in an English-language film as Francesca runs after Laura, followed by a solid half-minute of the two women wrestling as Curt watches. It appears to be the only time Khambatta had a stunt double; her face is hidden for most of the totally-necessary-for-the-story chase and wrestling, and there are two female stunt performers listed in the credits, Rosine "Ace" Hatem and Lynn Salvatori. One can only hope.

Khambatta's final scene in both *Deadly Intent* and films overall is also her second and last deadly game of cat-and-mouse, this time with a killer played by stuntman Solly Marx. As was so often the case with low-budget films from the late 1980s the scene is set in a warehouse full of cardboard boxes, and Marx gets the drop on Khambatta with a sword, slashing her wrist and then her throat.

In review, this is Khambatta's death roster in English-language films:

- *The Wilby Conspiracy*: falls down a mineshaft
- *Star Trek—The Motion Picture*: disintegrated
- *Nighthawks*: shot in the head
- *First Strike*: drowns (offscreen, implied)
- *Phoenix the Warrior*: explodes
- *Deadly Intent*: throat slashed by sword

Speaking of her career trajectory, on March 28, 1978, Khambatta had been on the dais for a press conference on the Paramount lot which was catered by Chasen's. Ten years later, she sat in a booth at Chasen's itself along with Maud Adams, Steve Railsback, Barbara Carerra, and other actors appearing upcoming projects by producer Chuck Fries during the American Film Market on February 29, 1988.[23]

This Is a Lowe

Two months after *Nighthawks* flopped in 1981, Sylvester Stallone signed with Mike Ovitz's Creative Artists Agency. Stallone was still with the

CAA in 1988 when he appeared in a much-hyped *Barbara Walters Special* on ABC on May 11 in which Walters interviewed Stallone in his house in Beverly Hills to promote the upcoming *Rambo III*. It was Peak Stallone: he was such a big star that CBS ran his 1985 hit *Rocky IV* in the same timeslot opposite the Barbara Walters interview.[24]

Two months after *Nighthawks* flopped in 1981, Persis Khambatta re-signed with David Moss as her agent after a few years with Jay Bernstein. In 1985 she left Moss for either Talent International or Contemporary Korman Artists (or possibly both) and returned to Moss in April 1988. On the day after the national broadcast of Ovitz client Sylvester Stallone's interview on *The Barbara Walters Special*, Moss client Persis Khambatta ventured into the American Cablesystems studios where she and actor Ed Fury were guests on the public access show *Skip E. Lowe Looks at Hollywood* on local cable channel 37.[25]

There is not enough space available in this book, or possibly in the observable universe, to give celebrity interviewer Skip E. Lowe his due. Martin Short based his character of Jiminy Glick to an extent on Lowe, and the best shorthand to describe Lowe is something Short said to David Letterman in 2001 and which was reprinted in articles noting Lowe's 2014 passing: when Lowe talked to people, he got "confused with tremendous enthusiasm."[26]

Though it was a "poking her with a stick" interview, what kept Lowe's tone-deafness from being *Oui*-like was his lack of guile, and his introduction did not lack enthusiasm: "Persis Khambatta.... Persis Khambatta ... what a nice name! Bombay, India.... Miss India ... tell me about yourself." And before Khambatta is able to start telling him about herself, Lowe continues: "Miss India! Good God, that's a great title. Beauty ... come to California, or Hollywood, or New York, or where?"[27]

Lowe was not wrong about Persis Khambatta being a nice name or Miss India being a great title, and there may be no better example of Lowe's "confused enthusiasm" than when he held up a picture of Robot Ilia but could not recall the name of the multi-billion dollar franchise it was from: "Tell me about Star.... Str ... tell me about this. This is Persis Khambatta."[28]

Khambatta admitted in the interview that she used to do things that made her feel bad in order to please other people—she didn't cite examples, but one has to wonder if letting Shatner and Koenig kiss her bald head was among those things—and that while "guilt is an Indian tradition," she no longer did things which made her feel bad, and that she had no regrets. Asked by Lowe, "what makes Persis have a good time? What does it take to have a good time for Persis Khambatta?" she gave what may be one of her most unguarded responses: "I have a link with the universe, and there's a child in me, I communicate with the child, and I protect the child, and I've begun to like myself."[29]

Khambatta herself brought up the E-bomb in the context of her American co-stars being "sort of protective" of her because she came from a foreign country, but, "you also get scared of being exotic." As Khambatta tried to explain that being considered exotic was a problem because it made people afraid to approach her, Lowe interrupted her: "Do you want to know why they're afraid to approach you?" The camera remained on a close-up of Lowe while Khambatta muttered "yeah" offscreen and Lowe proceeded to tell Khambatta what she knew all too well: "Because you're exotic and beautiful. Let's show the clip why they're afraid to approach Persis Khambatta, 'cuz you're so beautiful and exotic and different … and daring. From the wonderful film Star Trek, let's see that clip of Persis Khambatta." The clip was a montage of Robot Ilia scenes which make no sense out of context and not much more in context, after which Lowe said, "Persis Khambatta, that's so beautiful. Spiritual, and loving." Which are all words, and they are almost formed into complete sentences. To Lowe's credit, he did not focus on Khambatta having been bald in that one movie that one time, nor did he treat it as the end-all and be-all of her as a person or a performer.[30]

But even a spry little pixie like Skip E. Lowe was not immune to the male tendency in both reality and fiction to not believe what a woman says until a man confirms it. Khambatta described her problems with the Indian film industry: "In one day they will shoot two hours for one producer, and in the evening, they'll go for two hours for another producer, so they'll do about three or four films a day shooting. It's a different system completely. When I go there, and I don't do a lot of films, it's because they can never give me six weeks complete to shoot a film. They will say, could you come back in two months? And I couldn't afford to do that."[31]

To which Lowe replied with another one of his trademarks, a non-sequitur which was somehow also on topic: "They're all in English!" Except they were not all in English, and Khambatta corrected him: "No, in Hindi!" Speaking from the depths of his knowledge of a subject he knew nothing about, Lowe rebutted with, "They're in Hindi? None in English? There are some in English! No?" It was only when the hunky Ed Fury stepped in to verify that Hindi films are not in English, and that he had experienced the same weird shooting patterns, that Lowe seemed to believe Khambatta.[32]

Asked if she has any films coming up, Khambatta replied, "Yes, *Deadly Intent* with Steve Railsback, and I'm doing another one next month in Manila." There is no way to know if that Manila film got made without Khambatta or not at all, and it's all the same in the end.[33]

* * *

Celebrity is a mill which grinds humans down to their most marketable elements, such as the 1988 book *Christensen's Celebrity Autographs* in which Khambatta's signature from a *Nighthawks* press photo was one of 6,000 self-identifying scrawls, sandwiched between those of Evelyn Keyes and Guy Kibbie.[34] Meanwhile, as *Phoenix the Warrior* flew off video store shelves into the hands of furtive masturbators in mid-December 1988, a close friend of Khambatta's introduced her to a visiting relative, Rui Ninnian Saldanha. A member of Britain's field hockey team in the 1972 Olympics, Saldanha was presently a business insurance specialist for New York Life Insurance. Not in New York, mind you, but their office in Des Moines, Iowa.[35]

But Khambatta was smitten, and she had never been one to let geography hold her back.

1989-1990

The Triillusion Dissolution

Khambatta would do what was necessary to become Rui Saldanha's beloved wife—but not all at once, and not instantly, to be sure. She participated in the January 24 unveiling of the 1989 Golden Globe nominees; on January 25 she and Kabir Bedi were among the Indian celebrities who turned out in force at the Writers Guild Theater for the premiere of Jagmohan Mundhra's latest English-language film, *The Jigsaw Murders*; and on January 28 she attended but did not otherwise participate in the Golden Globes show.[1]

There was also the matter of Triillusion.

Khambatta had taken over the duties of her corporation's Secretary and Chief Financial Officer from Waldo Brain and Sukhbir Kang as of August 1988, and she had always been the Chief Executive Officer and its only Director. That simplified matters considerably when she signed the Certificate of Election to Wind Up and Dissolve as Triillusion's President and Secretary, and she signed the Certificate of Dissolution as its sole Director. Both documents were dated April 15, 1989, and the latter read[2]:

PERSIS KHAMBATTA certifies that:

1. She constitutes a majority of the directors now in office of TRIILLUSION CO, a California Corporation. (C 1057069)

2. The corporation has been completely wound up.

3. The corporation's known debts and liabilities have been adequately provided for by their assumption by Persis Khambatta, care of: Brain Bookkeeping & Tax Service, 19138 Hartland Street, Reseda, CA 91335

4. The corporation's known assets have been distributed to the persons entitled thereto.

5. The corporation is dissolved.

I further declared under the penalty of perjury under the laws of the State of California that the matters set forth in this certificate are true and correct of my own knowledge.

DATE: April 15, 1989[3]

Part of the reason Khambatta euthanized her company was that she'd had enough of the struggle; whatever God's plan may have been, it did not involve her producing movies under the aegis of her own stock-issuing corporation. One sign had come earlier in 1989 when *Megaforce*'s production company Golden Harvest offered to buy the unmade *Bandit Queen* property. Khambatta and Susie Coelho both sold their preproduction material, as did *Cosmopolitan* and all the other magazines which had run stories about Phoolan Devi. Golden Harvest producer John Strong III (of the early Indian themed *For Your Eyes Only* treatment) was currently casting for the lead role, and he noted that "the actress does not have to be an Indian," but "she has to be a newcomer. She could, of course, be an Indian. Or a Pakistani. Or someone from Spain, Italy, Portugal or South America." So, whoever from wherever, because one exotic woman is as good as another. The film never got made, at least not by Golden Harvest.[4]

Exile on Main Street: Des Moines

Another reason for Khambatta to dissolve Triillusion was that while State law did not require a California corporation's head honcho to be a California resident, she was now an Iowa resident—at least according to the list of people who had applied for marriage licenses in Polk County printed in the April 27, 1989, *Des Moines Register*:

> Rui N. Saldanha, 41, Des Moines, and Persis Khambatta, 42, Des Moines.[5]

Khambatta's second confirmed wedding was more laid-back than her first to Cliff Taylor at La Cage in 1981: she tied the knot with Saldanha at the Polk County Courthouse on May 14, 1989. She managed to stay under the radar in their West Des Moines apartment for the first few months, but word soon spread, and she consented to a request from *Des Moines Register* writer Julie Gammack. Khambatta had stopped shaving her head in January 1979, but the headline for Gammack's July 24, 1989, feature was "Bald Beauty of 'Star Trek' Film Beams Down Snugly in W.D.M." In case the headline did not remind the reader that Khambatta had been bald in that one movie that one time, the article kicked off with it.[6]

> That mysterious bald-headed woman from "Star Trek, the Motion Picture" moved to town just weeks ago. No kidding.
> So did the sultry Indian woman who portrayed Sylvester Stallone's nemesis in "Nighthawks." The Trekkie and the nemesis are one and the same, and she has appeared in films with Michael York, Sidney Poitier and Michael Caine.
> Persis Khambatta, now of West Des Moines, may be one of the few folks here roaming the grocery store video aisles who is actually featured in the film credits.[7]

The header picture was of Khambatta and Saldanha outside the Des Moines Art Center, Khambatta's hair long and lush. The article's other photo was the now-familiar murky, confounding, and unpleasant image of William Shatner and his hairy left arm clutching Khambatta's right shoulder, the caption for which misspelled her first name: "Bald Khambatta mystifies William Shatner in 'Star Trek, the Motion Picture.'" Gammack never used words to acknowledge that Khambatta was no longer bald in 1989, though she did write that Khambatta "actually shaved her head for the performance" in 1979, while also observing that while there was a lot of competition for the role, "the Indian woman's exotic profile prevailed."[8]

As for what the exotic-profiled Indian woman would be doing with herself in 1989 Iowa, "she is hoping she will be able to commute to jobs in Los Angeles and New York. She knows it will be difficult, because she's no longer living where the acting jobs are. She plans to get involved in local theater productions and would like to work in television here. She has faith in destiny. 'If I'm not meant to act, I'll accept that,' she said."[9]

Khambatta did her best to sound resigned to this change in direction.

> I'm really beginning to enjoy it here now. My first impression of America was Los Angeles and New York. This place gives you a calmness. It's safe. Everything is so chaotic in big cities.
>
> I've worked since I was 13, now I feel God has given me a holiday. I'm reading and listening to subliminal self-improvement tapes, and I have more time to meditate. But I would love to work.[10]

The work she did do while in Iowa was social, including joining the board of the Community Living Foundation, a privately-owned organization which raised money to grant financial assistance to caregivers as an alternative to institutionalization, thus helping developmentally disabled people remain at home, with their families.[11]

This included appearing in a commercial which ran on the local NBC affiliate WHO-TV in the autumn of 1990. It began with a starfield and a photo of Robot Ilia with the caption "Persis Khambatta as ILIA in Star Trek the Motion Picture," as she speaks in voiceover, "For most kids, it's fun to dream about the future." She then appeared onscreen identified as "Persis Khambatta, Board Member, Community Living Foundation for Iowans," and explained the organization's mission of providing wheelchairs and other such services for disabled children. The final shot is of the Bob Peak poster for the first Star Trek movie, but with Khambatta's, Shatner's, and Nimoy's faces airbrushed out and the title replaced with the organization's name and telephone number, as she asked for support "so all of Iowa's children can dream about the future."[12]

By the time it aired, Khambatta was dreaming about a different future.

* * *

Everyone has their own definition of rock bottom. There's no telling what the threshold was for Persis Khambatta—the isolation of Midwest life, the emotional toll of working for the Community Living Foundation, or again feeling like marriage had made her legally half a woman—but within a year of the October 1990 airing of the commercial, she was no longer living in Iowa.

Her God-given holiday was over.

The Nineties

1991–1993

Exile on Main Street: Los Angeles

Persis Khambatta was back in Los Angeles in time to be photographed by Ron Galella on June 21, 1991, at a party at the Beverly Hills home of Joseph Bologna and Renee Taylor. That autumn was packed with Indian-community events, including providing star power at the ribbon-cutting of *India West*'s new Artesia offices on October 24 as well as the annual fundraiser for the Nargis Dutt Foundation in Buena Park the next day. She returned to Artesia on November 25, where she was joined by the current Misses Artesia and California for the opening of the new Bhindi Jewellers building, and a few days later she was one of the judges of the fourth annual Miss L.A. India pageant. The event itself was kicked off by former Miss L.A. India and current Miss India USA and Miss India Universe winner Bela Bajaria, who told the audience that winning Miss L.A. India had encouraged her "to take a deeper look into myself, into my culture and into the inner beauty of the young Indian woman," and taught her "to overcome the steepness of adversity and the pitfalls of uncertainty."[1]

In 1965, Khambatta was crowned Miss India. In 1981, she founded Triillusion Co. to produce her own projects. In 1989, she wound up and dissolved the company without getting a single project off the ground.

In 1991, Bela Bajaria was crowned both Miss L.A. India and Miss India-Universe. In 2011 Bajaria became the president of Universal Television, where she helped to develop Mindy Kaling's *The Mindy Project* and Aziz Ansari's *Master of None*, and in 2016 she was named Vice President of Content at Netflix.[2] During the writing of *Presenting Persis Khambatta* in 2019 it was announced that while retaining her title of Content VP, Bajaria would start to focus on "lead international non–English TV originals—scripted, unscripted, comedy—in all international markets where Netflix is available, excluding Asia but including India." The arc of history bends toward social justice—I could not find a single article referring to Bajaria as exotic—but it must also leave people behind, as it did Khambatta.[3]

1991 was the 25th anniversary of the Star Trek franchise, and the nostalgia was strong enough that she was invited to the Paramount lot for the first time in years for the premiere of *Star Trek VI: The Undiscovered Country* on December 3, 1991. There, Ron Galella photographed Khambatta hugging James Doohan, for time heals all aloofness.[4]

The New Old School

Even as representations of South Asian people in American films were improving, non-demeaning work was still difficult to find in 1992. On April 6, Khambatta attended a UNICEF benefit screening of Roland Joffé's Calcutta-set *City of Joy* at the Academy of Television Arts and Sciences. Though the film had a white-savior narrative and leaned heavily on the begging bowl image of India which Indira Gandhi had hoped was no more back in 1982—Roger Ebert's review described *City of Joy*'s depiction of Calcutta as having "borrowed more from Dickens than from India"—the Indian characters were played by Indian people, and unlike David Lean's *A Passage to India* a mere eight years earlier, there was no hint of brownface or accents based on racist Peter Sellers caricatures. But *City of Joy*'s expansive cast did not include Persis Khambatta or even *Passage*'s Victor Banerjee, whose own Hollywood career had long since stalled out.[5]

What little English-language work Khambatta scrounged up also resulted in Hindi producers becoming reluctant to hire her for fear that she would get a better offer back in Hollywood and leave India in the middle of the production. They were accusing her of the kind of unprofessionalism she had always found so distasteful about the Indian film industry, but other than leaving *Awam* due to the part being misrepresented, Khambatta had always finished whatever movie she started. She had both the scars and the medical records to prove it.[6]

Khambatta was considering bidding *adieu* to the whole Hollywood grind, and told as much to Michael Potts in a May 15 *India West* article which announced her decision "to return home to Bombay and explore new horizons." She put a topical spin on it[7]:

> The recession has caused the Hollywood studios and independent companies to cut back on production, "which means less work for (an) exotic actress, and I am exotic," Khambatta told India-West.
>
> "In a way, I'm a minority," she added, "and so I've decided I have more opportunities in India, endless opportunities, because every year when I went back to India I was offered work in television serials."[8]

Khambatta had been trying to shake off the word "exotic" since she arrived in London in 1971; she was no closer to doing so in 1981, and in 1992 she released herself from the struggle by accepting the word. But she was not one to rest on her laurels or stop bring productive, and she told Potts she was considering opening a modeling school upon her return to Bombay. She would put her time in the school of hard knocks to good use by mentoring the next generation, and the curriculum would go beyond how to stand in front of a camera.[9]

> I would help them, first of all, to get their own inner strength and use their own confidence, and I would guide them because of the experience I've had.
> Even now, I tell them that they have to be in control of themselves, what happens with managers and agents (is that) you tend to let them do the work, thinking that they'd are going to take care of you. I start smiling when people here say, "trust me," because in Hollywood "trust me" means you-know-what.[10]

She planned to invite representatives of the American beauty industry to speak at her Bombay school, but she would also be brutally frank with her potential students: "I would be very honest in telling them if they had the necessary qualities and talent to make it in this business. Just because someone puts up the financing, I couldn't in good conscience lead them on."[11]

Her planned school never opened, and while she did not return to Bombay for good until 1995, she was resigned to returning in the May 1992 interview: "'I've come to a stage in my life where I feel more comfortable being with my people in India. There's a part of me that feels happy and safe. Somehow I like the challenge of going back.'" Never one to entirely give up, she told Potts that returning to India didn't mean she was through with Hollywood: "'I will be back.'"[12]

To an outside observer it might have looked like she never left Hollywood, for in September she attended the pre-party for the Chabad Telethon at the Beverly Hills home of Shirley Jones and Marty Engel. In December Khambatta was the special guest at the Asian Indian Women's Network's annual holiday luncheon at the Radisson Hotel in Diamond Bar. The Network's founder Angela Anand described their new Mentor and Protégé Program, which was similar to Khambatta's vision for her own school: "Whether starting a new business, changing one's career, or venturing beyond convention in pursuit of one's own vision and dreams would be more manageable and less stressful when a fellow community member has gone through a similar situation or path." What Khambatta said in her own remarks was not recorded beyond talking about the media-generated "Year of the Woman"—not to be confused with the United Nations' long-forgotten International Women's Year and/or Decade for Women—while *Asianweek* wrote that she "also injected thoughts about women in general, including the perception that men who are successful are viewed positively while women are not." Whatever the reader's feelings about the world of competitive beauty whence she came, never let there be any doubt that at heart and in her actions, Persis Khambatta was a feminist. There is no doubt.[13]

Her final work in Hollywood came when she shot a guest appearance for the pilot episode of *Lois & Clark: The New Adventures of Superman* in the spring of 1993, around the time she appeared at her first and last Star Trek convention, held on April 3–4 at the Valley Forge Convention Center in King of Prussia, Pennsylvania. The newspaper ads for Spring Trek '93 noted that it was Khambatta's "1st Convention Ever." Creation Entertainment had advertised Khambatta as the special guest at a Los Angeles convention on February 27 of that year, but there is no evidence that the convention happened, so it can be concluded that the Spring Trek was indeed Khambatta's first convention ever. That it would also be her last ever was unknown at the time.[14]

Lois & Clark: The New Adventures of Superman's two-hour premiere was broadcast on September 12. Khambatta appears as the Chairperson of the Congress of Nations on television screens within the show's universe for about fifty seconds toward the end of the second act, providing exposition to set up the climax. It is a brief but very cool scene: Khambatta not only gets to say the words "Lex Luthor" aloud, but her character openly rebukes Luthor, who responds to her speech by flying into a fit of rage. Persis Khambatta's name is buried deep in the closing credits, but compared to her deaths in *Phoenix the Warrior* and *Deadly Intent*, getting to tell off Superman's greatest villain is not a bad final bow for the cameras in Hollywood.

Her final bow in front of motion picture cameras shooting narrative works, that is.

Persis Reaches Out

An earthquake measuring 6.5 on the Richter scale struck the Latur and Osmanabad districts of the Indian state of Maharashtra on September 30, with an early estimate of about 10,000 dead and several thousand injured. Persis Khambatta was in the United States, and she went to work calling in favors and pulling what strings she could.[15]

She took a break on November 20 to attend the 50th Golden Globes, where she was photographed arriving by Ron Galella. He captured Khambatta again on December 4 as she arrived with Pierce Brosnan at Wolfgang Puck's Spago for a $250-per-plate American Red Cross charity dinner to raise funds for the earthquake victims, about whom the numbers now stood at 30,000 people dead, 12,000 injured, and 130,000 homeless. Khambatta organized the event with Ashok Amritraj, and other attending celebrities included James Doohan, Robert Forster, and Bo Hopkins, while Amritraj co-hosted the event with Sally Kirkland and *Family Ties'* Michael Gross. Khambatta had the wonderful audacity to name the evening "Hollywood Reaches Out" in spite of having been discarded by Hollywood herself, telling *India West* that "nobody's ever done that, having Hollywood celebrities meet with the cream of the Indian community." She also described the event's target of $40,000 as "just a few pennies in the ocean compared with the needs of these unfortunate people, but each one of them together can make a difference for a devastated life."[16]

Apropos of nothing, it seems worth noting that David Wolper received the Jean Hersholt Humanitarian Award for being involved with the 1984 Olympics, while Khambatta's own humanitarian work was never acknowledged by the Academy. For as much as the entertainment industry likes to pat itself on the back for doing good things, the only contemporaneous accounts of the event I could find were in *India West* and *India Today*. It was even ignored by *Daily Variety* despite Army Archerd's previous interest in Khambatta's adventures, let alone the presence of Pierce Brosnan, who was red-hot because of his good supporting work in the bad but inexplicably popular movie *Mrs. Doubtfire*.

American Red Cross CEO James Haigwood presented Kirkland, Amritraj, and Gross with plaques recognizing their participation in Hollywood Reaches Out. Upon receiving his, Gross joked that it was great to get something just for showing up, and then added, "these all belong on Persis' wall, I think."[17]

Gross' joke was funny because it was true: the great strength of Khambatta was that she kept showing up. Until she didn't.

1994–1995

Persis Punches Back

Other Southern California locales where Khambatta showed up in 1994 included the third annual Super Model India Contest on March 26, at which Sona Patel won both the top prize and Miss Photogenic. Khambatta had worked with the contestants in the weeks leading up to the contest and was presented with a plaque honoring her achievements over the decades. On May 30 she was spotted at the restaurant Nirvana as a guest of *Jigsaw Murders* director Jagmohan Mundhra, who was celebrating the fact that his sixteenth and latest film *Improper Conduct* was his first to receive a domestic theatrical release, having recently opened in seven theaters in Los Angeles with releases planned in ten more cities.[1]

Heavily-accented *Terminator* star Arnold Schwarzenegger's era as a box-office attraction was beginning to wind down. The John McTiernan film *Last Action Hero* was 1993's most notorious flop, and Ivan Reitman's *Junior* and James Cameron's *True Lies* both underperformed in 1994, especially compared to Schwarzenegger's previous works with those directors, *Twins* and *Terminator 2: Judgment Day*. (*Junior* and *True Lies* also have the worst gender politics of Schwarzenegger's filmography, which is saying a lot.) But he would never go away, and still appeared in major films as recently as the aforementioned *Terminator: Dark Fate* in 2019. Schwarzenegger's success in the late 1980s also shepherded the career of another foreign-born action star with a thick accent, Jean-Claude Van Damme. Ashok Amritraj produced one of Van Damme's biggest hits, Sheldon Lettich's 1991 picture *Double Impact*, and though Van Damme's career in films which received wide theatrical distribution sputtered out by the end of the 1990s, he also never quite went away. At the core of both of Schwarzenegger's and Van Damme's personas was violence, for the spectacle of boys punching things cuts through all cultural barriers.

Those barriers were the subject of a letter by man named Michael Stein in the June 25, 1994, *Los Angeles Times*. Stein was wondering about the "pattern going on in Hollywood that has as much to say about America as it does about the movie industry. Where are the beautiful and talented actresses who have foreign accents?"²

> One way to stardom in movies is to create a sensation-get noticed in a really "showy" role.
> Persis Khambatta ("Star Trek-The Motion Picture"), Marthe Keller ("Bobby Deerfield"), Sonia Braga ("Kiss of the Spider Woman"), Nastassja Kinski ("Tess") and others have done that.
> But their careers in the United States did not skyrocket. Despite the legends, Greta Garbo and Sophia Loren, American audiences still are reticent to embrace performers with accents, and Hollywood doesn't want to make the effort to sell it to them.³

The letter struck a chord with Persis Khambatta, and the *Times* ran her response on July 11 with the headline "Put the Accent on Diversity." It had been over a year since she shot her brief appearance on *Lois & Clark*, but she still lived in Los Angeles and the 700-word column functioned as something of a post-mortem of her post–Trek Hollywood career.⁴

> I was asked to be a presenter at the Academy Awards. I was invited to the A-list parties; whisked to the best tables at the "power" restaurants. I had a growing career as a model and an actress in London—I had starred opposite Michael Caine and Sidney Poitier in "The Wilby Conspiracy"—but everyone told me to stay in Hollywood. This was the place, they said, and I could have a big career.
> What they failed to mention was that no one would quite know what to do with me. I knew I was not about to displace Florence Henderson as the mother of the "Brady Bunch," but America is a polyglot of accents, faces and backgrounds.⁵

If Khambatta knew about the *Octopussy* casting debacle she did not mention it, but she did write of her frustration that the role of an Indian woman in the 1984 HBO miniseries based on M.M. Kaye's *The Far Pavilions* went to the white actress Amy Irving. She also ruminated on the way Merle Oberon found it necessary to hide her Indian heritage decades earlier, or how CBS had been reluctant to buy *I Love Lucy* because they didn't think the public would accept a red-haired "All-American" woman being married to a man from Cuban.⁶

> Hollywood's trepidation with accents has become not just an archaic attitude, but an albatross limiting the textural realism today's directors, writers and producers crave. When I saw Isabella Rossellini—a second-generation Hollywood actress with an accent—portraying Jeff Bridges' wife in "Fearless," I thought perhaps we've made a little movement in the right direction.
> There are many of us—trained, seasoned actresses—available to continue the broadening of our American tapestry.⁷

Khambatta was not wrong about any of that, and while the broadening would be slow to arrive and not occur within her lifetime—and not without a great deal of pushback from many white Star Trek fans—it would eventually arrive.

* * *

Much as there is no telling what the final straw was that resulted in Persis Khambatta returning from Iowa to California, though she had been talking about doing so since 1992 it is unclear what finally convinced her to move back to India for good. Looking back in 1998, she said of her return, "There is no permanence in my life, in anything. I came to Mumbai for personal reasons and it took longer than I thought and I stayed."[8]

Logic thus demands that it was a coincidence that her final known public appearance in the western hemisphere was in this writer's hometown: Khambatta was on the panel of judges at the Miss Asian American Beauty Pageant on August 27, 1994, at the William Saroyan Theater in Fresno, California. She was also the pageant's guest of honor and modeled a sari which was in turn auctioned off for $1,200, and that money was donated to a local charity.[9]

I moved from Fresno to San Francisco on August 16 of that year; Persis Khambatta visited my hometown less than two weeks after I left it, and within the next six months she returned to Bombay to stay. The point being that while I cannot prove that finding herself in Fresno even just for a day or two was what made living in the United States untenable, I also cannot prove that it was not.

Her Journey Through the Past

Persis Khambatta moved into the apartment she had long ago purchased in Bombay's upscale Nepean Sea Road neighborhood in time for the launch of the 26th International Film Festival of India on January 10, 1995. She was present with directors Yash Chopra and Gautam Ghose for the event's highlight: famed art director Nitin Desai's extensive, million-rupee-transformation of the Nehru Centre into a simulacrum of the Grand Café in Paris where Auguste and Louis Lumière held the first screening of their cinematograph in 1895. It was quite the spectacle by all accounts, complete with fake snow, horse-drawn carriages—and plenty of can-canning, because they could. Not a bad welcome for India's erstwhile Film Princess, even if it wasn't for her as such.[10]

She was also one of the celebrity judges for the *Femina* Miss India contest at the Andheri Sports Complex in Bombay on January 14, her first time participating since she and Meher Mistry had walked the fashion show (and spied for Veena Sajnani) in 1970. The 1995 contest's panel included her old friend Vijay Amritraj as well as her old rival Zeenat Aman, but the audience was most excited about Hindi action film star Amitabh Bachchan, long known as "the angry young man" for his screen persona of a violent vigilante. (The spectacle of boys punching things cuts through all cultural barriers.)[11]

There was now a swimsuit round, and the contest was now broadcast live across the country on Doordarshan Television. As *Femina* editor Vimla Patil told Khambatta in *Pride of India*, this was part of a new respectability the contest had developed in recent years. The Miss World and Miss Universe contests relocated from the Western world to Asia in the early 1990s due to the recession in the United States and Britain, just as an increasingly liberalized India was becoming "the single biggest market of the free world" and satellite television was taking hold. Doordarshan Television had once refused to cover Miss India on the grounds that this contest which was run by women for women was derogatory to women, but they had since changed their mind, while the government began considering it a tourist attraction. The *Times of India* also started paying attention to the contest, and Bachchan later told Khambatta that he deigned to be a judge that year "'more out of a social, friendly relationship with the *Times*' than anything else."[12]

Miss India's profile had been further heightened when the previous year's winner Sushmita Sen went on to be crowned Miss Universe, and first runner-up Aishwarya Rai came in first at Miss World. Khambatta found the drama-fest that was the 1994 contest to be distasteful even by pageant standards, since the media had picked favorites during the sub contests leading up to the main event, and she was relieved it didn't happen again in 1995; even beyond the intense pressure of the contest, whoever won would do so in the shadow cast by Rai and Sen's high-profile victories. Those victories also functioned as cautionary tales: Sen had been offered roles in the United States soap opera *The Bold and the Beautiful* as well as the James Bond film *Goldeneye*, and she wanted to do them, but the Miss Universe organization crunched the numbers and realized that they could increase their own profits by sending Sen on a promotional tour, so they nixed her acting gigs. Miss India was run by women for women, but not Miss Universe, and this was before Donald Trump bought the latter organization.[13]

Meanwhile, the 1995 Miss India judges existed in Bachchan's shadow. Khambatta requested that they meet the contestants before the program began, and upon entering the room where the ten judges sat in a semicircle, all but one contestant walked straight to Bachchan. Manpreet Brar made a point of introducing herself to each of the judges, and though she was not considered a classic beauty, her assertiveness and mindfulness gave her an advantage: she won the title of Miss India that year, and was the first runner up at Miss Universe. Khambatta never got to start her modeling school, but if she had, Brar might have been a prize pupil.[14]

Another Dream Deferred

For all her frustrations with Hollywood, Khambatta was still not a fan of the Hindi film industry. She had told *India West* in early 1994 before moving back to Bombay that she watched "every single Hindi movie released" in the United States, but mostly "because I get homesick," and the writer of *Presenting Persis Khambatta* was relieved to learn that Khambatta also reached for the remote when the songs started.[15]

> I have realized that Hindi films are unreal, a fantasy. I always fast forward the songs. Indian movies never rivet me like American movies often do. Most of the time they play in the background while you go about your chores.[16]

But work is work, and in early July 1995 Persis Khambatta shot the pilot episode of a project which promised to keep her busy: *City of Dreams*, a lavish, 1.63-million-rupee 80-part television serial set in the Bombay film industry. Co-produced by Firoz Nadiadwala's Base Industries Group and the London-based Spotlight Leisure company, it was shot in English and directed by British helmer Tim Graham. The main character was a Bombay movie mogul played by real-world film star Suresh Oberoi, and Khambatta played his wife, who sleeps around with younger men. (The magazine *Sunday* referred to Oberoi and Khambatta as "Bollywood has-beens" whom the show might turn into "born-again stars.") *Dreams* also featured Khambatta's *Wilby Conspiracy* costar Saeed Jaffrey as a tabloid editor who would find plenty of muck to rack with what *India Today* described as the "set formula of cavorting lovers and underworld villains." But in spite of early interest from a few dozen European territories at the Cannes Film Market in May 1995, the projected September start date came and went, and the project was shelved.[17]

Also shelved that year was a far more modest television project, a Khambatta-hosted chatshow to be called *Talk of the Town*. Next was an Anant Balani film titled *Khafa*, in which Khambatta was to play what she described as "the role of a strong woman—not a vamp." (Persis Khambatta was a feminist. There is no doubt.) The project gained a fair amount of press attention, not due to Khambatta's presence but because of hunky model and television actor Milind Soman making his big-screen debut. It was slated to begin shooting in April 1996 and to be released by the end of the year, but it did not and thus was not.[18]

Khafa translates into English as "irritated" or "angry," which is an apt description of Khambatta's mood in an March 1996 interview with Saira Menezes for *Outlook India*'s 10 Questions column, after *City of Dreams* and *Talk of the Town* had collapsed but while *Khafa* was still a going concern. The quick-question-and-quick-answer format allowed for little nuance or reflection, so Menezes went straight for the ego jugular: "After Star Trek, why did you stop shining?" Khambatta parried with: "Every star, whether it's Harrison Ford or Robert De Niro, is remembered by one film. Persis is a star in the sky—how can a star be forgotten when all you have to do is look up and see her." Menezes asked if it wasn't "a comedown for a star" to return to the Indian film industry after working in Hollywood, and Khambatta again refused to buy into that narrative: "I was a star even before I left India. In any case, for an actor, getting work is important."[19]

Khambatta described the *Khufu* role as "challenging and different from anything that I have done abroad," and that she was "working on my Hindi and my dances." Menezes' ears perked up at that word, and she asked, "Dances? Are you going to prance around trees and get typecast?" But Persis Khambatta was never one to consent to feeling inferior: "I love what I do and I'm not doing anything either for money or for the sake of some unfulfilled ambition. So there's no question of getting typecast." She also walked unafraid of losing a gig due to speaking her mind: "I don't backstab and if something pisses me off, I say it in no uncertain terms." When Khambatta was unwilling to name her planned romantic lead in *Khafa*, Menezes asked who her real-life leading man was: "There's nobody right now in my life. I like it that way."[20]

1996–1997

Pride of India *Is Begun*

Persis Khambatta may have liked not having anybody in her life, but she didn't like not working. While talking to her old friend and *Shingora* and *Jazira* producer Nari Hira (whose Hiba Films had run out of steam by 1990) after *Khafa*'s April 1996 start date came and went, Khambatta brought up the idea she'd been tossing around ever since meeting Indira Gandhi in 1982: a book honoring Miss India, and by extension all the women of India. Hira's response that the book was a "million dollar idea" was a good start, and being introduced to publisher Surendra Somani was an even better one, though Khambatta didn't bring up the book at first. Part of this was her fear of someone else taking her idea. There were countless examples in Hollywood—the Phoolan Devi free-for-all was a minor case of it—but it had also happened to Khambatta in India, and not even in the film industry: she wrote a song about Mother Teresa and sent it to musician Bappi Lahiri, who promptly wrote and recorded his own Mother Teresa song instead.[1]

Several weeks after their initial introduction, Somani read of a personal crisis in Khambatta's family and called to express concern and offer his assistance. Khambatta described the book during that conversation; Surendra liked the idea enough to set up an in-person meeting for the next day, and *Pride of India* started down the road to becoming a thing. (In his blurb for the book's dust jacket, fashion guru Prasad Bidapa wrote that when Khambatta told him she was writing a book about all the Miss Indias, "I said, 'Why bother?' The story we want is hers, the Persis saga, for I cannot think of a more interesting subject." Fair point!)[2]

Khambatta began tracking down as many former Miss Indias as she could, both winners and runners-up. She included the recipients of the title no matter which publication bestowed it—*Femina*, *Eve's Weekly*, or neither—as well as anyone who represented India in other contests such as Teen Princess, Navy Queen, Indian Princess, or even *Femina*'s own short-lived Bharat Sundari, the winners of which had gone on to participate reflection, so Menezes went straight for the ego jugular: "After Star Trek, why did you stop shining?" Khambatta parried with: "Every star, whether it's Harrison Ford or Robert De Niro, is remembered by one film. Persis is a star in the sky—how can a star be forgotten when all you have to do is look up and see her." Menezes asked if it wasn't "a comedown for a star" to return to the Indian film industry after working in Hollywood, and Khambatta again refused to buy into that narrative: "I was a star even before I left India. In any case, for an actor, getting work is important."[19]

Khambatta described the *Khafa* role as "challenging and different from anything that I have done abroad," and that she was "working on my Hindi and my dances." Menezes' ears perked up at that word, and she asked, "Dances? Are you going to prance around trees and get typecast?" But Persis Khambatta was never one to consent to feeling inferior: "I love what I do and I'm not doing anything either for money or for the sake of some unfulfilled ambition. So there's no question of getting typecast." She also walked unafraid of losing a gig due to speaking her mind: "I don't backstab and if something pisses me off, I say it in no uncertain terms." When Khambatta was unwilling to name her planned romantic lead in *Khafa*, Menezes asked who her real-life leading man was: "There's nobody right now in my life. I like it that way."[20]

1996–1997

Pride of India *Is Begun*

Persis Khambatta may have liked not having anybody in her life, but she didn't like not working. While talking to her old friend and *Shingora* and *Jazira* producer Nari Hira (whose Hiba Films had run out of steam by 1990) after *Khafa*'s April 1996 start date came and went, Khambatta brought up the idea she'd been tossing around ever since meeting Indira Gandhi in 1982: a book honoring Miss India, and by extension all the women of India. Hira's response that the book was a "million dollar idea" was a good start, and being introduced to publisher Surendra Somani was an even better one, though Khambatta didn't bring up the book at first. Part of this was her fear of someone else taking her idea. There were countless examples in Hollywood—the Phoolan Devi free-for-all was a minor case of it—but it had also happened to Khambatta in India, and not even in the film industry: she wrote a song about Mother Teresa and sent it to musician Bappi Lahiri, who promptly wrote and recorded his own Mother Teresa song instead.[1]

Several weeks after their initial introduction, Somani read of a personal crisis in Khambatta's family and called to express concern and offer his assistance. Khambatta described the book during that conversation; Surendra liked the idea enough to set up an in-person meeting for the next day, and *Pride of India* started down the road to becoming a thing. (In his blurb for the book's dust jacket, fashion guru Prasad Bidapa wrote that when Khambatta told him she was writing a book about all the Miss Indias, "I said, 'Why bother?' The story we want is hers, the Persis saga, for I cannot think of a more interesting subject." Fair point!)[2]

Khambatta began tracking down as many former Miss Indias as she could, both winners and runners-up. She included the recipients of the title no matter which publication bestowed it—*Femina*, *Eve's Weekly*, or neither—as well as anyone who represented India in other contests such as Teen Princess, Navy Queen, Indian Princess, or even *Femina*'s own short-lived Bharat Sundari, the winners of which had gone on to participate in that year's Miss World. *Pride of India* documents the achievements and struggles of more than 80 women, or at least as many achievements and struggles as they were willing to reveal. Khambatta's own modeling/mentoring school never happened, but she hoped her book would inspire the women of tomorrow while allowing the past winners to relive what were often forgotten glories.³

As she described it in *Pride of India*'s introduction:

> This book needed the co-operation of all the beautiful people in it. And most have helped me unstintingly, though a few needed a little pampering and attention. Transforming my vision of the book into reality was more difficult than it appeared. I left my ego aside, pursued the slimmest of chances and followed the most unlikely leads. The roads to completion were unbeaten tracks that often lead nowhere and were paved with the cobbled stones of frustration. Trying to trace some of these girls who are now settled in different parts of the world, or making 20 calls to some of them for an interview only to be told they are sleeping, having lunch, in the bath or out, often had me wanting to cry off. Their parents, secretaries or servants took my number down and the call that came back was as rare as the Kohinoor. But I persisted.⁴

The project was no longer a secret as of November 1996 when *Sunday* announced that "Khambatta is coming out with a 180-page book detailing the lives and times of former Miss Indias" which would also "offer an overview of the beauty business and fashion industry and dole out tips to aspiring models," and that the book was timed "to coincide with the Miss World pageant." This last part was not strictly true; Miss World had been in the news due to controversies which are beyond the scope of this book, but Khambatta was more conscious that the 50th anniversary of Indian Independence was August 15, 1997. While it might not be possible to have the book out by that month, she was determined it would be published in the semicentennial year.⁵

This meant she could squeeze in the 1997 Miss India contest, and Khambatta attended in January to interview her old fan Hemant Trivedi, who was co-directing the festivities with Lubna Adam. In that year's contest, there would be three winners who would go on to compete in Miss Asia Pacific, Miss World, and Miss Universe. There was buzz backstage about the book, and during a rehearsal Khambatta told the contestants, "I will be interviewing three of you girls for my book." This excited Diana Hayden, who said to herself, "Persis, I promise you this. I will be one of them." Hayden kept that promise when she won the Miss India–World 1997 title, and she was interviewed in *Pride of India* along with Nafisa Joseph (Miss India–Universe 1997) and Divya Chauhan (Miss India–Asia Pacific 1997).⁶

Though there were over a dozen people whom Khambatta could not reach or who did not want to speak to her, in the final product she was able to interview 85 contestants. She also spoke to three organizers, ten judges (including "India's supernova" Amit Bachchan), and four designers and/or choreographers.[7]

She found the past Miss Indias across the spectrum of achievement. Khambatta interviewed Pamela Singh *née* Bordes (Miss India 1982) in the restroom at a gallery displaying Singh's latest photography exhibit as reporters swarmed outside. Wendy Vaz (runner-up for Miss India 1969) was the director of an Indian industrial safety equipment manufacturer, while Veena Prakash (delegate to Miss World 1977) had recently worked in public relations for an investment banking firm in the United States. Nafisa Ali (*Eve's Weekly* Miss India 1976) had appeared in the 1979 film *Junoon*, and told Khambatta she wanted to return to movies just so she could work with Amitabh Bachchan, which she later did in the 1998 film *Major Saab*. Both Shikha Swaroop (*Eve's Weekly* Miss India 1988) and Karminder Kaur (Miss India/2 1993) had wanted to act in movies, but at 5' 10" each they were considered too tall, since it would not be acceptable for the heroine to tower over the leading man.[8]

Roopa Satyan (Miss India 1972) had mixed feelings: "The negative aspect is that it generates a lot of envy among women and makes you an easy target for a lot of malicious gossip. And presently it is being used against me in a very bitter divorce." Being Miss India wasn't at the top of her list of regrets, however: "If I had to do it all over again, I wouldn't have married so early. A big mistake!" While Satyan had been Miss India in 1972 and went on to compete in Miss Universe, Malathi Basappa had won Bharat Sundari that year and competed in Miss World. When speaking to Khambatta in 1997, Basappa was not impressed by any of it: "Beauty is no achievement, I would rather have been a famous writer or doctor." Nor was she thrilled about being associated with the specific crown she never won: "It irks me that even after all these years I am still spoken of as a Miss India, sidelining all my other achievements and experiences. It has been nearly 25 years since the Miss India contest. I have grown older and hopefully, wiser. People tend to forget that the laws of nature apply to Miss Indias as well!"[9]

* * *

"In more difficult times," Khambatta wrote in *Pride of India*, "researching this book is like tracing wayward school friends who have wandered carelessly all over the globe." But it also offered opportunities for reconciliation, for whatever beef Zeenat Aman and Persis Khambatta may have once had with each other is not hinted at in the entry about Aman. Perhaps being Miss India judges together in the 1995 pageant had helped to heal those wounds.[10]

Though that 1995 Miss India contest had a swimsuit round, it hadn't been established by 1989 when Suzanne Sabloak won; as she later told Khambatta, at Miss Universe "they asked me if I had a bathing costume round in my country and when I said 'no' they were dumbfounded because I was the only girl at the pageant who had not entered the swimsuit section of the contest." Khambatta noted that "as the first Indian girl in 15 years to come in the final ten at the Miss Universe pageant," Sabloak had "a sadness to her story. Strangely, it echoes sentiments many former Miss Indias have conveyed to me subtly, and in veiled phrases. As another ex–Miss India put it, they just 'faded away into dust' after the contest."[11]

India's Pride Is Serenaded

Persis Khambatta was never not a multitasker, and even while she was occupied with her book *Pride of India* in June 1997, she accepted a role in a film which was supposed to begin production that September: Dev Benegal's *Split Wide Open*. The picture would go on to win the Special Jury Prize at the 13th Singapore International Film Festival in 2000, but Persis Khambatta was not in it, which was most likely due to her passing in August 1998.[12]

Khambatta did appear in a different kind of movie in a different context back in June 1997: David Dasharath Kalal's nine-minute video collage *Love Song for Persis K.*, which kicked off a program of shorts titled *The Quest for Home* at the Roxie Theater during the 21st San Francisco International Lesbian & Gay Film Festival. *Love Song* did not warrant a description in that year's Program Guide, but this synopsis was provided when the source VHS videocassette was donated to the San Francisco Public Library: "Through video effects and an ethereal soundtrack, Kalal pays homage to Persis Khambatta (you remember the first Star Trek) in all of her melodramatic splendor and sensual baldness." This accurate description nevertheless fails to convey the pleasingly eye-searing qualities of the short, which uses footage from not only the 1983 version of that movie you remember but also *The Wilby Conspiracy*, *Megaforce*, and *Warrior of the Lost World*. Kalal often isolates Khambatta in the frame with brightly colored video effects, and the entire short is color-tinted in ways that almost make up aggressively monochromatic palette of that one movie. (Almost.) The voiceover narration read by Isobel Kalal is culled from Susan Sackett's *The Making of Star Trek—The Motion Picture*, which in the mid-1990s was the only source of information about Khambatta, and the soundtrack also includes Shobana Ramasubramanian singing lines from the Bee Gees' "More Than a Woman."[13]

Kalal's Khambatta-related follow-up *Five Minutes to Cloud Boundary* had its world premiere in November 2001 at MIX: The New York Lesbian & Gay Experimental Film/Video Festival. The title is a reference to Real Ilia's last line of dialog before her murder, and the Program Guide's description is "an extended trance remix of the former Miss India's appearance in a Star Trek episode." *Boundary* is not available online at the time of this writing, though Kalal uploaded *Love Song to Persis K.* to YouTube in 2016. He continues to post Persis-related visual art including paintings and animations on his website; though *Love Song* used footage from films in which Khambatta had hair, Kala's preferred image in works as recent as 2019's *Persistent Sky* and 2020's *Persistence 154–133* is of Khambatta as Robot Ilia.[14]

But back in 1997, Khambatta was working hard to ensure that she was remembered for more than being bald in that one movie that one time.

Pride of India *Is Published*

Nothing that is worth doing is without frustration, and as an impartial party I can verify that it goes double when researching and writing a nonfiction book. Khambatta no longer felt the need to hide her own frustration by the time she finished her book *Pride of India*, and she was more than willing to vent about the difficulty of tracking down her interview subjects when she talked to the web portal Rediff a few days before the book was published in mid–October 1997:

> I mean, these women have the time to go for parties, to do all kinds of things except return the call of a person who has called them at least 30 times. Come on, I was a professional, I know. I used to return home at night after a hectic day of shooting, be ready to drop dead and find 20 messages on my answering machine. And I'd return each and every call. Those that were not urgent, I would explain that I was tired and could I talk to them later. And these women could not even return one call? Don't they respect other people's time?[15]

Even as the book was being sent to the printer, Khambatta had one last white whale to pursue: Mother Teresa. *Pride of India* was dedicated to her, and part of the royalties of the regular Rs. 1,495 edition (about $40 in 1997 dollars) would go to her organization the Missionaries of Charity. There would also be 50 copies signed by many of the Miss Indias which would sell for Rs. 5,000 (about $140 in 1997 dollars), the full proceeds of which would go to the Missionaries.[16]

But what Khambatta wanted more than anything was for Mother Teresa to inaugurate the book in person. After sending as many letters as it took to get a response—and call those letters legion, for they were many—Khambatta spoke to her idol on the phone on September 1.[17]

Mother appreciated my effort in doing this book. She told me that, since her health was indifferent, she would not be able to come to Bombay for the book release. I told her we'd come to Calcutta. She told me to write to Sister Nirmala and then, four days later....[18]

Though she tried to do good things, Khambatta had no illusions about the limits of her own selflessness.

Not everyone can be as selfless as she was. Everyone might feel like doing charity—I do too, in fact, I collected a lot of money for the victims of the Latur earthquake—but not everyone can help a diseased person. I don't, for example, think I could touch a person who had leprosy sores all over his body.[19]

Maybe if Khambatta had been willing to touch lepers, the Academy would have recognized her humanitarian work or even acknowledge her post-1980 existence. (Just kidding! Khambatta could have resurrected Jean Hersholt or even Irving Thalberg, and the Academy would still have ignored her.)

Sponsored by the oral-care product company Smyle, the launch for the 227-page coffee-table book *Pride of India* was held on or around October 15. About two dozen Miss Indias appeared onstage with Khambatta, and if Mother Teresa couldn't be there, Mother India could. At least, Mother India was what the streamlined and dreamlined OG Miss India Pramila told photographers to call her.[20]

An equally exhausted and exhilarated Khambatta put it into perspective when speaking to a news crew backstage.

I used to ask God: God, I want to go abroad, I want to succeed, I want a Star Trek movie, I want this movie, and I used to get it. Now my prayer was: God, give me what you think is best for me. And, this came about. And it was so ... it fell into place. Like, I got help from publishers giving me advice, other authors giving me advice, so it was like a teamwork that worked out for me.[21]

Miss India had been a defining aspect of Khambatta's identity long before a frame of Star Trek was broadcast, but the association with the franchise was inescapable. *Pride of India*'s publisher Parijat House referred to Khambatta in their promotional material as having returned "this time on her own trek." Though the cover photo—conceived of by Khambatta, styled by Hemant Trivedi, and photographed by Farrokh Chothia—was of an unidentified model wearing a Miss India sash, the back cover was a close-up of one of the most flattering photos of Khambatta as Robot Ilia. Her face is tinted orangish-red, but the rest of her head is airbrushed into enough shadow that a viewer who did not know the origin of the picture could reasonably believe she had hair. Among the dust jacket blurbs was from Robert Wise: "It took a lot of courage to lose all her hair and become the bald character in *Star Trek*. I admire Persis for that, along with her performance. It made her portrayal of Ilia quite unique." Which has nothing to do with the Miss India contest, but by and large all the blurbs were about Khambatta, not about Miss India. Though she had no way of knowing that she would be dead less than a year after the book's publication, it was as if she knew this would be her chance to make a monument to herself as well.[22]

It is not a criticism on this writer's part to say that Khambatta used the book to celebrate herself as well as other Miss Indias, especially since the vast majority of *Pride of India* is about the others. But some did criticize her, such as *India Today*'s Nandita Chowdhury, whose review of *Pride of India* was written in the form of first-person plural open letter to Khambatta. Chowdhury admits at the start that "your coffee-table book achieves in a limited way what it sets out to achieve: giving readers of the '90s a rewind of the beauty business, 1947 onwards," but since "not all former Miss Indias and winners of other beauty pageants have the charisma or the mystique of, let us say, movie stars," the net result is that "unlike similar books inspired by cinema, after a few pages your glossy tome simply fails to enthrall."[23]

In Chowdhury's estimation, the greater crime is that "after a point, the book disappoints. In places, particularly the beginning and the end, it sounds more like a paean to yourself, Miss India 1965. We also notice that you are the only one of the 86 very beautiful women who gets six pages in the book. Inadvertent, I am sure. Midway, the book sags." Chowdhury also noted that "the expensive look or tasteful design cannot make up for the clichéd pictures, most of which appear to have been hurriedly put together from portfolios and collections of photographers." Well, yes: Khambatta acknowledges in her introduction that the massive book was put together over the course of a year, which is a fast turnaround by any standard, and she thanks "the many talented photographers, advertising agencies and magazines who dug into their photographic libraries."[24]

Chowdhury ends with what was no doubt meant to be a devastating mic drop:

> At best, *Pride of India* is a chronicle of change in styles, from demure contests back home to glitzy passages to international shores. At its worst, it is an expensive repetition. Most of all, Persis, we must thank you for reminding us all about yourself.[25]

What *India Today* said with sarcasm, this author says in all honesty: thank you, Persis.

1998

So Long, It Has Not Been Nice to Know You

Persis Khambatta's world line continued to point toward television despite the collapse of *City of Dreams* and *Talk of the Town*, and after *Pride of India* was published, she got to work developing scripts for a proposed serial based on her book. She was also excited to be one of the guests for the April 1998 tapings of the Star Plus channel's *Not a Nice Man to Know*, which featured octogenarian *Train to Pakistan* author Khushwant Singh talking with a series of 13 women who "registered on his emotional and literary radar over the years." The baker's dozen "have a mystique about them," producer Sadia Dehlvi told the *Telegraph*, "and Persis has more than her fair share." Khambatta and Singh got together the night before the taping to chat off-camera about old times, including Khambatta's belief that through regular prayer, God would give her what was best for her. But whether in the United States or in India people didn't watch chatshows to see middle-aged women achieving self-actualization, and *Outlook India*'s Glitterati column used this charming anecdote as an example of why *Not a Nice Man to Know* "promises to be rip-roaring good fun"[1]:

> Khushwant asks Persis, "So you didn't do the nude centerspread for Stern magazine?" Persis, "No Khushwant, I wanted to do India proud." Khushwant's riposte: "I'm sure you'd have done India proud even if you'd done it!"[2]

Oh, we do have fun! While this writer has not been able to watch the interview in question and thus does not know exactly what Khambatta said beyond the Glitterati retelling, there is also no evidence that Khambatta ever did a nude shoot for *Stern* or any other publication. This seems like the sort of thing the Internet would have discovered by the late 2010s, and as previously discussed, Khambatta is clothed in all available photos and stills from Kobi Jaeger's *Kamasutra*, even those in which her character of Nanda appears to be having sex. Khambatta did tell Singh during the interview that she would have gotten much more work in Hollywood had she agreed to appear nude onscreen, but again, a middle-aged woman talking about her decision to *not* appear nude isn't why people watched shows like *Not a Nice Man to Know*. Like the movie audiences in the United States that cheered her death in *Nighthawks* and were lured to the box office by images of her torture in *Warrior of the Lost World*, television audiences in India were in it for the rip-roaring good fun of a woman being shamed for doing wrong. Whether or not the woman had in fact done what she was being shamed for was a minor detail at best.[3]

Singh had been the *Illustrated Weekly of India*'s editor from 1969 through 1978. In a 2005 *Outlook India* interview when he was 91 years old and Khambatta had been dead for seven years, Singh boasted of the things he got away with at the *Weekly* because "fortunately, I had no boss." One fun example was "we published a cover picture of Simi Garewal with very little on" from Conrad Rooks' 1972 *Siddhartha*. "They were shocked. I said, but it's taken from the stills of the film!" Asked by the interviewer what Garewal had said, Singh replied that Garewal "didn't say a word—who was she to say anything?" A woman having any input into how a man exploits her image? Not on Khushwant Singh's watch! Unless they supplicated themselves before him, that is[4]:

> But the one who took great umbrage was Persis Khambatta. Her pictures had appeared in Playboy magazine or perhaps a German magazine, again, nude. And when she heard that I had got hold of the pictures and was planning to publish them, she came and threatened me. I told her: Go to hell—you appear like that before a foreign magazine and when it comes to your own people you have qualms? Then she pleaded with me, begged me not to publish it and so I didn't. With that change of attitude, how could I?[5]

Since Singh brought up *Playboy* as one of the magazines which Khambatta's nonexistent nude pictures had "perhaps" appeared in, it is worth considering Singh's own history with that magazine and with porn overall. The same 1969 *Life Asia Edition* article which profiled Khambatta as an Indian woman who defied the kissing taboo also observed that *Illustrated Weekly* editor Singh "faces prosecution because seven *Playboys* were sent to him by mail." After Singh passed in 2014, lawyer and novelist Bhaichand Patel recalled that when Patel started working for the United Nations in the 1970s, "I used to smuggle in for him banned copies of *Playboy* magazine in the diplomatic pouch. [Singh] loved to see pictures of naked, voluptuous women." They always do, don't they?[6]

Again, Singh told this story of Khambatta pleading and begging several years after her death when she was no longer able to tell her side of the story, though she always denied the existence of the photos when she was alive due to the photos not existing. But Singh was able to make the story extra-salacious in 2005 while becoming the hero by revealing a heart of gold underneath the gruff exterior—provided the woman acknowledges male supremacy by begging for his mercy. The picture of Khambatta that ran with the charming anecdote in *Outlook India* was from a 1979 photoshoot with Harry Langdon: the bald Khambatta leaning against a tall reflective surface, head resting in her hand, unclothed but only displaying the slightest suggestion of cleavage. It was presumably the most scandalous photo the *Outlook India* editors could find in a Google search, but it is also not a picture Singh could have run in the *Illustrated Weekly* even if he had wanted to, since he left that paper on July 25, 1978—the day *before* Khambatta's head was shaved, and several months before the photo was taken.[7]

When the 96-year-old Singh retired as a columnist after what *Outlook India* called "more than 70 uninterrupted years of ceaselessly needling readers" in 2011, his bold exposure of Khambatta's nonexistent nudity became another facet of his self-described skill at providing "some gossip, some titillation, some tearing up of reputations, some amusement"; the magazine summarized his 2005 anecdote as "Persis Khambatta came to plead not to publish her pictures that had appeared in *Playboy*, disarming him by falling at his feet." Khambatta had been dead for 13 years by 2011, and she had never appeared in *Playboy*, but who's counting? Oh, Khushwant Singh, you ceaseless needler you! This writer is glad she never knew you, since you don't sound very nice.[8]

The Pre-Mortem

Though the show would not be broadcast until August, *Not a Nice Man to Know*'s halo was bright enough to land Khambatta a feature story titled "The Star's Trek" by Samita Bhatia in the April 26 *Telegraph*. Khambatta revealed that what had made her not so much embittered, cynical, or even plain ol' angry but rather "hugely mad" about *Khafa, City of Dreams*, and *Talk of the Town* falling through was that nobody bothered to tell her those projects fell through. The producers ghosted her, which is rude by any standard but was all the more hurtful to Khambatta, who felt she had earned the right to work and to a modicum of communication when the promised work was taken away from her. She also felt that she was not given the recognition she deserved for the work she been able to accomplish.[9]

> She says, "Gulshan Grover and Shabana Azmi have done films abroad but they've done them and come back home." So why have Indian awards ceremonies and film festivals ignored her completely, she wonders.
>
> She smoulders on, "Inspired by Hollywood, they call themselves Bollywood, they even copy Hollywood films but they've not accepted me into the fold. They want to be around Cindy Crawford and Richard Gere when they come to India but they overlook the only Hollywood star they have in India."[10]

There may be no better example of the double standard Khambatta faced than when Bhatia, switching to an Esquireman-esque second person, suggested that refusing to do a nude shoot was somehow a form of hypocrisy on Khambatta's part.

> Says Persis, "I wanted India to be proud of me while I was abroad." So though *Playboy* pursued her for ten years to pose in the nude for the magazine, she consistently turned down the offer.
>
> Bold enough to shave off her hair but not bold enough to pose for *Playboy*, you quiz her. She retorts, "When I shaved my hair I had confidence in myself as a woman. I found that if I portrayed nudity in a film, no matter how successful I became people would always hold it against me."[11]

Persis Khambatta was not wrong about that; see again the career of Nastassja Kinski, whose talent was overshadowed by her willingness to be naked on camera in films like *Cat People*, which Khambatta had turned down. But that refusal contributed to Khambatta's "straight as an arrow" reputation which had made it difficult to find work in Hollywood, made more painful by how often she was let down by people she trusted. "You feel hurt, you cry. You start putting on weight, you feel that nobody loves you. It's a destruction that you go through." It also didn't help that she was attacked for her inability to live up to the impossible standards of strangers: "People take it upon themselves to fling at me—'Your face hasn't changed, but you're fat' or 'You kissed on screen so my husband thinks you're a whore.'" Kissing made her a whore in some eyes, while not doing nudity made her a coward in others.[12]

Khambatta took solace in being a "successful human being" on a spiritual level: "I believe in charity and humility. In my path to success if I had to step aside to let someone pass I did it. I'm happy that I didn't cross over someone's body to get there." Though she had not ruled out returning to television, her main plan was once again to open a modeling school or agency to be run "on strictly professional lines."[13]

* * *

It is a never a good idea to read the comments whether analog or digital, and the three letters published in the print edition of the June 7 *Telegraph* were no less hostile than those by *Starlog* readers. A *Telegraph* reader from Calcutta wrote that "'as an Indian, one feels proud of her successful stint as a model and actress for several prestigious assignments,' but that since 'time has left its scars on a woman who was once a bewitching beauty and the toast of Hollywood,'" it would perhaps be best for "to make a graceful exit as a successful Hollywood star and open a professional modelling agency or a training school instead of trying her luck on the small screen." A Durgapur resident acknowledged that Khambatta "might be the first Indian to make it big in Hollywood," but criticized her for staying in Hollywood as long as she did, saying Khambatta "should have returned earlier to repeat the feat in Bollywood. The fact that she managed to 'further her career abroad' should be consolation enough now." And a reader from Jamshedpur welcomed Khambatta's return to India, but also thought that Khambatta needed to work harder: "She should devote more time and energy for charity work in the country where 36 per cent of the population lives below the poverty line. She still possesses a big and beautiful smile which should come in handy for any humanitarian work."

Why was there so much poverty in India? Because Persis Khambatta didn't smile enough.

Persis in the Tower, When the Birds Came

Unaware of how Khushwant Singh would continue to tear up her reputation after her death, Khambatta had fun taping *Not a Nice Man to Know*, and she was excited to see the interview when it was finally aired at 9:30 p.m. on Friday, August 14. She was having dinner that night at the Taj with Sanjeev Choudhary, the vice-consul of the Canadian Embassy. They had met at a party on New Year's Eve and had attended many events together as friends since then, but she left him early that night in order to watch the *Not a Nice Man to Know* broadcast. The show and her appearance on it got good reviews, which pleased her to the end.[14]

Accounts differ as to the chain of events during her final hours, but what seems to have happened is that on the night of Monday, August 17, 1998, she began experiencing some combination of chest pains, headaches, and vomiting. She called her niece Diane, who rushed Persis to the Marine Hospital. After receiving medication, she asked to be taken back home. Diane obliged over the doctor's objection, but around five in the morning on Tuesday, August 18, Persis was having trouble breathing—possibly a stroke—and Diane took her back to the hospital. Soon thereafter, she was pronounced dead.[15]

Funeral rites were conducted on the morning of August 19 at the Tower of Silence in the Doongerwadi forest. In accordance with Parsi custom, her body was laid out in the sun, where it was consumed by vultures, crows, and other birds of prey. Among the few non-family members to attend the funeral was Kabir Bedi, whose other former partner Protima Gauri had died the same day as Khambatta.[16]

Khambatta's death was noted in "Final Farewells" box in *Starlog* #261 the following March, a mere seven months after her passing. She was listed between Shari Lewis ("Friend to Lambchop") and Leo Penn ("father to actors Sean & Chris").[17]

Persis Khambatta (August) Once the ill-fated Deltan Ilia of *Star Trek: The Motion Picture*. See STARLOG #37.[18]

The December 1998/January 1999 issue of *Star Trek Communicator* featured what was promoted as "the last interview," in which Khambatta spoke to Luke Montgomery "about her life, her career, and of course, her time on *Star Trek*, conducted by phone from her native India, not long before her unexpected passing." The phoner was most likely preliminary research for the 20th anniversary of the first Star Trek movie, and the transcript may not have seen the light of day had it not been for Khambatta's death. It is preceded by a cobbled-together, typo-heavy obituary which observed that "with her role in Star Trek's first silver-screen adventure, Khambatta beat Patrick Stewart to the punch in proving that bald could be sexy." The majority of the interview is about the filming of the movie, including Khambatta trotting out the old chestnut about the "sensual feeling" of showering with her bald head. (She also claimed that the leg-revealing properties of Robot Ilia's leisure robe had been her suggestion, but there is no other evidence that she had any input into the costume design.)[19]

Montgomery observed that Khambatta shaving her head for the film was "a potentially risky career move," and while he was not wrong about that, Khambatta used it as an opportunity to discuss the deeper issues she had faced.[20]

> One thing about me, as far as my career is concerned, is that I'm very confident. I know I'm good. Having shaved my head for the role put a spotlight on me. After *Star Trek*, I was with the top agencies, but producers and directors did not know what to make of me.
>
> Everybody told me to stay in Hollywood. This is where they said I could have a big career. What they failed to mention was that no one would quite know what to do with me. How many roles are there for actors with accents or foreign looks? I knew I was not about to displace the Florence Henderson types as the mother on shows like *The Brady Bunch*. If there is an exotic woman it's always the terrorist role. The American audience's limited expectations cause Hollywood's trepidation, and like an albatross, they limit the textural realism that today's writer and director can create.[21]

Montgomery followed up Khambatta's thoughtful comments on the problems caused by being Othered with a question about whether or not being Othered had caused any problems: "Ilia had a strong effect on male members of the Enterprise crew. Do people react differently because of your looks?"[22]

> Well, on *Star Trek*, Stephen Collins came up to me and said, "You're so exotic. You're foreign, you're intelligent, you're beautiful, and it scares me to talk to you." *(Laughs)* This happened to me a lot in America. People would say, "My God, she's a princess. She's a real lady." I sort of have that aura about me. In a way I was very shy deep inside because of it. People were afraid of me.[23]

But let's return to her previous answer and its most salient point:

> The American audience's limited expectations cause Hollywood's trepidation, and like an albatross, they limit the textural realism that today's writer and director can create.[24]

"Textural realism" a beautiful way to put it. The world is not made up of just one kind of person, and for sure the United States is not. When I look outside my own front door, I don't see just white people. Persis Khambatta would have been happy to see that an Indian performer like Rekha Sharma who in the 1980s would have been held back because she was exotic was instead cast in *Star Trek: Discovery* in 2017 as a character named Ellen Landry. And this was after eleven years after Sharma's first appearance on *Battlestar Galactica* as a character named Tory Foster—who, like *Discovery*'s Ellen Landry, was not defined by her skin color or exoticness.

Being a part of Star Trek is all fine and good, but by some standards, becoming a reference question is the sign of having truly made it. The "General Awareness" section of the State Bank of India Probationary Officers' Examination held in February 1999 was what it sounded like: multiple-choice questions about the test-takers' awareness of things in general, such as "Which of the following rays of sunlight help the solar cooker in its heating?" or "Which of the following countries attacked Iraq in December 1998?" (The five options for the latter question were "Britain and USA," "USA and Kuwait," "France and USA," "Germany and USA," and "USA and Italy.") For the question "Which of the following combinations of the books and their authors is not correct?," one of the options was "*Pride of India*—Persis Khambatta." If you were a functioning professional in 1999 India, it was expected that you knew who Khambatta was, and not just because she was bald in that one movie that one time.[25]

* * *

It is human nature to look for patterns in chaos, and while reading her words from the months leading up to her death cannot help but feel like a summation, I do not believe Khambatta intended to go quietly into that good night, and certainly not so soon. As she wrote in her author's note to *Pride of India*:

> To all the people who feature in this book, their families and especially the Miss Indias, I express my sincere gratitude for all their support for this book—my tribute to them. They have helped me to achieve my dream, a dream which was born spontaneously from my heart. But let me tell you honestly, this is only the beginning. There are many more boundaries to transcend and many battles to be won. And if somehow, the beautiful Miss Indias inspire someone, then I know that all my efforts have not been in vain.[26]

For sure, I can say that Miss India 1965 has inspired me. Persis Khambatta's efforts were not in vain.

Chapter Notes

Introduction

1. Persis Khambatta, *Pride of India: A Tribute to Miss India* (Mumbai: Parijat Media, 1997), 15.
2. Khambatta, 15.
3. Khambatta, 15.
4. Khambatta, 15; Ashish Rajadhyaksha and Paul Willemen, *Encyclopaedia of Indian Cinema* (New Delhi: Oxford University Press, 1995), 12.
5. Khambatta, 9–10.
6. Khambatta, 70.

Prologue

1. Don Morrison, "A Friendly Time Warp," *Minneapolis Star*, December 5, 1979.
2. Morrison.
3. Morrison.
4. Roderick Mann, "Shear Terror for Khambatta," *Los Angeles Times*, July 25, 1978; Charles Champlin, "Bald is Beautiful for 'Star Trek' Star," *Los Angeles Times*, November 29, 1979; Caroline Cushing, "Lt. Ilia Lets Down Her Hair," *Los Angeles Herald-Examiner*, November 29, 1979; Peter Rose, "Actress's Cleanshaven Image Lands Role in Star Trek Movie," *Arizona Republic*, December 2, 1979; Howard Pearson, "Bald is Beautiful in Star Trek Movie," *Deseret News*, December 4, 1979.
5. Bloomingdale's, "Bloomingdale's Has a Sunday Kind of Love for Christmas," Advertisement, *New York Times*, December 2, 1979; "Panorama," *Questar* 2 no. 3 (June 1980), 12; Sue Reilly, "Additional Material from Sue Reilly," December 20, 1979, *People Carbons*, Margaret Herrick Library, Beverly Hills.
6. Morrison.
7. Morrison.
8. Morrison.
9. Morrison.
10. Will Jones, "After Last Night," *Minneapolis Tribune*, December 6, 1979.
11. Reilly, December 20, 1979; Sue Reilly, "Persis Khambatta Suffered the Scrape of Her Locks, but 'Star Trek' Justified the Loss," *People* (January 7, 1980), 30; Dolores Barclay, "Bald-headed Discovery Just 'Old-Fashioned Girl,'" *Globe and Mail*, December 20, 1979.
12. Allan Asherman, *The Making of Star Trek II: The Wrath of Khan* (New York: Pocket Books, 1982: 192.
13. *RARE 1979 STAR TREK: The Motion Picture PREMIERE!!*, YouTube video, 18:03, posted by "Hezakya Newz & Music," May 29, 2016, https://www.youtube.com/watch?v=aMahpAHN2Xw&; "Rambling Reporter," *Hollywood Reporter*, June 26, 1979; Paramount Pictures, "Persis Khambatta of 'Star Trek—The Motion Picture' Discovers that Bald is Beautiful but Also Traumatic," Paramount Pictures press release, October 1979.
14. Susan Sackett, "Star Trek Report," *Starlog* no. 26 (September 1979), 53; Sue Reilly, "Persis Khambatta—Screen Lookahead," *People Carbons*, November 27, 1978; Army Archerd, "Just for Variety," *Daily Variety* 185, no. 60 (November 28, 1979), 3; Khambatta, 29.
15. *Motion Picture PREMIERE!!*; Jurate Kazickas, "Trekking Down to a World Premiere," *Washington Star*, December 7, 1979.
16. Karen E. Willson, "An Interview with Star Trek's Deltan Navigator Persis Khambatta," *Starlog* no. 37 (August 1980), 52.

Chapter Notes: 1946–1965; 1966–1969; 1970–1973

1946–1965

1. Caroline Cushing, "Lt. Ilia Lets Down Her Hair," *Los Angeles Herald-Examiner*, November 29, 1979; Crawley, July 1979, 33; Lalit Mohan Joshi, "Obituary: Persis Khambatta: A Model Career," *The Guardian*, August 28, 1998; Khambatta, 28; Reilly, January 7, 1980; Vernon Scott, "Scott's World: Exotic is the Word for Persis," *UPI*, April 18, 1981; Ann Guarino, "Off Camera," *New York Daily News*, August 3, 1975; Khambatta, 30; James Fuller Blumhardt, *Catalogue of the Library of the India Office Vol. II, Part V: Marathi and Gujarati Books* (London: Eyre and Spottiswoode, 1908), 179–180, 240.
2. Khambatta, 31; Lydia Lane, "Actress with a Sense of Destiny," *Los Angeles Times*, December 15, 1978; Samita Bhatia, "The Star's Trek," *Telegraph*, April 26, 1998.
3. Khambatta, 26; Jack Ong, "From Miss India To 'Star Trek': Presenting Persis Khambatta," *California Goodlife* (December 1979), 74; Rexona, "Day by Day. Lovelier with Rexona," Advertisement, *Indian Express*, February 28, 1965; Guarino.
4. Khambatta, 26, 28; Charles Champlin, "Bald is Beautiful for 'Star Trek' Star," *Los Angeles Times*, November 29, 1979; Bhatia; Ong.
5. Khambatta, 26, 210.
6. Khambatta, 195, 210–211; Ann Guarino, "Off Camera," *New York Daily News*, August 3, 1975.
7. Khambatta, 24, 26.
8. Joan Crosby, "TV Scout Reports," *World*, September 27, 1979.
9. "International Sound Track," *Variety* 239, no. 7 (July 7, 1965), 22; Khambatta, 26–27.
10. *Miss Universe 1965 Full Broadcast*, YouTube video, 14:35, posted by "ลูกโป่ง ลอยฟ้า ซึ่งซ่าลวรรค์," June 12, 2013, https://www.youtube.com/watch?v=egCgLygLHRM&; Scott.
11. John Cocchi, "Beauty from India Hopes to Become American Star," April 1977; Khambatta, 26, 27; "All Wasn't Quiet on Pageant's Eve," *Dayton Daily News*, July 21, 1965.
12. Khambatta, 27, 34; Arthur Pais, "Amazing Grace," *India Abroad*, December 1, 2006.
13. Kuldip Singh, "Obituary: Persis Khambatta," *Independent*, August 19, 1998; Khambatta, 26.

1966–1969

1. Ashish Rajadhyaksha and Paul Willemen, *Encyclopaedia of Indian Cinema* (New Delhi: Oxford University Press, 1995), 11.
2. Google, "Meena Kumari's 85th Birthday," Google Doodles, August 1, 2018, https://www.google.com/doodles/meena-kumaris-85th-birthday; *Pinjre Ke Panchhi (1966) Hindi Full Movie | Balraj Sahni, Meena Kumari | Hindi Classic Movies*, YouTube video, 2:14:30, posted by "Cinecurry Classics," September 24, 2016, https://www.youtube.com/watch?v=eHYsfekKJv0.
3. Bhatia; Rajadhyaksha and Willemen, 363; Monojit Lahiri, "What Has Zeenat that Zahirra Hasn't?", *Film World* 10, no. 1–2 (January-February 1974), 40.
4. Rajadhyaksha and Willemen, 363; "Persis Khambatta Biography," Paramount Pictures, October 1979.
5. *Bambai Raat Ki Bahon Mein Full Hindi Movies | Vimal Ahuja | Surekha | Hindi Movies*, YouTube video, 2:03:03, posted by "Cinema Scope Movies," April 8, 2014, https://www.youtube.com/watch?v=H-npFFaXVCk&t.
6. Khambatta, 27, 31; Gerry Levin, "India's Persis Khambatta Gambling on U.S. Career," *Hollywood Reporter*, April 11, 1977.
7. Khambatta, 26; Peter Rose, "Actress's Cleanshaven Image Lands Role in Star Trek Movie," *Arizona Republic*, December 2, 1979; Jones, *Return to Tomorrow*, 230.
8. "Two Exports from India," *Sydney Morning Herald*, October 13, 1968; "Kobi Jaeger in 'Kama Sutra' Suit," *Variety* 261, no. 10 (January 20, 1971), 17.
9. James Shepherd, "India's Crisis: To Kiss or Not To.", *Life Asia Edition* (December 8, 1969), 22, 25.
10. Smita Sajnani, "60—Winner of the 1970 Miss India Crown," *Indian Memory Project*, n.d., http://www.indianmemoryproject.com/60/.
11. Shobha Dé, *Shooting from the Hip* (New Delhi: UBS Publishers' Distributors Ltd., 1994), 234–235.
12. Dé, 235.
13. Dé, 235.
14. Dé, 235.

1970–1973

1. "Brodsky-Gould Pic R, 'Kama Sutra'

Goes X," *Variety* 261 no. 3 (December 2, 1970), 3.

2. "Kama Sutra," *San Francisco Chronicle*, December 11, 1970; "'Kama Sutra' Maker Charges AIP 'Butchered' The Film,'" *Daily Variety* 150, no. 8 (December 16, 1970), 8; "AIP As To 'Sutra' Pic: Innocent of Editing and 'Mutilations,'" *Variety* 261, no. 7 (December 30, 1970), 20; Howard Thompson, "Dull Double Bill," *New York Times*, March 18, 1971.

3. "Kama Sutra," *Daily Girl* 1, no. 3 (1971); Beutelwolf, "Persis Khambatta," *Vintage Erotica Forums*, last modified March 4, 2011, http://vintage-erotica-forum.com/showpostphp?p=1493949&postcount=1.

4. "Irmin Schmidt, Inner Space Production–Kamasutra—Vollendung Der Liebe," *Discogs*, n.d., https://www.discogs.com/-Irmin-Schmidt-Inner-Space-Production-Kamasutra-Vollendung-Der-Liebe/release/2053796.

5. "Irmin Schmidt, Inner Space Production–Kamasutra—Vollendung Der Liebe."

6. "Irmin Schmidt, Inner Space Production–Kamasutra—Vollendung Der Liebe."

7. *Kamasutra—Perfection of Love*, Amazon Prime, 38:00, n.d., https://www.amazon.com/Kamasutra-Perfection-Love-Persis-Khambatta/dp/B01HN8AV4Q/; Thompson.

8. Lydia Lane, "Persis Khambatta Had Plan for Life," *Los Angeles Times*, July 10, 1981; S.N. Khosla, "Good Head, Good Heart, Good Body," *Telegraph*, July 6, 1986.

9. Scott; *Skip E. Lowe with Guest Ed Fury, Persis Khambatta, Mark Hudson Bernice Altschul*, YouTube Video, 57:27, posted by "Romeo Carey," May 19, 2018, https://www.youtube.com/watch?v=vyNHPUgUzbo.

10. Khambatta, 27; "Squash," *Eton College Chronicle* no. 3359 (February 28, 1964), 5366.

11. Khambatta, 27; Scott.

12. "1971: Post Strike Ends with Pay Deal," *BBC News*, n.d., http://news.bbc.co.uk/onthisday/hi/dates/stories/march/8/newsid_2516000/2516343.stm.

13. Lane.

14. Barclay; Alison Castle, *The Stanley Kubrick Archives* (Köln, Germany: Taschen, 2013), 411.

15. Khambatta, 27; Scott.

16. "Actress Persis Khambatta," *Shutterstock*, n.d., https://www.shutterstock.com/editorial/image-editorial/actress-persis-khambatta-1352089a; *Index to the Times, March-April 1971* (London: Times Newspapers, 1971), 127, 172.

17. "Persis, Persis Khambatta, Indian model and actress, 1st August 1972," *Getty Images*, n.d., http://gettyimages.com/detail/news-photo/persis-persis-khambatta-indian-model-and-actress-1st-august-news-photo/119109100; Bhatia.

18. Earl Wilson, "Bombay Beauty Balks at Baring," *Philadelphia Daily News*, March 27, 1975; Rebecca Morehouse, "Persis Khambatta: A Star Is Shorn," *North American Newspaper Alliance*, January 3, 1980; George Anderson, "Timing, Toughness Help Persis Khambatta's Trek to Stardom," *Pittsburgh Post-Gazette*, April 8, 1981.

19. Khambatta, 27–28, 47.

20. Wilson, March 27, 1975.

21. Ann Guarino, "Off Camera," *New York Daily News*, August 3, 1975; Shirley Eder, "Caine Muzzles Actress Wife," *Detroit Free Press*, March 13, 1975.

22. Jones, Winter 1979, 47; Crawley, 33.

23. *Namaste: A Day in the Life of an Air India Hostess (1962)* | *British Pathé*, YouTube video, 1:35, posted by "British Pathé," April 13, 2014, https://www.youtube.com/watch?v=-ZwoBX1XWEI.

24. *1970s Air India "Hostess Welcome" Commercial*, YouTube video, 0.44, posted by "United Jet Mainliner," Feb 20, 2019, https://www.youtube.com/watch?v=egCgLygLHRM&.

25. *1970s Air India "Hostess Welcome" Commercial*.

26. Michael W. Potts, "Persis Khambatta: Proud of Being a Parsi," *India West*, May 15, 1981; "Indian Actress and Model Persis Khambatta (2 October 1948 A 18 August 1998). Appeared in Air India Advertisements," *Shutterstock*, n.d., https://www.shutterstock.com/editorial/image-editorial/indian-actress-and-model-persis-khambatta-2-october-1948-a-18-august-1998-appeared-in-air-india-advertisements-1976627a; Bhatia; "'Sophia Loren of India' is Out to Captivate American Viewers," *El Paso Herald-Post*, May 21, 1977; Wilson, March 27, 1975.

27. Bhatia; Potts, May 15, 1981.

28. Anthony Burton, "People," *New York Daily News*, March 12, 1975; Khambatta, 29.

1974–1977

1. "Persis Khambatta," *Getty Images*, n.d., https://www.gettyimages.com/detail/news-photo/actresses-prunella-gee-and-persis-khambatta-photo-call-to-news-photo/888805248; Khambatta, 30; "Films in the Future," *Daily Variety* 162, no. 35 (January 25,1974), 20; Jones, *Return to Tomorrow*, 311.
2. Khambatta, 29; Lahiri.
3. "Actress Turns Bald Head into an Asset," *Newspaper Enterprise Association*, February 5, 1979; Khambatta, 29; Savera R. Someshwar, "Persist Khambatta," *Rediff on the Net*, last modified October 10, 1997, http://www.rediff.com/style/oct/10persis.htm; Anderson; "Listen," *Los Angeles Times*, October 24, 1980.
4. "Films in the Future," *Daily Variety* 165, no. 50 (November 15, 1974), 6.
5. Guarino; Khambatta, 29; Burton; Wilson, March 27, 1975.
6. Guarino.
7. Charles McHarry, "On the Town," *New York Daily News*, March 10, 1975; "Italo B.O. Wilts in Heat; Brooks' 'Frankenstein' Tops," *Variety* 279, no. 6 (June 18, 1975), 33; "The Wilby Conspiracy," *Daily Variety* 168, no. 1 (June 20, 1975), 3; Stanley Eichelbaum, "The Rover Boys in South Africa," *San Francisco Examiner*, August 21, 1975; Vincent Canby, "Screen: A Frothy 'Wilby Conspiracy,'" *New York Times*, September 4, 1975.
8. Aram Goudsouzian, *Sidney Poitier: Man, Actor, Icon* (Chapel Hill, N.C.: University of North Carolina Press, 2004), 351.
9. A.H. Weiler, "Screen: British 'Conduct Unbecoming,'" *New York Times*, October 6, 1975.
10. "International Women's Year (1975)," *Harvard Library*, n.d., https://guides.library.harvard.edu/schlesinger_IWY; Hari Narain Verma and Amrit Verma, *Indian Women Through the Ages* (New Delhi: Great Indian Publishers, 1976), i, vi, 129, 153.
11. Levin; "Persis Khambatta," *On TV* (April 1982), 32; Sunil Sethi, "Indian Look Invades Western Market Again," *India Today*, November 30, 1976; "Princess Anne and Helena Rubinstein at the Tower," *Chemist & Druggist* 205, no. 5019 (June 12, 1976), 833.
12. Khambatta, 30.
13. Rex Reed, "At Last: A Producer Who Really Produces," *New York Daily News*, April 3, 1977.
14. Khambatta, 31; Julie Gammack, "Bald Beauty of 'Star Trek' Film Beams Down Snugly in W.D.M.," *Des Moines Register*, July 24, 1989.
15. Persis, Khambatta, "Persis Khambatta Cordially Invites You," Advertisement, *Variety* 287, no. 2 (May 18, 1977), 6; "Hollywood TV Production Chart," *Daily Variety* 174, no. 63 (March 3, 1977), 20; Scott.
16. "News of the Stars," *Star Trek Action Group* no. 40 (April 1980), 5.
17. Levin.
18. Bill Roeder, "Newsmakers," *Newsweek* 89, no. 20 (May 16, 1977), 47; Cocchi; "'Sophia Loren of India' is Out to Captivate American Viewers."
19. Persis Khambatta, "Persis Khambatta Cordially Invites You," Advertisement, *Variety* 287, no. 2 (May 18, 1977), 6; Persis Khambatta, "Persis Khambatta Cordially Invites You," Advertisement, *Daily Variety* 175, no. 56 (May 23, 1977), 8.
20. Aretha Franklin, "Aretha Franklin, Atlantic Records Recording Artist," Advertisement, *Variety* 287, no. 2 (May 18, 1977), 6.
21. Crawley, 31; Robert Kerwin, "Trekkie Treat," *Chicago Tribune*, June 3, 1979; Rose.
22. Crawley, 31.
23. Judith and Garfield Reeves-Stevens, *Star Trek Phase II: The Lost Series* (New York: Simon & Schuster, 1997), 48; Susan Sackett, "Star Trek Report," *Starlog* no. 12 (March 1978), 30; Crawley, 31.
24. J.M. Dillard, *Star Trek, "Where No One Has Gone Before": A History in Pictures* (New York: Pocket Books, 1994), 67; Gross, 46–57; "The Original Series Woman's Starfleet Uniform," *Christie's*, n.d., https://www.christies.com/lotfinder/lot/the-original-series-womans-starfleet-uniform-4780536-details.aspx.
25. Reeves-Stevens, 1997, 48; David Alexander, *Star Trek Creator: The Authorized Biography of Gene Roddenberry* (New York: Penguin, 1994), 443; Crawley, 31.
26. Aaron Gold, "Tower Ticker," *Chicago Tribune*, November 15, 1977.

1978

1. Sunil Sethi, "Bombay's Rapidly Rising Race of Beauty Models," *India Today*, June

30, 1978; "The Cut-Throat but Lucrative World of Advertising Photography," *India Today*, June 30, 1978.

2. Tom Sullivan, "Breakfast with the Trekkies," *Herald-News*, April 7, 1978; K. P. Sunil, "Not Making It," *Illustrated Weekly of India*, July 29, 1984; Charles Champlin, "Another 'Star' is Born," *Los Angeles Times*, March 31, 1978.

3. Forrest J. Ackerman, "Star Trek 23rd Century Style," *Famous Monsters* no. 145 (July 1978), 33.

4. "Star Trek II," *Star Trek Action Group* no. 25 (October 1977), 3.

5. Hank Grant, "Hollywood Reporter," *San Francisco Examiner*, June 18, 1978.

6. "Indian Actress Persis Khambatta (2 October 1948 A 18 August 1998)," *Shutterstock*, n.d., https://www.shutterstock.com/editorial/image-editorial/indian-actress-persis-khambatta-2-october-1948-a-18-august-1998-1974646a.

7. Fashion78, "Listen," *Los Angeles Times*, July 14, 1978; Anderson; Robin Leach, "Bald Beauty Loses 10G Gems," *New York Post*, April 7, 1980.

8. Susan Sackett and Gene Roddenberry, *The Making of Star Trek—The Motion Picture* (New York: Pocket Books, 1980), 139–140.

9. Sackett and Roddenberry, 139–140.

10. Mann, July 25, 1978; Vernon Scott, April 18, 1981; Vic Partipilo, "On Location," *Oakland Post*, December 25, 1979; Champlin, November 29, 1979; Jon Denny, "Small Talk with a Lady in the Big Time: Persis Khambatta," *Oui* (March 1981), 88.

11. Mann, July 25, 1978.

12. Shirjee, "Khaas Baat," *Sunday* 6, no. 23 (August 20, 1978), 35.

13. Shirjee; Jones, *Return to Tomorrow*, 144; Mann, July 25, 1978.

14. *Star Trek the Motion Picture Vintage*, YouTube video, 10:19, posted by "Rengav," October 1, 2016, https://www.youtube.com/watch?v=aaYLmdun8hs; Sackett and Roddenberry, 6; Koenig, 150–151; Morrie Gelman, "Par TV Closes Prod'n Gap with 'Laugh,'" *Daily Variety* 182, no. 53 (February 21, 1979), 10; "Trekkies Hear Roddenberry," *Chacahoula* 49 (1982), 77.

15. Sackett and Roddenberry, 6–7; Jones, *Return to Tomorrow*, 210; "Lookout," *People*, August 25, 1980; Karen E. Willson, "An Interview with Star Trek's Deltan Navigator Persis Khambatta," *Starlog* no. 37 (August 1980), 50.

16. *Star Trek the Motion Picture Vintage*.
17. *Star Trek the Motion Picture Vintage*.
18. Crawley, 32.
19. *Star Trek the Motion Picture Vintage*.
20. *Star Trek the Motion Picture Vintage*; Sackett and Roddenberry, 1–7; "Persis Makes a 'Bold' Move—Shaves Her Head," *India West*, October 20, 1978; Crawley, 33.
21. Jones, *Return to Tomorrow*, 118.
22. Crawley, 33; David Chierichetti, "How to Dress Buck Rogers—and Other Sci Fi Tales," *Los Angeles Times*, October 26, 1979; Jones, Winter 1979, 47.
23. Cushing; Howard Pearson, "Bald is Beautiful in Star Trek Movie," *Deseret News*, December 4, 1979; Bob Lardine, "She's Looking for Reel Love," *Daily News*, February 17, 1982.
24. "What's Up, Drac? Barbra's Back and So Is Cowboy Bob," *People*, December 25, 1978.
25. Denny, 90.
26. Khambatta, 30; Jones, *Return to Tomorrow*, 231; Sackett and Roddenberry, 162.
27. Jones, *Return to Tomorrow*, 231–232.
28. "Persis Khambatta's Class-A Uniform Shirt," *Christie's*, n.d., https://www.christies.com/LotFinder/lot_details.aspx?from=salesummary&intObjectID=4780404; "Ilia's Class-B Uniform Shirt," *Christie's*, n.d., https://www.christies.com/lotfinder/lot/ilias-class-b-uniform-shirt-4780392-details.aspx?from=salesummery&intobjectid=4780392.
29. Koenig, 20, 107; Rose; Jones, *Return to Tomorrow*, 143; Khambatta, 30.
30. Susan Sackett, "Star Trek Report," *Starlog* no. 18 (December 1978), 64; Koenig, 36.
31. Peter Mikelbank, "The Boss Speaks: 'Star Trek' Lives!" *Washington Post*, August 29, 1977; Koenig, 36; Khambatta, 29; Susan Sackett, "Star Trek Report," *Starlog* no. 29 (December 1979), 31.
32. Koenig, 37; Willson, August 1980, 50; Gene Roddenberry and Harold Livingston, *Star Trek—The Motion Picture Shooting Script*, July 19, 1978, Margaret Herrick Library, Beverly Hills, 951.f-S-1333.
33. Roddenberry and Livingston, July 19, 1978.
34. Roddenberry and Livingston, July 19, 1978.
35. Roddenberry and Livingston, July 19, 1978.

36. Roddenberry and Livingston, July 19, 1978.
37. Roddenberry and Livingston, July 19, 1978.
38. Jones, *Return to Tomorrow*, 410.
39. Jones, *Return to Tomorrow*, 410.
40. Jones, *Return to Tomorrow*, 410.
41. Jones, *Return to Tomorrow*, 144; Sackett and Roddenberry, 107.
42. Sackett and Roddenberry, 107.
43. Sackett and Roddenberry, 107–108.
44. Sackett and Roddenberry, 108.
45. Sackett and Roddenberry, 108.
46. Sackett and Roddenberry, 108.
47. Sackett and Roddenberry, 108.
48. Cushing.
49. Koenig, 60; Jones, *Return to Tomorrow*, 564.
50. Koenig, 56.
51. Koenig, 57, 63.
52. Koenig, 63.
53. Koenig, 69.
54. Jones, *Return to Tomorrow*, 330.
55. Jones, *Return to Tomorrow*, 330.
56. "Indian Actress and Model Persis Khambatta (2 October 1948 A 18 August 1998)," *Shutterstock*, n.d., https://www.shutterstock.com/editorial/image-editorial/indian-actress-and-model-persis-khambatta-2-october-1948-a-18-august-1998-1976621a; Roddenberry and Livingston, July 19, 1978.
57. Roddenberry and Livingston, August 17, 1978.
58. Koenig, 106; Roddenberry and Livingston, July 19, 1978; Judith and Garfield Reeves-Stevens, *The Art of Star Trek* (New York: Pocket Books, 1995), 188–191.
59. Roddenberry and Livingston, July 19, 1978.
60. Koenig, 107.
61. Reilly, November 27, 1978; Garry Abrams, "Eye," *Women's Wear Daily* 137, no. 50 (September 13, 1978), 4; Marilyn Beck, "Trekkie Goes Bald," *Kenosha News*, September 29, 1978.
62. Beck, September 29, 1978; "Singer-actor Sonny Bono, 46, and actress-model Susie Coelho, 26," *UPI*, January 1, 1982.
63. Reilly, November 27, 1978.
64. Reilly, January 7, 1980, 29.
65. Koenig, 111, 117 126; "Persis and Nimoy Behind-The-Scenes Birthday," October 2, 1978, *Roddenberry*, last modified October 1, 2016, https://www.facebook.com/roddenberry/posts/10153885839298144/; Khambatta, 63.
66. Koenig, 115, 134; Roddenberry and Livingston, September 27, 1978.
67. "A New Farrah She Isn't," *Los Angeles Magazine*, October 1978.
68. Roderick Mann, "Ferreting Out Dudley Moore," *Los Angeles Times*, October 10, 1978.
69. Mann, October 10, 1978; Roderick Mann, "Sellers: No Way to Treat 'Prisoner,'" *Los Angeles Times*, April 10, 1979.
70. Wayne Warga, "Prepare to Beam Aboard! 'Star Trek' at the Movies," *Los Angeles Times*, October 15, 1978.
71. Koenig, 147.
72. Roddenberry and Livingston, July 19, 1978.
73. Jones, *Return to Tomorrow*, 232; Gene Siskel, "'Trek' Is Ok, But Not Out of this World," *Chicago Tribune*, December 7, 1979.
74. Jones, *Return to Tomorrow*, 233.
75. Sackett and Roddenberry, 162–163; Crawley, 33.
76. Savera R. Someshwar, "Persist Khambatta," *Rediff on the Net*, last modified October 10, 1997, http://www.rediff.com/style/oct/10persis.htm; Sackett and Roddenberry, 140; Willson, August 1980, 52.
77. "Ilia's Off-Duty Tunic and Deltan Headband," *Christie's*, n.d., https://www.christies.com/lotfinder/lot/ilias-off-duty-tunic-and-deltan-headband-4780393-details.aspx.
78. Fashion79, "Listen," *Los Angeles Times*, November 23, 1979; Jones, *Return to Tomorrow*, 233; Willson, August 1980, 52.
79. "Persis Makes a 'Bold' Move—Shaves Her Head."
80. Kerwin.
81. Kerwin.
82. Kerwin.
83. Vijaya Irani, "West Slide Story," Sunday 6, no. 32 (October 22, 1978), 21.
84. Irani, 22.
85. Koenig, 176–177.
86. Koenig 168, 176; Don Shay, "Star Trek—The Motion Picture," *Cinefantastique* 8, no. 2–3 (Spring 1979), 92; "Actress Jane Fonda," *World*, November 8, 1978.
87. Koenig, 177; George Anthony, "Trekkies Rejoice, the Bold Journey Resumes," *Whitehorse Star*, February 2, 1979.
88. Anthony.
89. Gene Roddenberry and Harold Livingston, *Star Trek—The Motion Picture*

Shooting Script, November 5, 1978, Margaret Herrick Library, Beverly Hills, 951.f-S-1336.

90. R.H. Martin, "Chattin' with Stratton," *Fangoria* 3, no. 39 (November 1984), 34; Don Shay, "Into the V'ger Maw with Douglas Trumbull," *Cinefex* 1, no. 1 (1980), 19–20; Ben Bova, *Vision of the Future: The Art of Robert McCall* (New York: Harry N. Abrams, 1982), 143.

91. Gene Roddenberry and Harold Livingston, *Star Trek The Motion Picture Shooting Script*, November 29, 1978, Margaret Herrick Library, Beverly Hills, 951.f-S-1336; Jones, *Return to Tomorrow*, 273.

92. Earl Wilson, "Will Girls Shave Heads?" *Indianapolis Star*, December 4, 1978.

93. Phil Roura and Tom Poster, "A Bright Spot," *New York Daily News*, December 10, 1978; Shepherd, 25.

94. Lane, December 15, 1978; "Thursday," *Carlsbad Current-Argus*, December 24, 1978.

1979

1. Sackett and Roddenberry, 169; Army Archerd, "Just for Variety," *Daily Variety* 182, no. 37 (January 29, 1979), 3; Jones, *Return to Tomorrow*, 310.

2. Jones, *Return to Tomorrow*, 311; "Log Entries," *Starlog* no. 26 (September 1979), 12.

3. Jones, *Return to Tomorrow*, 311.

4. Archerd, January 29, 1979; Jones, *Return to Tomorrow*, 317, 310; Willson, August 1980, 52.

5. Susan Sackett, "Star Trek Report," *Starlog* no. 22 (May 1979), 29; Crawley, 33; Army Archerd, "Just for Variety," *Daily Variety* 182, no. 38 (January 30, 1979), 3; Willson, August 1980, 52.

6. Susan Sackett, "Star Trek Report," *Starlog* no. 22 (May 1979), 29.

7. James Delson, "A Comprehensive Interview with Robert Wise," *Fantastic Films* no. 10 (September 1979), 62.

8. "Today's TV," *New York Daily News*, March 7, 1979.

9. Suzy, "So California Invaded London Town," *New York Daily News*, March 22, 1979; "Indian Actress and Model Persis Khambatta (2 October 1948 A 18 August 1998)," *Shutterstock*, n.d., https://www.shutterstock.com/editorial/image-editorial/indian-actress-and-model-persis-khambatta-2-october-1948-a-18-august-1998-1976621a; Eve Ronan, "Star Trek Star Persis Khambatta Sheds Her Locks for Luck!" *Akron Beacon Journal*, April 26, 1979.

10. Denny, 88; Tom Davies, "Court of the Rich," *Observer*, May 20, 1979.

11. Davies.

12. "Rambling Reporter," June 26, 1979; "Berlin Offers Hefty Coin Help in Pitch to Revive Film Prod," *Variety* 291, no. 7 (June 21, 1978), 6; Susan Sackett, "Star Trek Report," *Starlog* no. 27 (October 1979), 31.

13. "Rambling Reporter," *Hollywood Reporter*, April 3, 1979; "Rambling Reporter," June 26, 1979; Roderick Mann, "Arkin to Film 'Arigo' in Brazil," *Los Angeles Times*, June 19, 1979; Morrison.

14. STAR TREK THE MOTION PICTURE interviews. The multi coloured SWAP SHOP, YouTube video, 18:47, posted by "trekkertos," November 6, 2015, https://www.youtube.com/watch?v=kkagXm_R7Nc.

15. *P M Magazine on Star Trek The Motion Picture—1979!!*, YouTube video, 6:56, posted by "videoholicULTIMATE," June 2, 2013, https://www.youtube.com/watch?v=qvJB9E86xRw.

16. *P M Magazine on Star Trek The Motion Picture—1979!!*

17. Willson, August 1980, 52, "Star Trek—The Motion Picture," *Star Trek Action Group* no. 38 (December 1979), 6; "International Sound Track," *Variety* 297, no. 6 (December 12, 1979), 40; Christine Hogan, "Hair, or Lack of It, the Measure of Her Success," *Sydney Morning Herald*, December 20, 1979.

18. Barclay, "Bald-headed Discovery Just 'Old-Fashioned Girl'"; Dolores Barclay, "East Indian Actress Maintains She's Just an Old-Fashioned Gal," *San Bernardino County Sun*, December 18, 1979; Dolores Barclay, "Persis Baldly Accepts Stardom," *Ottawa Journal*, December 20, 1979; Dolores Barclay, "Actress Cherishes Old Values of India," *Wisconsin State Journal*, December 26, 1979; Dolores Barclay, "Actress Goes Bald for Role," *Tennessean*, December 30, 1979; Dolores Barclay, "Miss India is Hollywood Star," *Canadian India Times*, January 10, 1980; Dolores Barclay, "'Star Trek' Actress Old Fashioned Gal," *Santa Fe New Mexican*, January 11, 1980.

19. Hogan.
20. Cushing; Liz Smith, *New York Daily News*, January 22, 1980.
21. Marilyn Beck, "'Serpentine' Director Looking for Superstar," *Journal News*, March 10, 1980.

1980

1. Thomas Schnurmacher, "Bujold, Gould Affair Was a Best-kept Showbiz Secret," *Montreal Gazette*, January 5, 1980.
2. Reilly, January 7, 1980, 29; Christopher Stone, Chuck Crandall, and Susan Stone, "'Star Trek' Blasts Off for the 80s with Kirk, Spock and a Bald Sexpot," *Us Weekly* (January 8, 1980), 18.
3. "Daytime Programs," *Detroit Free Press*, January 9, 1980; "Tuesday TV Highlights," *Albany Democrat-Herald*, January 12, 1980; "Monday TV Highlights," *Albany Democrat-Herald*, January 12, 1980; "Radio," *San Francisco Examiner*, January 14, 1980.
4. Bruce Smith, "State Woos Flick Dollars," *New York Daily News*, January 17, 1980; "Film Production: Universal," *Variety* 297, no. 12 (January 23, 1980), 32; Robin Leach, "Bald Beauty Loses 10G Gems," *New York Post*, April 7, 1980; Khambatta, 29; Roderick Mann, "Monroe Quote Draws Hot Words," *Los Angeles Times*, April 22, 1980.
5. "37th Annual Golden Globe Awards," Getty Images, n.d., https://www.gettyimages.com/detail/news-photo/persis-khambatta-during-37th-annual-golden-globe-awards-at-news-photo/105852757; "Halos Going to Par 'Trek' and 'Shirley,'" *Daily Variety* 186, no. 41 (February 4, 1980), 6; Sherwood Oaks Experimental College, "Star Trek Seminar: The Making of a Film," Advertisement, *Los Angeles Times*, February 3, 1980.
6. D.J. Saunders and Fred Kerber, "A Corker for Studio 54," *New York Daily News*, March 1, 1980; "Briefly," *Kingsport Times-News*, March 2, 1980.
7. "Wednesday's TV," *New York Daily News*, March 5, 1980.
8. Earl Wilson, "Right Back Atcha, Says Wry Mrs. Sly," *Indianapolis Star*, March 7, 1980.
9. Beck, March 10, 1980.
10. "A New Look for a Once-Bald Beauty," *New York Post*, March 11, 1980; "Persis Khambatta at a Party at 'Laboite' Disco," *Getty Images*., n.d., https://www.gettyimages.ae/detail/news-photo/persis-khambatta-was-asked-to-shave-her-head-again-for-the-news-photo/531077250; "Martin's Sideliners," *New York Post*, March 13, 1980; "The New Star Wars: Celebrity Politics Becomes Part of the Game," *People*, March 31, 1980; Suzy, "Tanya Says Yes to Young Earl Smith," *New York Daily News*, March 19, 1980.
11. Tom Buckley, "On a Tramway to High Film Drama," *New York Times*, March 25, 1980.
12. "Pix, People, Pickups," *Daily Variety* 187, no. 17 (March 28, 1980), 5; "Sorry Priyanka, You're Not the First Indian to Present an Oscar," *New Indian Express*, February 3, 2016.
13. Leach.
14. Curry Kirkpatrick, "He's Not a Man to Take it Lying Down," *Sports Illustrated*, May 12, 1980; *William Shatner and Persis Khambatta Present Documentary Oscars® in 1980*, YouTube video, 5:28, posted by "Oscars," April 13, 2014, https://www.youtube.com/watch?v=xwbLZNpaSjg&; Rex Reed, *New York Daily News*, April 16, 1980.
15. Mann, April 22, 1980.
16. Mann, April 22, 1980.
17. Leach; Marilyn Beck, "'Angel' Wings Are Being Fitted Again," *New York Daily News*, February 21, 1980; Joey Sasso, "Through Channels," *South Idaho Press*, April 4, 1980; "Persis Turns Down Offer to be an 'Angel,'" *Arizona Republic*, April 20, 1980; "Persis Khambatta with Dann Moss," *Borsari Images*, n.d., http://www.borsariimages.com/archive/public/AssetDetail.cfm?aid=P-ABK-788-PB&fol=AA-7575-PB&rdir=folders&rpage=ViewFolderContents; Rip Taylor, "Thanks Chuck," Advertisement, *Daily Variety* 187, no. 49 (May 13, 1980), 2.
18. Jack Martin, "Bald Beauty Gets Brushoff," *New York Post*, May 27, 1980; Marilyn Beck, "Hollywood," *Ithaca Journal*, May 29, 1980.
19. Nels Nelson, "Newest Angel Almost a '10,'" *Philadelphia Daily News*, June 4, 1980.
20. Nelson.
21. Nelson.
22. Denny, 89–90; Bert Reisfeld, "The Persis Khambatta Story," 1981.
23. Sony Pictures Publicity, "CHARLIE'S ANGELS Production Information," *Sony*

Pictures Press Release, November 4, 2019, https://sonypicturespublicity.com/dom/secured/mediaassets/viewMediaAssets Level2.jsf; Walt Disney Studios, "Aladdin Press Kit," *Walt Disney Studios*, n.d., http://www.wdsmediafile.com/media/Aladdin/-writen-material/Aladdin5ce30bcaa76f4.pdf; Disney, "5 Things You Didn't Know About Aladdin's Naomi Scott," *Vogue India*, May 15, 2019, https://www.vogue.in/story/-things-you-didnt-know-about-aladdins-naomi-scott/.

24. Disney, May 15, 2019.

25. "YouTube Star Lilly Singh is the First Woman of Indian-Origin to Host a U.S. Late Night Show," *Rolling Stone India*, last modified March 16, 2019, https://rollingstoneindia.com/lilly-singh-late-night-show/; *OLAY #MAKESPACEFORWOMEN | SUPER BOWL LIV OFFICIAL COMMERCIAL*, 0:30, posted by "Olay North America," January 30, 2020, https://www.youtube.com/watch?v=Q-0Ll60FkLg.

26. "Meet Ilia of 'Star Trek—The Motion Picture,'" *Palm Beach Post*, May 2, 1980.

27. "Meet Ilia of 'Star Trek—The Motion Picture.'"

28. "Meet Ilia of 'Star Trek—The Motion Picture.'"

29. Gwen Jones and Carole Lalli, "Simply Hair-Raising," *L.A. Herald-Examiner*, June 13, 1980.

30. Willson, August 1980, 52.

31. "Communications," *Starlog* no. 39 (October 1980), 8.

32. Suzy, March 19, 1980; Jane Carroll, "The Raiderettes in Las Vegas," *San Francisco Examiner*, September 21, 1980; Anderson.

33. "People," *Press Democrat*, June 19, 1980; Lee Grant, "Parties: Parking Lot Becomes a 'Paradise'," *Los Angeles Times*, June 23, 1980.

34. "Persis Khambatta with John Phillip Law," Borsari Images, n.d. http://www.borsariimages.com/archive/public/AssetDetail.cfm?aid=P-ABK-778-PB&fol=AA-7575-PB&rdir=folders&rpage=ViewFolderContents; Army Archerd, "Just for Variety," *Daily Variety* 188, no. 38 (July 30, 1980), 3; Committee to Cure Cancer through Immunization, "2nd Annual Celebrity Racquetball Tournament," Advertisement, *Los Angeles Times*, July 27, 1980; Tia Gindick, "Wrapped Up in Their Art," *Los Angeles Times*, August 12, 1980; Bettijane Levine,

"Fonda's Nontoxic Waists," *Los Angeles Times*, September 26, 1980.

35. L. T. Brown, "A Watch on the Time," *Indianapolis News*, October 17, 1980; "Nat'l Film Society Tips Hat to Some of the Big Names," *Daily Variety* 189, no. 36 (October 28, 1980), 6; "Science-Fiction Awards," *New York Times*, November 24, 1980; "$250,000 Raised: 'Jazz Singer' Benefit Breaks Records," *Los Angeles Times*, December 19, 1980; Jody Jacobs, "Seeing in the New Year on an Upbeat," *Los Angeles Times*, January 5, 1981.

36. Michael W. Potts, "Persis Khambatta to Return to Bombay," *India West*, May 15, 1992; Tim Boxer, "Persis' a Terror," *New York Post*, April 4, 1981; "Pix, People, Pickups," *Daily Variety* 189, no. 43 (November 5, 1980), 1; Joan Crosby, "TV Scout Short Subjects," *Morning Call*, January 18, 1981; Crawley, 30.

37. Paramount Pictures, "Paramount Television Welcomes Harve Bennett," Advertisement, *Daily Variety* 190, no. 2 (December 9, 1980), 28.

38. Rich Handley, "Star Trek II at 20: Still Feeling Young," *Star Trek Communicator* no. 139 (August/September 2002), 53.

39. Handley.

1981

1. Khambatta, 30; "Cat People (1982)," *Mr. Skin*, n.d., https://www.mrskin.com/-cat-people-nude-scenes-t1615; Boxer.

2. "Khambatta on 'Hour,'" *Hollywood Reporter*, January 9, 1981; Gary Collins, *The Hour Magazine Cookbook* (New York: G.P. Putnam's Sons, 1995), 113; "Listen," *Los Angeles Times*, January 23, 1981.

3. Denny, 88.
4. Denny, 89.
5. Denny, 91.
6. Denny, 89.
7. Denny, 89.
8. Denny, 89.
9. Denny, 89.
10. Denny, 89.
11. Denny, 89.
12. Denny, 90.
13. Denny, 90.
14. Denny, 90.
15. Denny, 91.
16. Denny, 91.
17. Denny, 90.

18. Universal Studios, "Persis Khambatta—'Nighthawks,'" Universal Studios press release, February 26, 1981; Potts.
19. Potts; Denny, 88.
20. Reilly, January 7, 1980, 29.
21. Potts.
22. Aljean Harmetz, "Quick End of Low-Budget Horror-Film Cycle Seen," *New York Times*, October 2, 1980.
23. Potts, May 15, 1981; Janet Maslin, "'Nighthawks' With Sylvester Stallone," *New York Times*, April 10, 1981.
24. "Persis Khambatta Sighting at Ma Maison Restaurant—March 2, 1981," *Getty Images*, n.d., https://www.gettyimages.com/detail/news-photo/persis-khambatta-during-persis-khambatta-sighting-at-ma-news-photo/106203948; Jody Jacobs, "Phyllis Diller to Get Double Honors," *Los Angeles Times*, March 26, 1981; "An Evening with Michelle Phillips," *Esquire* (March 1981), 80.
25. "An Evening with Persis Khambatta," *Esquire* (July 1981), 53.
26. "An Evening with Persis Khambatta," 53.
27. "An Evening with Persis Khambatta," 55.
28. "An Evening with Persis Khambatta," 55.
29. "An Evening with Persis Khambatta," 55.
30. Khambatta, 28; "An Evening with Persis Khambatta," 55.
31. "An Evening with Persis Khambatta," 55.
32. "An Evening with Persis Khambatta," 55.
33. "An Evening with Persis Khambatta," 55; Cushing.
34. Tia Gindick, "Auction Benefits Four Organizations," *Los Angeles Times*, April 20, 1981; "An Evening with Persis Khambatta," 55.
35. Anderson.
36. Anderson.
37. Scott.
38. Scott.
39. Scott.
40. Scott.
41. "Eye," *Women's Wear Daily*, April 13, 1981; Army Archerd, "Just for Variety," *Daily Variety* 191, no. 37 (April 27, 1981), 3.
42. Khambatta, 91; Potts; Reisfeld; "Rambling Reporter," *Hollywood Reporter*, April 18, 1981.
43. "Persis Khambatta with Cliff Taylor," *Borsari Images*, n.d., http://www.borsariimages.com/archive/public/AssetDetail.cfm?aid=P-ABK-755-PB&fol=AA-7575-PB&rdir=folders&rpage=ViewFolderContents; "Persis Khambatta with Cliff Taylor," *Borsari Images*, n.d., http://www.borsariimages.com/archive/public/AssetDetail.cfm?aid=P-ABK-735-PB&fol=AA-7575-PB&rdir=folders&rpage=ViewFolderContents; "Bradbury Honored," *Spectrum*, May 31, 1981; "Rambling Reporter," *Hollywood Reporter*, May 29, 1981; "Rambling Reporter," *Hollywood Reporter*, June 10, 1981; "Emmy Award Presenters Named," *Los Angeles Times*, June 1, 1981.
44. George Christy, "The Great Life," *Hollywood Reporter*, June 19, 1981; Liz Smith, *New York Daily News*, May 5, 1981.
45. Christy; Marylouise Oates, "Pickfair Party for Jerry Buss: It was a Magic Evening for Celebrities," *Los Angeles Times*, June 19, 1981.
46. Army Archerd, "Just for Variety," *Daily Variety* 192, no. 18 (July 1, 1981), 3; Lane, July 10, 1981; Khambatta, 30.
47. Lane, July 10, 1981; Alan L. Gansberg, "Hollywood Strip," *Copley News Service*, June 9, 1981; Marilyn Beck, "Marilyn Beck," *San Francisco Examiner*, November 6, 1981.
48. Khosla.
49. Khosla.
50. Liz Smith, *New York Daily News*, August 19, 1981; "Sideliners," *New York Post*, September 2, 1981.
51. Triillusion Co., *Articles of Incorporation*, October 12, 1981; Triillusion Co., *Statement by Domestic Stock Corporation*, October 31, 1987.
52. *New York Post*, June 22, 1982; Lardine; Michael W. Potts, "Actress Persis Khambatta Succumbs to Heart Attack," *India West*, August 21, 1998; "Fame," *Richmond Review*, December 30, 1981.
53. Bill Willard, "Producer Albert Ruddy Hosts NATO to Megaforce' Shoot-Out, Lunch," *Daily Variety* 193, no. 49 (November 12, 1981), 21; Jeff Szalay, "Starlog Preview: Megaforce," *Starlog* no. 57 (April 1982), 19; Beck, November 6, 1981.
54. Beck, November 6, 1981.
55. Bill Willard, "Producer Albert Ruddy Hosts NATO to Megaforce' Shoot-Out, Lunch," *Daily Variety* 193, no. 49 (November 12, 1981), 21; Louise J. Esterhazy, "Louise

on the Scent," *Women's Wear Daily* Vol. 142, Iss. 104 (Nov 25, 1981), 4–5.; Lardine.

56. Bob Thomas, "Bald Beauty from 'Star Trek' Still Has Mega-Career," *Courier-News*, December 17, 1981.

57. Thomas, December 17, 1981; Bob Thomas, "Young Actress' Hairy Experience," *Santa Cruz Sentinel*, December 24, 1981; Bob Thomas, "Baldness, 'Star Trek' Spur Persis' Career," *Indianapolis Star*, December 24, 1981; Bob Thomas, "Baldness Made Actress Famous," *Morning News*, December 25, 1981; Bob Thomas, "'Star Trek' Baldy's Career Moving Along Nicely," *Longview News-Journal*, December 27, 1981; Roderick Mann, "This is a Trek Shatner Doesn't Mind," *Los Angeles Times*, December 22, 1981.

58. Anthony Bowen, "Celebrity Resolutions," *Tampa Tribune*, December 28, 1981.

59. Bowen.

60. "Hayes Proud of Son, But Plans to ss-*Tribune*, February 24, 1982; "Megaforce," *AFI Catalog*, n.d., https://catalog.afi.com/Film/56845-MEGAFORCE; Khambatta, 26.

1982

1. Ramesh P. Murarka, "1981—A Milestone Year for the Indian Community in the U.S.," *India West*, January 8, 1982; Lardine; Marilyn Beck, "Marilyn Beck," *San Francisco Examiner*, February 17, 1982.

2. Khambatta, 32.

3. Twentieth Century-Fox Corporation, "The Hair-Raising Adventures of Persis Khambatta," Twentieth Century-Fox Corporation press release, 1982.

4. Twentieth Century-Fox Corporation, "The Hair-Raising Adventures of Persis Khambatta."

5. Twentieth Century-Fox Corporation, "The Hair-Raising Adventures of Persis Khambatta."

6. Twentieth Century-Fox Corporation, "The Hair-Raising Adventures of Persis Khambatta."

7. Twentieth Century-Fox Corporation, "The Hair-Raising Adventures of Persis Khambatta."

8. Twentieth Century-Fox Corporation, "The Hair-Raising Adventures of Persis Khambatta."

9. Twentieth Century-Fox Corporation, "The Hair-Raising Adventures of Persis Khambatta."

10. Twentieth Century-Fox Corporation, "The Hair-Raising Adventures of Persis Khambatta."

11. Twentieth Century-Fox Corporation, "The Hair-Raising Adventures of Persis Khambatta."

12. Twentieth Century-Fox Corporation, "The Hair-Raising Adventures of Persis Khambatta."

13. Twentieth Century-Fox Corporation, "The Hair-Raising Adventures of Persis Khambatta."

14. *On TV*, 33.

15. "Portrait de Persis Khambatta en 1982," *Getty Images*, n.d., https://www.gettyimages.ae/detail/news-photo/actrice-indienne-persis-khambatta-a-paris-en-mars-1982-news-photo/954039500; "Premiere of 'She Dances Alone'—April 20, 1982," *Getty Images*, n.d., https://www.gettyimages.com/detail/news-photo/persis-khambatta-and-kip-whitman-during-premiere-of-she-news-photo/105922971; "Persis Khambatta with Gary Sandy," *Borsari Images*, n.d., http://www.borsariimages.com/archive/public/AssetDetail.cfm?aid=-P-ABK-751-PB&fol=AA-7575-PB&rdir=folders&rpage=ViewFolderContents.

16. Ed Naha, "The Young and the Weightless," *Starlog* no. 59 (June 1982), 64; Janet Maslin, "New 'Star Trek' Full of Gadgets and Fun," *New York Times*, June 4, 1982.

17. "Hollywood Soundtrack," *Variety* 306, no. 5 (March 3, 1982), 22; *New York Post*, June 22, 1982; "TV Tomorrow," *San Francisco Examiner*, June 10, 1982; "TV Tonight," *San Francisco Examiner*, June 22, 1982; Anderson; Earl Wilson, "It Happened Last Night," *Tyler Morning Telegraph*, June 23, 1982; "International Sound Track: Rome," *Variety* 307, no. 8 (June 23, 1982), 40.

18. "Pix, People, Pickups," *Daily Variety* 196, no. 13 (June 23, 1982), 14; *Mega Force (1982) movie review—Sneak Previews with Roger Ebert and Gene Siskel*, YouTube video, 5:16, posted by "Eric Stan," Jun 25, 2019, https://www.youtube.com/watch?v=PpzCTP7EGaY.

19. *Mega Force (1982) movie review—Sneak Previews with Roger Ebert and Gene Siskel*.

20. Jim Murray, "Real Men Don't Give it a Thought," *Los Angeles Times*, May 4, 1982;

Clint Walker, "'Megaforce' Remains a Guilty Pleasure," *Journal Gazette*, May 11, 2019.
21. "Pix, People, Pickups," *Daily Variety* 196, no. 13 (June 23, 1982), 14; John Dodd, "Not Even Day-Glo Hides the Tackiness," *Edmonton Journal*, June 26, 1982; Ernest Leogrande, "Mega Bomb," *New York Daily News*, June 26, 1982.
22. Janet Maslin, "'Megaforce' Is a Mix of Joviality and Stunts," *New York Times*, June 27, 1982.
23. Gene Siskel, "'Megaforce' Action, Laughs Don't Mix," *Chicago Tribune*, June 29, 1982; Roger Ebert, "'Megaforce' Waste of Money and Time," *Asbury Park Press*, July 2, 1982.
24. Daryl Miller, "Adventure Is Childish Megaflop," *Arizona Daily Star*, June 30, 1982; Malcolm L. Johnson, "Comically Inept 'Megaforce' Lacks Power to Seem Relevant or Amusing," *Hartford Courant*, July 1, 1982; Paulette Henderson, "'Megaforce' Is 'Mega-dull,'" *Waterloo Courier*, July 2, 1982.
25. Harry F. Thermal, "Latest Action, Sci-Fi Movies Make Crash Landings," *News Journal*, July 4, 1982.
26. Mike Mayo, "Megaforce," *Cinefantastique* 13, no. 1 (September-October 1982), 45, 47.
27. Joe Lovitt, "'Rocky III' Plot No Secret to Fans," *Queen City Mail*, July 7, 1982.
28. Aljean Harmetz, "'E.T.,' at $87 Million, Hit of Summer Box Office," *New York Times*, July 7, 1982.
29. "Communications," *Starlog* no. 65 (December 1982), 8.
30. Roderick Mann, "'Megaforce' Spends Megabucks on Arms," *Los Angeles Times*, November 22, 1981.
31. Mayo.
32. Diana Maychick, "Poor Persis Khambatta: No Kisses, No Romance," *New York Post*, July 10, 1982; Twentieth Century-Fox Corporation, "'MEGAFORCE' Production Information," Twentieth Century-Fox Corporation press release, 1982.
33. Twentieth Century-Fox Corporation, "'MEGAFORCE' Production Information."
34. Twentieth Century-Fox Corporation, "'MEGAFORCE' Production Information."
35. Twentieth Century-Fox Corporation, "'MEGAFORCE' Production Information."
36. Twentieth Century-Fox Corporation, "'MEGAFORCE' Production Information."
37. Twentieth Century-Fox Corporation, "'MEGAFORCE' Production Information."
38. Twentieth Century-Fox Corporation, "'MEGAFORCE' Production Information"; Khambatta, 47.
39. Twentieth Century-Fox Corporation, "'MEGAFORCE' Production Information."
40. Twentieth Century-Fox Corporation, "'MEGAFORCE' Production Information."
41. Maychick, July 10, 1982.
42. Sackett and Roddenberry, 139.
43. Twentieth Century-Fox Corporation.
44. Harold Livingston, *Star Trek II: "In Thy Image" Rough First Draft*, October 20, 1977, Margaret Herrick Library, Beverly Hills, 953.f-S-1353.
45. "Stunts Unlimited Opens Its Membership to Women," *Daily Variety* 173, no. 10 (September 20, 1976), 10; "Land Speed Record," *Los Angeles Times*, September 23, 1976; Will Tusher, "Multifunction Camera Car Bows to Acclaim, Orders," *Daily Variety* 210 no. 40 (February 3, 1986), 20; "Kitty Zooms 524 MPH, Eyes 600," *Dayton Daily News*, December 6, 1976.
46. "Kitty Zooms 524 MPH, Eyes 600."
47. "Needham Blocked Speed Effort," *York Daily Record*, December 10, 1.
48. "Farrah Fawcett Double Files 'Cannonball' Suit," *Daily Variety* 192, no. 4 (June 11, 1981), 3.
49. Robin Adams Sloan, "Gossip Column," *Asbury Park Press*, July 15, 1982.
50. Denny Boyd, "Jim Checks Up on All the Dirty Talk," *Vancouver Sun*, July 17, 1982.
51. Maychick, July 10, 1982.
52. Maychick, July 10, 1982.
53. Koenig, 36; Maychick, July 10, 1982.
54. A.P. Kamath & V. Bhuvana, "The Bandit Queen Rides Again," *Illustrated Weekly of India*, March 19, 1989.
55. "Maud Enjoys 'Chicago Story,'" *Mansfield News-Journal*, April 9, 1982; Dave Kaufman, "40 TV Series Get the Heave-Ho from Net Skeds," *Daily Variety* 196 no. 9 (June 17, 1982), 15.
56. Janet Hirshenson, Jane Jenkins, and Rachel Kranz, *A Star Is Found: Our Adventures Casting Some of Hollywood's Biggest*

Chapter Notes: 1983

Movies (Orlando, Fl: Harcourt, 2009), 34–36.

57. "Maud Adams Signs for Bond Film," *Daily Herald*, August 9, 1982; Hirshenson, Jenkins, and Kranz, 36.

58. Hirshenson, Jenkins, and Kranz, 127–128.

59. Amit Roy, "Licence to write about BOND," *Telegraph*, last modified September 9, 2016, https://www.telegraphindia.com/entertainment/licence-to-write-about-bond/cid/1421856; Ajay Chowdhury and Matthew Field, *Some Kind of Hero: The Remarkable Story of the James Bond Films* (Chicago: The History Press, 2015), 435.

60. Ramesh P. Murarka, "A Weary Prime Minister Meets Some Prominent California Indians," *India West*, August 6, 1982; Michael W. Potts, "Over 10,000 Attend India I-Day Celebrations in Los Angeles," *India West*, August 20, 1982; K. P. Sunil, "Not Making It," *Illustrated Weekly of India*, July 29, 1984.

61. Murarka, August 6, 1982.

62. Khambatta, 8.

63. Potts, August 20, 1982; Bettijane Levine, "Fendis Pipe Furs to Russia," *Los Angeles Times*, September 10, 1982.

64. Fashion82, "Listen," *Los Angeles Times*, October 8, 1982.

65. Fashion82, October 8, 1982.

66. "Wednesday," *Leader-Post*, October 20, 1982; Army Archerd, "Just for Variety," *Daily Variety* 197, no. 45 (November 5, 1982), 3; "Hollywood Soundtrack," *Variety* 309, no. 3 (November 17, 1982), 36; Rajen S. Anand, "Rohini Hattangady Attends L.A. Premiere of 'Gandhi,'" *India West*, December 24, 1982.

67. "Khambatta to Star," *Hollywood Reporter*, October 29, 1982.

1983

1. Harold Martin, "Time Exposure," *Popular Photography* 72, no. 1 (January 2008), 132; "January 12, 1983," *Los Angeles Times*, January 9, 1983.

2. Margo Skinner, "Art & Entertainment," *Asian Week*, January 13, 1983; Michael W. Potts, "California is Leading Source of Tourist Business to India," *India West*, February 11, 1983; Army Archerd, "Just for Variety," *Daily Variety* 198, no. 50 (February 15, 1988), 3; Jill Jackson, "India Awards 'Gandhi' Director," *Palm Beach Daily News*, March 10, 1983.

3. "India's Bandit Queen Selects Her Captors," *San Francisco Examiner*, February 11, 1983; Michael W. Potts, "Persis to Star as Phoolan Devi in her Own Film, 'The Bandit Queen,'" *India West*, April 27, 1984; Alan L. Gansberg, "Khambatta Eyes 'Bandit Queen,'" *Hollywood Reporter*, March 16, 1984.

4. Dick Kleiner, "Susie Bono Eyes an Exotic Role," *Times and Democrat*, July 16, 1984; Michael London, "Actresses Vie to Screen Bandit Queen's Saga," *Los Angeles Times*, May 16, 1984; Vernon Scott, "Scott's World: Susie Bono Went Calling on India's Bandit Queen," UPI, May 11, 1983; Scott, April 18, 1981.

5. Kleiner.

6. Scott, May 11, 1983; Phoolan Devi, Marie-Thérèse Cuny, and Paul Rambali, I, *Phoolan Devi: The Autobiography of India's Bandit Queen* (London: Warner Books, 1997), 499–500; London.

7. Linda Gross, "Movies of the Week," *Los Angeles Times*, February 20, 1983.

8. Ramesh P. Murarka and Michael W. Potts, "Nation-Wide Tour Nets $275,000 for Nargis Dutt Memorial Foundation," *India West*, April 8, 1983; Academy of Motion Picture Arts and Sciences, "William Shatner, David Wolper Set For All-Star Oscar Show," Academy of Motion Picture Arts and Sciences press release, April 1, 1983; Academy of Motion Picture Arts and Sciences, "Wise to Moderate Foreign Language Oscar Symposium," Academy of Motion Picture Arts and Sciences press release, April 1, 1983; Academy of Motion Picture Arts and Sciences, "David L. Wolper Academy Awards Acceptance Speech," *Academy Awards Acceptance Speech Database*, n.d., http://aaspeechesdb.oscars.org/link/057-24/.

9. End Hunger, "The End Hunger Televent," Advertisement, *Los Angeles Times*, March 3, 1983; "Pix, People, Pickups," *Daily Variety* 199, no. 27 (April 12, 1983), 19.

10. George Michael and Rae Lindsay, *George Michael's Complete Hair Care for Men* (Garden City, N.Y.: Doubleday & Company, 1983), 111.

11. Michael W. Potts, "'Warrior of the Lost World' Means Greater Exposure for Persis," *India West*, June 24, 1983.

12. Potts, June 24, 1983.

13. Continental Motion Pictures, "Warrior of the Lost World," Advertisement, *Variety* 310, no. 13 (April 27, 1983), 14; Potts, June 24, 1983.
14. Potts, June 24, 1983.
15. Potts, June 24, 1983; Ed Naha, "Through a Glass Lightly," *Starlog* no. 46 (July 1983), 63.
16. Alan L. Gansberg, "Hollywood Strip," *Copley News Service*, August 10, 1983.
17. Khosla.
18. David McDonnell, "Log Entries," *Starlog* no. 76 (November 1983), 10–11; Gayle Duke, "Pageant Countdown," *Tampa Tribune*, August 20, 1983.
19. "Saturday Television Listings," *Daily Republican-Register*, August 26, 1983.
20. Jay Bobbin, "NBC Plans 2-Hour Special," *Asheville Citizen-Times*, September 10, 1983.
21. "Television and Radio Briefs," *Daily Variety* 201, no. 49 (November 11, 1983), 12.

1984

1. Edna Gundersen, "India's Influence Remains With El Paso Couple," *El Paso Times*, August 26, 1983.
2. Kathleen Halloran, "Hairless Woman Has Sense of Humor, Wonder, Adventure," *News-Press*, February 27, 1984.
3. "A Mysterious Swedish Model Named Jenny O Makes a Bald Fashion Statement," *People*, April 23, 1984.
4. John Duka, "Reporter's Notebook: Fashion as Art in Milan," *New York Times*, March 18, 1984; Jill Gerston, "The Gender Blenders," *Philadelphia Inquirer*, May 31, 1984; "Style News," *Vogue* 174, no. 8 (August 1, 1984), 153.
5. Paula Span, "House of Pectorals," *Washington Post*, December 19, 1985; Alex Kayser, *Heads* (New York: Abbeville Press, 1985), 66.
6. "U.S.-Based Actress Persis Khambatta to Co-Produce Film," *India Today*, March 15, 1984; "Thursday's Television," *New York Daily News*, March 1, 1984; Alan L. Gansberg, "Khambatta Eyes 'Bandit Queen,'" *Hollywood Reporter*, March 16, 1984.
7. Gansberg, March 16, 1984; Potts, April 27, 1984; London; Diana Maychick, "Sari Time in H'wood for 2 Actresses," *New York Post*, May 16, 1984.
8. Potts, April 27, 1984; London.
9. Potts, April 27, 1984.
10. "Short Takes," *Daily Variety* 203 no. 16 (March 27, 1984), 25; Rajadhyaksha and Willemen, 510, 538; Meheli Sen and Anustup Basu, *Figurations in Indian Film* (London: Palgrave Macmillan UK, 2013), 23.
11. Coomi Kapoor, "Film Makers Face the Brunt of Censor Board Whims and Fancies," *India Today*, April 15, 1985; Rajendra Ojha, *Screen World Publication*'s 75 Glorious Years of Indian Cinema (Bombay: Screen World Publication, 1988), 83; "Sarika to Join Growing Gaggle of Single Parents," *India Today*, September 30, 1985; "Sarika to Join Growing Gaggle of Single Parents," *India Today*, September 30, 1985.
12. Phoolan Devi, Marie-Thérèse Cuny, and Paul Rambali, I, *Phoolan Devi: The Autobiography of India's Bandit Queen* (London: Warner Books, 1997), 481.
13. Richard S. Ehrlich, "Notorious 'Bandit Queen,' Stewing in Indian Prison, Rues Day She Surrendered," *San Francisco Examiner*, July 13, 1986.
14. Mary A. Fischer, "Two Actresses Vie to Escape Hollywood's Caste System—by Playing India's Bandit Queen," *People*, June 11, 1984; Maychick, May 16, 1984; Marilyn Beck, "Marilyn Beck," *St. Cloud Times*, June 16, 1984.
15. Sunil.
16. Fischer.
17. Fischer.
18. Fischer.
19. Hank Werba, "Breakthroughs for Milan Mart," *Variety* 316, no. 13 (October 24, 1984), 1.
20. Cannon Films, "Breakin' 2 is Electric Boogaloo," Advertisement, *Variety* 316, no. 13 (October 24, 1984), 23; RGH International Film Enterprises Inc., "First Strike," Advertisement, *Variety* 316, no. 13 (October 24, 1984), 199.
21. "Film and TV Casting News," *Daily Variety* 206, no. 3 (December 10, 1984), 18.
22. Bunny Mars, "Do Tell...," *Los Angeles Times*, April 15, 1984; Bunny Mars, "Do Tell," *Los Angeles Times*, May 13, 1984.
23. Michael W. Potts, "Persis to Star in CBS TV Episode After Completing Film in India," *India West*, April 17, 1987; Ritu Singh, *Stark Raving Ad: A Giddy Guide to Indian Ads You Love (or Hate)* (Gurugram, India: Hachette India, 2018); Khambatta, dust jacket.

24. Michael W. Potts, "Houston's India Week Draws Large Crowds; Ends on Sour Note," *India West*, May 11, 1984.
25. "Film Castings," *Daily Variety* 204, no. 42 (August 3, 1984), 35; Lawrence Cohn, "170 'Secret' Features Filmed in 1984," *Variety* 318 no. 13 (May 1, 1985), 5.
26. "Motion Picture Producer & Director," *Allankuskowski.com*, n.d., http://allankuskowski.com/.
27. "'Stars of Today' Program Set," *Los Angeles Times*, August 11, 1984; Hollywood International, "Hollywood International's Celebration II," Advertisement, *LA Weekly*, September 6, 1984.
28. Alex Gordon, "The Pit & the Pen," *Fangoria* 40, no. 3 (December 1984), 57–58.
29. "MPAA Tags 13 Pix for Week," *Daily Variety* 205, no. 63 (December 4, 1984), 2.
30. "TPE Goes After Two Barter Pilots on Show Biz Folk," *Variety* 316 no. 13 (October 24, 1984), 402.

1985

1. Robin Leach and Judith Rich, *Lifestyles of the Rich and Famous* (Garden City, N.Y.: Doubleday, 1986), 24–25.
2. Television Program Enterprises, "The Start of Something Big," Advertisement, *Daily Variety* 287 no. 28 (April 12, 1985), 9.
3. "Visto Int'l Puts 2 Independent Pix in Release," *Daily Variety* 206, no. 42 (February 5, 1985), 11; "Videos," *Statesman Journal*, May 17, 1985.
4. "Film Reviews," *Variety* 319, no. 7 (June 12, 1985), 18; "Continental Loaded for AFMarket; Sarluis Seeking Production Topper," *Variety* 310, no. 5 (March 2, 1983), 258.
5. "Warrior of the Lost World," *VHS Collector.com*, last modified August 8, 2012, https://vhscollector.com/movie/warrior-lost-world.
6. Phantom of the Movies, "Spiders and Maggots and Flies, Oh My!" *New York Daily News*, September 11, 1985.
7. Roderick Mann, "He's Booked His Passage to Hollywood," *Los Angeles Times*, January 29, 1985.
8. "Hollywood Celebrities Grace Glittering Opening Ceremony of Bombay Palace," *India West*, February 22, 1985; Jeff Wagner, "Success of David Lean's Film Triggers Victor Banerjee's 'Passage' to Hollywood," *India West*, March 1, 1985.
9. Nan Robertson, "Victor Banerjee—India Personified," *New York Times*, March 17, 1985; Arthur Pais, "Films Winners: Romance and Revenge," *India Abroad*, January 6, 1989.
10. *Festival of India in the United States, 1985–1986* (New York: Harry N. Abrams, 1985), cover copy; Kirsten Gallagher, "Celebration of India," *Orlando Sentinel*, June 13, 1985; "All-Time Film Rental Champs (of U.S.-Canada Market)," *Variety* 321, no. 11 (January 8, 1986), 26, 58, 62.
11. National Gallery of Art, "The Sculpture of India: 3000 B.C.–1300 A.D. Marks Beginning of Festival of India 1985–1986," National Gallery of Art press release, April 16, 1985; Phil Roura and Tom Poster, "Here & There," *New York Daily News*, June 12, 1985.
12. Jeff Wagner, "Rajiv Meets Indian Community in 2 Affairs," *India West*, June 23, 1985; "Agents Alley," *Daily Variety* 208, no. 7 (June 14, 1985), 15; "Persis Khambatta pacted," *Hollywood Reporter*, May 31, 1985; Edward Lozzi, "A Tribute to Persis Khambatta," *Edward Lozzi & Associates*, n.d., http://www.lozzipr.com/persis.html; Phil Roura and Tom Poster, "Here & There," *New York Daily News*, May 16, 1985; Wagner, June 23, 1985.
13. Bonny Mukherjee, "London-Based American TV and Film Company to Make Mini-Series on Indira Gandhi," *India Today*, April 15, 1985.
14. "Judith De Paul Spells Determination," *Daily Variety* 209, no. 38 (October 29, 1985), 9, 118.
15. Roger Watkins, "De Paul's Silver Chalice Wraps 'Klarsfeld' on Budget, on Time," *Variety* 323, no. 10 (July 2, 1986), 42; "De Paul is Catalyst In HBO, Soviet Coprod," *Variety* 325, no. 9 (December 24, 1986), 77; Brian Lowry, "Procter & Gamble Prods. Ups Telefilm Production," *Daily Variety* 228, no. 2 (June 7, 1990), 20.
16. "Film Reviews," *Variety* 320, no. 4 (August 21, 1985), 16.
17. "HFPA Gives 11G in Grants to Industry-Related Orgs," *Daily Variety* 208, no. 30 (July 18, 1985), 29; "LA I-Day Celebrations a Symphony of Color, Curry, and Culture," *India West*, August 23, 1985.
18. Ramesh P. Murarka, "Glittering 'Tribute to India' Presented in Los Angeles," *India West*, September 20, 1985.
19. S.H. Venkatramani, "Businessmen

Set to Flood the Market with Hindi, Tamil Films Made Exclusively for Video," *India Today*, September 15, 1986.
  20. Mohammed Aslam, "Neeta Puri, Winner of the Miss India Contest of New York in 1983, Enters Bollywood," *India Today*, August 31, 1986.
  21. "Star Trek Actress Persis Khambatta Lands Role in Nari Hira's Shingora," *India Today*, November 30, 1985; Harry Haun, "What's Cooking? Ross in Hot Role as Baker," *New York Daily News*, August 29, 1985.

1986–1988

  1. Welcome Home, "Official National Welcome Home Celebration for Our Vietnam Veterans," Advertisement, *Los Angeles Times*, February 9, 1986.
  2. "Khambatta to Star in Indian Film," *Los Angeles Daily News*, February 20, 1986.
  3. "Khambatta to Star in Indian Film."
  4. Khosa.
  5. Khosa; "Without Comment," *Sunday* 13, no. 37 (July 20, 1986), 77.
  6. "It's Such a Compliment to Have Lady Di Wearing My Dress," *India Today*, September 30, 1986; "Rambling Reporter," *Hollywood Reporter*, August 29, 1986; B.R. Srikanth and Shameem Akhtar, "Things of Beauty," *Outlook India*, August 31, 1998.
  7. Michael W. Potts, "'Kamla' Screened in LA in Hopes of American Release," *India West*, October 17, 1986.
  8. Michael W. Potts, "Khambatta to Co-Produce $2-Million Feature Film," *India West*, December 12, 1986; Triillusion Co., *Statement by Domestic Stock Corporation*, October 31, 1987.
  9. Noel de Sousa, "Ahmed Lateef," *Golden Globes*, last modified August 21, 2015, https://www.goldenglobes.com/goldenglobes/ahmed-lateef-31324.
  10. Morrie Gelman, 'Star Trek' Feature Reported Presold by Par to ABC-TV," *Daily Variety* 182, no. 37 (January 29, 1979), 1, 6; Dale Pollock, "ABC Stocks Up on Films for the '80s," *Daily Variety* 186, no. 9 (December 18, 1979), 24.
  11. "Monday," *New York Daily News*, March 8, 1987.
  12. Potts, April 17, 1987; P. Chaltanya, "Small Screen," *Sunday* 14, no. 43 (September 13, 1987), 76.
  13. Potts, April 17, 1987.
  14. Potts, April 17, 1987; "Keach Directing Seg of 'New Mike Hammer,'" *Daily Variety* 215, no. 9 (March 16, 1987), 77.
  15. "Premiere of Distortions," *Getty Images*, n.d., https://www.gettyimages.com/detail/news-photo/persis-khambatta-during-premiere-of-distortions-at-academy-news-photo/109667001; Lor, "Homevideo Reviews," *Variety* 327, no. 13 (July 22, 1987), 47; "War Prison Camp Series," *VHSCollector.com*, n.d., https://vhscollector.com/distributor-series/war-prison-camp-series.
  16. Lor.
  17. "Action Intl. Means What Its Title Says," *Variety* 327, no. 2 (May 6, 1987), 247; "New Film Starts," *Variety* 329, no. 1 (October 28, 1987), 24.
  18. Doch, "Cannes Market," *Variety* 331, no. 5 (May 25, 1988), 28.
  19. Doch.
  20. "Homevideo Briefs," *Daily Variety* 220, no. 16 (August 29, 1988), 16; Al Stewart, "Newsline," *Billboard* 100, no. 37 (September 10, 1988), 52.
  21. "1987–88 Film Production," *Variety* 331, no. 2 (May 4, 1988), 162.
  22. Lor, "Cannes Market," *Variety* 331, no. 4 (May 18, 1988), 124.
  23. Army Archerd, "Just for Variety," *Daily Variety* 218, no. 60 (March 2, 1988), 3.
  24. Army Archerd, "Just for Variety," *Daily Variety* 192, no. 13 (June 24, 1981), 3; "TV Wednesday," *San Francisco Examiner*, May 11, 1988.
  25. "Agents Alley," *Daily Variety* 219, no. 34 (April 22, 1988), 14; Skip E. Lowe with Guest Ed Fury, Persis Khambatta, Mark Hudson Bernice Altschul.
  26. Mike Barnes, "Skip E. Lowe, Talk Show Host and Inspiration for Martin Short's Jiminy Glick, Dies at 85," *Hollywood Reporter*, last modified September 23, 2014, https://www.hollywoodreporter.com/news/skip-e-lowe-dead-talk-735285.
  27. Skip E. Lowe with Guest Ed Fury, Persis Khambatta, Mark Hudson Bernice Altschul.
  28. Skip E. Lowe with Guest Ed Fury, Persis Khambatta, Mark Hudson Bernice Altschul.
  29. Skip E. Lowe with Guest Ed Fury, Persis Khambatta, Mark Hudson Bernice Altschul.
  30. Skip E. Lowe with Guest Ed Fury,

Persis Khambatta, Mark Hudson Bernice Altschul.
  31. *Skip E. Lowe with Guest Ed Fury,* Persis Khambatta, Mark Hudson Bernice Altschul.
  32. *Skip E. Lowe with Guest Ed Fury,* Persis Khambatta, Mark Hudson Bernice Altschul.
  33. *Skip E. Lowe with Guest Ed Fury,* Persis Khambatta, Mark Hudson Bernice Altschul.
  34. Roger Christensen and Karen Christensen, *Christensen's Celebrity Autographs* (San Diego, CA: Cardiff-by-the-Sea Publishing Company, 1988), 118.
  35. Gammack.

1989–1990

  1. "Aletter Keeps HFPA Custom As '89 Miss Golden Globe," *Daily Variety* 222, no. 18 (December 30, 1988), 3; Michael W. Potts, "Mundhra's 'The Jigsaw Murders' Premieres in Los Angeles," *India West*, February 3, 1989; "The 46th Annual Golden Globe Awards—Arrivals," *Getty Images*, n.d., https://www.gettyimages.com/detail/news-photo/persis-khambatta-during-the-46th-annual-golden-globe-awards-news-photo/105923076.
  2. Triillusion Co., *Statement by Domestic Stock Corporation*, August 15, 1988.
  3. Triillusion Co., *Certificate of Dissolution*, April 15, 1989.
  4. Kamath and Bhuvana.
  5. "Marriages," *Des Moines Register*, April 27, 1989.
  6. Gammack.
  7. Gammack.
  8. Gammack.
  9. Gammack.
  10. Gammack.
  11. Mary Kay Shanley, "A Little Help Keeps Disabled in Own Homes," *Des Moines Register*, March 29, 1987.
  12. *NBC commercials (October 21, 1990),* YouTube video, 18:42, posted by "SchfiftyThreeRetroTV," June 25, 2019, https://www.youtube.com/watch?v=kGUuUMjKslU.

1991–1993

  1. "Persis Khambatta Sighting at Bologna-Taylor's Home—June 21, 1991," *Getty Images*, n.d., https://www.gettyimages.com/detail/news-photo/persis-khambatta-during-persis-khambatta-sighting-at-news-photo/107132639; Michael W. Potts, "Film Stars Grace Opening of India-West Office in L.A.," *India West*, November 1, 1991; Ramesh P. Murarka and Ramesh Gune, "Calif. Chapters of Nargis Dutt Foundation Collect $95,000 at This Year's Events," *India West*, November 1, 1991; Michael W. Potts, "Bay Area Woman Crowned "Miss L.A. India," *India West*, December 6, 1991.
  2. Nellie Andreeva, "Bela Bajaria Joins Netflix: Former Universal TV President Named VP Content," *Deadline*, last modified October 5, 2016, https://deadline.com/2016/10/bela-bajaria-netflix-former-universal-tv-president-vp-content-1201831053/.
  3. Nellie Andreeva, "Bela Bajaria to Lead International Non-English TV Originals for Netflix, Erik Barmack Segues to Producing," *Deadline*, last modified March 6, 2019, https://deadline.com/2019/03/bela-bajaria-lead-international-non-english-tv-originals-for-netflix-erik-barmack-segues-to-producing-1202570698/.
  4. "Premiere of 'Star Trek VI,'" *Getty Images*, n.d., https://www.gettyimages.com/photos/persis-khambatta?events=75331072&family=editorial&phrase=persis%20khambatta&sort=best.
  5. Michael W. Potts, "Director Joffé Attends Unicef Benefit Screening," *India West*, April 10, 1992; Roger Ebert, "Doctor Drops Out, Tunes in to Calcutta," *Wisconsin State Journal*, April 17, 1992.
  6. Potts, May 15, 1992.
  7. Potts, May 15, 1992.
  8. Potts, May 15, 1992.
  9. Potts, May 15, 1992.
  10. Potts, May 15, 1992.
  11. Potts, May 15, 1992.
  12. Potts, May 15, 1992.
  13. "Chabad Pre-Telethon Party," *Getty Images*, n.d., https://www.gettyimages.com/detail/news-photo/persis-khambatta-news-photo/75786406; "Ron Galella Archive—File Photos," *Getty Images*, n.d., https://www.gettyimages.com/detail/news-photo/-actress-marina-sirtis-attending-chabad-pre-telethon-party-news-photo/81606618; Archana Dongre, "Women's Network Launches Mentor-Protege Program," *India West*, December 18, 1992; Beulah Ku, "Indo-

American Women Show Success, Variation," *Asianweek*, January 8, 1993.
 14. Spring Trek '93, "Spring Trek '93," Advertisement, *Philadelphia Daily News*, April 2, 1993; Creation Entertainment, "Creation Presents," Advertisement, *Starlog* no 189 (April 1993), 14; "Dear Starfleet," *Starfleet Communique* no. 56 (April/May 1993), 12.
 15. "Nearly 10,000 Die as Earthquake Rocks Two Districts of Maharashtra," *Indian Express*, October 1, 1993; Michael W. Potts, "Hollywood Reaches Out to Earthquake Victims in India," *India West*, December 10, 1993.
 16. "TV Taping of "Golden Globe Awards 50th Anniversary," *Getty Images*, n.d., https://www.gettyimages.com/detail/news-photo/persis-khambatta-during-tv-taping-of-golden-globe-awards-news-photo/105923067; Potts, December 10, 1993.
 17. Potts, December 10, 1993.

1994–1995

 1. Michael W. Potts, "Sona Patel Crowned 'Super Model,'" *India West*, April 1, 1994; Preeti Shah, "Mundhra's Film Released in LA Theaters," *India West*, June 3, 1994.
 2. Michael Stein, "Accent on U.S. Stars," *Los Angeles Times*, June 25, 1994.
 3. Stein.
 4. Persis Khambatta, "Counterpunch: Put the Accent on Diversity," *Los Angeles Times*, July 11, 1994.
 5. Khambatta, July 11, 1994.
 6. Khambatta, July 11, 1994.
 7. Khambatta, July 11, 1994.
 8. Bhatia.
 9. Michael W. Potts, "LA's Zarin Dastur Named Miss Asian American Princess," *India West*, September 2, 1994.
 10. "Art Director Nitin Desai Recreates the Grand Cafe at Bombay's Nehru Centre," *India Today*, January 31, 1995; Tejaswini Ganti, *Producing Bollywood: Inside the Contemporary Hindi Film Industry* (Durham, NC: Duke University Press, 2012), 60–61.
 11. Vaishali Honawar, "The New Queens," *Telegraph*, February 5, 1995.
 12. Honawar; Khambatta, 211, 218; "Ms Persis Khambatta," *TimesContent*, n.d., https://timescontent.com/syndication-photos/reprint/fashion/264707/ms-persis-khambatta.html.

 13. Khambatta, 180, 190; "Briefly," *Los Angeles Times*, October 24, 1996.
 14. Khambatta, 186.
 15. Preeti Shah, "The Poor Quality of Indian Videos: Whose Fault Is It?" *India West*, March 11, 1994.
 16. Shah.
 17. Lekha Rattanani, "Big as in Bollywood," *India Today*, July 15, 1995; William Rhode, "Like a Dream," *Sunday* 22, no. 27 (July 2, 1995), 66.
 18. Shafquat Ali, "Role Model," *Sunday* 23, no. 13 (March 31, 1996), 43; Saira Menezes, "10 Questions: Persis Khambatta," *Outlook India*, March 20, 1996.
 19. Menezes.
 20. Menezes.

1996–1997

 1. Khambatta, 8; Someshwar.
 2. Khambatta, 8, dust jacket.
 3. Khambatta, 8.
 4. Khambatta, 8.
 5. "Don't Miss This One," *Sunday* 23, no. 43 (November 9, 1996), 56.
 6. Khambatta, 224, 202–207; Someshwar.
 7. Khambatta, 218.
 8. Khambatta, 53, 93, 99, 123, 156, 174–175.
 9. Khambatta, 71–73.
 10. Khambatta, 76.
 11. Khambatta, 158.
 12. Anupama Chopra, "Crop of Directors Make Waves in Film Industry with Brash New Themes," *India Today*, June 30, 1997; "2000: SGIFF 13," Singapore International Film Festival, n.d., https://www.sgiff.com/past-editions/2000-sgiff-13/.
 13. *Love Song For Persis K*, YouTube video, 8:59, posted by "David Dasharath Kalal," March 4, 2016, https://www.youtube.com/watch?v=uDXUZ2yFLEI&t.
 14. *Love Song For Persis K*; "Paint," David Dasharath Kalal, n.d., https://www.davidkalal.net/paint.html.
 15. Someshwar.
 16. Someshwar.
 17. Someshwar.
 18. Someshwar.
 19. Someshwar.
 20. *Tribute to Miss India—Launch of Pride of India | Archival Footage*, YouTube video, 1:55, posted by "WildFilmsIndia,"

Sep 25, 2019, https://www.youtube.com/watch?v=hM5R5D4T0DM; "Mama Hindustani," *Outlook India*, October 20, 1997.
21. Tribute to Miss India—Launch of Pride of India | Archival Footage.
22. Michael W. Potts, "Persis Khambatta's Latest Trek: Book of Miss Indias," *India West*, August 29, 1997; Khambatta, dust jacket.
23. Nandita Chowdhury, "Catwalk Memories," *India Today*, October 20, 1997.
24. Chowdhury; Khambatta, 8–9.
25. Chowdhury.

1998

1. Srikanth and Akhtar; "Khushwant Singh to Shoot Chat Show for Star Plus," *India Today*, April 13, 1998; Namrata Joshi, "Watch Highlights of Music Show, Chat Show & Feature," *India Today*, August 17, 1998; "Indian Beauty Queen Who Made It to Hollywood: Persis Khambatta, 49, Died in Mumbai After a Cardiac Arrest," *India in New York*, August 28, 1998.
2. "Glitterati," *Outlook India*, April 20, 1998.
3. Kuldip Singh, August 19, 1998.
4. Sheela Reddy, "'I Don't Know One Editor in India Who is Well-Read,'" *Outlook India*, October 17, 2005.
5. Reddy.
6. Shepherd, 22, 24; Bhaichand Patel, "Festival of Lightness," *Outlook India*, March 31, 2014.
7. Reddy.
8. Sheela Reddy, "'I May Die Any Day Now,'" *Outlook India*, October 24, 2011.
9. Bhatia.
10. Bhatia.
11. Bhatia.
12. Bhatia.
13. Bhatia.
14. "Persis Khambatta, 49, Dies," *Indian Express*, August 18, 1998; "Persis Dead," *Rediff on the Net*, last modified August 18, 1998, http://www.rediff.com/news/1998/aug/18peroio.htm.
15. Potts, August 21, 1998; Jeswant Kaur, "So Long, Persis," *Malay Mail*, September 15, 1998.
16. Elliot Hannon, "Vanishing Vultures a Grave Matter for India's Parsis," *NPR*, last modified September 5, 2012, https://www.npr.org/2012/09/05/160401322/vanishing-vultures-a-grave-matter-for-indias-parsis; Srikanth and Akhtar.
17. "Final Farewells," *Starlog* no. 261 (April 1999), 8.
18. "Final Farewells."
19. Luke Montgomery, "Persis Khambatta: The Last Interview," *Star Trek Communicator* no. 120 (December 1998/January 1999), 67–68.
20. Montgomery, 69.
21. Montgomery, 69.
22. Montgomery, 69.
23. Montgomery, 69.
24. Montgomery, 69.
25. V. V. K. Subburaj, *Probationary Officers' Examination* (Chennai, India: T. Krishna Press), 213.
26. Khambatta, 9.

Bibliography

Abrams, Garry. "Eye." *Women's Wear Daily* 137, no. 50 (September 13, 1978), 4.

Academy of Motion Picture Arts and Sciences. "David L. Wolper Academy Awards Acceptance Speech." *Academy Awards Acceptance Speech Database.* n.d. http://aaspeechesdb.oscars.org/link/057-24/.

———. "William Shatner, David Wolper Set for All-Star Oscar Show." Academy of Motion Picture Arts and Sciences press release, April 1, 1983.

———. "Wise to Moderate Foreign Language Oscar Symposium." Academy of Motion Picture Arts and Sciences press release, April 1, 1983.

Ackerman, Forrest J. "Star Trek 23rd Century Style." *Famous Monsters* no. 145 (July 1978), 32–37.

"Action Intl. Means What Its Title Says." *Variety* 327, no. 2 (May 6, 1987), 247.

"Actress Jane Fonda." *World*, November 8, 1978.

"Actress Persis Khambatta." *Shutterstock.* n.d. https://www.shutterstock.com/editorial/image-editorial/actress-persis-khambatta-1352089a.

"Actress Turns Bald Head into an Asset." *Newspaper Enterprise Association*, February 5, 1979.

"Agents Alley." *Daily Variety* 208, no. 7 (June 14, 1985), 15.

———. *Daily Variety* 219, no. 34 (April 22, 1988), 14.

Alexander, David. *Star Trek Creator: The Authorized Biography of Gene Roddenberry.* New York: Penguin, 1994.

Ali, Shafquat. "Role Model." *Sunday* 23, no. 13 (March 31, 1996), 43.

"All Wasn't Quiet on Pageant's Eve." *Dayton Daily News*, July 21, 1965.

"All-Time Film Rental Champs (of U.S.-Canada Market)." *Variety* 321, no. 11 (January 8, 1986), 26, 58, 62.

Anand, Rajen S. "Rohini Hattangady Attends L.A. Premiere of 'Gandhi.'" *India West*, December 24, 1982.

Anderson, George. "Timing, Toughness Help Persis Khambatta's Trek to Stardom." *Pittsburgh Post-Gazette*, April 8, 1981.

Andreeva, Nellie. "Bela Bajaria Joins Netflix: Former Universal TV President Named VP Content." *Deadline.* Last modified October 5, 2016. https://deadline.com/2016/10/bela-bajaria-netflix-former-universal-tv-president-vp-content-1201831053/.

———. "Bela Bajaria to Lead International Non-English TV Originals for Netflix, Erik Barmack Segues To Producing." *Deadline.* Last modified March 6, 2019. https://deadline.com/2019/03/bela-bajaria-lead-international-non-english-tv-originals-for-netflix-erik-barmack-segues-to-producing-1202570698/.

Anthony, George. "Trekkies Rejoice, the Bold Journey Resumes." *Whitehorse Star*, February 2, 1979.

Archerd, Army. "Just for Variety." *Daily Variety* 182, no. 37 (January 29, 1979), 3.

———. "Just for Variety." *Daily Variety* 182, no. 38 (January 30, 1979), 3.

———. "Just for Variety." *Daily Variety* 185, no. 60 (November 28, 1979), 3.

———. "Just for Variety." *Daily Variety* 188, no. 38 (July 30, 1980), 3.

———. "Just for Variety." *Daily Variety* 191, no. 37 (April 27, 1981), 3.

———. "Just for Variety." *Daily Variety* 192, no. 13 (June 24, 1981), 3.

———. "Just for Variety." *Daily Variety* 192, no. 18 (July 1, 1981), 3.

_____. "Just for Variety." *Daily Variety* 197, no. 45 (November 5, 1982), 3.
_____. "Just for Variety." *Daily Variety* 198, no. 50 (February 15, 1988), 3.
_____. "Just for Variety." *Daily Variety* 218, no. 60 (March 2, 1988), 3.
"Art Director Nitin Desai Recreates the Grand Cafe at Bombay's Nehru Centre." *India Today*, January 31, 1995.
Asherman, Allan. *The Making of Star Trek II: The Wrath of Khan*. New York: Pocket Books, 1982.
Aslam, Mohammed. "Neeta Puri, Winner of the Miss India Contest Of New York in 1983, Enters Bollywood." *India Today*, August 31, 1986.
Barclay, Dolores. "Actress Cherishes Old Values of India." *Wisconsin State Journal*, December 26, 1979.
_____. "Actress Goes Bald for Role." *Tennessean*, December 30, 1979.
_____. "Bald-headed Discovery Just 'Old-Fashioned Girl.'" *Globe and Mail*, December 20, 1979.
_____. "East Indian Actress Maintains She's Just an Old-Fashioned Gal." *San Bernardino County Sun*, December 18, 1979.
_____. "Miss India is Hollywood Star." *Canadian India Times*, January 10, 1980.
_____. "Persis Baldly Accepts Stardom." *Ottawa Journal*, December 20, 1979.
_____. "'Star Trek' Actress Old Fashioned Gal." *Santa Fe New Mexican*, January 11, 1980.
Barnes, Mike. "Skip E. Lowe, Talk Show Host and Inspiration for Martin Short's Jiminy Glick, Dies at 85." *Hollywood Reporter*. Last modified September 23, 2014. https://www.hollywoodreporter.com/news/skip-e-lowe-dead-talk-735285.
Beck, Marilyn. "'Angel' Wings Are Being Fitted Again." *New York Daily News*, February 21, 1980.
_____. "Hollywood." *Ithaca Journal*, May 29, 1980.
_____. "Marilyn Beck." *San Francisco Examiner*, February 17, 1982.
_____. "Marilyn Beck." *San Francisco Examiner*, November 6, 1981.
_____. "Marilyn Beck." *St. Cloud Times*, June 16, 1984.
_____. "Trekkie Goes Bald." *Kenosha News*, September 29, 1978.
"Berlin Offers Hefty Coin Help in Pitch to Revive Film Prod." *Variety* 291, no. 7 (June 21, 1978), 6.
Beutelwolf. "Persis Khambatta." *Vintage Erotica Forums*. Last modified March 4, 2011. http://vintage-erotica-forum.com/showpost.php?p=1493949&postcount=1.
Bhatia, Samita. "The Star's Trek." *Telegraph*, April 26, 1998.
Bloomingdale's. "Bloomingdale's Has a Sunday Kind of Love for Christmas." Advertisement. *New York Times*, December 2, 1979.
Bobbin, Jay. "NBC Plans 2-Hour Special." *Asheville Citizen-Times*, September 10, 1983.
Bova, Ben. *Vision of the Future: The Art of Robert McCall*. New York: Harry N. Abrams, 1982.
Bowen, Anthony. "Celebrity Resolutions." *Tampa Tribune*, December 28, 1981.
Boxer, Tim. "Persis' a Terror." *New York Post*, April 4, 1981.
Boyd, Denny. "Jim Checks Up on All the Dirty Talk." *Vancouver Sun*, July 17, 1982.
"Bradbury Honored." *Spectrum*, May 31, 1981.
"Briefly." *Kingsport Times-News*, March 2, 1980.
_____. *Los Angeles Times*, October 24, 1996.
"Brodsky-Gould Pic R, 'Kama Sutra' Goes X." *Variety* 261 no. 3 (December 2, 1970), 3.
Buckley, Tom. "On a Tramway to High Film Drama." *New York Times*, March 25, 1980.
"Bulletin." *Starlog* no. 8 (September 1977), 33.
Burton, Anthony. "People." *New York Daily News*, March 12, 1975.
Canby, Vincent. "Screen: A Frothy 'Wilby Conspiracy.'" *New York Times*, September 4, 1975.
Carroll, Jane. "The Raiderettes in Las Vegas." *San Francisco Examiner*, September 21, 1980.
Castle, Alison. *The Stanley Kubrick Archives*. Köln, Germany: Taschen, 2013.
"Cat People (1982)." *Mr. Skin*. n.d. https://www.mrskin.com/cat-people-nude-scenes-t1615.
"Chabad Pre-Telethon Party." *Getty Images*. n.d. https://www.gettyimages.com/detail/news-photo/persis-khambatta-news-photo/75786406.
Chaltanya, P. "Small Screen." *Sunday* 14, no. 43 (September 13, 1987), 76.
Champlin, Charles. "Another 'Star' is Born." *Los Angeles Times*, March 31, 1978.
_____. "Bald is Beautiful for 'Star Trek'

Bibliography

Star." *Los Angeles Times*, November 29, 1979.
Chierichetti, David. "How to Dress Buck Rogers—and Other Sci-Fi Tales." *Los Angeles Times*, October 26, 1979.
Chopra, Anupama. "Crop of Directors Make Waves in Film Industry with Brash New Themes." *India Today*, June 30, 1997.
Chowdhury, Ajay and Matthew Field. *Some Kind of Hero: The Remarkable Story of the James Bond Films*. Chicago: The History Press, 2015).
Chowdhury, Nandita. "Catwalk Memories." *India Today*, October 20, 1997.
Christensen, Roger and Karen Christensen. *Christensen's Celebrity Autographs*. San Diego, CA: Cardiff-by-the-Sea Publishing Company, 1988.
Christy, George. "The Great Life." *Hollywood Reporter*, June 19, 1981.
Cocchi, John. "Beauty from India Hopes to Become American Star." April 1977.
Cohn, Lawrence. "170 'Secret' Features Filmed in 1984." *Variety* 318 no. 13 (May 1, 1985), 5, 276.
Collins, Gary. *The Hour Magazine Cookbook*. New York: G.P. Putnam's Sons, 1995.
Committee to Cure Cancer through Immunization. "2nd Annual Celebrity Racquetball Tournament." Advertisement. *Los Angeles Times*, July 27, 1980.
"Communications." *Starlog* no. 39 (October 1980), 6–8.
_____. *Starlog* no. 65 (December 1982), 6–10.
"Continental Loaded for AFMarket; Sarluis Seeking Production Topper." *Variety* 310, no. 5 (March 2, 1983), 14, 258.
Continental Motion Pictures. "Warrior of the Lost World." Advertisement. *Variety* 310, no. 13 (April 27, 1983), 14.
Crawley, Tony. "The Star Trek Interviews—Part 2." *Starburst* 1, no. 11 (July 1979), 30–33.
Creation Entertainment. "Creation Presents..." Advertisement. *Starlog* no. 189 (April 1993), 14.
Crosby, Joan. "TV Scout Reports." *World*, September 27, 1979.
_____. "TV Scout Short Subjects." *Morning Call*, January 18, 1981.
Cushing, Caroline. "Lt. Ilia Lets Down Her Hair." *Los Angeles Herald-Examiner*, November 29, 1979.
"The Cut-Throat but Lucrative World of Advertising Photography." *India Today*, June 30, 1978.
Davies, Tom. "Court of the Rich." *Observer*, May 20, 1979.
"Daytime Programs." *Detroit Free Press*, January 9, 1980.
"Dear Starfleet." *Starfleet Communique* no. 56 (April/May 1993), 12–13.
Delson, James. "A Comprehensive Interview with Robert Wise." *Fantastic Films* no. 10 (September 1979), 18–23, 38, 58–62.
Denny, Jon. "Small Talk with a Lady in the Big Time: Persis Khambatta." *Oui* (March 1981), 89–90.
"De Paul is Catalyst In HBO, Soviet Coprod." *Variety* 325, no. 9 (December 24, 1986), 77.
Devi, Phoolan, Marie-Thérèse Cuny, and Paul Rambali. *I, Phoolan Devi: The Autobiography of India's Bandit Queen*. London: Warner Books, 1997.
Dillard, J.M. *Star Trek, "Where No One Has Gone Before": A History in Pictures*. New York: Pocket Books, 1994.
Disney. "5 Things You Didn't Know About Aladdin's Naomi Scott." *Vogue India*. May 15, 2019. https://www.vogue.in/story/-things-you-didnt-know-about-aladdins-naomi-scott/.
Doch. "Cannes Market." *Variety* 331, no. 5 (May 25, 1988), 18–19, 23–24, 28–30, 32–33.
Dodd, John. "Not Even Day-Glo Hides the Tackiness." *Edmonton Journal*, June 26, 1982.
Dongre, Archana. "Women's Network Launches Mentor-Protege Program." *India West*, December 18, 1992.
"Don't Miss This One." *Sunday* 23, no. 43 (November 9, 1996), 56.
Duka, John. "Reporter's Notebook: Fashion as Art in Milan." *New York Times*, March 18, 1984.
Duke, Gayle. "Pageant Countdown." *Tampa Tribune*, August 20, 1983.
Ebert, Roger. "Doctor Drops Out, Tunes in to Calcutta." *Wisconsin State Journal*, April 17, 1992.
_____. "'Megaforce' Waste of Money and Time." *Asbury Park Press*, July 2, 1982.
Eder, Shirley. "Caine Muzzles Actress Wife." *Detroit Free Press*, March 13, 1975.
Ehrlich, Richard S. "Notorious 'Bandit Queen,' Stewing in Indian Prison, Rues Day She Surrendered." *San Francisco Examiner*, July 13, 1986.

Eichelbaum, Stanley. "The Rover Boys in South Africa." *San Francisco Examiner*, August 21, 1975.
Fashion82. "Listen." *Los Angeles Times*, October 8, 1982.
End Hunger. "The End Hunger Televent." Advertisement. *Los Angeles Times*, March 3, 1983.
"An Evening with Michelle Phillips." *Esquire* (March 1981), 80–82.
"An Evening with Persis Khambatta." *Esquire* (July 1981), 52–55.
"Fame." *Richmond Review*, December 30, 1981.
"Farrah Fawcett Double Files 'Cannonball' Suit." *Daily Variety* 192, no. 4 (June 11, 1981), 3.
Fashion78. "Listen." *Los Angeles Times*, July 14, 1978.
Fashion79. "Listen." *Los Angeles Times*, November 23, 1979.
Festival of India in the United States, 1985–1986. New York: Harry N. Abrams, 1985.
Fields, Sidney. "Only Human." *New York Daily News*, December 8, 1979.
"Film and TV Casting News." *Daily Variety* 206, no. 3 (December 10, 1984), 18.
"Film Castings." *Daily Variety* 204, no. 42 (August 3, 1984), 35.
"Film Production: Universal." *Variety* 297, no. 12 (January 23, 1980), 32.
"Film Reviews." *Variety* 319, no. 7 (June 12, 1985), 15, 16, 18.
_____. *Variety* 320, no. 4 (August 21, 1985), 16.
"Films in the Future." *Daily Variety* 162, no. 35 (January 25,1974), 20.
_____. *Daily Variety* 165, no. 50 (November 15, 1974), 6.
Fischer, Mary A. "Two Actresses Vie to Escape Hollywood's Caste System—by Playing India's Bandit Queen." *People*, June 11, 1984.
"The 46th Annual Golden Globe Awards—Arrivals." Getty Images. n.d. https://www.gettyimages.com/detail/news-photo/-persis-khambatta-during-the-46th-annual-golden-globe-awards-news-photo/105923076.
Franklin, Aretha. "Aretha Franklin, Atlantic Records Recording Artist." Advertisement. *Variety* 287, no. 2 (May 18, 1977), 6.
Gallagher, Kirsten. "Celebration of India." *Orlando Sentinel*, June 13, 1985.
Gammack, Julie. "Bald Beauty of 'Star Trek' Film Beams Down Snugly in W.D.M." *Des Moines Register*, July 24, 1989.

Gansberg, Alan L. "Hollywood Strip." *Copley News Service*, August 10, 1983.
_____. "Hollywood Strip." *Copley News Service*, August 26, 1983.
_____. "Hollywood Strip." *Copley News Service*, June 9, 1981.
_____. "Khambatta Eyes 'Bandit Queen.'" *Hollywood Reporter*, March 16, 1984.
Ganti, Tejaswini. *Producing Bollywood: Inside the Contemporary Hindi Film Industry*. Durham, NC: Duke University Press, 2012.
Gelman, Morrie. "Par TV Closes Prod'n Gap with 'Laugh.'" *Daily Variety* 182, no. 53 (February 21, 1979), 10.
Gerston, Jill. "The Gender Blenders." *Philadelphia Inquirer*, May 31, 1984.
Gindick, Tia. "Auction Benefits Four Organizations." *Los Angeles Times*, April 20, 1981.
_____. "Wrapped Up in Their Art." *Los Angeles Times*, August 12, 1980.
"Glitterati." *Outlook India*, April 20, 1998.
Gold, Aaron. "Tower Ticker." *Chicago Tribune*, November 15, 1977.
Google. "Meena Kumari's 85th Birthday." Google Doodles. August 1, 2018. https://www.google.com/doodles/meena-kumaris-85th-birthday.
Gordon, Alex. "The Pit & the Pen." *Fangoria* 40, no. 3 (December 1984), 57–58.
Grant, Hank. "Hollywood Reporter." *San Francisco Examiner*, June 18, 1978.
Grant, Lee. "Parties: Parking Lot Becomes a 'Paradise.'" *Los Angeles Times*, June 23, 1980.
Gross, Linda. "Movies of the Week." *Los Angeles Times*, February 20, 1983.
Guarino, Ann. "Off Camera." *New York Daily News*, August 3, 1975.
Gundersen, Edna. "India's Influence Remains With El Paso Couple." *El Paso Times*, August 26, 1983.
Halloran, Kathleen. "Hairless Woman Has Sense of Humor, Wonder, Adventure." *News-Press*, February 27, 1984.
"Halos Going to Par 'Trek' and 'Shirley.'" *Daily Variety* 186, no. 41 (February 4, 1980), 6.
Handley, Rich. "Star Trek II at 20: Still Feeling Young." *Star Trek Communicator* no. 139 (August/September 2002), 52–59.
Hannon, Elliot. "Vanishing Vultures a Grave Matter for India's Parsis." NPR. Last modified September 5, 2012. https://www.npr.org/2012/09/05/160401322/vanishing-vultures-a-grave-matter-for-indias-parsis.

Harmetz, Aljean. "'E.T.,' at $87 Million, Hit of Summer Box Office." *New York Times*, July 7, 1982.

———. "Quick End of Low-Budget Horror-Film Cycle Seen." *New York Times*, October 2, 1980.

Haun, Harry. "What's Cooking? Ross in Hot Role as Baker." *New York Daily News*, August 29, 1985.

"HBO Miniseries: 'Far Pavilions.'" *Variety* 307, no. 4 (May 26, 1982), 47.

Henderson, Paulette. "'Megaforce' Is 'Megadull.'" *Waterloo Courier*, July 2, 1982.

"HFPA Gives 11G in Grants to Industry-Related Orgs." *Daily Variety* 208, no. 30 (July 18, 1985), 29.

Hirshenson, Janet, Jane Jenkins, and Rachel Kranz. *A Star Is Found: Our Adventures Casting Some of Hollywood's Biggest Movies*. Orlando, Fl: Harcourt, 2009.

"Hollywood Celebrities Grace Glittering Opening Ceremony of Bombay Palace." *India West*, February 22, 1985.

Hollywood International. "Hollywood International's Celebration II." Advertisement. *LA Weekly*, September 6, 1984.

"Hollywood Soundtrack." *Variety* 306, no. 5 (March 3, 1982), 22.

———. *Variety* 309, no. 3 (November 17, 1982), 36.

"Hollywood TV Production Chart." *Daily Variety* 174, no. 63 (March 3, 1977), 20.

"Homevideo Briefs." *Daily Variety* 220, no. 16 (August 29, 1988), 16.

Honawar, Vaishali. "The New Queens." *Telegraph*, February 5, 1995.

"Ilia's Class-B Uniform Shirt." *Christie's*. n.d. https://www.christies.com/lotfinder/lot/ilias-class-b-uniform-shirt-4780392-details.aspx?from=salesummery&intobjectid=4780392.

"Ilia's Off-Duty Tunic and Deltan Headband." *Christie's*. n.d. https://www.christies.com/lotfinder/lot/ilias-off-duty-tunic-and-deltan-headband-4780393-details.aspx.

"In Camera: The Nelson Affair." *Films and Filming* 20, no. 2 (November 1973), 76.

Index to the Times, March-April 1971. London: Times Newspapers, 1971.

"Indian Actress and Model Persis Khambatta (2 October 1948 A 18 August 1998)." *Shutterstock*. n.d. https://www.shutterstock.com/editorial/image-editorial/-indian-actress-and-model-persis-khambatta-2-october-1948-a-18-august-1998-1976621a.

"Indian Actress and Model Persis Khambatta (2 October 1948 A 18 August 1998). Appeared in Air India Advertisements." *Shutterstock*. n.d. https://www.shutterstock.com/editorial/image-editorial/-indian-actress-and-model-persis-khambatta-2-october-1948-a-18-august-1998-appeared-in-air-india-advertisements-1976627a.

"Indian Actress Persis Khambatta (2 October 1948 A 18 August 1998)." *Shutterstock*. n.d. https://www.shutterstock.com/editorial/image-editorial/indian-actress-persis-khambatta-2-october-1948-a-18-august-1998-1974646a.

"Indian Beauty Queen Who Made It to Hollywood: Persis Khambatta, 49, Died In Mumbai After A Cardiac Arrest." *India in New York*, August 28, 1998.

"India's Bandit Queen Selects Her Captors." *San Francisco Examiner*, February 11, 1983.

"International Sound Track." *Variety* 239, no. 7 (July 7, 1965), 22.

———. *Variety* 297, no. 6 (December 12, 1979), 40.

"International Sound Track: Rome." *Variety* 307, no. 8 (June 23, 1982), 40, 42.

"International Women's Year (1975)." *Harvard Library*. n.d. https://guides.library.harvard.edu/schlesinger_IWY.

Irani, Vijaya. "West Slide Story." *Sunday* 6, no. 52 (October 22, 1978), 21–22.

"Irmin Schmidt, Inner Space Production–Kamasutra—Vollendung Der Liebe." *Discogs*. n.d. https://www.discogs.com/Irmin-Schmidt-Inner-Space-Production-Kamasutra-Vollendung-Der-Liebe/release/2053796.

"Italo B.O. Wilts in Heat; Brooks' 'Frankenstein' Tops." *Variety* 279, no. 6 (June 18, 1975), 33.

Jackson, Jill. "India Awards 'Gandhi' Director." *Palm Beach Daily News*, March 10, 1983.

Jacobs, Jody. "Phyllis Diller to Get Double Honors." *Los Angeles Times*, March 26, 1981.

———. "Seeing in the New Year on an Upbeat." *Los Angeles Times*, January 5, 1981.

"January 12, 1983." *Los Angeles Times*, January 9, 1983.

Johnson, Malcolm L. "Comically Inept 'Megaforce' Lacks Power to Seem Relevant or Amusing." *Hartford Courant*, July 1, 1982.

Jones, Gwen and Carole Lalli. "Simply Hair-Raising." *L.A. Herald-Examiner*, June 13, 1980.

Jones, Preston Neal. *Return to Tomorrow: The Filming of Star Trek—The Motion Picture*. Sierra Madre, CA: Creature Features, 2014.

_____. "Star Trek—The Motion Picture." *Cinefantastique* 9, no. 2 (Winter 1979), 40–47.

Jones, Will. "After Last Night." *Minneapolis Tribune*, December 6, 1979.

Joshi, Lalit Mohan. "Obituary: Persis Khambatta: A Model Career." *The Guardian*, August 28, 1998.

Joshi, Namrata. "Watch Highlights of Music Show, Chat Show & Feature." *India Today*, August 17, 1998.

"Judith De Paul Spells Determination." *Daily Variety* 209, no. 38 (October 29, 1985), 9, 34, 118.

"Kama Sutra." *Daily Girl* 1, no. 3 (1971).

"'Kama Sutra' Maker Charges AIP 'Butchered' The Film." *Daily Variety* 150, no. 8 (December 16, 1970), 8.

Kamath, A.P., and V. Bhuvana. "The Bandit Queen Rides Again." *Illustrated Weekly of India*, March 19, 1989.

Kapoor, Coomi. "Film Makers Face the Brunt of Censor Board Whims and Fancies." *India Today*, April 15, 1985.

Kaufman, Dave. "40 TV Series Get the Heave-Ho from Net Skeds." *Daily Variety* 196 no. 9 (June 17, 1982), 1, 15.

_____. "Par Wants 3-Hour Slice of TV." *Daily Variety* 175, no. 57 (May 24, 1977), 1, 7.

Kaur, Jeswant. "So Long, Persis." *Malay Mail*, September 15, 1998.

Kaye, Jeffrey. "Trekkie Alert." *New West* (March 26, 1979), 60.

Kayser, Alex. *Heads*. New York: Abbeville Press, 1985.

Kazickas, Jurate. "Trekking Down to a World Premiere." *Washington Star*, December 7, 1979.

"Keach Directing Seg of 'New Mike Hammer.'" *Daily Variety* 215, no. 9 (March 16, 1987), 77.

Kerwin, Robert. "Trekkie Treat." *Chicago Tribune*, June 3, 1979.

Khambatta, Persis. "Counterpunch: Put the Accent on Diversity." *Los Angeles Times*, July 11, 1994.

_____. "Persis Khambatta Cordially Invites You..." Advertisement. *Daily Variety* 175, no. 56 (May 23, 1977), 8.

_____. "Persis Khambatta Cordially Invites You..." Advertisement. *Variety* 287, no. 2 (May 18, 1977), 6.

_____. *Pride of India: A Tribute to Miss India*. Mumbai: Parijat Media, 1997.

"Khambatta to Star." *Hollywood Reporter*, October 29, 1982.

"Khambatta on 'Hour.'" *Hollywood Reporter*, January 9, 1981.

"Khambatta to Star in Indian Film." *Los Angeles Daily News*, February 20, 1986.

Khosla, S.N. "Good Head, Good Heart, Good Body." *Telegraph*, July 6, 1986.

"Khushwant Singh to Shoot Chat Show for Star Plus." *India Today*, April 13, 1998.

Kirkpatrick, Curry. "He's Not a Man to Take It Lying Down." *Sports Illustrated*, May 12, 1980.

"Kitty Zooms 524 MPH, Eyes 600." *Dayton Daily News*, December 6, 1976.

Kleiner, Dick. "Susie Bono Eyes an Exotic Role." Times and Democrat, July 16, 1984.

"Kobi Jaeger in 'Kama Sutra' Suit." *Variety* 261, no. 10 (January 20, 1971), 17.

Koenig, Walter. *Chekov's Enterprise: A Personal Journal of the Making of Star Trek—The Motion Picture*. New York: Pocket Books, 1980.

Ku, Beulah. "Indo-American Women Show Success, Variation." *Asianweek*, January 8, 1993.

Lahiri, Monojit. "What Has Zeenat that Zahirra Hasn't?" *Film World* 10, no. 1–2 (Jan–Feb 1974), 40.

"Land Speed Record." *Los Angeles Times*, September 23, 1976.

Lane, Lydia. "Actress with a Sense of Destiny." *Los Angeles Times*, December 15, 1978.

_____. "Persis Khambatta Had Plan for Life." *Los Angeles Times*, July 10, 1981.

Lardine, Bob. "She's Looking for Reel Love." *Daily News*, February 17, 1982.

Leach, Robin. "Bald Beauty Loses 10G Gems." *New York Post*, April 7, 1980.

Leach, Robin, and Judith Rich. *Lifestyles of the Rich and Famous*. Garden City, N.Y.: Doubleday, 1986.

Leogrande, Ernest. "Mega Bomb." *New York Daily News*, June 26, 1982.

Levin, Gerry. "India's Persis Khambatta Gambling on U.S. Career." *Hollywood Reporter*, April 11, 1977.

Levine, Bettijane. "Fendis Pipe Furs to Russia." *Los Angeles Times*, September 10, 1982.

_____. "Fonda's Nontoxic Waists." *Los Angeles Times*, September 26, 1980.
"Listen." *Los Angeles Times*, October 24, 1980.
_____. *Los Angeles Times*, January 23, 1981.
Livingston, Harold. *Star Trek II: "In Thy Image" Rough First Draft*. October 20, 1977. Margaret Herrick Library, Beverly Hills, 953.f-S-1353.
"Log Entries." *Starlog* no. 26 (September 1979), 9–16.
London, Michael. "Actresses Vie to Screen Bandit Queen's Saga." *Los Angeles Times*, May 16, 1984.
"Lookout." *People*, August 25, 1980.
Lor. "Cannes Market." *Variety* 331, no. 4 (May 18, 1988), 124.
_____. "Homevideo Reviews." *Variety* 327, no. 13 (July 22, 1987), 47.
Lovitt, Joe. "'Rocky III' Plot No Secret to Fans." *Queen City Mail*, July 7, 1982.
Lowry, Brian. "Procter & Gamble Prods. Ups Telefilm Production." *Daily Variety* 228, no. 2 (June 7, 1990), 1, 20.
Lozzi, Edward. "A Tribute to Persis Khambatta." *Edward Lozzi & Associates*. n.d. http://www.lozzipr.com/persis.html.
"Mama Hindustani." *Outlook India*, October 20, 1997.
Mann, Roderick. "Arkin to Film 'Arigo' in Brazil." *Los Angeles Times*, June 19, 1979.
_____. "Ferreting Out Dudley Moore." *Los Angeles Times*, October 10, 1978.
_____. "He's Booked His Passage to Hollywood." *Los Angeles Times*, January 29, 1985.
_____. "'Megaforce' Spends Megabucks on Arms." *Los Angeles Times*, November 22, 1981.
_____. "Monroe Quote Draws Hot Words." *Los Angeles Times*, April 22, 1980.
_____. "Sellers: No Way to Treat 'Prisoner.'" *Los Angeles Times*, April 10, 1979.
_____. "Shear Terror for Khambatta." *Los Angeles Times*, July 25, 1978.
_____. "This is a Trek Shatner Doesn't Mind." *Los Angeles Times*, December 22, 1981.
"Marriages." *Des Moines Register*, April 27, 1989.
Mars, Bunny. "Do Tell...." *Los Angeles Times*, April 15, 1984.
Martin, Harold. "Time Exposure." *Popular Photography* 72, no. 1 (January 2008), 132.
Martin, Jack. "Bald Beauty Gets Brushoff." *New York Post*, May 27, 1980.
Martin, R.H. "Chattin' with Stratton." *Fangoria* 3, no. 39 (November 1984), 34–39.
"Martin's Sideliners." *New York Post*, March 13, 1980.
Maslin, Janet. "'Megaforce' is a Mix of Joviality and Stunts." *New York Times*, June 27, 1982.
_____. "New 'Star Trek' Full of Gadgets and Fun." *New York Times*, June 4, 1982.
_____. "'Nighthawks' With Sylvester Stallone," *New York Times*, April 10, 1981.
"Maud Adams Signs for Bond Film." *Daily Herald*, August 9, 1982.
"Maud Enjoys 'Chicago Story.'" *Mansfield News-Journal*, April 9, 1982.
Maychick, Diana. "Poor Persis Khambatta: No Kisses, No Romance." *New York Post*, July 10, 1982.
_____. "Sari Time in H'wood for 2 Actresses." *New York Post*, May 16, 1984.
Mayo, Mike. "Megaforce." *Cinefantastique* 13, no. 1 (September-October 1982), 45, 47.
McDonnell, David. "Log Entries." *Starlog* no. 76 (November 1983), 10–17.
McHarry, Charles. "On the Town." *New York Daily News*, March 10, 1975.
"Meet Ilia of 'Star Trek—The Motion Picture.'" *Palm Beach Post*, May 2, 1980.
Michael, George and Rae Lindsay. *George Michael's Complete Hair Care for Men*. Garden City, N.Y.: Doubleday & Company, 1983.
Mikelbank, Peter. "The Boss Speaks: 'Star Trek' Lives!" *Washington Post*, August 29, 1977.
Miller, Daryl. "Adventure Is Childish Megaflop." *Arizona Daily Star*, June 30, 1982.
"Monday." *New York Daily News*, March 8, 1987.
"Monday TV Highlights." *Albany Democrat-Herald*, January 12, 1980.
Montgomery, Luke. "Persis Khambatta: The Last Interview." *Star Trek Communicator* no. 120 (December 1998/January 1999), 66–69.
Morehouse, Rebecca. "Persis Khambatta: A Star Is Shorn." *North American Newspaper Alliance*, January 3, 1980.
Morrison, Don. "A Friendly Time Warp." *Minneapolis Star*, December 5, 1979.
"Motion Picture Producer & Director." *Allankuskowski.com*. n.d. http://allankuskowski.com/.
"Ms Persis Khambatta." *TimesContent*. n.d. https://timescontent.com/syndication-photos/reprint/fashion/264707/ms-persis-khambatta.html.

Mukherjee, Bonny. "London-Based American TV and Film Company to Make Mini-Series on Indira Gandhi." *India Today*, April 15, 1985.

Murarka, Ramesh P. "Glittering 'Tribute to India' Presented in Los Angeles." *India West*, September 20, 1985.

———. "1981—A Milestone Year for the Indian Community in the U.S." *India West*, January 8, 1982.

———. "A Weary Prime Minister Meets Some Prominent California Indians." *India West*, August 6, 1982.

Murarka, Ramesh P., and Michael W. Potts. "Nation-Wide Tour Nets $275,000 for Nargis Dutt Memorial Foundation." *India West*, April 8, 1983.

Murarka, Ramesh P., and Ramesh Gune. "Calif. Chapters of Nargis Dutt Foundation Collect $95,000 at This Year's Events." *India West*, November 1, 1991.

Murray, Jim. "Real Men Don't Give it a Thought." *Los Angeles Times*, May 4, 1982.

"A Mysterious Swedish Model Named Jenny O Makes a Bald Fashion Statement." *People*, April 23, 1984.

Naha, Ed. "Through a Glass Lightly." *Starlog* no. 46 (July 1983), 62–65, 87.

———. "The Young and the Weightless." *Starlog* no. 59 (June 1982), 30–33, 64.

National Gallery of Art. "The Sculpture of India: 3000 B.C.-1300 A.D. Marks Beginning of Festival of India 1985–1986." National Gallery of Art press release, April 16, 1985.

"Nat'l Film Society Tips Hat to Some of the Big Names." *Daily Variety* 189, no. 36 (October 28, 1980), 6.

"Nearly 10,000 Die as Earthquake Rocks Two Districts of Maharashtra." *Indian Express*, October 1, 1993.

Nelson, Nels. "Newest Angel Almost a '10.'" *Philadelphia Daily News*, June 4, 1980.

"A New Farrah She Isn't." *Los Angeles Magazine*, October 1978.

"New Film Starts." *Variety* 329, no. 1 (October 28, 1987), 6, 24.

"A New Look for a Once-Bald Beauty." *New York Post*, March 11, 1980.

"The New Star Wars: Celebrity Politics Becomes Part of the Game." *People*, March 31, 1980.

"News of the Stars." *Star Trek Action Group* no. 40 (April 1980), 5.

"Nominations for Sci-Fi, Fantasy Films Listed." *Los Angeles Times*, January 4, 1980.

Oates, Marylouise. "Pickfair Party for Jerry Buss: It Was a Magic Evening for Celebrities." *Los Angeles Times*, June 19, 1981.

Ojha, Rajendra. *Screen World Publication's 75 Glorious Years of Indian Cinema*. Bombay: Screen World Publication, 1988.

"1987–88 Film Production." *Variety* 331, no. 2 (May 4, 1988), 135, 140, 141, 146, 150, 154, 162, 166, 170, 174, 178–179, 183, 187, 191.

"1971: Post Strike Ends with Pay Deal." *BBC News*. n.d. http://news.bbc.co.uk/onthis day/hi/dates/stories/march/8/newsid_2516000/2516343.stm.

Ong, Jack. "From Miss India To 'Star Trek': Presenting Persis Khambatta." *California Goodlife* (December 1979), 70–74.

"The Original Series Woman's Starfleet Uniform." *Christie's*. n.d. https://www.christies.com/lotfinder/lot/the-original-series-womans-starfleet-uniform-4780536-details.aspx.

"Paint." *David Dasharath Kalal*. n.d. https://www.davidkalal.net/paint.html.

Pais, Arthur. "Amazing Grace." *India Abroad*, December 1, 2006.

———. "Films Winners: Romance and Revenge." *India Abroad*, January 6, 1989.

"Panorama." *Questar* 2 no. 3 (June 1980), 10–12.

Paramount Pictures. "Paramount Television Welcomes Harve Bennett." Advertisement. *Daily Variety* 190, no. 2 (December 9, 1980), 28.

———. "Persis Khambatta of 'Star Trek—The Motion Picture' Discovers that Bald is Beautiful but Also Traumatic." Paramount Pictures press release, October 1979.

Partipilo, Vic. "On Location." *Oakland Post*, December 25, 1979.

Patel, Bhaichand. "Festival of Lightness." *Outlook India*, March 31, 2014.

Pearson, Howard. "Bald is Beautiful in Star Trek Movie." *Deseret News*, December 4, 1979.

"People." *Press Democrat*, June 19, 1980.

"Persis Dead." *Rediff on the Net*. Last modified August 18, 1998. http://www.rediff.com/news/1998/aug/18persis.htm.

"Persis Khambatta." *Getty Images*. n.d. https://www.gettyimages.com/detail/news-photo/actresses-prunella-gee-and-persis-khambatta-photo-call-to-news-photo/888805248.

_____. *On TV* (April 1982), 32–33.
"Persis Khambatta at a Party at 'Laboite' Disco." *Getty Images.* n.d. https://www.gettyimages.ae/detail/news-photo/-persis-khambatta-was-asked-to-shave-her-head-again-for-the-news-photo/531077250.
"Persis Khambatta Biography." Paramount Pictures, October 1979.
"Persis Khambatta, 49, Dies." *Indian Express,* August 18, 1998.
"Persis Khambatta, Movie Actress, 49." *New York Times,* August 20, 1998.
"Persis Khambatta pacted..." *Hollywood Reporter,* May 31, 1985.
"Persis Khambatta Sighting at Bologna-Taylor's Home—June 21, 1991." *Getty Images.* n.d. https://www.gettyimages.com/detail/news-photo/persis-khambatta-during-persis-khambatta-sighting-at-news-photo/107132639.
"Persis Khambatta Sighting at Ma Maison Restaurant—March 2, 1981." *Getty Images.* n.d. https://www.gettyimages.com/detail/news-photo/persis-khambatta-during-persis-khambatta-sighting-at-ma-news-photo/106203948.
"Persis Khambatta with Cliff Taylor." *Borsari Images.* n.d. http://www.borsariimages.com/archive/public/AssetDetail.cfm?aid=P-ABK-735-PB&fol=AA-7575-PB&rdir=folders&rpage=ViewFolderContents.
_____. *Borsari Images.* n.d. http://www.borsariimages.com/archive/public/AssetDetail.cfm?aid=P-ABK-755-PB&fol=-AA-7575-PB&rdir=folders&rpage=ViewFolderContents.
"Persis Khambatta with Dann Moss." *Borsari Images.* n.d. http://www.borsariimages.com/archive/public/AssetDetail.cfm?aid=P-ABK-788-PB&fol=AA-7575-PB&rdir=folders&rpage=ViewFolderContents.
"Persis Khambatta with Gary Sandy." *Borsari Images.* n.d. http://www.borsariimages.com/archive/public/AssetDetail.cfm?aid=P-ABK-751-PB&fol=AA-7575-PB&rdir=folders&rpage=ViewFolderContents.
"Persis Khambatta with John Phillip Law." *Borsari Images.* n.d. http://www.borsariimages.com/archive/public/AssetDetail.cfm?aid=P-ABK-778-PB&fol=AA-7575-PB&rdir=folders&rpage=ViewFolderContents.
"Persis Khambatta's Class-A Uniform Shirt." *Christie's.* n.d. https://www.christies.com/LotFinder/lot_details.aspx?from=sale summary&intObjectID=4780404.
"Persis Makes a 'Bold' Move—Shaves Her Head." *India West,* October 20, 1978.
"Persis, Persis Khambatta, Indian model and actress, 1st August 1972." *Getty Images.* n.d. http://gettyimages.com/detail/news-photo/persis-persis-khambatta-indian-model-and-actress-1st-august-news-photo/119109100.
"Persis Turns Down Offer to be an 'Angel.'" *Arizona Republic,* April 20, 1980.
Phantom of the Movies. "Spiders and Maggots and Flies, Oh My!" *New York Daily News,* September 11, 1985.
"Pix, People, Pickups." *Daily Variety* 187, no. 17 (March 28, 1980), 5.
_____. *Daily Variety* 189, no. 43 (November 5, 1980), 1, 15.
_____. *Daily Variety* 196, no. 13 (June 23, 1982), 14.
_____. *Daily Variety* 199, no. 27 (April 12, 1983), 19.
Pollock, Dale. "ABC Stocks Up on Films for the '80s." *Daily Variety* 186, no. 9 (December 18, 1979), 1, 24.
"Portrait de Persis Khambatta en 1982." *Getty Images.* n.d. https://www.gettyimages.ae/detail/news-photo/actrice-indienne-persis-khambatta-a-paris-en-mars-1982-news-photo/954039500.
Potts, Michael W. "Actress Persis Khambatta Succumbs to Heart Attack." *India West,* August 21, 1998.
_____. "California is Leading Source of Tourist Business to India." *India West,* February 11, 1983.
_____. "Director Joffé Attends UNICEF Benefit Screening." *India West,* April 10, 1992.
_____. "Film Stars Grace Opening of India-West Office in L.A." *India West,* November 1, 1991.
_____. "Hollywood Reaches Out to Earthquake Victims in India." *India West,* December 10, 1993.
_____. "'Kamla' Screened in LA in Hopes of American Release." *India West,* October 17, 1986.
_____. "Khambatta to Co-Produce $2-Million Feature Film." *India West,* December 12, 1986.
_____. "LA's Zarin Dastur Named Miss Asian American Princess." *India West,* September 2, 1994.
_____. "Over 10,000 Attend India I-Day

Celebrations in Los Angeles." *India West*, August 20, 1982.
_____. "Persis Khambatta to Return to Bombay." *India West*, May 15, 1992.
_____. "Persis Khambatta: Proud of Being a Parsi." *India West*, May 15, 1981.
_____. "Persis Khambatta's Latest Trek: Book of Miss Indias." *India West*, August 29, 1997.
_____. "Persis to Star as Phoolan Devi in her Own Film, 'The Bandit Queen,'" *India West*, April 27, 1984.
_____. "Persis to Star in CBS TV Episode After Completing Film in India." *India West*, April 17, 1987.
_____. "Sona Patel Crowned 'Super Model.'" *India West*, April 1, 1994.
_____. "'Warrior of the Lost World' Means Greater Exposure for Persis." *India West*, June 24, 1983.
"Premiere of Distortions." *Getty Images*, n.d. https://www.gettyimages.com/detail/news-photo/persis-khambatta-during-premiere-of-distortions-at-academy-news-photo/109667001.
"Premiere of 'She Dances Alone'—April 20, 1982." *Getty Images*. n.d. https://www.gettyimages.com/detail/news-photo/persis-khambatta-and-kip-whitman-during-premiere-of-she-news-photo/105922971.
"Premiere of 'Star Trek VI.'" *Getty Images*. n.d. https://www.gettyimages.com/photos/persis-khambatta?events=75331072&family=editorial&phrase=persis%20khambatta&sort=best.
"Princess Anne and Helena Rubinstein at the Tower." *Chemist & Druggist* 205, no. 5019 (June 12, 1976), 833.
"Prunella Gee and Persis Khambatta." *Getty Images*. n.d. https://www.gettyimages.com/license/830874050.
"Radio." *San Francisco Examiner*, January 14, 1980.
Rajadhyaksha, Ashish and Paul Willemen. *Encyclopaedia of Indian Cinema*. New Delhi: Oxford University Press, 1995.
"Rambling Reporter." *Hollywood Reporter*, April 3, 1979.
_____. *Hollywood Reporter*, April 18, 1981.
_____. *Hollywood Reporter*, August 29, 1986.
_____. *Hollywood Reporter*, January 10, 1985.
_____. *Hollywood Reporter*, June 10, 1981.
_____. *Hollywood Reporter*, June 26, 1979.
_____. *Hollywood Reporter*, May 29, 1981.

Rattanani, Lekha. "Big as in Bollywood." *India Today*, July 15, 1995.
Reddy, Sheela. "'I Don't Know One Editor in India Who is Well-Read.'" *Outlook India*, October 17, 2005.
_____. "'I May Die Any Day Now.'" *Outlook India*, October 24, 2011.
Reed, Rex. "At Last: A Producer Who Really Produces." *New York Daily News*, April 3, 1977.
_____. *New York Daily News*, April 16, 1980.
Reeves-Stevens, Judith and Garfield. *The Art of Star Trek*. New York: Pocket Books, 1995.
_____. *Star Trek Phase II: The Lost Series*. New York: Simon & Schuster, 1997.
Reilly, Sue. "Additional Material from Sue Reilly." *People Carbons*, December 20, 1979. Margaret Herrick Library, Beverly Hills.
_____. "Persis Khambatta—Screen Lookahead." *People Carbons*, November 27, 1978. Margaret Herrick Library, Beverly Hills.
_____. "Persis Khambatta Suffered the Scrape of Her Locks, but 'Star Trek' Justified the Loss." *People* (January 7, 1980), 29–30.
Reisfeld, Bert. "The Persis Khambatta Story." 1981.
Rexona. "Day by Day...Lovelier with Rexona." Advertisement. *Indian Express*, February 28, 1965.
RGH International Film Enterprises Inc. "First Strike." Advertisement. *Variety* 316, no. 13 (October 24, 1984), 199.
Rhode, William. "Like a Dream." *Sunday* 22, no. 27 (July 2, 1995), 66.
Robertson, Nan. "Victor Banerjee—India Personified." *New York Times*, March 17, 1985.
Roddenberry, Gene, and Harold Livingston. *Star Trek—The Motion Picture Shooting Script*. July 19, 1978. Margaret Herrick Library, Beverly Hills, 951.f-S-1333.
_____. *Star Trek—The Motion Picture Shooting Script*. November 29, 1978. Margaret Herrick Library, Beverly Hills, 951.f-S-1336.
_____. *Star Trek—The Motion Picture Shooting Script*. November 5, 1978. Margaret Herrick Library, Beverly Hills, 951.f-S-1336.
Roeder, Bill. "Newsmakers." *Newsweek* 89, no. 20 (May 16, 1977), 47.
"Ron Galella Archive—File Photos." *Getty*

Bibliography 215

Images. n.d. https://www.gettyimages.com/detail/news-photo/actress-marina-sirtis-attending-chabad-pre-telethon-party-news-photo/81606618.

Ronan, Eve. "Star Trek Star Persis Khambatta Sheds Her Locks for Luck!" *Akron Beacon Journal*, April 26, 1979.

Rose, Peter. "Actress's Cleanshaven Image Lands Role in Star Trek Movie." *Arizona Republic*, December 2, 1979.

Roura, Phil, and Tom Poster. "A Bright Spot." *New York Daily News*, December 10, 1978.

———. "Here & There." *New York Daily News*, June 12, 1985.

———. "Here & There." *New York Daily News*, May 16, 1985.

Roy, Amit. "Licence to write about BOND." *Telegraph*. Last modified September 9, 2016. https://www.telegraphindia.com/entertainment/licence-to-write-about-bond/cid/1421856.

Sackett, Susan. "Star Trek Report." *Starlog* no. 12 (March 1978), 30.

———. "Star Trek Report." *Starlog* no. 18 (December 1978), 64–65.

———. "Star Trek Report." *Starlog* no. 22 (May 1979), 29.

———. "Star Trek Report." *Starlog* no. 26 (September 1979), 52–53.

———. "Star Trek Report." *Starlog* no. 27 (October 1979), 31.

———. "Star Trek Report." *Starlog* no. 29 (December 1979), 31.

Sackett, Susan, and Gene Roddenberry. *The Making of Star Trek—The Motion Picture*. New York: Pocket Books, 1980.

Sajnani, Smita. "60—Winner of the 1970 Miss India Crown." *Indian Memory Project*. n.d. http://www.indianmemoryproject.com/60/.

Santangelo, Elaine. "Close Up: Star Trek's Lee Cole." *Questar* 2, no. 3 (June 1980), 48–49.

"Sarika to Join Growing Gaggle of Single Parents." *India Today*, September 30, 1985.

Sasso, Joey. "Through Channels." *South Idaho Press*, April 4, 1980.

"Saturday Television Listings." *Daily Republican-Register*, August 26, 1983.

Saunders, D.J., and Fred Kerber., "A Corker for Studio 54." *New York Daily News*, March 1, 1980.

Schnurmacher, Thomas. "Bujold, Gould Affair Was a Best-kept Showbiz Secret." *Gazette*, January 5, 1980.

"Science-Fiction Awards." *New York Times*, November 24, 1980.

Scott, Vernon. "Scott's World: Exotic is the Word for Persis." *UPI*, April 18, 1981.

———. "Scott's World: Susie Bono Went Calling on India's Bandit Queen." *UPI*, May 11, 1983.

Sen, Meheli, and Anustup Basu. *Figurations in Indian Film*. London: Palgrave Macmillan UK, 2013.

Sethi, Sunil. "Bombay's Rapidly Rising Race of Beauty Models." *India Today*, June 30, 1978.

———. "Indian Look Invades Western Market Again." *India Today*, November 30, 1976.

Shah, Preeti. "Mundhra's Film Released in LA Theaters." *India West*, June 3, 1994.

———. "The Poor Quality of Indian Videos: Whose Fault Is It?" *India West*, March 11, 1994.

Shanley, Mary Kay. "A Little Help Keeps Disabled in Own Homes." *Des Moines Register*, March 29, 1987.

Shay, Don. "Into the V'ger Maw with Douglas Trumbull." *Cinefex* 1, no. 1 (1980), 4–33.

———. "Star Trek—The Motion Picture." *Cinefantastique* 8, no. 2–3 (Spring 1979), 88–95.

Shepherd, James. "India's Crisis: To Kiss or Not To..." *Life Asia Edition* (December 8, 1969), 21–26.

Sherwood Oaks Experimental College. "Star Trek Seminar: The Making of a Film." Advertisement. *Los Angeles Times*, February 3, 1980.

Shirjee. "Khaas Baat." *Sunday* 6, no. 23 (August 20, 1978), 35.

"Short Takes." *Daily Variety* 203 no. 16 (March 27, 1984), 25.

"Sideliners." *New York Post*, September 2, 1981.

"Singer-actor Sonny Bono, 46, and actress-model Susie Coelho, 26,..." *UPI*, January 1, 1982.

Singh, Kuldip. "Obituary: Persis Khambatta." *Independent*, August 19, 1998.

Singh, Ritu. *Stark Raving Ad: A Giddy Guide to Indian Ads You Love (or Hate)*. Gurugram, India: Hachette India, 2018.

Siskel, Gene. "'Megaforce' Action, Laughs Don't Mix." *Chicago Tribune*, June 29, 1982.

———. "'Trek' Is Ok, But Not Out of this World." *Chicago Tribune*, December 7, 1979.

Skinner, Margo. "Art & Entertainment." *Asian Week*, January 13, 1983.
Sloan, Robin Adams. "Gossip Column." *Asbury Park Press*, July 15, 1982.
Smith, Bruce. "State Woos Flick Dollars." *New York Daily News*, January 17, 1980.
Smith, Liz. *New York Daily News*, August 19, 1981.
_____. *New York Daily News*, January 22, 1980.
_____. *New York Daily News*, May 5, 1981.
Someshwar, Savera R. "Persist Khambatta." *Rediff on the Net*. Last modified October 10, 1997. http://www.rediff.com/style/oct/10persis.htm.
Sony Pictures Publicity. "*Charlie's Angels* Production Information." Sony Pictures Press Release, November 4, 2019. https://sonypicturespublicity.com/dom/secured/mediaassets/viewMediaAssetsLevel2.jsf.
"'Sophia Loren of India' is Out to Captivate American Viewers." *El Paso Herald-Post*, May 21, 1977.
"Sorry Priyanka, You're Not the First Indian to Present an Oscar." *New Indian Express*, February 3, 2016.
Span, Paula. "House of Pectorals," *Washington Post*, December 19, 1985.
Spring Trek '93. "Spring Trek '93." Advertisement. *Philadelphia Daily News*, April 2, 1993.
"Squash." *Eton College Chronicle* no. 3359 (February 28, 1964), 5366.
Srikanth, B.R., and Shameem Akhtar. "Things of Beauty." *Outlook*, August 31, 1998.
"Star Trek Actress Persis Khambatta Lands Role in Nari Hira's Shingora." *India Today*, November 30, 1985.
"STAR TREK Meeting—August 3, 1977." August 5, 1977. https://www.facebook.com/pg/TheTrekFiles/photos/?tab=album&album_id=1025809107593336.
"Star Trek—The Motion Picture." *Star Trek Action Group* no. 38 (December 1979), 6.
Star Trek—The Motion Picture Shooting Schedule, August 29, 1978.
"Star Trek II." *Star Trek Action Group* no. 25 (October 1977), 3.
"'Stars of Today' Program Set." *Los Angeles Times*, August 11, 1984.
Stein, Michael. "Accent on U.S. Stars." *Los Angeles Times*, June 25, 1994.
Stewart, Al. "Newsline." *Billboard* 100, no. 37 (September 10, 1988), 52.
Stone, Christopher, Chuck Crandall, and Susan Stone. "'Star Trek' Blasts Off for the 80s with Kirk, Spock and a Bald Sexpot." *Us Weekly* (January 8, 1980), 18–21.
"Stunts Unlimited Opens Its Membership to Women." *Daily Variety* 173, no. 10 (September 20, 1976), 10.
"Style News." *Vogue* 174, no. 8 (August 1, 1984), 153.
Subburaj, V. V. K. *Probationary Officers' Examination*. Chennai, India: T. Krishna Press.
"Sues to Halt AIP 'Kama' Distrib'n." *Daily Variety* 150, no. 20 (January 5, 1971), 1, 4.
Sullivan, Tom. "Breakfast with the Trekkies." *Herald-News*, April 7, 1978.
Sunil, K. P. "Not Making It." *Illustrated Weekly of India*, July 29, 1984.
Suzy. "So. California Invaded London Town." *New York Daily News*, March 22, 1979.
_____. "Tanya Says Yes to Young Earl Smith." *New York Daily News*, March 19, 1980.
Szalay, Jeff. "Starlog Preview: Megaforce." *Starlog* no. 57 (April 1982), 10–14, 16–19.
Taylor, Rip. "Thanks Chuck." Advertisement. *Daily Variety* 187, no. 49 (May 13, 1980), 2.
"Television and Radio Briefs." *Daily Variety* 201, no. 49 (November 11, 1983), 12.
Television Program Enterprises. "The Start of Something Big." Advertisement. *Daily Variety* 287, no. 28 (April 12, 1985), 9.
Thermal, Harry F. "Latest Action, Sci-Fi Movies Make Crash Landings." *News Journal*, July 4, 1982.
"37th Annual Golden Globe Awards." *Getty Images*. n.d. https://www.gettyimages.com/detail/news-photo/persis-khambatta-during-37th-annual-golden-globe-awards-at-news-photo/105852757.
Thomas, Bob. "Bald Beauty from 'Star Trek' Still Has Mega-Career." *Courier-News*, December 17, 1981.
_____. "Baldness Made Actress Famous." *Morning News*, December 25, 1981.
_____. "Baldness, 'Star Trek' Spur Persis' Career." *Indianapolis Star*, December 24, 1981.
_____. "'Star Trek' Baldy's Career Moving Along Nicely." *Longview News-Journal*, December 27, 1981.
_____. "Young Actress' Hairy Experience." *Santa Cruz Sentinel*, December 24, 1981.
Thompson, Howard. "Dull Double Bill." *New York Times*, March 18, 1971.

"Thursday." *Carlsbad Current-Argus*, December 24, 1978.
"Thursday's Television." *New York Daily News*, March 1, 1984.
"Today's TV." *New York Daily News*, March 7, 1979.
"TPE Goes After Two Barter Pilots on Show Biz Folk." *Variety* 316 no. 13 (October 24, 1984), 402, 406.
"Trekkies Hear Roddenberry." *Chacahoula* 49 (1982), 77.
Trillusion Co. *Articles of Incorporation*. October 12, 1981.
———. *Certificate of Dissolution*. April 15, 1989.
———. *Certificate of Election to Wind Up and Dissolve*. April 15, 1989.
———. *Statement by Domestic Stock Corporation*. August 15, 1988.
———. *Statement by Domestic Stock Corporation*. October 31, 1987.
"Tuesday TV Highlights." *Albany Democrat-Herald*, January 12, 1980.
Tusher, Will. "Multifunction Camera Car Bows to Acclaim, Orders." *Daily Variety* 210 no. 40 (February 3, 1986), 3, 20.
"TV Taping of "Golden Globe Awards 50th Anniversary." *Getty Images*. n.d. https://www.gettyimages.com/detail/news-photo/persis-khambatta-during-tv-taping-of-golden-globe-awards-news-photo/105923067.
"TV Tomorrow." *San Francisco Examiner*, June 10, 1982.
"TV Tonight." *San Francisco Examiner*, June 22, 1982.
"TV Wednesday." *San Francisco Examiner*, May 11, 1988.
Twentieth Century-Fox Corporation. "The Hair-Raising Adventures of Persis Khambatta." Twentieth Century-Fox Corporation press release, 1982.
———. "'MEGAFORCE' Production Information." Twentieth Century-Fox Corporation press release, 1982.
"'$250,000 Raised: 'Jazz Singer' Benefit Breaks Records." *Los Angeles Times*, December 19, 1980.
"2000: SGIFF 13." *Singapore International Film Festival*. n.d. https://www.sgiff.com/past-editions/2000-sgiff-13/.
Universal Studios. "Persis Khambatta—'Nighthawks.'" Universal Studios press release, February 26, 1981.
"US-Based Actress Persis Khambatta to Co-Produce Film." *India Today*, March 15, 1984.

Venkatramani, S.H. "Businessmen Set to Flood the Market with Hindi, Tamil Films Made Exclusively for Video." *India Today*, September 15, 1986.
"Videos." *Statesman Journal*, May 17, 1985.
"Visto Int'l Puts 2 Independent Pix in Release." *Daily Variety* 206, no. 42 (February 5, 1985), 11.
"Voices." *India Today*, January 15, 1983.
Wagner, Jeff. "Rajiv Meets Indian Community in 2 Affairs." *India West*, June 23, 1985.
———. "Success of David Lean's Film Triggers Victor Banerjee's 'Passage' to Hollywood." *India West*, March 1, 1985.
Walker, Clint. "'Megaforce' Remains a Guilty Pleasure." *Journal Gazette*, May 11, 2019.
Walt Disney Studios. "Aladdin Press Kit." *Walt Disney Studios*. n.d. http://www.wdsmediafile.com/media/Aladdin/-writen-material/Aladdin5ce30bcaa76f4.pdf.
"War Prison Camp Series." *VHSCollector.com*. n.d. https://vhscollector.com/-distributor-series/war-prison-camp-series.
Warga, Wayne. "Prepare to Beam Aboard! 'Star Trek' at the Movies." *Los Angeles Times*, October 15, 1978.
"Warrior of the Lost World." *VHSCollector.com*. Last modified August 8, 2012. https://vhscollector.com/movie/warrior-lost-world.
Watkins, Roger. "De Paul's Silver Chalice Wraps 'Klarsfeld' on Budget, on Time." *Variety* 323, no. 10 (July 2, 1986), 42.
"Wednesday." *Leader-Post*, October 20, 1982.
"Wednesday's TV." *New York Daily News*, March 5, 1980.
Weiler, A.H. "Screen: British 'Conduct Unbecoming.'" *New York Times*. October 6, 1975.
Welcome Home. "Official National Welcome Home Celebration for Our Vietnam Veterans." Advertisement. *Los Angeles Times*, February 9, 1986.
Wells, Joyce. "No-Sweat Look Grows, but Peak Not in Sight." *Women's Wear Daily* 139, no. 100 (November 20, 1979), 1, 9.
Werba, Hank. "Breakthroughs for Milan Mart." *Variety* 316, no. 13 (October 24, 1984), 1, 266.
"The Wilby Conspiracy." *Daily Variety* 168, no. 1 (June 20, 1975), 3, 16.
Willard, Bill. "Producer Albert Ruddy Hosts

NATO to Megaforce' Shoot-Out, Lunch." *Daily Variety* 193, no. 49 (November 12, 1981), 21.

Willson, Karen E. "An Interview with Star Trek's Deltan Navigator Persis Khambatta." *Starlog* no. 37 (August 1980), 48–52.

Wilson, Earl. "Bombay Beauty Balks at Baring." *Philadelphia Daily News*, March 27, 1975.

_____. "It Happened Last Night." *Tyler Morning Telegraph*, June 23, 1982.

_____. "Right Back Atcha, Says Wry Mrs. Sly." *Indianapolis Star*, March 7, 1980.

_____. "Will Girls Shave Heads?" *Indianapolis Star*, December 4, 1978.

"Without Comment." *Sunday* 13, no. 37 (July 20, 1986), 77.

"YouTube Star Lilly Singh is the First Woman of Indian-Origin to Host a U.S. Late Night Show." *Rolling Stone India*. Last modified March 16, 2019. https://rollingstoneindia.com/lilly-singh-late-night-show/.

Index

Aaron, Salome 29
Abbas, Khwaja Ahmad 15–16
ABC (television network) 44, 67, 73, 110, 117, 145, 151
Academy Awards 1, 69–71, 83, 90, 93, 117, 120, 137, 165
Academy of Motion Picture Arts and Sciences 117, 163, 175
Academy Theater 147
Ackerman, Forrest J. 34–35, 67
Action International Pictures 148
Adam, Lubna 171
Adams, Maud 90, 110–113, 149–150
Adamson, Al 24
After the Fall of New York 134
Ahuja, Vimal 15–16
Air India 24–26, 29; analysis of Khambatta's commercial 24–25
Akhtar, Shameem 144
Aladdin (2019 film) 72–73
The Alan Thicke Show (1980 television series) 113
Alfie (1966 film) 77
Ali, Nafisa 172
Alien Seed 148
All-Star Family Feud 124
Allen, Woody 76
Alley, Kirstie 98
Alonso, Maria Conchita 149
Alopecia Universalis 122
Aman, Zeenat 17, 34, 37, 55, 166, 172
Amazon Prime 20–21
Ambassador Hotel 75
Les Ambassadeurs 26
American Cablesystems 151

American Film Market 129, 149–150
American International Pictures 19–21, 148
American Red Cross 162–163
Amritraj, Ashok 112, 114, 137, 162–164
Amritraj, Vijay 70, 112, 114
Anderson, George 88, 93
Anderson, Loni 75–76
Anderson, Michael 27
Anderson, Richard Dean 142
Andheri Sports Complex 166
Andrews, Julie 115
Anne (Princess) 29
Annie (1982 film) 99
Anthony, George 57
Antonioni, Michelangelo 55
The Appointment (1981 film) 149
Aquarius (film distributor) 133–136
Archerd, Army 62, 71, 75, 129, 163
Arnaz, Desi, Jr. 59
Arrants, Rod 143
Art on the Runway 75
Artistry in Cinema Awards 76
As the World Turns 140
Asian Indian Women's Network 161
Asian Week 115, 121
Asianweek 161
The Assassinator see *Warrior of the Lost World*
Associated Press 63, 65, 93–94, 115–116
Athaiya, Bhanu 117
Atkins, Christopher 75
Attack see *Nighthawks*
Attila (male model) 123

Avedon, Richard 22
Avery, Tex 15
Avildsen, John G. 77
Awam 143, 160
Aylesworth, Anne 76
Aylesworth, John 76

Baba, Shirdi Sai 9, 86
Babi, Parveen 37
Bach, Barbara 72
Bachchan, Amitabh 166–167, 172
Bacon, Francis 9, 11
Bailey, David 10, 63
Bajaria, Bela 159
Bambai Raat Ki Bahon Mein 3, 15–16, 26, 35, 136, 140–141
Bancroft, Anne 139
The Bandit Queen (unmade Golden Harvest film) 155
The Bandit Queen (unmade Persis Khambatta film) 124–128, 135, 144
The Bandit Queen (unmade Susie Coelho film) 124–128, 155
The Bandit Queen, the Warrior Queen, and Me 125
Banerjee, Victor 136–139, 160
Banks, Elizabeth 72
Bapa 21, 23, 75
The Barbara Walters Special 151
Barclay, Dolores 65, 94
Barrett, Majel 37–38, 48–49
Barris, Chuck 71
Barth, Carl 37–38
Basappa, Malathi 172
Base Industries Group 168
Batman (1966 television series) 130

219

220 Index

Battlestar Galactica (2004 television series) 183
Baum, Martin 25
BBC (British television network) 6, 24, 64
Bechdel Test 49
Beck, Marilyn 50, 68–69, 71, 91, 93, 95, 127–128
Bedi, Kabir 37, 50, 95, 112, 120, 129, 137, 140, 144, 154, 181
Bee Gees 173
Beloved India see *Kamasutra—Vollendung Der Liebe*
Beltz, Heidi Von 108
Benegal, Dev 172
Benetton boutique 7
Bennett, Harve 77–78
Benson, Robby 59
Berenger, Tom 71
Bergman, Ingrid 82, 103
Bergman, Sandahl 79, 121
Bernstein, Jay 74, 146, 151
The Best of Everything 121
Betaab 124–125
Beverly Hills People 76
Beverly Hilton 68, 117, 140
Beverly Wilshire 75, 88
Bharat Sundari contest 170, 172
Bharucha, Cyrus 6
Bhatia, Samita 179–180
Bheegi Raat 3, 14–15, 91, 136
Bhindi Jewellers 159
Biarritz 75
Bidapa, Prasad 170
Birch, Patricia 102
Birds of Prey and the Fantabulous Emancipation of One Harley Quinn 149
The Black Hole (1979 film) 145
Black Sunday (1977 film) 30
Blade Runner (1982 film) 99
Blair, Linda 139
Blazing Stewardesses (1975 film) 24
Bloomingdale's (New York) 5–6
The Blue Lagoon (1980 film) 75–76
Bluhdorn, Charles 77–78
La Boite Disco 69
The Bold and the Beautiful 167
Bologna, Joseph 159
Bombay Dyeing 10

Bombay Palace (Indian restaurant) 137
Bond, Alicia 130
Bono, Sonny 50, 72, 116
Bono, Susie see Coelho, Susie
Boone, Debbie 98
Bora Bora (1968 film) 19
Bostwick, Barry 93, 95, 100–102 105–106, 136, 142
Bowen, Anthony 94
Boyd, Denny 109
Bradbury, Ray 90
The Brady Bunch (1969 television series) 165, 182
Braga, Sonia 165
Brain, Waldo 145, 154
Brando, Marlon 26
Brar, Manpreet 167
Brave New World (1932 book) 135
Breakin' 2: Electric Boogaloo 128, 130
Breakin' 2 Is Electric Boogaloo see *Breakin' 2: Electric Boogaloo*
Breedlove, Lee 107–108
Bridges, Jeff 117, 165
Bring 'Em Back Alive (1982 television series) 120
Brinkley, Christie 123
British Raj 21, 28, 132
Brooks, Bob 110
Brosnan, Pierce 162–163
Brown, Jerry 50
Brown, L.T. 76
Brown, Nicole 91
Brynner, Yul 35–36, 59, 71, 74, 118, 123
Bunny Mars see Rouilard, Richard
Bush, George 138
Buss, Jerry 91
Butler, Harry 124

Cable T.V. Party 98
La Cage Aux Folles (supper club) 90–91, 110, 155
Caine, Michael 23–25, 29, 144, 155, 165
Caine, Shakira 23–25, 29
California Suite (1978 film) 63
Cameron, James 133, 149, 164
Campaign for Economic Democracy Education Fund/Cancer Project 75

Can (German rock group) 20
Canadian India Times 66
Canby, Vincent 28
Cannes Film Festival 63, 71, 148
Cannes Film Market 118, 147–150, 168
Cannon Films 128, 130
The Cannonball Run 93, 105, 108
Cardin, Pierre 16–17
Carerra, Barbara 150
Carpenter, John 99
Carradine, David 148
Carrera, Barbara 30
Carroll, Diahann 76
Carroll, Jane 75
carrot juice-plus 59
Carson, Johnny 70, 98
Carter, Jimmy 69
Carter, Lynda 48
Cartier 35, 69
Casablanca (American television series) 3, 114–115, 117, 142; analysis of Khambatta's character 120–121; production 114; release and reception 120
Casablanca (Michael Curtiz film) 114
Le Castel 86–87
Castro Theatre 44
Cat People (1982 film) 79–80, 118, 180
Celebrity Racquetball Tournament 75
Central Board of Film Certification 125
Century Plaza Hotel 90, 112, 121
Chabad Telethon 161
Chakraborty, Mithun 146
Champlin, Charles 34
Charlie's Angels (1976 television series) 71–72, 75–76, 109–110
Charlie's Angels (2019 film) 72–73
Chase, Chevy 50
Chasen's 34, 48, 150
Chatwal, Sant Singh 137
Checker, Chubby 14
Chevillot, Pascal 7–8, 79, 91
Chez Moi 62
Chez Régine 63
Chicago Story (1982 television series) 110

Index 221

Chicago Sun-Times 101
Chicago Tribune 33, 53, 55, 100
China Love (unmade film) 145
Chopin, Frédéric 8
Chopra, B.R. 143
Chopra, Priyanka 1, 69
Chopra, Yash 166
Chothia, Farrokh 175
Choudhary, Sanjeev 181
Chowdhury, Ajay 112
Chowdhury, Nandita 176
Choudhury, Salil 15
Christ Church (Oxford University) 21
Christensen's Celebrity Autographs 153
Christie's 40 Years of Star Trek: The Collection Auction 33, 41, 54
Cinefantastique 41, 54, 102
Cinefex 58
City of Dreams (unmade television series) 168, 177, 179
City of Hope Medical Center 90
City of Joy 160
Clark, Dick 76
Clarke, Logan 124
Clayburgh, Jill 77, 118, 146
Click Modeling Agency 123
Clinic Les Champs 113
Clive, Doris 35
A Clockwork Orange (1971 film) 22, 133
Coelho, Susie 50, 68, 72, 110, 125–126, 155; meeting Phoolan Devi 116; negotiating the rights to *The Bandit Queen* 121; press rivalry with Khambatta 126–128
Coffee, Tea or Me? (1967 book) 24
Coffee, Tea or Me? (1973 telefilm) 24
Collins, Gary 79
Collins, Joan 63
Collins, Phil 140
Columbia Drug Store 32
Comi, Paul 130
Committee to Cure Cancer through Immunization 75
Communist Party of India 15

Community Living Foundation 156–157
Conan the Barbarian (1982 film) 77, 79, 118
Conduct Unbecoming 3, 70, 129, 145; analysis of Khambatta's character 28–29; production 27; release 28
Connelly, Sherilyn: *The First Star Trek Movie: Bringing the Franchise to the Big Screen, 1969–1980* 3, 33, 103, 117–118
Connery, Sean 13
Contemporary Korman Artists 139, 151
Continental Films 37
Continental Motion Pictures 117–118, 130, 132
Coppola, Francis Ford 115
Corman, Roger 20
Cort, Bud 149
Cosby, Bill 98
Cosmopolitan 155
The Cotton Club (1984 film) 115
Courier-News (Bridgewater, NJ) 94
Crawford, Annahella 11
Creation Entertainment 162
Creative Artists Agency 150–151
The Creator 50
Crist, Paula 60
Crosby, Cathy Lee 98–99
Crosby, Joan 11, 77
Cuny, Marie-Thérèse 116

Daddy Warbucks 59, 72
Daily Girl 19–20
Daily Mail (UK Newspaper) 25
Daily Variety 32, 62, 69, 71, 75, 77, 112, 117, 121, 128–130, 132, 139, 163
Darden, Bijou 90
Davenport, Nigel 83
Davies, Tom 63
Dawber, Pam 75, 132
Day, Gerry 145
Dayton Journal-Herald 101
DCM 10
Dé, Shobha: *Shooting from the Hip* 18, 22
The Deadly Flower (unmade Sidney H. Levine film) 125, 128

deadly games of cat-and-mouse 149–150
Deadly Intent 3, 150, 152, 162; production 149; release and reception 149–150; analysis of Khambatta's character 150
DeFries, Tony 22
Dehlvi, Sadia 177
Dempster, Nigel 71–72
De Niro, Robert 68, 76, 119–120, 169
De Paul, Judith 139–140
Denny, Jon 79–81
Derek, Bo 53
Dern, Bruce 110
Des Moines Art Center 156
Des Moines Register 155–156
Desai, Morarji 31
de Sousa, Noel 130, 144–145
Detroit Free Press 24
Devi, Phoolan 115–116, 121, 124–128, 135, 155, 170
Dick, Nigel 149
Dickens, Charles 22, 160
Dietrich, Bruno 19
Dillard, J.M.: *Star Trek: "Where No One Has Gone Before": A History in Pictures* 33
Diller, Barry 77
Dinah! & Friends 63, 68
Dire Straits 14
Dirty Tricks (1981 film) 89
Distortions (1987 film) 147
D'Moro, Pierre 125
Dodd, John 100
The Dogs of War (1980 film) 71
Donna (Italian magazine) 123
Donner, Clive 105
Doohan, James 41, 160, 163
Doongerwadi forest 181
Doordarshan Television (television network) 167
Dornhelm, Robert 98
Double Impact 164
DuBois, Marta 92
Dunhill cigarettes 86, 137
Dynamite Kids' Page 63

Eastwood, Clint 99, 146
Ebert, Roger 99–101, 160
Eden, Barbara 76
Eder, Shirley 24
Edinburgh Film Festival 140

Index

Edmonton Journal 100
Edrick, Bobbie 6, 74
Edward Lozzi & Associates 139
Edwards, Blake 76, 137
Ehrlich, Richard S. 126
Eichelbaum, Stanley 28
Eilbacher, Lisa 150
Eisenstein, Sergei 60
Eisner, Michael 77–78
El Paso Times 122
The Electric Flag 20
Elves (1989 film) 148
Embassy Auditorium 149
Empire Theatre Leicester Square 65
End Hunger 117
Engel, Marty 161
Equal Rights Amendment 29, 81
Esquire 85, 87–88, 91
Esquireman 85–89, 91, 93, 95, 180
Estrada, Erik 148
E.T. (1982 film) 99
Etienne, Bobby 90
Evans, Robert 30, 115
Eve's Weekly 170, 172
Ewing, John Christy 130
Exciting People, Exotic Places 131–132
Exciting People in Exotic Places see *Exciting People, Exotic Places*
The Exterminator (1980 film) 133
The Exterminator 2 (1984 film) 133
Eye of Katmandu (unmade film) 145
Eyecatchers 141

The Fall of Saigon 142
Famous Monsters of Filmland 34–35
Fangoria 130–131, 133
Fantastic Films 62
The Far Pavilions (1984 miniseries) 165
Faria, Reita 12–14
Farrow, Mia 51, 64, 117
Fawcett, Farrah 51–52, 66, 74, 205
Fazeli, Hossein Martin 126
Fearless (1993 film) 165
Femina 10–11, 17, 166–167, 170

Fendi 113
Ferris, Irene 72
Ferry, Virginia 115
Festival of India 1985–1986 138, 140
Fiddler on the Roof (1971 film) 103, 106
Film World 26
Firefox (1982) 99
First Strike 3, 128, 136, 140, 148, 150; analysis of Khambatta's character 147; production 129–130; release and reception 147
Firstenberg, Sam 128
F.I.S.T. 70
Five Minutes to Cloud Boundary (2001 video) 174
Fleischer, Richard 76
Fletcher, Robert 39, 41, 47, 54
Fonda, Jane 56, 75
For Whom the Bell Tolls (1943 film) 82, 103
For Your Eyes Only (1981 film) 109, 155
Ford, Harrison 169
The Formula (1980 film) 77
Forster, Robert 163
Fortnum & Mason 22
Four Seasons Hotel (Washington, D.C.) 7
Fox, Roy 25
Frankenheimer, John 30
Franklin, Aretha 32
Frears, Stephen 140
Fredrick, William 107–108
Freeman, Paul 71
Fries, Chuck 149–150
Funt, Allen 53
Furth, George 105
Fury, Ed 151–152
Future Force 148

Gable, Clark 76
Gabor, Eva 35
Galella, Ron 85, 159–160, 162
Gammack, Julie 155–156
Gandhi (1982 film) 113–114, 116–117, 138
Gandhi, Indira 10, 31, 112–113, 131, 138–140, 143, 160, 170
Gandhi, Rajiv 138–139
Gansberg, Alan L. 124

Garbo, Greta 165
Garden Vareli 129
Garewal, Simi 55–56, 178
Gauri, Protima 37, 181
Gaylord's (New York restaurant) 7
Gee, Prunella 26
Gelfan, Gregory 92
Georgette Klinger Skin Care Salon 36
Ghose, Gautam 166
Gilbert, Lewis 13
Ginty, Robert 118–119, 131, 133, 142
Glam Rock 22, 93
Glen, John 112
Glitterati (newspaper column) 177
Globe and Mail 65
Going Ape! (1981 film) 89
Gold, Aaron 33
Goldberg, Leonard 71
Golden Globes 68, 154, 162
Golden Halos 68
Golden Harvest Group 93, 155
Goldeneye (1995 film) 167
Goldsmith, Jerry 8, 20, 38
The Gong Show Movie 71
Good Morning America 67
Google Doodle 15
Gordon, Alex 130–131, 133
Gordon, David 76, 79
Goudsouzian, Aram 28
Grabowski, Marilyn 95
Graham, Tim 168
Grand Café 166
Grant, Hank 35
Grant, Lee 75
Gray, Spalding 3
Grease 2 (1982 film) 102
Greenfeld, Gillian 126
Gremlins (1984 film) 131
Gross, Linda 117
Gross, Michael 163
Guarino, Ann 27
Guiding Light 140
Gypsies (Los Angeles restaurant) 7, 47

Hafeez, Ray 124–125
Haggerty, Dan 148
Haigwood, James 163
Hakoba 10
Halloween (1978 film) 133
Hama, Mie 109
Hamilton, Guy 110

Index

Hanky Panky (1982 film) 102
Hardly Working (1980 film) 89
Hare Krishnas 36
Harper's (British magazine) 22
Hartford Courant 101
Hatem, Rosine "Ace" 150
Hauer, Rutger 82–83
Hawks see *Nighthawks*
Hawn, Goldie 127
Hayden, Diana 171
Hayes, Isaac 50
Heathrow Airport 21
Hefner, Hugh 96
Henderson, Florence 165, 182
Henderson, Paulette 101
Hendry, Gloria 109
Hepburn, Audrey 31
Hersholt, Jean 175
Hiba Films 140, 146, 170
Hildebrand, Frank 117–118
Hilton, Francesca 91
Hira, Nari 140, 146, 170
Hogan, Christine 65–66
Holliday, Judy 67
Hollywood Foreign Press Association 140, 145
Hollywood International's Celebration II 130–131
Hollywood Reaches Out 162–163
Hollywood Reporter 31, 35, 64, 90, 94, 114, 124, 139, 144
Hopkins, Bo 163
Hotel Mayflower 68
Houghton, Adrian 74
Hour Magazine 79
Hour Magazine Cookbook 79
Howard, Sheila 148
Howards End (1992 film) 138
Humperdinck, Engelbert 75
Hunter (1984 American television series) 3, 142–144
Hussain, Waris 95
Hussey, Olivia 91
Huston, John 23–24, 99
Hutton, Lauren 80

I, Phoolan Devi: The Autobiography of India's Bandit Queen 116, 126
Illustrated Weekly of India 127, 144, 178–179
Improper Conduct (1994 film) 164

India Festival Committee 129
India Film Journalists' Association 2, 16; Best Newcomer of the Year award 16
India Independence Day 113, 120, 140
India Today 34, 124–126, 139, 141, 144, 163, 168, 176
India West 55, 82, 85, 95, 113, 117–119, 137, 139–140, 144, 146, 159–160, 163, 168
Indian Independence 2, 9, 171
Indian Princess contest 170
Indiana Jones and the Temple of Doom (1984 film) 131, 138
Indianapolis Star 94
Indira Gandhi: A Tryst with Destiny see *Indira Gandhi—If I Die Tomorrow*
Indira Gandhi—If I Die Tomorrow (unmade television miniseries) 139
Indo-U.S. Subcommission on Education and Culture 138
International Film Festival of India 166
International Women's Year 29, 161
Introvision 106, 135
Invasion of the Body Snatchers (1956 film) 27
Invasion USA (1985 film) 149
Irani, Vijaya 55–56
Irving, Amy 165
The Island of Dr. Moreau (1977 film) 30
It Happened One Night (1934 film) 76
The Italian Stallion see *The Party at Kitty and Stud's*
Ivory, James 138
Iyer, Padma 129

Jacobs, Jody 77
Jaeger, Kobi 17, 19–21, 177
Jaffrey, Madhur 139
Jaffrey, Saeed 28, 168
Jagger, Bianca 69
Jarrett, Jimmy 25
Jay, Ricky 98
Jazira 3, 146, 170
The Jazz Singer (1980 film) 76

Jenkins, Jane: *A Star Is Found* 110–112
Jewels by Edwar 76
Jewison, Norman 71, 106, 110
Jhabvala, Ruth Prawer 138
Jhangiani, Dr. K.D. 10
The Jigsaw Murders (1989 film) 154
Joffé, Roland 160
Johnson, Lyndon 12
Johnson, Malcolm L. 101
Johnson Space Center 129
Jones, Grace 112
Jones, Preston Neal: *Return to Tomorrow: The Filming of Star Trek: The Motion Picture* 41, 44, 47, 54, 58, 61
Jones, Shirley 161
Jones, Will 7
Jordan, Louis 111
Joseph, Nafisa 171
Junior (1994 film) 164
Junoon 172
Just Passing Through (unmade film) 77

Kachler, Robert S. 107
Kahani Phoolan Ki see *Kahani Phoolvati Ki*
Kahani Phoolvati Ki (1984 film) 125–126
Kalal, David Dasharath 173–174
Kalank Ka Tika 146
Kalidas 14
Kaling, Mindy 1, 159
Kama Sutra see *Kamasutra—Vollendung Der Liebe*
Kamala (textile mill) 10
Kamasutra—Vollendung der Liebe (Irmin Schmidt score) 20
Kamasutra—Vollendung der Liebe (Kobi Jaeger film) 3, 19–21, 141, 143, 148, 177
Kang, Sukhbir 145, 154
Kapoor, Raj 10
Karlan, Richard 130
Karloff, Boris 34–35, 67
Katzenberg, Jeffrey 36, 77–78
Kaur, Karminder 172
Kaye, M.M. 165
Kayser, Alex: *Heads* 124

223

Index

Kazickas, Jurate 8
Keller, Marthe 30, 165
Kelley, DeForest 7, 41, 52, 60, 65, 68
Kennedy, Edward 69
Kennedy, Jayne 72, 76, 121
Kennedy, Robert 12
Kerwin, Robert 55
Keyes, Evelyn 153
"Khaaan!" 49
Khafa (unmade film) 168–170, 179
Khambatta, Diane 181
Khambatta, Dinshi 9, 38, 86, 91, 94
Khambatta, Feroze 9
Khambatta, Jeroo 7, 9–11, 13, 23, 27, 38–39, 64, 66, 86, 91–92, 94, 141
Khatau (textile mill) 10
Kibbie, Guy 153
The King and I (1956 film) 35, 59
Kinmont, Kathleen 148–149
Kinski, Nastassja 80, 165, 180
Kirkland, Sally 163
Kishnani, Monica 129
Kleiner, Dick 116
Kline, Richard H. 39
Koenig, Walter 151; *Chekov's Enterprise* 41–42, 47, 49, 108
Kohinoor diamond 171
Kojak (1973 television series) 35, 79
Krieger, Alan 75
Kriendler, Jeff 98
Kroll, Jack 84–85
Kronsberg, Jeremy Joe 89
KSAN (radio station) 68
KTCA (television station) 6
Kumar, Pradeep 14
Kumari, Meena 15
Kuskowski, Allan 128–130

LA Weekly 130
Ladd Company 75
Laforet, Bertrand 98
Lahiri, Bappi 170
Lakeland Civic Arena 120
Lakme 29–30
Lane, Lydia 59, 91
Langdon, Harry 179
Las Vegas Hilton 75
Last Action Hero 164
Last Call (1991 film) 144

The Last Orgy of the Third Reich (1977 film) 147
Lateef, Ahmed 95, 145
Law, John Philip 75
Lawrence, Margaret: *Seven Thunders* 145
Lawrence of Arabia (1962 film) 137
Lawson, Terry 101
Leach, Robin 70
Lean, David 137–138, 160
Lee, Norma A. 6, 30–31
Leogrande, Ernest 100
Leone, Alfredo 98
Lesso, Elke 91
Letterman, David 151
Lettich, Sheldon 164
Levin, Gerry 31
Levin, Henry 24
Levine, Sidney H. 125
Lewis, Jerry 89
Lewis, Shari 181
Lichfield, Patrick 22
Life Asia Edition 17, 59, 178
Lifestyles of the Rich and Famous (1984 television series) 131
Lifestyles of the Rich and Famous (1986 book) 132
Lisberger, Steven 99
Live Aid 140
Live and Let Die (1973 film) 109
Livingston, Harold 42, 48, 51, 57, 107
Lloyd's of London 35–36
Loane, Janice 11
Locke, Sam 125
The Locket (unmade film) 145
Lois & Clark: The New Adventures of Superman 162, 165
Longbotham, Brian 61–62
Longview News-Journal 94
The Lone Ranger (1949 television series) 55
Loren, Sophia 31, 52, 80, 165
Los Angeles Area Emmy Awards 90
Los Angeles Civic Center Mall 113, 120
Los Angeles Daily News 143
Los Angeles Herald-Examiner 74
Los Angeles Magazine 51
Los Angeles Museum of Art 50

Los Angeles Times 5, 34–36, 52, 54, 59, 64, 75, 77, 91, 113, 117, 126, 129, 139, 164–165
Love Song for Persis K. (1997 video) 173–174
Lowe, Skip E. 151–152
Lucas, George 89, 133
Lumière, Auguste 166
Lumière, Louis 166
Lumley, Joanna 115

Ma Maison 7, 85
MacArthur Theater (Washington, D.C.) 5, 7–8, 65–66, 75
MacGyver (1985 American television series) 3, 142–144
Magique Disco 69
Magnum, P.I. (1980 television series) 92
Maizlish, Leonard 36
Major Saab 172
Maksoud, Hala 115
Malmuth, Bruce 66
The Man Who Would Be King (1975 film) 23–24
The Man with the Golden Gun (1974 film) 6, 110
The Man with the Power 3, 6, 70, 130, 135; analysis of Khambatta's character 31; production 30–31; release and reception 32
Manhattan's 20th Precinct 69
Mann, Roderick 36–37, 52, 64, 70, 94, 96, 136
Mann's Chinese Theatre 65
Margaret Herrick Library 42
Marquette Hotel (Minneapolis) 5
Martin, Jack 71
Marx, Solly 150
Masada (1981 television miniseries) 88
Maslin, Janet 85, 98, 100
Master of None (2015 series) 159
Masterpiece Theater 6
Mastroianni, Armand 147
Mathur, Rakesh 116
Maxwell, Lois 111
Maychick, Diana 109
Mayo, Mike 102

Index 225

McCall, Robert: *Vision of the Future: The Art of Robert McCall* 58
McCarthy, Kevin 27
McKenna, Mary 37
McKenna, Paula 37
McTiernan, John 164
McWilliams, Debbie 110
Megaforce 3, 63, 107–109, 119–120, 134–136, 143, 146, 148, 155, 173; analysis of Khambatta's character 103–107; production 92–94; promotional materials 95–98; release and reception 99–103
Megaforce: Deeds Not Words (unmade film) 98
Mehta, Zubin 112
Men Who Rate a '10' 76, 121
Menezes, Saira 168–169
Mental Health Association 90
Merchant, Ismail 138
Merchant-Ivory 138–140
The Merv Griffin Show 59, 98, 115
Michael, George: *George Michael's Complete Hair Care for Men* 118
Michael Levine Public Relations 139
Michelson, Harold 60
MIFED 128, 130
The Mike Douglas Show 48, 68
Milius, John 77
Miller, Daryl 101
The Mindy Project 159
Minelli, Liza 90, 119–120
Mini Page 73–74
Minneapolis Star 5–7
Minneapolis Tribune 5, 7
Minster, Barbara 37
Mirza, Katy 34, 56
Miss Angel Face *see* Miss Bombay
Miss Asian American Beauty Pageant 166
Miss Bombay 11
Miss India (contests) 1–2, 10–12, 14, 17, 122, 166–167, 176, 197
Miss India (title) 2–3, 7, 11–12, 15–18, 20, 33, 35, 56, 66, 69, 73, 79, 86, 101, 108, 125, 141, 151, 170–175, 183;

India Film Journalists' Association Award for Miss India 2; Miss India-Asia Pacific 171; Miss India-Universe 159, 171; Miss India USA 129, 141, 159; Miss India-World 171; Miss L.A. India 159
Miss Piggy 67
Miss Teen USA 120–121
Miss Universe 11–13, 60, 108, 167, 171–173
Missionaries of Charity 174
Mr. Skin (website) 79
Mistry, Meher 11, 17, 166
MIX: The New York Lesbian & Gay Experimental Film/Video Festival 174
Moarsi, Mila 113
Mollo, John 117
Monroe, Marilyn 26
Montalban, Ricardo 98
Montgomery, Luke 182
Montreal Gazette 67
Moore, Roger 111
Moreno, Rita 124
Morgan, Andre 107
Morning News (Wilmington, DE) 94
Morrison, Don 6–7, 64
Morton's 75
Moss, Dann 71
Moss, David 30, 91, 151
Moss Agency 91
Mother Teresa 170, 174–175
Motion Picture Association of America 19, 131
Movie Movie (1978 film) 100
Mrs. Doubtfire 163
MST3K *see Mystery Science Theater 3000*
Swami Muktananda 91
Multi-Coloured Swap Shop 64
Mundhra, Jagmohan 144, 154, 164
Murder in Music City 50
MV Britannia 109
My Beautiful Laundrette 140
Myers, Carmel 76
Mystery Science Theater 3000 (1988 television series) 134–136

Nadiadwala, Firoz 168
Nardino, Gary 77
Naren, Sandy 144

Nargis Dutt Memorial Foundation 117, 159
Nath, Rajenda 91
National Association of Theatre Owners (NATO) 93
National Film Society 76
Navy Queen contest 170
Nazi Hunter: The Beate Klarsfeld Story 139–140
Nazi Love Camp 27 (1977 film) 147
Needham, Hal 63, 92–93, 94, 101–103, 105–108, 118, 135, 146; Kitty O'Neil lawsuit 107–108; *Stuntman!* 108
Nehru Centre 166
Nelson, Nels 72
Nelson, Ralph 25
Netflix 159
The New Mike Hammer (1984 American television series) 3, 146–147
New York Daily News 27, 30, 59, 63, 69–70, 95, 100, 133, 141, 146
New York Post 69–72, 92, 103, 109, 126
New York Times 19–20, 28, 84–85, 98, 100, 102, 123, 137
News Journal (Wilmington, DE) 101
News-Press (Fort Myers, FL) 122
Newsweek 20, 31, 52, 85
Nichols, Nichelle 42–43, 49, 91
Nicholson, Sam 61, 119
Night Eyes (1990 film) 144
Nighthawks 3, 8, 66, 68–71, 74, 81–85, 88–89, 92, 95, 97, 99, 101, 103, 105, 108–109, 127, 136, 146, 149–151, 153, 155, 178
Nimoy, Leonard 7, 33, 36, 39, 41, 52, 57, 60, 142, 156
Sister Nirmala 175
Not a Nice Man to Know (chatshow) 177–179, 181

O, Jenny 123–124
Oberoi, D.L. 34
Oberoi, Suresh 168
Oberon, Merle 165
Observer (UK Magazine) 63

226 Index

Octopussy 109, 111–113, 149, 165
Official National Welcome Home Celebration for Our Vietnam Veterans 142
On Top All Over the World 132
On TV 97–98
O'Neil, Kitty 107–108
Operation California 115
Orlando, Tony 75
Oscars *see* Academy Awards
O'Shea, Busty 90
Ottawa Journal 65–66
Oui 72, 79–82, 144, 151
Out of this World (1950 Broadway musical) 76
Outlook India 144, 168, 177–179
Ovitz, Mike 150

Pacific Theatres' Cinerama Dome 75
Paciocco, Lou 90
Pais, Arthur 137
Pal, Pratapaditya 50
Pan Am 29, 31, 98
Panama, Norman 24
Paradise Alley 70
Paramount Pictures 8, 15–17, 32–36, 39, 47, 50, 53, 60, 62–64, 77, 82, 150, 160
Paramount Television 77, 145
Parekh, Naren 144
Parijat House 175
Paris Blues 76
Parsis 6, 9, 11–12, 40, 56, 82, 104, 141 181
The Party (1968 film) 137
The Party at Kitty and Stud's (1970 film) 83
Pascal, Robert 90
A Passage to India (1984 film) 137–138, 160
The Passenger (1975 film) 55
Partition 2
Patel, Bhaichand 178
Patel, Praful 22
Patel, Sona 164
Patil, Vimla 10–11, 167
PBS (American television network) 6, 99
Peak, Bob 156
Pendennis 63
Penn, Chris 181

Penn, Leo 181
Penn, Sean 181
Penthouse 95
People (magazine) 37, 39, 50, 67, 123, 126–127
Persis Khambatta complex 56
Persistence 154–133 (2020 artwork) 174
Persistent Sky (2019 artwork) 174
Philadelphia Inquirer 123
Phillips, Fred 34, 37–39, 41
Phillips, Janna 37–38, 53–54
Phillips, Michelle 85, 87
Phoenix the Warrior 3, 150, 153, 162; analysis of Khambatta's character 149; production 148; release and reception 148–149
Phoolan (unfinished documentary) 126
Phoolan Devi (1984 Bengali-language film) 125
Photoplay Awards 64–65
Piccoli, Michel 8
Pickford, Mary 91
Pinewood Studios 26
Pinjre Ke Panchhi 3, 15, 136
Pittsburgh Post-Gazette 88
Playboy 26, 95–96, 178–180
Pleasence, Donald 118, 131, 136
PM Magazine 64–65
Poitier, Sidney 24–28, 76, 102, 155, 165
Ponds 10
Poonam 14–15
Popular Photography 115
Porter, Cole 76
Portfolio X 145
Poster, Tom 59
Potts, Michael 144, 160–161
Povill, Jon 58
Prakash, Veena 172
Pramila 2, 14
Presenting Rip Taylor (unwritten book) 109
Pride of India: A Tribute to Miss India 1–4, 10–11, 30, 104, 113, 167, 170–177, 183
Prince Charles 67
Procter & Gamble Productions 140
Prom Night (1980 film) 84
Puck, Wolfgang 162

Purcell, Lee 50
Puri, Neeta 141, 146

Queen City Mail 102

Raging Bull 68
Raiders of the Lost Ark 120
Railsback, Steve 150, 152
Rajadhyaksha, Ashish 2, 14; *Encyclopaedia of Indian Cinema* 2, 14
Rakoff, Alvin 89
Ramasubramanian, Shobana 173
Rambali, Paul 116
Rambling Reporter 35, 64, 144
Rambo: First Blood Part II 149
Rambo III 151
Ramsay, Todd 43–44, 46–47, 49, 51, 56
Rawail, Rahul 124–125
Ray, Satyajit 55
Reagan, Nancy 138
Reagan, Ronald 81
Reagan Administration 138
Real Men Don't Eat Quiche 100
Rediff 174–175
Reed, Rex 30, 70
Reilly, Sue 50, 67
Reisfeld, Bert 72
Reitman, Ivan 164
The Rejuvenator 149
The Remains of the Day (1993 film) 138
Rexona 10, 12
RGH International Film Enterprises Inc. 128
Rhodes, Zandra 35
The Road Warrior 134, 148
Roberts, Tanya 72, 75
Robertson, Nan 137
Robinson, Gavin 22
The Rocky Horror Picture Show (1975 film) 100
Rocky II 70
Rocky III 99
Rocky IV 99, 151
Roddenberry, Gene 3, 32, 36–42, 45–46, 48, 51–54, 56–57, 64, 67, 79, 88
Roddenberry Shop 42
Roeder, Bill 31
Rogers, Wayne 59
Rolle, Esther 48

Index

Rollerball (1975 film) 110
Romero, Cesar 130
Ronan, Eve 63
Rooks, Conrad 55, 178
A Room with a View (1986 film) 138
Roosevelt Island Tramway 69, 83
Rosemary's Baby (1968 film) 51
Rossellini, Isabella 165
Rothwell, John 36
Rouilard, Richard 129
Roura, Phil 59
Roxie Theater (San Francisco, CA) 173
Roy, Ashok 125–126
Rubinstein, Helena 29
Ruddy, Albert S. 93, 95, 105, 107

Sabloak, Suzanne 172
Sacchi, Robert 79
Sackett, Susan 38, 40, 62, 64; *The Making of Star Trek—The Motion Picture* 38–40, 173
Sainte-Chapelle 83
Saiyam Shivam Sundaram (1978 film) 37
Sajnani, Veena 17, 166
Saldanha, Rui Ninnian 153–156
Salvatori, Lynn 150
San Bernardino County Sun 65
San Francisco Examiner 28, 35, 75
San Francisco International Lesbian & Gay Film Festival 173
San Francisco Public Library 173
Sand, George 8
Sandy, Gary 98
Santa Cruz Sentinel 94
Santa Fe New Mexican 66
Sarandon, Susan 90
Sarlui, Helen 130
Sasso, Joey 71
Sassoon, Vidal 51
Saturn Awards 75–76, 110, 120–121
Satyan, Roopa 172
Savalas, Telly 35–36, 59, 71–72, 74, 118, 123
Saxon, John 91

Schmidt, Irmin 20
Schneider, Maria 55
Schnurmacher, Thomas 67
Schrader, Paul 79
Schwarzenegger, Arnold 164; as the Governator 133
Scorsese, Martin 68
Scott, Christopher 73
Scott, Naomi 72–73
Scott, Ridley 99, 106
Scott, Usha 73
Scott, Vernon 89, 93, 116
Screen Actors Guild 29
Segovia, Jimmy 90
Selleck, Tom 92
Sellers, Peter 137, 160
Sen, Sushmita 167
Sethna, Ratanji Framji 9, 11, 39–40, 92
Shaft (1971 film) 98
Shankar, Ravi 112
Sharif, Omar 124
Sharma, Rekha 183
Sharpe, Cornelia 72
Shashikala 14
Shatner, William 7, 33, 41, 49, 52, 57, 60–61, 65, 68–70, 82, 94, 117, 151, 156; hairy left arm 57, 73, 146–147, 156
Shay, Don 58
She Dances Alone 98
Sheen, Martin 140
Shepherd, Cybill 76, 112
Shepherd, James 17
Sheraton-Universal 88
Sherwood Oaks Experimental College 68
Shields, Brooke 75–76
Shingora 3, 140–144, 146, 170; analysis of Khambatta's character 141; production 140; release and reception 140
Shirjee 37
Shore, Dinah 63
Shoreham Hotel 139
Short, Martin 151
Showtime (cable network) 139
Shrimpton, Jean 10
Siddha Yoga 91
Siddhartha (1972 film) 55–56, 178
Sideliners 92
Siegel, Don 27
Signal 30 16

Silliman, Al, Jr. 24
Silva, Henry 93
Silver Chalice Productions 139–140
Silver Eye Productions 145
Silverheels, Jay 55
Simpson, O.J. 91
Simpsons of Piccadilly 22
Singapore International Film Festival 173
Singh, Gurmeet 10, 34
Singh, Khushwant 56, 177–179, 181
Singh, Pamela 172
Siskel, Gene 3, 53, 85, 99–101, 104, 136, 141
Sisson, Dave 64–65
Skinner, Margo 115, 121
Skip E. Lowe Looks at Hollywood 151–152
Sledge Hammer! (1986 television series) 143
Sloan, Robin 108
Small, Michele 47–48
SMI Motivator 107–108
Smith, Liz 90, 92
Smokey and the Bandit 92, 107
Smyle 175
The Snake (unmade film) 98
Sneak Previews (1975 television series) 99–100
Soman, Milind 168
Somani, Surendra 170
Some Kind of Hero: The Remarkable Story of the James Bond Films 112
Sone Ka Pinjra 146
Sony Video Software 148–149
Soul, David 142
Southern California Motion Picture Council 68
Southtown Theater (Minneapolis, MN) 5
Spago 162–163
Spencer, Alan 143
Spencer, Ronald 22
Spencer Sisters 34
Spielberg, Steven 99
Split Wide Open 172
Spotlight Leisure 168
Spring Trek '93 162
Srikanth, B.R. 144
Stallone, Sylvester 8, 68–70, 81–83, 99, 108, 150–151, 155
Star Plus (television network) 177

Index

Star Trek (franchise) 3, 34, 133–134, 160
Star Trek (1966 television series) 5, 24, 34, 36, 175
Star Trek Action Group 31
Star Trek Communicator 77–78, 182–183
Star Trek: Discovery 183
Star Trek—The Motion Picture 1, 3–5-6, 15–17, 19–20, 29–30, 33, 34, 62–65, 67–69, 73–75, 77–78, 80, 82, 85–86, 92, 94, 96–97, 99–103, 105–106, 108–109, 113, 115, 117–119, 112, 122–123, 127, 134–135, 145–146, 150, 152, 155–156, 165, 169, 173–176, 182; ABC television broadcast 44, 73, 117, 145; Blu-ray release (1979 theatrical version) 45, 49, 56; DVD release (2001 Director's Edition) 33, 44–45, 48–49, 56; press conference (March 28, 1978) 34–35, 150; principal photography 41–58, 60–62; shaving of Khambatta's head 37–39; soundtrack LP 8; as that one movie 3, 8, 62, 69, 71–72, 74, 79, 85, 92–93, 96–98, 103, 119, 122, 133, 152, 155, 173–174, 183; theatrical release 43–45, 48–49; VHS and Beta release (1979 version) 73; VHS and Beta release (1983 Special Longer Version) 44–45, 48–49, 56, 117; videodisc release (1979 theatrical version) 73, 146
Star Trek: The Next Generation (1987 television series) 145
Star Trek II (unmade television series) 3, 32–33
Star Trek II: The Wrath of Khan 49, 58, 77, 98–99, 135
Star Trek II Writer's Guide 42
Star Trek III: The Search for Spock 58
Star Trek IV: The Voyage Home 112, 117

Star Trek VI: The Undiscovered Country 160
Star Wars (1977 film) 89
Star Wars: The Last Jedi (2017 film) 146
Starburst (UK magazine) 32
Stardust Ballroom 56
Starlog 62, 64, 74, 98, 102–103, 119, 180–182
Starting Over 178
State Bank of India Probationary Officers' Examination 183
Stead, C.K. 86
Stein, Michael 164–165
Stern (German magazine) 177
Stévenin, Jean-François 71
The Stewardesses (1969 film) 24
Stewart, Kristen 72
Stewart, Patrick 182
Stonewall Riots 91
Stratton, Rick 57
Strasberg, Lee 26
Streisand, Barbra 127
Strong, John, III 109, 155
Studio 54 40, 68
Stunts Unlimited 107
Sullivan, Tom 34
Sunday (Indian magazine) 37, 55–56, 146, 168, 171
Sunil, K.P. 127
Super Model India contest 164
Suzy 63, 69
Swanson, Gloria 76
Swaroop, Shikha 172
Swimming to Cambodia (1987 film) 3
Swit, Loretta 76, 115, 121
Sydney Morning Herald 17, 65–66

Taj Hotel 16
Takei, George 35, 56
Talent International 139, 151
Tales of the Gold Monkey 120
Talk of the Town (unmade chatshow) 168, 177, 179
Talsky, Ron 79
Tampa Tribune 94
Tanen, Ted 138
Tattletales 71
Tattoo (1981 film) 110
Taxi Driver 76
Taylor, Cliff 90–91, 144, 155

Taylor, Don 30
Taylor, Renee 159
Taylor, Rip 71, 109, 113
Teen Princess contest 170
Tejani, Anil 140
Telegraph (Indian newspaper) 91, 112, 143–144, 177, 179–181
10 (1979 film) 53, 76
Ten Years of Gold (Aretha Franklin record) 32
Tennessean 66
The Terminator (1984 film) 133, 164
Terminator: Dark Fate (2019 film) 133
Terminator 2: Judgment Day (1991 film) 164
TerraCon (1977 convention) 35
Thalberg, Irving 175
Thermal, Harry F. 101
The Thing (1982 film) 99
Thomas, Bob 93–94
Thompson, Howard 19–21
Thorn EMI/HBO Video 132–134
Three in Love (unmade film) 125
Thunderball (1965 film) 13
THX 1138 (1971 film) 133
Tidyman, Ernest 98
Tiegs, Cheryl 123
Times of India 167
The Tonight Show 98
Tower of Silence 181
Towner, Ken 35
Train to Pakistan 177
Trans Northern Television 130
Treasures of Tutankhamun 56
Triillusion Co. 92, 115, 124, 144–145, 148, 154–155, 159
The Trip (1967 film) 20
Trivedi, Hemant 129, 171, 175
Tron (1982 film) 99
True Lies 164
Trumbull, Douglas 58
Trump, Donald 167
TV Scout 11
Twentieth Century–Fox 95–96, 103, 107
21 (British magazine) 22
Twin Peaks: Fire Walk with Me 84

Index 229

Twins (1988 film) 164
Twist (dance) 14–16, 26, 126, 136
Twisted Sex: Trailers from the Sick Sick 60s 20

UCLA 62
UK Immigrants Advisory Service 22
UNICEF 113, 160
United Artists 24, 28
United Nations 29, 161, 178
United Nations Decade for Women 29, 161
United Producers Organization 19
Universal Studios 68, 82, 95, 103
Universal Television 159
University of Bombay 17, 19
An Unmarried Woman 178
The Unterman (unmade film) 139
UPI 56, 68, 89, 116
Us Weekly 67

Vallejo, Boris 149
Valley Forge Convention Center 162
Valley, Mick 58
Vancouver Sun 109
Van Damme, Jean-Claude 164
Vanity, Inc. 37
Variety 12, 19, 32, 118, 128–130, 133, 138–139, 147–148, 150
Vaswani, Danny 122
Vaswani, Lavina 122
Vaz, Wendy 172
Verma, Amrit: *Indian Women Through the Ages* 29
Verma, Hari Narain: *Indian Women Through the Ages* 29
Versace 129
Viacom 139
Victor Awards 75
Video City Productions 147–148
Vijayvergiya, V.N. 129
Visto International 131–133
Vogue (American magazine) 123
Vogue India 73
Vraney, Mike 20

Walken, Christopher 71
Walters, Barbara 151
Wanted: Dead or Alive (1986 film) 149
Warga, Wayne 52
Warrior of the Lost World 3, 105, 118, 121, 129, 146, 148, 173, 178; analysis of Khambatta's character 134–136; production 118–119; release and reception 130–134
Washington Post 123
Washington Star 8
Waterloo Courier 101
West, Adam 130
What Do You Say to a Naked Lady? (1970 film) 53
What's New, Pussycat? (1965 film) 105
When a Stranger Calls (1979 film) 84
Whitehorse Star 57
Whitman, Kip 98
Whittaker, James 107
WHO (television station) 156
The Wilby Conspiracy 3, 6, 29, 70, 95, 102, 119, 129, 150, 165, 168, 173; analysis of Khambatta's character 28, 106; production 25–27; release and reception 27–28, 102
Willemen, Paul 2, 14; *Encyclopaedia of Indian Cinema* 2, 14
William Saroyan Theater 166
Williams, Billy Dee 68, 84, 142
Williamson, Fred 99, 131, 150
Wilson, Earl 22–23, 58, 68, 98
Winters, David 148
Wisconsin State Journal 66
Wise, Robert 1, 39, 50–54, 56–57, 60–62, 64–65, 91, 117, 175–176
WKRP in Cincinnati 98
Wolper, David 114, 117, 120, 163
Woman's Own 22
Worth, David 118, 133, 135
Writers Guild Theater 154

Xenon Nightclub 69

Yablans, Irwin 91
Yan, Cathy 149
yellowface 13
York, Michael 145
You Only Live Twice (1967 film) 13–14
Young, Terence 13
Yuki 93
Yuvaraj of Dhrangadhra *see* Bapa
Yves Saint Laurent 35

Zellermayer, Alexander Markus 63–64
Zmed, Adrian 124
Zoroaster 9, 86
Zuber, Marc 141, 144

www.ingramcontent.com/pod-product-compliance
Ingram Content Group UK Ltd.
Pitfield, Milton Keynes, MK11 3LW, UK
UKHW041947140426
5217IPUK00014B/684